Sovereignty, the WTC
Fundamentals of Int

The last decade of the twentieth century and the first of the twenty-first century will certainly rank high as a challenging period for the generally accepted assumptions of international law. The forces of "globalization," accompanied by striking changes in government institutions, a remarkable increase in NGO activity and advocacy, an intense emphasis on market economic ideas and a backlash against them, have chipped away at the fragile theoretical foundations of the international legal system as it has been generally accepted for centuries. The objective of this book is to explore the relationship between general international law (and its sovereignty-based assumptions) with the legal "constitution," jurisprudence, and practice of the WTO as an empirical case study of international economic law, all in the context of these twenty-first-century developments.

JOHN H. JACKSON is University Professor of Law at the Georgetown University Law Center. He joined the Georgetown Faculty after a distinguished career as Hessel E. Yntema Professor of Law at the University of Michigan. He has advised the United States and other governments and international organizations on international trade law, and has published widely in the area. In June of 2003, Professor Jackson was awarded the honorary degree, "Doctor Iuris Honoris Causa" from Hamburg University Faculty of Law. Also in June 2003, he was appointed by WTO Director-General, Dr. Supachai Panitchpadki, to the WTO Consultative Board, composed of eight "eminent persons," and chaired by Peter Sutherland. The Board released a report entitled "The Future of WTO: Addressing Institutional Challenges in the New Millennium," in January 2005. He has published widely in the area of international trade law, including his book *The Jurisprudence of GATT and the WTO: Insights on Treaty Law and Economic Relations* (Cambridge University Press).

Recent books in the Hersch Lauterpacht Memorial Lecture series

JAN PAULSSON
Denial of Justice in International Law
0 521 85118 1

FRANCISCO ORREGO VICUNA
International Dispute Settlement in an Evolving Global Society:
Constitutionalization, Accessibility, Privatization
0 521 84239 5

MARTTI KOSKENNIEMI
The Gentle Civilizer of Nations:
The Rise and Fall of International Law 1870–1960
0 521 62311 1 hardback
0 521 54809 8 paperback

THOMAS M. FRANCK
Recourse to Force:
State Action against Threats and Armed Attacks
0 521 82013 8

Sovereignty, the WTO and Changing Fundamentals of International Law

JOHN H. JACKSON

CAMBRIDGE
UNIVERSITY PRESS

CAMBRIDGE UNIVERSITY PRESS
Cambridge, New York, Melbourne, Madrid, Cape Town, Singapore, São Paulo, Delhi

Cambridge University Press
The Edinburgh Building, Cambridge CB2 8RU, UK

Published in the United States of America by Cambridge University Press, New York

www.cambridge.org
Information on this title: www.cambridge.org/9780521748414

© John H. Jackson 2006

This publication is in copyright. Subject to statutory exception
and to the provisions of relevant collective licensing agreements,
no reproduction of any part may take place without
the written permission of Cambridge University Press.

First published 2006
First paperback edition 2009

Printed in the United Kingdom at the University Press, Cambridge

A catalogue record for this publication is available from the British Library

ISBN 978-0-521-86007-9 hardback
ISBN 978-0-521-74841-4 paperback

Cambridge University Press has no responsibility for the persistence or accuracy of URLs
for external or third-party internet websites referred to in this publication, and does not
guarantee that any content on such websites is, or will remain, accurate or appropriate.
Information regarding prices, travel timetables and other factual information given in this
work are correct at time of first printing but Cambridge University Press does not
guarantee the accuacy of such inforamtion thereafter.

To Joan, who deserves much for constant support and intellectual companionship.

Contents

Preface	xi
Table of statutes and regulations	xiv
Table of cases	xx

Part I Challenges to fundamental assumptions of international law

1 Introduction: international law and international economic law in the interdependent world of the twenty-first century — 3
1.1 A time of challenge and changing assumptions — 3
1.2 Facts on the ground: the world situation landscape – change, interdependence, globalization, adjustment — 8
1.3 Implications for international law and its role for international relations: challenges to the fundamental logic and axioms of international law (a brief overview of things to come) — 13
1.4 Contours and road map – the structure of this book — 15

2 The real world impinges on international law: exploring the challenges to the fundamental assumptions of international law and institutions — 18
2.1 Introduction to exploring the challenges and their impacts on international law — 18
2.2 Circumstances and conditions — 20
2.3 International law and its discontents — 32
2.4 International economic law — 46

	2.5	International institutional law	49
	2.6	Some conclusions: the international law system challenged	54

3 Sovereignty-modern: a new approach to an outdated concept   57
	3.1	Sovereignty and the fundamental logic of international law	57
	3.2	Traditional Westphalian sovereignty concepts: outmoded and discredited?	62
	3.3	Potentially valid policy objectives of sovereignty concepts	70
	3.4	Perceptions and reflections for Part I: changing fundamentals of international law	76

Part II The WTO

4 The WTO as international organization: institutional evolution, structure, and key problems   81
	4.1	The WTO as international economic law and its relationship to general international law	81
	4.2	The policy objectives and preferences for a WTO	84
	4.3	Historical background: from Bretton Woods to Cancún and Hong Kong	91
	4.4	The World Trade Organization: structure of the treaty and the institution	104
	4.5	Institutional problems of the WTO	110
	4.6	WTO Rules and members' domestic legal systems	122
	4.7	Scope of the subject matter agenda for the WTO: the question of competence	128

5 The WTO dispute settlement system   134
	5.1	The WTO dispute settlement system – unique, a great achievement, controversial	134
	5.2	The bottom-up trial and error history of the GATT dispute settlement system and the Uruguay Round makeover	137
	5.3	The multiple policy goals of international dispute settlement: dilemmas, balancing, and competing principles	145

5.4	The current structure and operation of the WTO dispute settlement system	152
5.5	A decade of WTO dispute settlement activity, 1995–2005	159
5.6	Key jurisprudential questions I: the relation of WTO law to international law – sovereignty tensions	163
5.7	Key jurisprudential questions II: structural doctrines channeling juridical techniques of decision	173
5.8	Key jurisprudential questions III: treaty interpretation	182
5.9	Key jurisprudential questions IV: dispute settlement reports and national law	192
5.10	Key jurisprudential questions V: compliance and implementation	195
5.11	Dispute settlement structural problems and proposed reforms	199
5.12	Perspectives and conclusions for Part II: the lessons of the GATT/WTO system	204

Part III The search for solutions

6 Policy analytical approaches and thought experiments — 211

6.1	Introduction to Part III and Chapter 6	211
6.2	The sovereignty conundrum: slicing the concept	214
6.3	Towards a policy analysis matrix: a three-dimensional puzzle (at least)	217
6.4	Economics and markets: a thought experiment about market failure in the era of globalization	220
6.5	Thinking constitutional	222
6.6	The growing importance of juridical institutions	227
6.7	Interface theory: managing globalization in a world of wide variation	230

7 Illustrative applications — 234

7.1	Illustrative applications – grappling with detail and diversity	234
7.2	The WTO and its "constitution": institutional detail and dynamic evolution	236
7.3	Investments and international rules	240

	7.4	Environmental policies	243
	7.5	Health, globalization, and international institutions	245
	7.6	Human rights and nation-state sovereignty	248
	7.7	Federalism examples: US and EU struggles with the allocation of power	252
	7.8	The United Nations and the use of force: constitutionalism evolving	256
8	**Perspectives and implications: some conclusions**		258
	Appendix: Outline of the Uruguay Round treaty establishing the World Trade Organization		269

Notes 271
Index 353

Preface

When I was invited in May 2001 to deliver the annual international law lecture series at the Cambridge University Lauterpacht Research Centre in November 2002, I was honored and also challenged to pursue further some thinking and writing about the interrelationship of international law and international economic law which I had already begun.

Little did I then realize, however, how complex and elaborate a preoccupation this task would be. At the time of the invitation, the events of September 11, 2001, had not yet occurred, and those events suddenly created an eruption of thinking and writing about general international law and its meaning for twenty-first-century international relations.

By the time I had prepared the lectures, it was apparent to me that there were added dimensions to the landscape which required exploration. The intellectual journey became longer, more perilous, and yet more interesting. The book is therefore substantially longer than the lectures, but still pursues the goal of being relatively compact.

Chapter 1 sets forth the overall logical structure of the book, and outlines the roadmap for the intellectual journey it represents, so that these need not be repeated here. However, a few general remarks may alert the reader to certain features of this book. For example, it is not designed to be a complete text on its subjects (international law and international economic law as represented by the World Trade Organization). This book only purports to provide an overall framework for thinking about those two subjects and how they interrelate, and an overview of their numerous conceptual problems and puzzles. In some sense this is two books pasted together, with bridges between them. It was not an easy project.

This book also is not designed to provide any "grand theory" of these subjects, but as stated several times in the text is about "queries rather than theories." Its logic rests a great deal on empirical observation of one very complex, relatively new, and decidedly important international law institution, namely the World Trade Organization and particularly its dispute settlement system. The book's objective (hopefully at least partly realized) is to outline fundamental logical problems about existing international law concepts, and to use the WTO legal system as a source of empirically observed data to shed light on those logical problems of international law generally. The journey herein ends with Chapter 8, which reviews the way this is accomplished.

I wish to express my gratitude to the Cambridge University Lauterpacht Research Centre for inviting me to deliver the annual series of international law lectures which occurred in November 2002. The delightful hospitality both physical and intellectual of the Lauterpacht center for those lectures, and of its founder Professor Sir Elihu Lauterpacht and its director Professor James R. Crawford, as well as some of their colleagues such as Professor Phillip Allott, provided an extraordinary and memorable launch for further struggles with the conceptual difficulties of the subject of general international law and its relationship with international economic law. Certainly the Center and its colleagues truly represent the best perspectives of its namesake, Judge Sir Hersch Lauterpacht, who has inspired so many thoughtful participants and observers of international relations and its relation to legal norms.

I am also grateful for the support of the Georgetown University Law Center, its Dean Judy Areen, dean during most of the efforts for this book, and the remarkable GULC library regarding its subject. In addition I wish to recognize the support of the University of Michigan School of Law (where I continue to hold the title of Emeritus Professor) for many decades of sustenance in the then novel and difficult task of exploring the minefields (and boiler room) of international economic law.

In addition I particularly want to recognize and appreciate the remarkable and diligent assistance of my principal editorial and administrative assistant, Joanna Sokolow. Her research ability and computer command, as well as her constantly pleasant demeanor and interaction with others including my students, are hard to replicate in any environment. I also express my appreciation and gratitude to several student research assistants, particularly Isabelle Van Damme and Helge Zeitler.

Likewise I am indebted intellectually to many colleagues and other professional friends and associates, long conversations with whom have helped shape my thinking. In particular, some of the editors of the *Journal of International Economic Law* and the *American Journal of International Law* with which I am associated, have assisted my thinking.

Over many decades of activity, observation, and thinking concerning international law and economic law I have benefited enormously from many profound and interesting writings of authors of many viewpoints, as well as numerous intense discussions (over dinners or otherwise) with friends and colleagues too numerous to mention here. Likewise I am grateful to a number of students and their work and discussions with me. Many of these students have gone on to remarkable careers in subjects related to these discussions, and maintain close contact with me so as to continue the learning process on both sides.

Finally, but distinctly not least, I thank my wife Joan not only for the family support and sustenance, but for the intellectual companionship she has provided, often stimulating directions of my thinking.

Table of statutes and regulations

Act of 24 September 1789, ch. 20, 9(b), 1 Stat. 73, 77, 287n–24

Act to Extend the Authority of the President under section 350 of the 1930 US Tariff Act, as amended, and for other purposes, 5 July 1945, Pub. L. 79–130, 59 Stat. 410, 304n11, 305n18

Agreement on Trade-Related Aspects of Intellectual Property Rights (TRIPS), WTO Charter Annex 1C, 105, 227, 247, 347n29

Agricultural Adjustment Act, 1951 Amendments to Section 22 (f) of, , 66 Stat. 75 (US), 317n11

Agriculture, Agreement on, WTO Charter Annex 1A, Article 13, 336n6

Alien Tort Claims Act (ATC Act), 28 U.S.C. 1350 (2000) (US), 41, 287n–24

Antidumping Act of 1916 (US), 179–180

Articles of Agreement of the International Bank for Reconstruction and Development (IBRD), Jul. 22, 1944, 60 Stat. 1440, 2. U.N.T.S. 134, amended Dec. 16, 1965, 16 U.S.T. 1942, 606 U.N.T.S. 294, 338n11

Articles of Agreement of the International Monetary Fund (IMF), Jul. 22, 1944, 60 Stat. 1301; 2 U.N.T.S. 39, 338n11

Bill of Rights passed by Congress September 25, 1789, ratified December 15, 1791 (US), 349n9

Bretton-Woods Agreements Act of 1945, 22 U.S.C.A. secs. 286–86gg, 274n9, 312n3

Central America-Dominican Republic-United States Free Trade Agreement (CAFTA) (Final Text) (May 28, 2004), 340n8

Conference on Security and Cooperation in Europe, Final Act of, Helsinki, Aug. 1, 1975, 289n35

Constitution of the Netherlands, Article 94, 23

Cotonou Agreement, 2000 O.J. L317/3 (Dec. 15, 2000), 280n27, 298n28

DSU (Understanding on Rules and Procedures Governing the Settlement of Disputes). *See* WTO Charter, Annex 2

Table of statutes and regulations

Europe, Treaty Establishing a Constitution for, 2004 O.J. (C 310), Rome, Oct. 29, 2004, 44, 292n8, 313n15, 337n3, 349n7, 350n6

European Convention on Human Rights (Convention for the Protection of Human Rights and Fundamental Freedoms), Rome, Nov. 4, 1950, Council of Europe CETS No. 005, 226, 249, 348n3

European Economic Community, Treaty Establishing (Treaty of Rome) Mar. 25, 1957, 306n45

Financial Services Agreement (GATS Annex), 115

Framework Convention on Tobacco Control, WHO Doc. A/FCTC/INB2/2, 9 Jan. 2001, 246, 346n13

General Agreement on Tariffs and Trade (GATT)
   1947, 105, 106
   1994, 105, 128
   Preamble, 84
   Article I, 275n8
   Article II, 96
   Article III, 131, 142, 161, 178, 247, 275n8
   Article III(2), 142–143, 186
   Article III(4), 131, 186
   Article XVI(1), 106
   Article XX, 161, 165, 189–90
   Article XX(g), 189
   Article XXIII, 138–140, 152, 196–97
   Article XXIV, 314n22
   Article XXIV(12), 128
   Article XXV, 107, 140
   Article XXXIII, 298n27
   Part I, 95
   Part II, 95–96
   Part III, 95
   Protocol of Provisional Application (PPA), 82, 94–96

General Agreement on Trade in Services (GATS). See WTO Charter Annex 1B,

Havana Charter for an International Trade Organization, Mar. 24, 1948, 84, 92–93, 129, 138, 314n1
   Article 1, 85
   Articles 92–97, 316n2

ICC Statute (Statute of the International Criminal Court), Article 98, 289n37

ICJ Statute. See Statute of the International Court of Justice

International Health Regulations (IHRs), 245, 246, 341n11, 346n6, 347n22

Luxembourg Accords, Jan. 29, 1966, 292n3

Mercosur Treaty Establishing a Common Market Between the Argentine Republic, the

Federal Republic of Brazil, the Republic of Paraguay and the Republic of Uruguay, Mar. 26, 1991, 30 ILM 1041, 277n2, 280n26, 340–341n9
Mercosur Protocol of Brasilia for the Solution of Controversies, Decision 1/91, Art. 23 (Dec. 17, 1991) 36 ILM 691 (1997), 341n10
North American Free Trade Agreement (NAFTA), Dec. 17, 1992. Can.–Mex.–U.S., 32 ILM 289 & 605 (1993) (entered into force Jan. 1, 1994), 21, 126, 227, 340n7
North American Free Trade Agreement Act, P. L. No. 103-182, 102, 107 Stat. 2057, 2062 (1993), 19 U.S.C.A. sec. 3312 (a) (1), 279n20
Organisation for Economic Co-operation and Development (OECD), Declaration on International Investment and Multinational Enterprises & Principles of Corporate Governance, 289n35
Public Company Accounting Reform and Investor Protection Act of 2002, P. L. No. 107–204, 116 Stat. 745 (2002) (US), 278n11
Reciprocal Trade Agreements Act (1934/1945) (US), 92–94
Restatement (Third) of the Foreign Relations Law of the United States, Section 114 (1987), 280n24
Rome, Treaty of (Treaty Establishing the European Economic Community), Mar. 25, 1957, 306n45
Rules of Professional Responsibility for Attorneys (Sarbanes-Oxley Act), 15 U.S.C.S. 7201 (2003), 278n11
Safeguards, Agreement on, WTO Charter Annex 1A, Article 12(5), 333n15
Sanitary and Phytosanitary Measures, Agreement on the Application of (SPS), WTO Charter Annex 1A, 161, 247, 347n26
Sarbanes-Oxley Act (Rules of Professional Responsibility for Attorneys), 15 U.S.C.S. 7201 (2003), 278n11
Statute of the International Court of Justice
   Article 38(1), 35, 284n5
   Article 38(1)(b), 39
   Article 38(3), 285n12
   Article 59, 175, 326n8
Statute of the International Criminal Court (ICC), Article 98, 289n37
Tariff Act (1930) (US), 92
Technical Barriers to Trade (TBT), Agreement on, WTO Charter Annex 1A, 247, 318n23, 347n27
Telecomms Agreement (GATS Annex), 115
Tobacco Control, Framework Convention on, WHO Doc. A/FCTC/INB2/2, Jan. 9, 2001, 246, 346n13
Trade Act of 1974 (US), Sections 301–310, 178–79, 313n4, 327n19, 327n21, 334n1

Trade Act of 2002 (US), Title XXI, 307n57
Trade Policy Review Mechanism (TRPM), WTO Charter Annex 3, 105, 107
Trade Promotion Authority Act of 2002 (TPA Act) (US), 307n57
Treaty Establishing a Common Market Between the Argentine Republic, the Federal Republic of Brazil, the Republic of Paraguay and the Republic of Uruguay (Mercosur), Mar. 26, 1991, 30 ILM 1041, 277n2, 280n26, 340–41n9
Treaty Establishing a Constitution for Europe, 2004 O.J. (C 310), Rome, Oct. 29, 2004, 44, 292n8, 313n15, 337n3, 349n7, 350n6
Treaty Establishing the European Economic Community, Mar. 25, 1957 (Treaty of Rome), 306n45
Treaty of Westphalia (1648), 62–63
TRIPS (Agreement on Trade-Related Aspects of Intellectual Property Rights), WTO Charter Annex 1C, 105, 227, 247, 347n29
TRPM (Trade Policy Review Mechanism), WTO Charter Annex 3, 105, 107
UN Charter, 223, 225
   Article 2(4), 256
   Article 17(2), 292n7
   Article 51, 256
   Article 94, 168
   Chapter VII, 256
UNCLOS III (Third UN Conference on the Law of the Sea), Rule 37, UN Doc. A/Conf/62/30/Rev.1; 13 ILM 1205 (1974), 280n28
UNCTAD (UN Conference on Trade and Development), UN Doc. A/5479, 280n28
Understanding on Rules and Procedures Governing the Settlement of Disputes (DSU). See WTO Charter, Annex 2
Understanding Regarding Notification, Consultation, Dispute Settlement and Surveillance, Nov. 28, 1979, GATT B.I.S.D. (26th Supp.) at 210 (1980), 140–141, 317n10, 318n17
UPU Congresses, Art. 19.1 of the Rules of Procedures of, 280n28
Uruguay Round Agreements Act (US)
   P. L. No. 103-465, 102, 108 Stat. 4815, 19 U.S.C.A. sec. 3512(a)(1) (US), 279n20
   section 102, Pub. L.No. 103–182, 102, 107 Stat. 2057, 289n40
US–Australia Free Trade Agreement (Final Text) (May 18, 2004), 340n8
US–Chile Free Trade Agreement (Final Text) (Jun. 6, 2003), entered into force Jan. 1, 2004, 340n8
US–Singapore Free Trade Agreement (Final Text) (May 6, 2003), entered into force Jan. 1, 2004, 340n8

Table of statutes and regulations

Vienna Convention on the Law of Treaties (VCLT), 4, 14, 45, 52, 161, 170, 176, 183, 187, 193, 194, 196, 212, 225, 268, 289n34, 328n3
    Article 2.1(a), 288n32
    Article 31(1), 291n14, 292n5
    Article 31(3), 323n12
    Article 31(3)(b), 331n3
    Articles 31 and 32, 158, 166–67, 184
Westphalia, Treaty of (1648), 62–63
World Health Organization (WHO) Constitution, 246
    Preamble, 345–346n1, 346n7
    Article 19, 346n12
    Article 22, 346n15
    Article 75, 347n21
WTO Charter *(Agreement Establishing the World Trade Organization)*, 104–106, 269–70, 306n36
    Annex 1A, Multilateral Agreements on Trade in Goods
        Agreement on Agriculture, Article 13, 336n6
        Agreement on Implementation of Article VI, 324n17, 324n20
        Agreement on Safeguards, Article 12(5), 333n15
        Agreement on Technical Barriers to Trade (TBT), 247, 318n23, 347n27
        Agreement on the Application of Sanitary and Phytosanitary Measures (SPS), 161, 247, 347n26
        GATT 1994, 105, 128 (*See also* General Agreement on Tariffs and Trade)
    Annex 1B, *General Agreement on Trade in Services (GATS)*, 105, 162–163, 242, 315n11
        Annex on Financial Services & *Annex on Negotiations on Basic Telecommunications*, 115
        Article VI(4), 133
    Annex 1C, *Agreement on Trade-Related Aspects of Intellectual Property Rights (TRIPS)*, 105, 227, 247, 347n29
    Annex 2, *Understanding on Rules and Procedures Governing the Settlement of Disputes (DSU)*, 105, 113, 144–145, 152, 158–59
        Article 1, 145, 319n4
        Article 3, 146, 147
        Article 3(2), 148, 183, 191, 332n7
        Article 3(3), 147–48
        Article 3(8), 318n24, 332n11
        Article 5, 319n2
        Article 11, 154, 180, 327n25
        Article 12, 320n14

Table of statutes and regulations

Article 12(2), 183
Article 13, 155, 181
Article 15, 320n14
Article 16, 320n14, 320n15
Article 17(6), 170, 180, 181, 324n18, 324n19, 325n23, 325n25, 327n26, 328n29
Article 17(6)(i), 328n30
Article 17(6)(ii), 170–71
Article 19(1), 332n10
Article 19(2), 332n7
Article 21(1), 324n16
Article 21(6), 324n16
Article 22, 332n12
Article 22(1), 324n14
Article 22(2), 324n15
Article 22(4), 327n23
Article 22(6), 327n23, 332n13
Article 23, 319n4
Article 23(2), 124
Article 25, 319n3
Amendments to, Proposed Text by Mexico, WTO Doc. TN/DS/W/40, Jan. 27, 2003, 332n14
Appendix 3, 320n14
Rules of Conduct, WTO Doc. WT/DSB/RC/1, Dec.11, 1996, 319n5
Annex 3, *Trade Policy Review Mechanism (TRPM)*, 105, 107
Annex 4, Plurilateral Agreements, 106, 115
Preamble, 84–86
Article IX, 108, 159, 310n6, 310n7
Article IX(2), 343n1
Article IX(8), 310n9
Article X, 343n2
Article XI, 308n8, 309n6
Article XII, 308n8
Article XIII, 109, 308n8
Article XVI, 91
Article XVI(1), 176
Article XVI(3), 332n5
Article XVI(4), 124
Wye River Memorandum, Oct. 23, 1998, 1sr.-PLO, 37 ILM 1251 (1998), 298n26

Table of cases

Alvarez-Machain case
  SOSA v. Alvarez-Machain, No 03-339 and 03-485, June 29, 2004, 124 S.Ct. 2739, 279n23, 287n23
  United States v. Alvarez-Machain, 504 U.S. 655 (1992), 40–41, 287n22
Arrest Warrant of 11 April 2000 (Dem. Rep. Congo v. Belg.), 41 ILM 536 (2002) (International Court of Justice), 294n3
Asbestos case
  EC – Measures Affecting the Prohibition of Asbestos and Asbestos Products, WTO Doc. WT/DS135/AB/R, adopted Mar. 12, 2001, 186, 247, 320n17, 330n9, 331n2
  EC – Measures Affecting Asbestos and Asbestos-Containing Products, WTO Doc. WT/DS135/AB/R, adopted Apr. 5, 2001, 327n27
Australia – Measures affecting Importation of Salmon, WTO Doc. WT/DS18/AB/R, adopted Nov. 6, 1998, 347n28
Australian Subsidy on Ammonium Sulphate, Apr. 3, 1950,GATT B.I.S.D. (Vol. II) at 188 (1952), 317n6, 317n7
Banco Nacional de Cuba v. Sabbatino, 376 U.S. 398, 84 S.Ct. 923, 11 L.Ed.2d 804 (1964), 40, 287n21
Beef Hormones case
  EC – Measures Concerning Meat and Meat Products (Hormones), WTO Docs. WT/DS26 & 48/AB/R, adopted Jan. 16, 1998, 328n31, 328n33
  EC – Measures Concerning Meat and Meat Products (Hormones), WTO Docs. WT/DS26 & 48/AB/R, adopted Feb. 13, 1998, 154, 155, 161, 171, 182, 247, 319n7, 322n12, 325n26, 325n27, 329n4, 347n28
  US – Continued Suspension of Obligations in the EC – Hormones Dispute (WT/DS320) and *Canada – Continued Suspension of Obligations in the EC*

Table of cases

- *Hormones Dispute (WT/DS321)*, WTO Docs. WT/DS320/8 & 321/8, of Aug. 2, 2005, 319–320n11
Biret International SA v. Council, Case C-93/02 P, 2003, ECR I-10497, 314n18
Bush v. Gore, 531 U.S. 98 (2000), 253, 350n1
Byrd Amendment case *(US – Continued Dumping and Subsidy Offset Act of 2000)*, WTO Docs. WT/ DS217 & 234/AB/R, adopted Jan. 16, 2003, 180, 323n9, 327n24
Canada – Import, Distribution, and Sale of Alcoholic Drinks by Canadian Provincial Marketing Agencies, GATT B.I.S.D. 37(1989), Mar. 22, 1988, and GATT B.I.S.D. 27 (1993), Feb. 18, 1992, 314n21
Canada – Measures Affecting the Export of Certain Aircraft, WTO Doc. WT/DS70/AB/R, adopted Aug. 20, 1999, 292n10
Certain Expenses of the United Nations (Art. 17, para. 2 of the Charter), *Advisory Opinion of 20 July 1962* (International Court of Justice), 292n7
Charming Betsy case *(Murray v. The Schooner Charming Betsy)*, 6 U.S. (2 Cranch) 64, 2 L.Ed. 208 (1804), 124–25, 193, 279n24, 287n20, 313n5, 331n4
Chevron U.S.A. Inc. v. Natural Resources Defense Council, Inc. et. al., 467 U.S. 837 (1984), 325n22
Citrus case *(EEC – Tariff Treatment of Citrus Products from Certain Mediterranean Countries)*, L/5776, 317n14
Commission v. Germany, Case 61/94, 1996 E.C.R. I-3989 (European Court of Justice), 290n40
Continental Shelf case (Tunisia/Libya), 1982 ICJ Rep. 18 (International Court of Justice), 291n15
Corus Staal BV v. Dept. of Commerce, Fed. Cir. No. 04–1107, Jan. 21, 2005, 395 F.3d 1343, 331n8
Cotton case *(US – Subsidies on Upland Cotton)*, WTO Docs. WT/DS267/AB/R & WT/DS267/R, both adopted Mar. 21, 2005, 283n52, 283n53, 308n57, 322n20, 336n6, 341n15, 341n16, 342n18
Dem. Rep. Congo v. Belg. (Arrest Warrant of 11 April 2000), 41 ILM 536 (2002) (International Court of Justice), 294n3
EC – Export Subsidies on Sugar (*Sugar* case), WTO Docs. WT/DS265/R, WT/DS266/R, WT/DS283/R, panel Reports on complaints by Australia, Brazil, and Thailand, adopted May 19, 2005, 283n52, 308n57, 322n21, 341n16, 342n18
EC – Imposition of Anti-Dumping Duties on Imports of Cotton Yarn from Brazil,

Table of cases

WTO Doc. ADP/137, adopted by the ADP Committee, Oct. 30, 1995, 323n1

EC – Measures Affecting the Approval and Marketing of Biotech Products (*GMO* case), WTO Docs. WT/DS291/27, WT/DS292/21, & WT/DS293/21 (ongoing case), 319n9, 328n32

EC – Measures Affecting Asbestos and Asbestos-Containing Products (*Asbestos* case), WTO Doc. WT/DS135/AB/R, adopted Apr. 5, 2001, 327n27

EC – Measures Affecting the Prohibition of Asbestos and Asbestos Products (*Asbestos* case), WTO Doc. WT/DS135/AB/R, adopted Mar. 12, 2001, 186, 247, 320n17, 330n9, 331n2

EC – Measures Concerning Meat and Meat Products (Hormones) (*Beef Hormones* case), WTO Docs. WT/DS26 & 48/AB/R
  adopted Jan. 16, 1998, 328n31, 328n33
  adopted Feb. 13, 1998, 154, 155, 161, 171, 182, 247, 319n7, 322n12, 325n26, 325n27, 329n4, 347n28

EEC – Payments and Subsidies Paid to Processors and Producers of Oilseeds and Related Animal Feed Proteins, Jan. 25, 1990, GATT B.I.S.D. (37th Supp.) at 37 (1990), 318n22

EEC – Tariff Treatment of Citrus Products from Certain Mediterranean Countries (*Citrus* case), L/5776, 317n14

Ethiopia v. South Africa/Liberia, 1966 ICJ Rep. 6 (International Court of Justice), 292n7

Filartiga v. Pena-Irala, 630 F.2d. 876 (2d Circ. 1980), 287n20

France v. Turkey (*S.S. Lotus* case), 1927 PCIJ (Ser. A) No. 10, 52, 262, 285n8, 292n9

French Assistance to Exports of Wheat and Wheat Flour, Nov. 21, 1958, GATT B.I.S.D. (7th Supp.) at 46 (1959), 318n16

FSC case *(US – Tax Treatment for "Foreign Sales Corporations")*
  Recourse to Article 21.5 of the DSU by the EC, WTO Doc. WT/DS108/AB/RW, adopted Jan. 29, 2002, 321n22
  WTO Docs. WT/DS108/R & WT/DS108/AB/R, adopted Mar. 20, 2000, 321n22, 342n21
  Recourse to Arbitration by the United States under Article 22.6 of the DSU and Article 4.11 of the SCM Agreement, WTO Doc. WT/DS108/ARB, circulated Aug. 30, 2002, 321n22

Fuji Film case *(Japan – Measures Affecting Consumer Photographic Film and Paper),* WTO Doc. WT/DS44/R, adopted Apr. 22, 1998 (not appealed), 181, 327n28

German Duty on Sardines case (Oct. 31, 1952), GATT B.I.S.D. (1st Supp.) at 53 (1953), 317n7

Table of cases

GMO case *(EC – Measures Affecting the Approval and Marketing of Biotech Products)*, WTO Docs. WT/DS291/27, WT/DS292/21, & WT/DS293/21 (ongoing case), 319n9, 328n32

Hermès v. FHT, Case C-53/96, 1998 E.C.R. I-3603 (European Court of Justice), 290n40

Interfood v. Hauptzollamt Hamburg, Case 92/71, 1972 E.C.R. 231 (European Court of Justice), 289–90n40

Japan – Measures Affecting Consumer Photographic Film and Paper (*Fuji Film* case), WTO Doc. WT/DS44/R, adopted Apr. 22, 1998 (not appealed), 181, 327n28

Japan – Taxes on Alcoholic Beverages, WTO Doc. WT/DS8, 10 & 11/AB/R, adopted Nov. 1, 1996, 161, 166–168, 176, 186, 187, 320n16, 322n10, 323n5, 323n11, 327n11, 329n7, 331n5

Korea – Measures Affecting Government Procurement, WTO Doc. WT/DS163/R, adopted Jun. 19, 2000, 291n16

Legal Consequences for States of the Continuing Presence of South Africa in Namibia (South West Africa) notwithstanding Security Council Resolution 276 (1970), Advisory Opinion 1971 ICJ Rep. 16 (International Court of Justice), 291–92n1

Léon Van Parys NV v. Belgisch Interventie-en Restitutiebureau (BIRB), Case C-377/02, Mar. 1, 2005 (not yet published), 314n18

Lotus case *(France v. Turkey)*, 1927 PCIJ (Ser. A) No. 10, 52, 262, 285n8, 292n9

Malaysia – Prohibition of Imports of Polyethylene and Polypropylene, WTO Doc. WT/DS1, requested Jan. 10, 1995, 323n3

Marbury v. Madison, 5 U.S. 137 (1803), 198, 317n6, 349n11

McCulloch v. Maryland, 4 Wheat. 316 (1819), 292n6

Murray v. The Schooner Charming Betsy, 6 U.S. (2 Cranch) 64, 2 L.Ed. 208 (1804), 124–125, 193, 279n24, 287n20, 313n5, 331n4

Netherlands Measures of Suspension of Obligations to the United States, Nov. 8, 1952, GATT B.I.S.D. (1st Supp.) at 32 (1953), 317n11, 332n9

Nicaragua Case, 1986 ICJ Rep. 3 (International Court of Justice), 291n15

Oil Fee or *Superfund* case *(US – Taxes on Petroleum and Certain Imported Substances)*, GATT B.I.S.D. (34th Supp.), at 136 (1988), 142, 143, 178, 317n13, 327n16

The Paquete Habana, 175 U.S. 677 (1900), 287n20

Planned Parenthood of Southeastern Pa. v. Casey, 505 U.S. 833 (1992), 174, 326n4

Roe v. Wade, 410 U.S. 113 (1973), 174, 326n5

Table of cases

SA CNL-SUCAL NV v. HAG GF AG, Case C-10/89, 1990 E.C.R., I-3711 (European Court of Justice), 326n6

Shrimp-Turtle case *(US – Import Prohibition of Certain Shrimp and Shrimp Products)*, WTO Doc. WT/DS58/AB/R, adopted Nov. 6, 1998), 150, 161, 177, 187–191, 276n2, 278n14, 294n5, 322n14, 327n14, 330n13, 330n17, 331n19, 331n21

SOSA v. Alvarez-Machain, No 03-339 and 03-485, June 29, 2004, 124 S.Ct. 2739, 279n23, 287n23

South West Africa (Ethiopia v. South Africa/Liberia), 1966 ICJ Rep. 6 (International Court of Justice), 292n7

South West Africa (Legal Consequences for States of the Continuing Presence of South Africa in Namibia notwithstanding Security Council Resolution 276 (1970)), Advisory Opinion 1971 ICJ Rep. 16 (International Court of Justice), 291–92n1

Spain – Measures Concerning Domestic Sale of Soybean Oil, June 17, 1981, L/5142, 318n16

S.S. Lotus Case (France v. Turkey), 1927 PCIJ (Ser. A) No. 10, 52, 262, 285n8, 292n9

Steel Safeguards case *(US – Definitive Safeguard Measures on Imports of Certain Steel Products)*, WTO Docs. WT/DS248, 249, 251–254, 258, & 259/R, adopted Nov. 10, 2003, 176, 198, 327n12, 341n15

Sugar case *(EC – Export Subsidies on Sugar)*, WTO Docs. WT/DS265/R, WT/DS266/R, WT/DS283/R, panel Reports on complaints by Australia, Brazil, and Thailand, adopted May 19, 2005, 283n52, 308n57, 322n21, 341n16, 342n18

Superfund or *Oil Fee* case *(US – Taxes on Petroleum and Certain Imported Substances)*, GATT B.I.S.D. (34th Supp.), at 136 (1988), 142, 143, 178, 317n13, 327n16

Timken Company v. United States, Jan. 16, 2004, 354 F.3d 1334, 331n8

Tuna-Dolphin cases
  US – Prohibition of Imports of Tuna and Tuna Products from Canada, GATT Docs. L/5198 – 29S/91, adopted Feb. 22, 1982, 190, 331n22
  US – Restrictions on Imports of Tuna (Tuna I), GATT Docs. DS21/R – 39S/155, adopted Sept. 3, 1991, 190, 278n14, 331n22
  US – Restrictions on Imports of Tuna (Tuna II), GATT Doc. DS29/R, adopted Jun. 16, 1994, 27n14, 190, 323n1, 331n22

Tunesia/Libya Continental Shelf Case, 1982 ICJ Rep. 18 (International Court of Justice), 291n15

United States – Anti-Dumping Act of 1916, WTO Docs. WT/DS136/AB/R & WT/DS162/AB/R, adopted Sept. 26, 2000, 325n25

Table of cases

United States v. Alvarez-Machain, 504 U.S. 655 (1992), 40–41, 287n22

United States v. Palestine Liberation Organization, 695 F.Supp. 1456 (S.D.N.Y. 1988), 313n6

Uruguayan Recourse to Article XXIII, Nov. 16, 1962, GATT B.I.S.D. (11th Supp.) at 95 (1963), 318n15

US – Anti-Dumping Act of 1916, WTO Docs. WT/DS136/R & WT/DS136/AB/R, adopted Sept. 26, 2000, 327n22

US – Continued Dumping and Subsidy Offset Act of 2000 (*Byrd Amendment* case), WTO Docs. WT/ DS217 & 234/AB/R, adopted Jan. 16, 2003, 180, 323n9, 327n24

US – Continued Suspension of Obligations in the EC – Hormones Dispute (WT/DS320) and *Canada – Continued Suspension of Obligations in the EC – Hormones Dispute (WT/DS321)* (*Beef Hormones* case), WTO Docs. WT/DS320/8 & 321/8, of Aug. 2, 2005, 319–320n11

US – Countervailing Measures Concerning Certain Products from the European Communities, WTO Doc. WT/DS212/AB/R, adopted Jan. 8, 2003, 315n10

US – Definitive Safeguard Measures on Imports of Certain Steel Products (*Steel Safeguards* case), WTO Docs. WT/DS248, 249, 251–254, 258, & 259/R, adopted Nov. 10, 2003, 176, 198, 327n12, 341n15

US – Import Prohibition of Certain Shrimp and Shrimp Products (*Shrimp-Turtle* case), WTO Doc. WT/DS58/AB/R, adopted Nov. 6, 1998, 150, 161, 177, 187–91, 276n2, 278n14, 294n5, 322n14, 327n14, 330n13, 330n17, 331n19, 331n21

US – Imposition of Countervailing Duties on Certain Hot-Rolled Lead and Bismuth Carbon Steel Products Originating in France, Germany and the United Kingdom
WTO Doc. SCM/185, Nov. 15, 1994 (not adopted), 323n1
WTO Doc. WT/DS138/AB/R, adopted Jun. 7, 2000, 325n21

US – Measures Affecting Alcoholic and Malt Beverages, GATT B.I.S.D. 39 (1992) 206, 314n21

US – Measures Affecting the Cross-Border Supply of Gambling and Betting Services, WTO Doc. WT/DS285/R, adopted Apr. 20, 2005 (subject to appellate changes), 322n18, 322n19

US – Measures Affecting Imports of Woven Wool Shirts and Blouses from India, WTO Doc. WT/DS33/R, adopted 23 May 1997, 325n26

US – Prohibition of Imports of Tuna and Tuna Products from Canada, GATT Docs. L/5198 – 29S/91, adopted Feb. 22, 1982, 190, 331n22

US – Restrictions on Imports of Cotton and Man-Made Fibre Underwear
WTO Doc. WT/DS24/AB/R, adopted Feb. 25, 1997, 308n57, 319n3, 341n16

WTO Doc. WT/DS24/R, adopted Feb. 25, 1998, 325n26

US – Restrictions on Imports of Tuna (Tuna I), GATT Docs. DS21/R – 39S/155, adopted Sept. 3, 1991, 190, 278n14, 331n22

US – Restrictions on Imports of Tuna (Tuna II), GATT Doc. DS29/R, adopted Jun. 16, 1994, 27n14, 190, 323n1

US – Sections 301–310 of the Trade Act of 1974, WTO Doc. WT/DS152/R, adopted Jan. 27, 2000 (not appealed), 313n4, 327n19, 327n21, 334n1

US – Standards for Reformulated and Conventional Gasoline
 WTO Doc. WT/DS2/AB/R, adopted Jan. 29, 1996, 161, 165–166, 177, 278n14, 320n18
 WTO Doc. WT/DS2/AB/R, adopted Apr. 26, 1996, 322n9
 WTO Doc. WT/DS2/AB/R, adopted May 20, 1996, 323n2
 WTO Doc. WT/DS4/AB/R, adopted May 20, 1996, 161, 165–166, 177, 278n14, 320n18

US – Subsidies on Upland Cotton (*Cotton* case), WTO Docs. WT/DS267/AB/R & WT/DS267/R, both adopted Mar. 21, 2005, 283n52, 283n53, 308n57, 322n20, 336n6, 341n15, 341n16, 342n18

US – Sunset Reviews of Anti-Dumping Measures on Oil Country Tubular Goods from Argentina, WTO Doc. WT/DS268/AB/R, adopted Dec. 17, 2004, 327n15

US – Tax Treatment for "Foreign Sales Corporations" (*FSC* case)
 Recourse to Article 21.5 of the DSU by the EC, WTO Doc. WT/DS108/AB/RW, adopted Jan. 29, 2002, 321n22
 WTO Docs. WT/DS108/R & WT/DS108/AB/R, adopted Mar. 20, 2000, 321n22, 342n21
 Recourse to Arbitration by the United States under Article 22.6 of the DSU and Article 4.11 of the SCM Agreement, WTO Doc. WT/DS108/ARB, circulated Aug. 30, 2002, 321n22

US – Taxes on Petroleum and Certain Imported Substances (*Oil Fee* or *Superfund* case), GATT B.I.S.D. (34th Supp.), at 136 (1988), 142, 143, 178, 317n13, 327n16

PART I

Challenges to Fundamental Assumptions of International Law

1

Introduction: international law and international economic law in the interdependent world of the twenty-first century

I feel about globalization a lot like I feel about the dawn. Generally speaking, I think it is a good thing that the sun comes up every morning. It does more good than harm. But even if I didn't much care for the dawn, there isn't much I could do about it. I didn't start globalization, I can't stop it – except at a huge cost to human development – and I'm not going to waste time trying. All I want to think about is how I can get the best out of this new system, and cushion the worst, for the most people.

Thomas L. Friedman, The Lexus and the Olive Tree[1]

1.1 A time of challenge and changing assumptions

The last decade of the twentieth century and the first of the twenty-first century may not be the most challenging period for the generally accepted assumptions of international law, but this period will certainly rank high on any such list. The growing depth, speed of change, and adjustment required by "globalization," accompanied by striking changes in government institutions, a remarkable increase in nongovernment activity and advocacy, an intense emphasis on market economic ideas, and a backlash against them, have all chipped away at the relatively fragile (perhaps already crumbing) theoretical foundations of the international legal system as it has been generally accepted for centuries.

The goal of this book, based partly on a series of lectures invited by and delivered at Cambridge University in 2002,[2] is to explore the legal "constitution" and practice of the World Trade Organization (WTO) in the context of international law generally, and as a major "case study" example of that general international law and its particular context of international economic law. It is obvious to most observers of these subjects that the WTO, as surely the most intricate and profound legal component of international economic law, is linked in profound ways to general international law. Thus, it is not surprising that the WTO legal framework, and the slightly more general framework of international economic law, cannot escape the many challenges and other conceptual problems about international law which are currently the subject of great academic and official government debate in many parts of the world. These debates are manifested in the recent meetings of major international law societies such as the American Society of International Law (ASIL) and its counterparts in other countries,[3] as well as in important governmental documents, reports, and activities, not the least of which include the wealth of writings, speeches, and other communications relating to the cosmic geopolitical controversies of the post-September 11, 2001, years at the United Nations and elsewhere.[4] Questions being discussed include the legitimacy of many basic international law norms (especially those of customary international law), and the structure, efficacy, and creditability of important international institutions.

It is no surprise that international economic law (IEL), and the WTO in particular, is enmeshed in these broader issues of international law, but also that the subject of IEL, and its currently most important example, have practices and experiences that are extremely relevant to discussions in the broader context. Discussions probe the role of "sovereignty" concepts in the many tensions arising in the application of international norms which impinge, sometimes deeply, on nation-state government actions and responsibilities. These discussions also engage deep jurisprudential issues about the appropriate role of international juridical systems (such as the WTO dispute settlement procedures). Also subject to critical and disputed attention are issues of institutional structures, decision making, voting, criteria for membership, and obligation to perform the results of dispute resolution procedures. Many contemporary circumstances cast doubt on international legal "axioms," such as the role of the Vienna Convention on the Law of Treaties.

These criticisms and concerns have been increasing for some decades, but appear to be more acutely relevant now, in both affirmative and negative senses, than they were during many other periods of recent history. The methodology of this book is to describe and analyze these criticisms and concerns, often expressed by many innovative and thoughtful minds,[5] with reflections from this author based on academic, government, and

1.1 A time of challenge and changing assumptions

private sector experiences, and with particular reference to the practice and experience of international economic law.

The lessons to be learned from this material have implications relevant to many other areas of international law and its actual application in the affairs of the world and its widely varied societies.

It is not this author's claim that the thinking and concerns about international law are only recent, or that they are more acute now than they have been at any other time. History and other careful scholarship show various periods of momentous impact on international law by currents of thought,[6] some instigated by colossal events such as World War II. But in a less cataclysmic way, though nevertheless likely to be equally profound, current world trends of recent decades have required the traditional institutions and patterns of thinking about general international law to confront concepts and opinions about those institutions and thoughts which have been stimulated or caused by such activity of the real world, and by thoughtful but often divergent reflections of participants and observers.[7]

Consider, for example, the decade and a half of transition from the twentieth century to the twenty-first century, roughly 1989 to 2002. On November 9, 1989, the Berlin Wall came down, ushering in several years of astonishing events resulting in a fundamental makeover of eastern Europe. A sense of optimism was widespread, with visions of economic benefits from the "peace dividend" dancing in people's heads. The United Nations faced challenges of localized turbulence, partly caused by the revision of the east European map. But in 1991 the United Nations faced and conquered an overt act of aggression perpetrated by Iraq. International law, with the United Nations as its protector, has seldom looked better. The United States, as the sole remaining superpower, seemed a welcome complement to the strengthening of world law and institutions, with NATO providing the military backbone. Europe was continuing a path towards greater unity,[8] expanding its horizons partly to accommodate the remade map.

In economic matters, equally momentous events and optimism were prevalent. The largest trade negotiation ever held (GATT (General Agreement on Tariffs and Trade) Uruguay Round (UR)), was winding to its April 1994 close, fostered by the United States and the European Community. The UR results were nothing short of astonishing, extraordinarily fulfilling most of its agenda set at the 1986 Punta del Este launching conference. The results in some respects exceeded the original agenda, with the establishment of a new international organization – the World Trade

Organization – to take over in 1995 from the troubled GATT (1948–94). In a sense the new WTO completed the triad of institutions contemplated by the 1944 Bretton Woods Conference.[9]

Equally remarkable were the fundamental reforms made in the dispute settlement procedures which had evolved in GATT. Central to these reforms was compulsory jurisdiction over all disputes arising under the UR "covered agreements," a totally new and unique Appellate Body and process, and virtually automatic adoption by the WTO of the dispute settlement reports, with not only an international law obligation to comply, but also a series of possible temporary "compensatory" measures designed the better to induce such compliance.[10]

In this context also, international law (or international economic law) seemed ascendant and strongly reinforced by the rule-oriented procedures set forth in the UR treaty.

Throughout this period, and indeed throughout the last half century, the world has changed in ways that required new approaches and greater abilities to adjust. As the twentieth century drew to a close, trouble began to cast longer shadows. The forces of globalization and interdependence posed increasing challenges to traditional concepts of nation-state actors in international affairs. International law, both in its general sense and the economic context, was profoundly tested.

Horrifically brutal events in Somalia, Kosovo, and Rwanda posed further challenges to international law and institutions. Many commentators described these and other situations as failures of the United Nations (and its members). On the economic front, the Asian financial crisis of 1997–98 tested the capacities of the Bretton Woods financial institutions. The WTO found itself the target of strident and even violent criticism, as most poignantly demonstrated in Seattle in December 1999. World trade and other economic developments towards greater international interdependence demanded that societies and citizens adjust more quickly. These circumstances were seen to create greater risks to citizens and their lifestyle expectations, and this induced a sense of fear. With forces operating in the world beyond the control of any one national government, political leaders felt frustrated by their inability to deliver remedies to their constituents.

Soon after the turn of the millennium came the disaster of September 11, 2001. It was as if the 1989 fall of the Berlin Wall, and the 2001 fall of New York's twin towers, were allegorical bookends to a transition period portending momentous changes in the world as it was previously understood, and in the expectations of both leaders and constituents about what was to come.

1.1 A time of challenge and changing assumptions

Law at any level of government or human institution will forever be affected by the "facts on the ground," namely the circumstances of the societies or institutions which both desperately need legal norms and legal institutions, but also feel constrained by them when they seem out of date or otherwise unable to cope with changing "facts on the ground." So it is no surprise that international law and institutions would be so challenged also.

It is one purpose of this book to explore many of these challenges, not with the unachievable ambition of "solving" or completely meeting them, but rather with the desire to set forth ways to think about them, which hopefully could lead in time to constructive solutions. In short, this book is more about queries than theories.

This opening chapter will next (in section 1.2) describe the current circumstances or situation "landscape," which positions international law and with which such law must cope in order to be relevant and useful. Section 1.3 will briefly describe the implications for international law caused by the circumstances and situation, and outline some themes about these implications which will repeatedly occur and be addressed throughout this book. Finally, section 1.4 will describe the logical structure for this book – its "road map" to guide the reader's thinking and understanding of this book's goals. "Road map" is an appropriate term, because the logic of this book's structure is a bit intricate, reflecting the complexity of the subjects concerned and their many varied relationships.

Of course, many of the considerations and thoughts dealt with in this purposely short book can only be presented in brief, "tip of the iceberg" form. The literature relevant to a number of the subjects found in this book is extraordinarily voluminous, with literally thousands of book titles available.[11] This book will not extensively catalogue or appraise this literature. Instead, it will endeavor to outline some of the key issues of "jurisprudence and constitution" related to the fundamental concepts of international law and international economic law. Many of the subjects so treated could each easily be the subject of an entire book (and some are, including books by this author).[12] The goal here is to focus on the broad landscape of the many issues, and how these issues interrelate to each other, both in logic and in fact. In that sense, the "road map" analogy is apt here also. It is this author's hope that the reader will benefit from this approach and from the framework for thinking about the many issues and their relationships put forward. A limited number of footnotes will assist the reader to pursue more deeply many of the subjects indicated.

Introduction

1.2 Facts on the ground: the world situation landscape – change, interdependence, globalization, adjustment

Every explanation of change in legal structures as part of societal institutions requires at least some appreciation of the exogenous facts which condition, constrain, and motivate institutional change. With reference to the topic of this book – fundamental change in international law – it will be obvious to most readers that the changes legal systems currently face are enormous, whether compared with previous decades or with previous centuries. A brief inventory of some of these changes which are most relevant to this book's topic is therefore necessary for laying the groundwork for discussion of the changing fundamentals of international law.[1]

A complete inventory of such change could be very extensive, and will not be attempted here. But a few salient facts and conditions can easily be identified. To some extent, most of these circumstances can be understood within the broad and often ambiguous term "globalization."[2] It is a word indeed so ambiguous as to often lead to overuse and some misuse. Nevertheless, most persons know at least generally what is meant by the term. Not only does it often generate thought about broad, sometimes theoretical, and occasionally distant relationships and events, but the term can also evoke worries and fears as well as pleasurable thoughts closely relevant to the lives of individuals. "Globalization" can be blamed for economic distress such as job loss or insecurity, or credited with greater variety and stimulus for fuller lives because of increased economic efficiencies or cultural opportunities. The term clearly connotes conditions of interdependence in world economic and political relationships, which means that events or circumstances in one part of the world can have remarkably large and often swift effects in other distant parts of the world.

Likewise, these circumstances can force individuals and their association groups, including economic enterprises, to change strategies and thought processes which sometimes have gainfully guided their behavior over long periods of time. For individuals and their families who have been fortunate to enjoy a satisfying and relaxed lifestyle, these forced changes can be traumatic indeed. In some cases, expertise developed by individuals over a considerable portion of their lifetime is rendered relatively useless by such change, a situation bound to be challenging for governments and other social institutions. Leaders discover frustration in not being able to affect economic and social conditions in ways demanded by their constituents, and even sometimes find themselves made redundant by the rapidly shifting parameters of their lives.

1.2 Facts on the ground: the world situation landscape

In some contexts and some discussions the term globalization has been used to embrace two or more different concepts. On the one hand it refers to exogenous forces in the world over which humans and their institutions have little influence or effect. On the other hand it refers to directions of political and economic policies and institutions which are in some views misdirected and could be countered by appropriate human political, economic, or legal action. This would perhaps be termed "endogenous." To this author it seems that both definitions can be justified, but clarification is needed to indicate which meaning is utilized. Unfortunately the same word has these two meanings, or even a third, which would be to embrace both concepts. Even if exogenous, of course, globalization could be side-tracked by certain types of world events such as war, terror, or natural disasters.

Some observers feel that the inevitability of global forces has been overemphasized.[3] It is argued that various human endeavors including government action can actually affect and maybe counter globalization and its development, for better or worse. It seems true that governments (and markets) can in theory have important effects of this type, but it is also true that governments and human efforts can do harm. Furthermore, constraints of law, constitutions, markets, and culture (*inter alia*) may prevent governments and other human institutions from achieving effects which could be appropriate and advisable, even when they are in theory possible. Consequently, it seems that there are some aspects of globalization which are clearly exogenous (technology changes over the last half century, for example), and that other aspects may not be so fixed in theory, but in practice operate to impose great constraints on what can effectually be changed in the trends of "globalization." The problem then becomes not how to *reverse* globalization, or any part of it, but how to *cope* with it through policies which can capture the benefits of globalization while offsetting or ameliorating effects which are harmful to individuals or their families (or to world peace). The many concerns about globalization which motivate strident and even violent movements of opposition and protest, or which (as recently manifested in the European negative referenda votes) cause important political results clearly are linked to the downside potential of globalization as well as (and perhaps even more significantly) to widespread fears of those downside potentials. This clearly poses challenges which governments and other human institutions face in the current world of "globalization" in its broad and multifaceted meanings.

Despite the complexity and chameleon characteristics of globalization and its many subsidiary forms, certain concrete factors can almost always be considered on any list of causes. At least three of these factors are primarily a result of technological changes over the last century, but especially during the last half century. A number of other factors which can then also be discussed are to a large extent derivative from the core three technological changes mentioned below.

Some writers have expressed the view that "globalization," meaning relatively free movement across national borders and over long distances in the world of persons, goods, money, services, and ideas, is now no greater than at other periods such as the time at the end of the nineteenth century and the earliest decades of the twentieth century.[4] Certainly there have been such periods of importance in commerce and migration, but the argument here is that due to new technological and other factors, the world we face today is orders of magnitude different, with a vast difference in kind, and not just degree, from that of a century ago. What are these factors? They include changes in transport, communication, and weapons. These and other changes are often seen as beyond the effective control of any government, and often require responses that cannot be effective when undertaken only by individual nation-states.[5]

Transport has dramatically changed because of technologies that have vastly reduced both the time and cost of moving goods (and some services) throughout the world. Today, the consumer in many societies (especially those that do not unduly restrain international commerce) has choices never before realized. Fresh foods of enormous variety are moved swiftly, often by huge freight airplanes, so that goods which cannot endure long journeys can reach eager buyers thousands of miles distant from the site of production.[6] Other goods, such as high fashion items like women's shoes, can be produced and moved to market before the fashions change. The cost of such transport is usually a much smaller percentage of the value of the items than was the case even several decades ago. Thus, whereas transport time and cost in 1900 was a substantial *natural* barrier to trade, giving some protection to the local producers against foreign competition, this protection is now often nonexistent.

Communication has also benefited from striking reductions in cost and time, due to technology changes hardly imagined a century ago. Ideas and even products (e.g. designs, advertisements, and documents) move at the speed of light between continents, often at a cost of mere pennies. A few keystrokes on a computer can move millions of dollars. Telephone calls from London to the United States are reputed to cost less than it costs to call from inner London to its suburbs, and the marginal cost of transcontinental telephone calls (not including the capital cost of the transmittal techniques) is often fractions of 1 cent.[7] Of course, both of

1.2 Facts on the ground: the world situation landscape

these attributes – reduced cost and time – for both transport and communication have their perils. A financial crisis (or diseases) in one part of the world can flow sickeningly fast to other regions, and dangerous products or non-domestic species of plants and animals can quickly cause difficulties far from home. These factors are also dramatically affecting world production techniques. Enterprises can now, thanks to lower transport and communication costs as well as increased speed and efficiency of communication, move materials through several countries in order to complete a product, taking advantage of lower costs for varied stages of added value. Old ideas that a particular product has a "national origin," still somewhat embedded in international law rules such as trade rules, appear to be increasingly outmoded.[8]

A third major technological force with enormous impact on world affairs is the change in weapons which the world has witnessed in the last half century. The impact of new weapons on international relations was great even in the 1940s.[9] When combined with the previous factors relating to transport and communication, the increased peril to the world from misuse of weapons is easily understood. This implicates the danger from a growing variety and potency of weapons of mass destruction, but also the lethal potential of more traditional weapons combined with technologies of delivery and control (communications) that appear awesome and frightening. The risk is not only of international conflict, but of arms use within nations, whether due to civil conflict or misuse by rogue governments against their own citizens in order to perpetuate corrupt regimes, also making the world less safe. Nongovernment actors with criminal or terrorist intents add greatly to the risks.

If the three factors discussed above are not enough to distress and frighten citizens, some other factors can also be mentioned. While less scary, or in most cases even potentially beneficial, these factors can also create the type of change which calls for new evaluation and institutional structures. These factors also influence the international law system.

One of these factors, which is intimately related to governments and other societal conditions, is the striking increase in number and participation of nongovernmental actors in national and international political and economic affairs. Whether they are non-profit "NGOs" or business enterprises, the world has witnessed an enormous increase in such activity, particularly prominent in press and media reports of international conferences and structures. An important example was the published reports about the World Summit on Sustainable Development held in South Africa in 2002, described in Chapter 2.[10] Likewise the very important Fifth Ministerial

Meeting of the WTO held at Cancún, Mexico, on September 10–14, 2003, was instructive, not only for its failure to fulfill its agenda ambitions, but also for the extensive activity of NGOs and their representatives, in some cases ably assisting poor countries in their diplomatic efforts, but also allegedly playing official roles in some national diplomatic missions to the conference. Clearly the changes in costs and time of transport and communication have assisted the efforts of NGOs and turned them into forces to be reckoned with. A corollary factor partly related to this phenomena is the blurring of differences between private and public activity. What is the relationship of some nongovernment actors to the often broader and more complex policy objectives of the official government representatives?[11]

Another circumstance to contend with is the fall of the Berlin Wall. The dissolution of socialist economic and societal structures, particularly accelerated in the decade after the fall, has brought a strong upsurge in "market economic" thinking for the structuring of national and international governmental and economic institutions. The WTO is certainly one manifestation of this – but not the only one – as many national governmental systems have turned to market economic thinking as a means to better deliver more satisfying lives to their constituents.[12] These sentiments are not exempt from criticism, of course, particularly when shifts from non-market structures to more market-oriented activities create adjustment costs which are sometimes not shared appropriately among all citizens,[13] or when special interests profit excessively from opportunities caused by these shifts.

Another related factor is the alleged hegemony of a single great power (after the demise of the Soviet Union). The awesome military and economic power of the United States has been much discussed and also criticized. When what one national entity in the world spends on military capacity and armaments each year is more than the total amount spent for those purposes by all the other nations which make up the next nine ranking military powers, there is reason for concern.[14] One can be partly thankful that it is the United States, rather than some other powers which could be imagined in that role. Yet the structure of the US government, democratic and constitutional as it may be, has not always been regarded as oriented toward long-term, worldwide policy objectives, making many people uncomfortable with the apparent monopoly on power the US controls. Democratic deficiencies with respect to electoral procedures and parliamentary campaign contributions lead to worries about a hegemonic approach to world affairs. Perhaps the ideas that note the relative importance of "soft power" as opposed to "hard" military might will prove to have force[15] as the world experiences the new circumstances and failures of unilateralist tendencies. Yet what alternatives may fill in the apparent failures of existing international institutions? One must doubt the ability of "balance of power" theories, or various other constructions of international relations which have been influential in the past. These are matters to which this text will return in later chapters.

In the light of the risks and circumstances requiring speedy and therefore uncomfortable change, it is not surprising that many massive manifestations of protest against "globalization" have been witnessed in the last few years. Yet what can be done? Is international law a solution? Or even a helpful addition to a set of solutions? That is part of what this book is tackling. But the *New York Times* author Thomas Friedman in his book, *The Lexis and the Olive Tree*, eloquently drives home an important and poignant reality[16] with his depiction of the "electronic herd" as the new form of international economic "governance."

1.3 Implications for international law and its role for international relations: challenges to the fundamental logic and axioms of international law (a brief overview of things to come)

In the light of the circumstances outlined in the preceding section, what are some of the implications for international law, including implications for international economic law as a subdivision of international law (a concept returned to in a later chapter)? In addition, one should ask whether the experience of international economic law (and particularly the experience of the WTO, as discussed in Chapters 4 and 5) is relevant to changes in international law generally. This section is designed only to introduce some of these questions, and also to mention some themes which will reoccur in various later chapters.

One of the clear implications of the facts outlined in the previous section is that nation-state governments are facing greater difficulties than ever in "governing," in the sense of offering policies which can be adopted at the nation-state level which have a reasonably good chance of "delivering" the benefits sought by constituents. If traditional barriers to risks spreading from one nation to another have been diminished through reduced costs and time for transport and communications, governments may try to use governmental barriers to reduce those risks. But as the world becomes more interdependent, the potential utility and effectiveness of those governmental barriers is increasingly doubtful. Thus, there should be inevitable pressures to turn to international cooperation of various sorts,

Introduction

often necessitating reliance on institutional mechanisms (e.g., international organizations), either existing or yet to be formed. However, the experience of some international institutions has not been satisfactory.[1]

When one adds to the mix the problem of weapons and the complexity of nongovernmental actors (including terrorist actors), some of the older paradigms of international law increasingly appear antiquated and inappropriate. Can the system rely on "state consent" as the basis of all international norm legitimation? What about "rogue states"? What about the forces of the world market which often can ignore international legal norms when no effective "compliance pressures" seem to exist? Do the ancient and outdated concepts of Westphalian sovereignty, granting a state monarch power to do his will, regardless of its impact on his own citizens, still apply? Can the largely fictional notion of equality of nation-states really work when it operates in particular contexts with a different reality? What is the appropriate allocation of international institutional power among states with vast differences in population, natural resources, military force, and economic power?

Can treaties always solve the problems that the international legal system faces? To what degree can reliance be placed on customary international law given its extreme ambiguity and indefiniteness in some cases? What is to be done about the "hold-out states" that refuse to recognize a developing customary norm and also refuse to sign a treaty?

Even as to treaties which have been adopted, is the international system constructed in a way that allows the treaties to operate efficiently, or does the often extremely difficult process for amendment render treaties so rigid that governments avoid them?

On a more detailed level, can the current rules about interpreting a treaty, such as those expressed in the Vienna Convention on the Law of Treaties (VCLT) as embodying customary international law, operate effectively in twenty-first-century circumstances, when major treaties with large memberships do not neatly fit into paradigms which seem to have derived from concepts associated with bilateral or small group membership treaties?

Can a strict rule of non-interference in a nation-state's "sovereignty" really work in a world that includes governments that have been willing to undertake horrible actions against their own citizens or against humanity? If not, what should external action regarding such governments entail, and what are appropriate limits to such action?

What legal entities should be considered as the appropriate beneficiaries of treaties or other international law? Clearly beneficiaries are

1.4 Contours and road map – the structure of this book

not only governments. Which individuals should benefit? Which nongovernmental organizations? What type of nongovernmental enterprises? Which should be considered deserving of legal operations for their benefit (e.g. market participants regarding WTO rules, or individuals when rules should protect human rights)? In what situations should nongovernment actors be given privileges of participating in the formation and application of international law rules?

Examination of the extensively documented practice of the operation of international economic law reveals not only detailed experiences which bear on many of the questions posed above, but also provides analysis of some of those questions in greater depth and detail than can be found in any other sources.[2] It also reveals the necessity of an institutional framework for world markets to work successfully, and arguably establishes the rationale for a juridical (dispute settlement) type of institution as vitally important for such an institutional framework. At least for economic activity based largely on market-oriented frameworks, a juridical system with at least modest precedent recognition is likely to be central to lower the "risk premium" for many international transactions. The WTO jurisprudence also demonstrates the importance of nongovernment beneficiaries of the rule-based system, particularly the market participants.[3]

1.4 Contours and road map – the structure of this book

This book consists of eight chapters, grouped in an overall structure of three parts. These parts present the logic underlying this book as follows. Part I (Chapters 1, 2 and 3) mainly focuses on presenting the problems and circumstances challenging the fundamentals of international law and international economic law. Part II (Chapters 4 and 5) focuses on the WTO and its experience, history, and structure, and how these provide interesting examples and analyses relevant not only to international economic law, but to general international law. Part III (Chapters 6, 7 and 8) then explores various approaches for future thinking about the problems and applications, responding to them in their particular circumstances.

At the end of each part (in the last chapter and last section of each of the three parts), there is a brief reflection overview about how the materials of that part's chapters relate to the overall logic of the book, with the exception of the final chapter (Chapter 8) which is devoted to conclusions and overall perspectives for the book as a whole.

The following explains this structure in a bit more detail. For example, Part I ("problems presented") includes this chapter (introductory), and

Introduction

then moves on to Chapter 2 for an overview of international law subjects and the criticisms, concerns, and uncertainties of these. Chapter 2, after an introduction (2.1), explores (in 2.2) some of the conditions and circumstances of current international affairs, but, in contrast to Chapter 1, the focus is such conditions and circumstances which relate particularly to international law and international economic law. Then Chapter 2 takes up in turn some detail regarding challenges to fundamentals of international law (2.3), then international economic law (2.4), and next international institutions and their legal frameworks (2.5). A few preliminary perspectives and conclusions are presented in 2.6.

Chapter 3 is focused entirely on the subject of sovereignty, in order to explore what it means today (if anything) and the fallacies and hypocrisy with which it is laced. Also discussed is a newer way of looking at the subject of sovereignty which could be entitled "sovereignty modern" or "sovereignty in slices."

Next, in Part II ("WTO") Chapters 4 and 5 take up two separate groups of functions and institutional activities of the WTO. Chapter 4 is devoted to the non-dispute settlement functions, experiences, and responsibilities of the WTO. This entails discussion of WTO and GATT history ("constitutional evolution"), the treaty structure, the decision making processes (including "consensus"), various institutional and systemic problems (some resulting from nation-state members clinging to "sovereignty" notions), the scope of subject-matter competence of the organization, and the legal relationship of the WTO to its members' domestic laws. The emphasis here is on the diplomatic and political side of the WTO.

Chapter 5 then turns to the all-important WTO dispute settlement system, and explores what such a system means for nation-state sovereignty, as well as for the effectiveness and viability of the WTO and its ability to achieve its goals established by its nation-state members.

WTO is chosen for focus in Part II, not only because this author has special expertise, but also because of the importance of this organization in world affairs, and the detail and extent of its experience already in its ten years of existence. This organization is described by some as the most important international organization in existence, with the probable exception of the United Nations. The WTO activities poignantly and frequently illustrate many of the problems and policy tensions which exist in international relations, such as the meaning and evolution of "sovereignty" concepts, and the impact and "constitutional development" of a dispute settlement system which some describe as the most powerful and influential (in the sense of real world effects) of any international tribunal

1.4 Contours and road map – the structure of this book

type system. The number of front page news articles about the WTO dispute procedures is striking testimony to support these observations.

Finally, the three short chapters of Part III explore responses and approaches for analyzing the challenges to existing international law fundamentals, with the realization that these approaches to some extent are demonstrated by the experience and practice of international economic law as well as other sources, but also that international law and its approaches are relevant to the challenges for international economic law.

Chapter 6 presents several ideas about methods of thinking about the foundations of international law, including the elaboration of ideas presented in Chapter 3 regarding sovereignty. One concept noted in Chapter 3 suggests the idea of sovereignty really being about "allocating power," which seems central to some of the valid portions of "sovereignty-modern" ideas. Chapter 6 contains an illustration of how this idea could operate, and will also deal to a certain extent with the role of economic analysis in the international law context.

Chapter 7 is designed simply to suggest a variety of applications of the principles developed in the preceding chapters. It takes up a short selection of discrete and important international law and international institutional problems and activities in order to suggest how some of these principles might be relevant to subjects as widely varied as the environment, competition policy, the United Nations and use of force, human rights, health policies, and so on. The overall lesson is that there is not any single simple formula for approaching these many problems, but rather a need to "disaggregate and analyze" the subjects concerned, to recognize that supposedly singular "international law" concepts such as "treaty" or "dispute procedure" have varied forms which probably demand different institutional solutions.

Finally, Chapter 8 will present some broad reflections and conclusions, with some comments on some of the themes running throughout the book.

2

The real world impinges on international law: exploring the challenges to the fundamental assumptions of international law and institutions

> Our post-war institutions were built for an inter-*national* world, but we now live in a *global* world.
>
> UN Secretary-General Kofi Annan[1]

2.1 Introduction to exploring the challenges and their impacts on international law

International law, since Grotius at least, has often benefited from a presumption of superiority when it comes to comparisons with other legal systems (regional, national, sub-federal, etc.).[2] Nevertheless, there are many serious criticisms of international law as such, or of certain sub-parts or types of international law; not all of these criticisms are balanced or even cogent. This phenomenon is not particularly new. Older versions of this criticism have even denied that "international law" is "law" as such, mistakenly using nineteenth-century approaches (cf. John Austin, among others) to a definition of law that is well recognized as not careful or adequately descriptive of real-life effective implications of human measures termed "international law."[3] The fallacy is even more easily recognized in our contemporary world of "globalized" institutions, such as markets, communications, transport, and weaponry, as was briefly described in Chapter 1. There are vast empirically observable, real impacts on human institutional (governmental, business, academic, etc.) behavior due to norms embraced by the phrase "international law," even though those norms and their relationships to behavior are much more complex than some of the simple paradigms of legal norm application in national domestic and other legal systems.

2.1 Exploring the challenges and their impacts on international law

Some of the criticisms, however, have bite and cannot be easily dismissed without attention. Indeed, some of the criticisms require a thoughtful response, taking into account changes in the international law system generally, and in certain specific regimes. This is particularly true in our contemporary world, in which the circumstances that influence the formation of the international law regimes have so fundamentally changed.

This chapter is designed broadly to introduce the variety of detailed developments and conditions of our contemporary world which are logically and empirically affecting how a variety of human institutions are reacting to international law norms, or alleged norms. The subject is often discussed in relation to concepts of "sovereignty," which will be briefly mentioned in this chapter. The fundamental importance of the connection between sovereignty and many accepted assumptions of international law will be the detailed focus of Chapter 3.

Section 2.2, therefore, will give an overview of and briefly explore various current phenomena impinging on traditional notions of the international legal system and how it operates in the real world of participants in (or subjects of) that system, such as diplomats, governments, business entities, and civil society in general. Again, there is a very substantial literature (growing every day), inventorying these phenomena and attempting various explanations about their relationships to human and institutional behavior and to theories of "legitimacy" regarding norms. Clearly only a small part of the literature and the observable phenomena can be touched on here, but this portion of the whole will illustrate the necessity for some rethinking about fundamental principles and relationships.

Sections 2.3, 2.4, and 2.5 will each take up a segment of the very broad landscape of international norms, in order to reflect on the impacts of the phenomena overviewed in 2.2. First, section 2.3 will examine the field of public or "general" international law, with discussions about customary international law and treaties.

Section 2.4 will then turn to the subject of international economic law (IEL), which, in some ways, is the major theme of this book, in the sense that the World Trade Organization is the central illustration of legal and jurisprudential developments influenced by phenomena of our contemporary world (e.g. "globalization"). Nevertheless, as noted in Chapter 1, this book has the ambition of exploring relationships of international economic law to international law generally, and some of the concepts involved will be introduced in section 2.4.

Section 2.5 will turn to the increasingly important subject of international law institutions, such as intergovernmental organizations, not only in order to explore the impacts on those entities of the phenomena overviewed in section 2.2, but also to notice or suggest developments through which institutions may be part of the "answer" for increasing problems of the international legal system, and its fundamental axioms, such as "sovereignty."

Section 2.6 will conclude this chapter by noting some of the implications of the discussion in the preceding sections, and segue into Chapter 3, which takes up the concept of "sovereignty" in greater depth.

2.2 Circumstances and conditions

Section 2 of Chapter 1 introduced some of the fundamental phenomena characterizing our contemporary world, including ease of transport, communications, weaponry, and the way in which markets operate. Clearly, there is often a causal relationship between those more fundamental developments and a large variety of more specific and detailed phenomena which affect the way in which international legal norms apply or operate. This section, 2.2, now examines these various phenomena in somewhat greater detail (but still as an overview), to provide the groundwork for the discussions of international law in the later sections of this chapter. In essence, it seems possible to think of these phenomena as roughly grouped into categories of government and nongovernment phenomena. The first group below (Parts *a* to *e*) are the former; the other parts (*f* to *h*) can be grouped under the nongovernment impacts heading. However, as noted in Chapter 1, for virtually every illustration mentioned below, a fundamental fact of "globalization," as that term is used in this book, is the impact of the globalized market systems over which governments often have very limited control.[1] Bearing that in mind, the discussion below explores "markets" in the discussion of nongovernment impacts.

a. Governments and fragmentation or aggregation

A curious phenomenon concerning the way in which governments operate in more recent times can be detected. Two dimensions of this are sometimes described as "fragmentation," and "coalition of regional arrangements." It seems that government constituents or citizens are not always happy with a notion of applicable and significant government activities always applying at one level, such as the "nation-state." A number of

2.2 Circumstances and conditions

"nations" have either divided into separate entities, each sometimes claiming full "sovereignty," such as the former Soviet Union, the former Socialist Federal Republic of Yugoslavia, or former Czechoslovakia, or have taken moves in the opposite direction to join with other nation-states into regional governmental entities (often focused on trade or other economic matters). Examples of the latter include most notably the European Union, but also entities such as the customs union Mercosur[2] or the free trade area NAFTA,[3] and large numbers of other "free trade agreements" with various dimensions of integration of government authority.[4] Newer possibilities also exist on the horizon, especially in Asia.[5] Some countries, such as Belgium, have even moved in both directions.[6]

Clearly this creates perplexing conceptual questions for international (and national) law, including issues of "statehood," allocation of powers (see Chapter 3), dominion over land and minerals, ideas of "citizenship," concepts of state succession (such as related to sovereign debts), and many more. The developing complexity of gradations of "independence" or "sovereignty" challenges some of the established notions of international law.

b. Internal governance

Government entities at all levels, but particularly those that claim "sovereign statehood," with its supposed monopoly on the internal exercise of power, increasingly find themselves constrained in how they use this governing power. Most prominently, they are often constrained by more than fifty[7] treaties regarding human rights, but increasingly are subject to criticism, if not legal measures, relating to their methods of governance. Ideas have been floated that governments have an international law obligation to operate as a democracy – the "democratic entitlement" described by Professor Thomas Franck.[8] Treaties have been established to limit "corruption," and international organizations, particularly financial Bretton Woods organizations (the IMF and the World Bank) have imposed conditions of lending which very deeply constrain basic governmental policy decisions such as those bearing on taxation, social security, economic structures, and government spending. To put it mildly, in many such cases the meaning of "sovereign statehood" is highly attenuated. Apart from "hard" and even "soft" law of treaties, the concept of "rogue" or "failed" state has been developing in circumstances of extreme misgovernance or mistreatment of humans (citizens or otherwise) or of risks in relation to weapons of mass destruction. This has led to expressed and sometimes official government views of the need to interfere severely with such governments in ways that call for extremely different concepts of sovereignty.[9]

c. Extraterritorial measures of governments

Increasingly various measures of government regulation have "extraterritorial effects" beyond the regulating governments' territorial or citizen control limits. Brief mention of a number of such situations will suffice to recognize many problems that arise:

Anti-trust or competition law regulations, particularly by nations which have large markets that are intertwined with international effects (notable are the United States and the European Union) often impact on other nations.[10]

Securities laws regulating a variety of market entities (government and non-government) such as accounting standards, fraud on investors, transparency requirements, and a variety of other investment activities, some of which differ dramatically from one society to the next (such as insider trading rules), also are evidence of changing dimensions of governmental activities which affect or are subject to international legal norms in a variety of complex ways.[11] The enormous number of treaties relating to investment regulations of nation-states is a more detailed example.[12]

Taxes in some jurisdictions often have major effects outside jurisdictional borders.[13]

Various social and even cultural standards of individual governments sometimes try to apply various social and even cultural standards beyond their borders or to impose de facto pressures (such as trade restrictions) on foreign societies to reduce what are perceived as competitive advantages for a society without comparable social regulations, such as workplace standards, labor regulations, environmental standards, limits on foreign films, and so on.

Environmental measures designed to protect the "global commons" have been a particular source of contention, especially in the elaborate jurisprudence of the WTO.[14]

d. The relationship of international law to national domestic legal systems

One of the most misunderstood characteristics of international law (IL) is the its relationship to national domestic (often confusingly termed "municipal") law. Part of the reason for this confusion is the great variety of legal doctrines among nation-states regarding this subject. There has been a general concept that this question of how IL impacts domestic law is one which, absent explicit (treaty) agreement, is left to each nation-state to decide based on its constitutional and other societal circumstances.

2.2 Circumstances and conditions

Thus some states (sometimes termed "monist") view IL as integrally part of their domestic law, even without any specific national law measure (sometimes termed an "act of transformation") resulting from legislative or executive action to introduce the international norm into domestic jurisprudence.[15]

For example, Article 94 of the Constitution of the Netherlands stipulates that international treaties trump statutory laws, and the Netherlands courts apply international courts directly as such.[16] Other nations take an opposite view (termed "dualist") such that any international norm, especially a treaty norm but sometimes even customary international law, becomes part of domestic law only with such additional action.[17] In the United States for example, there is a fairly extensive debate about the degree of adoption in domestic law for IL norms, either at the federal or state levels. The United States has a mixed monist/dualist system (at least arguably) that is even more confusing than normal.[18]

There is a difference of viewpoint about the trends regarding this issue also. Some observers feel that there is a distinct trend among nations toward the "monist" view. In some cases these observers cite relatively new "constitutions" to support their view, although it has to be admitted that the record is mixed, and some constitutions actually take a different stance for certain subjects, such as human rights, than they would take for other subjects. The European Union Court of Justice has developed some jurisprudence on this subject which can, in the view of some, be termed "muddled."[19]

In the United States (and perhaps in other nations), there seems to be a distinct trend, spurred by explicit control of this issue by the Congress,[20] towards the view that specific major treaties shall not have "direct application" ("self executing") status in US domestic law. A statute is usually enacted applying the international norm in the manner in which the Congress desires, with congressional views about interpretation of those IL norms often fairly explicit (and not always upheld by international juridical bodies such as the WTO Appellate Body).[21] This "dualist" approach is advocated partly as a "check and balance" against international misconduct, or sometimes by broad ambiguous reference to "preserving sovereignty."[22] A recent case of the US Supreme Court has some interesting implications for the evolving US domestic jurisprudence on this subject, and there may be some international jurisprudence implications also.[23]

One confusion about these attributes relates to the domestic effect of a treaty which is not "directly applicable." It is sometimes stated, even in court opinions, that such a treaty is irrelevant, and need not even be discussed. This seems clearly wrong, because there are a variety of concepts, including the "consistency principle," which allow various effects of such a treaty, particularly the effects on the way in which a domestic court should interpret its own national statutes in the light of treaty or other international law obligations.[24] We return to this problem in section 4.6.

e. Diplomatic and other actions inside international organizations

The diplomatic and governance activities internal to international governmental organizations seem to have been changing during the past few decades. For one thing, the number of nation-state members has been dramatically increasing, and with notions of equality of members coupled with egalitarian voting structures, achieving the necessary agreement to move ahead on some subjects becomes increasingly difficult. In addition (as noted below in *f*), the activity of NGOs has become extremely significant, clearly causally related to the circumstances outlined in Chapter 1, particularly communication and transport (travel) speed and lower cost.

It does not escape the attention of nations, especially those which are more powerful, that despite their size they are nevertheless assigned one vote which is "equivalent" to the vote of very tiny nations with populations, economies, and land masses less than 1 percent of the size of those of the larger nation.[25] Numerical analysis can show that in an extreme (and therefore unlikely but still illustrative) case, less than 5 percent of the population of the world could control a majority of votes in an international organization such as the United Nations (or WTO).[26] Furthermore, some legal entities may control a number of votes in a particular institutional structure, such as the twenty-five votes which the European Union can vote as a unit in the WTO (sometimes assisted by affiliations with various association treaties which could allow mustering of sixty or eighty votes).[27] It is little wonder that the United Nations has offset some of these problems with a veto power, and that financial institutions such as the IMF and the World Bank utilize a weighted voting system, despite strident and increasing criticisms of each of the "unequal voting" systems.

One approach taken in some international institutions to help offset the risk of "unreal recognition of power" involved in one-nation–one-vote majority systems, is to demand use of a "consensus approach" that allows any party to veto a proposed measure. This has much value in preserving a broad measure of legitimacy for measures, but of course risks paralysis or extreme holdout techniques (sometimes for bargaining purposes unrelated to the measure proposed.).[28]

2.2 Circumstances and conditions

Another trend which can be noticed, albeit not yet with a large impact, is the increasingly made proposal that international organizations must be subject to "good governance" ideals, just as the nation-state should.[29] These ideals usually include "transparency," so that the public (NGOs included) can observe actions and decision making in "real time," that is in a way that gives opportunity for comment and input. In addition, sometimes lumped under the term "transparency" but conceptually different, is the ideal of "participation" by various entities and parties ("stakeholders, civil society, constituents") which will be affected by the measures of the international institution. The conceptual ideals of political science, which note the characteristics necessary for "good governance" often at the nation-state level, can be utilized for evaluating appropriate structures of international institutions.[30]

Another increasingly prominent concept which can be seen developing in international institutions is that which is sometimes ambiguously termed "variable geometry."[31] This is the idea that with regard to legal standards and norms which may be applied to nations and their societies (and economic structures), "one size does not fit all." Those special circumstances, such as poverty, or lack of governmental capacity, or extreme disease, or a natural disaster, may be a justification for measures which do not apply equally to all nations or all citizen groups.[32]

The fascinating "constitutional" developments of the European Union form an extremely interesting "case study" of the development of some of these international institutional concepts discussed above. The European Union has struggled for years with the problem of appropriate voting and majority requirements for decisions, and has recently developed proposals for relatively novel and intriguing ideas of variable geometry, while at the same time expressing the values involved in "subsidiarity."[33]

The increase in the size, complexity, variation, and budgets of many international institutions has also *affected* the "internal transparency and participation" dimension, a situation which is creating acrimony and distrust in some quarters. Some governments, often the smaller and poorer ones, complain that they have trouble learning about what is going on, and also have difficulty (often due to lack of "capacity," meaning personnel, travel budgets, mission office space, etc.) in participating effectively and therefore difficulty in protecting their own political and societal interests. Clearly, more attention will be focused on these aspects of "good governance" in international institutions.

Finally it must be noted that the international institutions are not immune from some of the difficulties often felt in nation-states relating to fraud, corruption, misapplication of resources, malfeasance by high officials, and misuse of power embodied in some officials or ruling sub-bodies of such institutions.[34] Even apart from misfeasance of this degree, there are also some perceptions that ruling elites become entrenched in certain international institutions, and this results in a dangerous lack of sensitivity to a broad range of local needs felt by nation-states or their sub-parts.

f. Nongovernment actors and organizations

Turning now to several phenomena affecting international law which can be grouped as "nongovernment" (although clearly intertwined with many of the governmental subjects discussed above), clearly one of the most profound and importantly impacting developments is the role of non-government actors and participants.[35] Many of these are termed NGOs (nongovernment organizations) even when particular "NGOs" comprise one individual or a loose grouping of individuals or legal or non-legal entities. These come in various "colors," which we can classify as "non-profit," "profit or business," and "illicit," although these terms probably do not exhaust the possible "colors" one will encounter. A brief discussion of each of these should "map the landscape" adequately for our purposes here.

Non-profit. The range, person-power participation, subject-matter scope, and financing of NGOs involved in international diplomacy and institutions today are truly astonishing, and clearly are causally related to the discussion in Chapter 1 of the circumstances of globalization such as reduced cost and time for communication and travel. The Internet and cell phones (worldwide access) are in great use by NGOs of all types. The number of such entities is overwhelming in some diplomatic situations.

The World Summit on Sustainable Development (Johannesburg, South Africa, August 26–September 4, 2002) was an interesting example of some of these trends. At that conference there were 60,000 people registered to attend. Governments had 5,000 registrants, and the media had 2,000. Thus there were 53,000 from nongovernmental entities (individuals, organizations, and other nongovernment players of some type or another). The number of NGOs registered for the Johannesburg Summit was 15,000. Some who watched any of the televised sessions of the summit have the impression that the NGOs were running the show, with many press interviews and so on. That, in turn, raises a series of questions. Is this level of NGO participation appropriate? democratic? legitimate? In some ways, many governments are more democratic than some of the

2.2 Circumstances and conditions

NGOs that are criticizing international governmental institutions for being undemocratic.[36] Nevertheless this is part of the context of modern diplomacy, and NGO participation can clearly enhance certain types and levels of policy making, as will be noted elsewhere in this book.

Similar phenomena are reported at a variety of other international diplomatic conferences, including some which have had responsibilities for developing concrete treaty obligations. The International Conference on Financing for Development (Monterrey, Mexico, March 18–22, 2002) accredited 557 NGOs, and 2,600 representatives of approximately 700 organizations attended a parallel Global NGO Forum.[37]

The Fifth Session of the WTO Ministerial Conference, held in Cancún on September 10–14, 2003, supposedly a definitive governmental negotiating meeting, is a good example of the added complexity brought about by the heavy presence of NGOs (some with constructive participation, some not). Seventy-six international intergovernmental organizations had observer status. The Cancún Ministerial attracted a presence of almost 800 NGOs and close to 1,600 of their representatives. This was the highest number of civil society representations at a WTO Ministerial Conference during the then nine years' existence of the WTO.[38] Some poor countries were aided greatly by some NGO assistance in preparing and advocating proposals, and in some cases NGO persons were incorporated into national diplomatic delegations to this ministerial meeting and so even had "speaking parts" as well as full access to all restricted documents. In itself this is not necessarily inappropriate, but it is recognized that there are certain risks in these developments, for example,[39]

NGO personnel and officials are generally not elected, and often not accountable to any true democratic constituency.

NGOs may be single-issue oriented, and use their position and leverage with some diplomats actively to pursue goals which are not balanced by a variety of opposing policy objectives which nation-states (particularly larger ones) must consider when balancing priorities.

NGOs assist poor governments which lack adequate staff and personnel with needed expertise and negotiation skills. This can be for the better, but some observers wonder whether in all cases the nongovernment assistance is directed toward achieving the goals of the assisted government.

NGOs are remarkably wealthy in some cases. For example, the annual budget of OXFAM (generally viewed as a highly constructive and responsible NGO) is over US$300 million – about three times the budget of the entire WTO. Such wealth gives power in the form of the ability to travel, provide research and documentary resources, entertain, and so on. For this reason some poorer developing countries are very antagonistic to NGO participation at the WTO, because they fear that such NGOs are funded by and therefore influenced by moneyed interests in the industrial countries which are contrary to the poorer countries' interests. Clearly this is a mixed picture, since there are a number of instances where the power exercised by NGOs, including church groups, have been very effective in aiding the development of appropriate policies to assist the third world poor.[40]

NGOs can be remarkably non-transparent, hiding the sources of their funding and thereby deceiving the particular institutions, diplomats, and governments about what goals they really seek to achieve. Sometimes it is conjectured that some NGOs seem to desire to disrupt more than to achieve.[41]

Of course, these various worries and risks are not absent at the nation-state level either, so perhaps it can be concluded that on balance the NGOs do more good than harm, and this certainly seems true for a relatively large number of NGOs, especially those that make a point of transparency including funding sources (often through their extensive web sites).[42]

But the bottom line for this book's analysis is that the NGO phenomenon has added a whole new dimension to the practice of "diplomacy" or conduct of international relations, particularly including the processes of international institutions.[43]

Profit organizations and businesses. Another phenomenon which demands adjustment by the older traditions of international law is the increased role of business organizations which go beyond national borders. The so-called "multinational corporation," or MNC, has been the subject of much study for many decades, some very critical, other complimentary. Again it is not the role of this text to take sides, except to note that there is a huge variety of such entities, and the roles they play in international relations and institutions vary enormously. Therefore international legal institutions must be sensitive to these roles, be sure to understand them, and adjust accordingly.

The immense power of some of these entities has been noted. The total annual revenue or business status of many MNCs is greater than the gross domestic product (GDP) of all but a dozen or so national economies in the world. This does not immediately translate into "power on the world scene," but the importance of this power cannot be dismissed, just as is the case for non-profit NGOs.

In a number of cases of international law importance, MNCs have a major interest in government regulatory measures, whether it be in food product standards, appliance and vehicle safety standards, or dozens of other regulatory measures including standards and rules applying to employment, the environment, financial transactions, taxation, and corporate good governance.[44] It is therefore quite clear that when an

2.2 Circumstances and conditions

international institution measure or other international law norm has an impact on a corporation or an economic sector association of such or similar entities, those parties will have an incentive to "weigh in" on the processes which could affect them. Manifestations of this are apparent in media reports almost every day. Mention can be made of pharmaceutical company interests in WTO negotiations, food processing company interests in World Health Organization (WHO) potential standards, film and publication company interests in intellectual property issues, and of course interest in investment, competition, and financial service rules in many countries, as well as coordination or harmonization efforts of international institutions.[45]

There has developed a fairly extensive literature about "regulatory competition," meaning the subject concerning the way in which different countries may compete for inward investment (or other international transactions such as exports or imports) by lowering standards protecting consumers or other groups.[46] This "race to the bottom" idea has been much worked over, and countered by ideas about "race to the top,"[47] but again the point here is that these policy issues must be reflected in the operation of relevant international law and institutional measures. One worry that is often expressed is that of "regulatory capture," by which the government regulators are "captured" by affiliation, conversation, access, political contributions, or even corruption, so that the regulators unevenly favor the regulated in their decisions. A key conceptual question for international affairs, particularly as to economic subjects, is whether the international institutions are so constituted as to make them "capture-able" by regulated interest groups, who can use the "leverage" of international norms to achieve their favored results in situations where they could not have achieved these results within their own nation-state (or even other nation-states).[48] Part of the heavy protests of the "anti-globalization" groups is tied to these worries. The international legal system must also cope with these phenomena.

Finally, at least brief reference must be made of nongovernment "*illicit operators.*" It is probably enough to remind readers of the very difficult problems of illegal drug trafficking, the similar problems of money laundering and fraudulent or illegal flows of funds internationally, and of course, even more serious, the question of nongovernment terrorist group operations which pose enormous worries about the international system, and all of which seem to benefit from some of the attributes of globalization and interdependence, including the ease of travel and transport and communication.

g. Markets and their operation

As noted before, the role of markets and their "globalization" is a leitmotif for this book, and is part of the "intellectual infrastructure" which is a logical foundation for exploring the phenomena currently impacting on the world legal and institutional structure. A few examples can be noted.

It has already been noted that production has been greatly changed by the transport/communication revolution, so that it is increasingly common for unfinished products to move through several economies for value-added operations, until finally becoming a completed product. Thus older international economic law concepts of the "origin of goods" often do not seem to be appropriate.[49] Likewise, older concepts of "reciprocity" tied to measuring the value of products in international exchange become more problematic.

Already implied by discussion above in this section are the problems of extraordinarily swift flow of funds (millions transferred with several computer key clicks). Problems exist even when all such transactions are legal and even ethical. Economic disturbances such as a collapsing national currency or the flight of capital from a disturbed nation, as in the Asian financial crisis of 1997–1998,[50] can evolve swiftly and cause great economic harm to far distant societies, thus suggesting the importance of international institutions and norms to assist in "crisis management."

Markets are also heavily influenced (and sometimes troubled) by the regulatory problems mentioned above. The operation of the global market can make it difficult and even impossible for a single nation or group of several nations to regulate effectively so as to achieve appropriate, democratically chosen societal goals. This can be noticed in connection with antitrust/competition problems, as well as with numerous different types of financial service problems. Very prominent in this regard are investment flow problems. The very large number of treaties (mostly bilateral) relating to government treatment of investment is a signal of the importance of this subject to norms of international law.[51]

The interdependence of the world market and its vulnerability to some national government decisions is poignantly demonstrated by elaborate negotiations in the WTO context with regard to agriculture subsidies. In a very important case at the WTO, Brazil complained against the United States for its subsidies related to cotton production, and part of the case which led the WTO first-level panel to conclude that the US practice was inconsistent with its WTO obligations concerning agricultural policy and subsidies was an academic study which demonstrated to the panel the damage which such US subsidies caused to cotton producers in Brazil.[52] The Appellate Body has largely supported the first-level rulings.[53] The impact of this decision on the Doha negotiating round is likely to be profound.

h. Transmittals: disease, finance, public opinion and information

Finally in this section, the discussion needs to note the impact on the international system and its institutions and norms of what may be termed "transmittals," referring to the now current relative ease with which certain types of problems can transfer from one nation to another, often due again to the globalization effects of both travel/transport and communication, *inter alia*. Often these transmittals are becoming even more serious problems because of the confused state of international affairs and institutional weaknesses.

The striking worldwide impact of certain communicable diseases is an easily appreciated example. SARS, HIV-AIDS, avian influenza, other types of influenza, and other diseases raise the risk of extreme loss of life, experienced in long past historical times of plague or early twentieth-century influenza. Clearly activity more widely applicable than just one or a few nation-states is imperative, and organizations such as the World Health Organization become essential and thus need to be understood.

The problem of rapid flow of funds has already been noted above, but in addition, the control of profoundly anti-social and illegal transactions, such as money supporting terrorism, or money proceeds of fraud or drug traffic, faces the problem presented by ease of transport/communication, as well as the advantage offered to criminal elements by the patchwork of individual legal systems and a lack of a coherent international legal framework which often exists.

Finally it can also be noted that the ease of travel and communication, combined with the operation of a "globalized market," can cause information which is extremely important and influential for political purposes and public opinion to flow very quickly in great amounts (and in some cases is fraudulent or otherwise untrue). A remarkable example of this speed was the incredible worldwide distribution of disturbing pictures of inappropriate treatment of prisoners in Iraq by personnel acting under the authority of the US government.[54] Less flamboyant, but still potentially very important, is the remarkable amount of information available worldwide on the Internet, which includes vast amounts relevant to government policies, and enables exchange and commentary by huge numbers of persons and entities, to say nothing about the potential for fund-raising for various political purposes. Much information relating to the application of international law norms, and to activities of international institutions, can now be accessed quickly and cheaply, providing the opportunity for a much broader policy participation and a greater spread of expertise on a worldwide basis. This means that international diplomacy and legal activity are no longer the sole domain of elite groups, but now must respond to the evaluation of concrete facts as well as wide-ranging opinions from great numbers of participants (including, this author must say, students worldwide who now read scholarly works and have little hesitation in querying and challenging the content through computer and Internet communications). It also means that many professional, high-level services can now be "outsourced," or performed from great distances, which can compel competitive adjustment in far-away societies at a remarkably fast rate, as author Thomas Friedman has so graphically portrayed.[55]

This also means that very complex material relating to international legal procedures and disputes such as the World Court, or the WTO dispute settlement system, or other juridical institutions, is readily available for appraisal and comment, again reducing the role of elite groups which may before now have had relatively exclusive access to such information.

2.3 International law and its discontents

Persons who have the misfortune of tangling deeply with the logic and sources of international law generally, know well the extensive history and literature of the subject, embracing the Greeks and the Romans and, more recently, eminent philosophers including Kant, Austin, Kelsen, Stone, and many more in recent decades.[1] These and others realize how, in some cases, a rigorous pursuit of the "holy grails" of universal truths can end in a recognition of "universal uncertainties." Indeed some of this phenomenon is an attribute of legal philosophy generally, with its many rich avenues of discourse and some remarkable contributions to understanding. To some extent, international law is but a sub-subject of the broader explorations of questions such as "what is law?" and numerous other jurisprudential main and side streets. An interesting question, not to be considered in depth here, is whether there is something about international law that renders these explorations "different in kind" and not just "different in degree." The complexity of multi-levels of power, legitimacy, monopolies of force, or lacks thereof, perhaps suggest some such difference.

2.3 International law and its discontents

In that light, and recognizing the limited goal of this chapter, a number of questions about international law can be mentioned (but only as a sample of a broader terrain). Here are some.

(1) What is the source of international law?
(2) Related to (1) what are the elements of legitimacy for international law norms?
(3) To what degree are those two questions related to and dependent on the concept of sovereignty (a concept under considerable criticism which Chapter 3 will overview)?
(4) What is the role of empirical observation (sometimes logically related to a concept termed "induction") in attempts to answer the questions above?
(5) How should "compliance" with the norms affect some of these questions, and if (as would be maintained in this work) compliance is a key to effectiveness of norms, what sort of practices might enhance the degree of compliance with IL norms?
(6) How do disciplines such as international relations (political science) and economics relate to these questions?

These and other questions are constant challenges to the broad subject of international law (and to law generally), but the goal here is to focus more particularly on the effects of "globalization"[2] on these and other questions as related to activity we can list under the phrase "international economic law" or, more particularly, the WTO. In other words, what are the actual or potential effects (including long-term effects) of the phenomena outlined in the previous section (2.2) on international law in general and international economic law (as part of international law) in particular? This is not an easy inquiry, but the object in this chapter is to outline the broader inquiry concerning international law, and then turn later (Chapters 4 and 5) to a study of the WTO as possibly furnishing empirical observations which provide examples of effects and responses which are important in themselves, but may also suggest lessons for other subjects of international law in general. Thus some of our questions narrow to the effects of conditions or circumstances mentioned in section 2.2, such as fragmentation of nations and multiplying of legal international law entities including groups of nations; the role of non-government entities and their impact; questions of interference in national societies and governments (especially of a non-military sort); impacts on government regulatory activity at various levels; constraints on government entities imposed by the operation of the globalized market;

33

relationship of the international norms to national or sub-federal (or super-national) "constitutions"; and, not least, how to think about the problems of achieving important governmental goals in the complex contexts of these many varied factors.

A significant amount of the criticism of international law concepts and "purported norms" points towards great uncertainties about some of the questions above. In some cases these uncertainties have existed for lengthy periods of time (they are not new), so this raises the question as to why anybody should worry about them seriously now (or some would say, only now). One answer may be that rather suddenly (within a matter of decades) international law has become remarkably important to much larger and varied populations of citizens. Larger political and economic entities may have found it possible largely to ignore international law in the past (an exception may be the relatively small states of Europe, and perhaps a few other places), since the average citizen-constituent would rarely encounter a need to understand it. With the remarkable developments of "globalization" and interdependence in the world developing more recently (as noted in Chapter 1 and section 2.2), the average citizen finds that his or her family circumstances (employment, business success, property ownership, pensions, health care, recreation and travel, civil unrest, investment and money flows, etc.) depend more and more on the international situation and its legal framework.

International law generally is mostly analyzed in two different parts related to what is often discussed as "sources." The two most prominent parts of IL analysis are customary international law, and "conventional" or treaty law. Of these two subject-sources of international law, that of "customary" international law has perhaps been the object of the most biting and exorbitant criticism, as expressed in a substantial literature of recent decades. But no one can assume that "treaties" and treaty-making and applying are subjects free from conceptual and operational problems. Both these subjects have great uncertainties embedded in them (which often undermine the policy goals for using international law) and they also have elements of dysfunction, stemming from weak institutional structures. These render the universe of international law as potentially unhelpful for solving some of the burning problems of globalization (e.g. weapons, economic crises, the regulatory needs of societies).

Bearing these introductory comments in mind, the remainder of this section is divided into three parts. The first part briefly addresses some "foundation" questions common to international law generally. The next focuses on customary international law, and the final part is devoted to treaties. Necessarily the comments which follow are only a brief overview of subjects which have been elaborately discussed in a vast, complex, and disputatious literature.

a. Foundations of international law

A starting point for many scholars and other observers exploring the basic premises of international law is the question: what is the "source" of such law? A truly analytic, rigorously logical approach sometime seems to come to a dead end, or suggests that such a quest is circular, because the starting norm is itself a norm of rule-making and depends on the source norm. Kelsen's *Grundnorm* comes to mind,[3] but more recent criticism (mostly focused on customary international law, as explored in the next sub-section) tries to go beyond that.[4] Some have suggested that Article 38(1) of the Statute of the International Court of Justice is itself authority for both treaties and customary international law, but others argue that that statute needs justification, and thus the circle continues.[5]

The familiar fundamental phrase "pacta sunt servanda" to give a legal norm legitimacy requiring treaties to be followed, is a possible beginning for treaty law, but the question of the validity of that phrase often leads to customary international law as its basis, and thus again is forced to face the validity question of customary international law. Indeed, one recent carefully thought through statement about international law in general states flatly:

> ... international law does not seem to have a constitution which regulates the nature, foundation and interrelation of sources. It is an all-pervading problem, one that will haunt us . . . It threatens to cripple the whole endeavour of "finding the law."[6]

A recent book, *The Limits of International Law*,[7] presents an intriguing and controversial analysis of international law which endeavors to explain international behavior on the basis of self-interest, arguing that such behavior is little affected by international law norms. The book seems partly to revert to older political science views about international relations, but uses more modern "rational choice" and game theoretic hypothetical problems to buttress its conclusions.

Clearly, the authors have important insights worth examining, some of which parallel views expressed in this book. However, pushing the paradigm of "self-interest" raises many important questions. One question is how broadly or narrowly you define "self-interest" (e.g., does it include a broad interest to "preserve peace" in the world? does it include an interest in the instrumental advantages argued on behalf of a rule-based international relations system?). A question can also always be raised about whether such interests are evaluated on a long-term or short-term frame of reference.

Likewise, there are difficult empirical problems, which authors Goldsmith and Posner acknowledge with candor and grace. Furthermore, some of the argumentation about the effect of international norms is very similar to some of the basic jurisprudential philosophical issues about law in general (international or national), which engender many different viewpoints (e.g., why do people obey the law? is there a moral obligation to obey law?).

An important traditional source for international rules is often stated to be "state consent."[8] This relates significantly to the concept of sovereignty as it is often defined (and which we explore in Chapter 3). If such concept posits that each "sovereign" is supreme in the international system, then it can follow that no "higher norm" can legitimately apply to that sovereign unless it has consented. Consent of each nation-state (or other entity with similar characteristics) is thus the crucial element for both treaties and customary international law. Such a concept also has led to other logical derivative notions (such as equality of nations, non-interference, monopoly of internal national authority, etc.). This set of arguments and concepts will be the focus of Chapter 3, but it is necessary to notice here its implications for the purposes of this chapter. If, as some recommend (and practice may be supporting), the concept of "sovereignty" no longer has or should have the implications mentioned above, then "state consent" is undermined as the legitimizing source of international norms. And that forces one to explore what appropriate substitutes (e.g. an "altered" or "evolving" sovereignty concept?) might exist. It also forces an exploration of whether there need to be alternative justifications for some of the other "derivative" concepts of "sovereignty."

Related to the "consent as source" idea is a more eclectic approach by the renowned American scholar, the late Professor Oscar Schachter. In one of his works he gives a "baker's dozen" list of "candidates" for the basis of international law norms, as follows:

(i)   consent of states
(ii) customary practice
(iii) a sense of "rightness" – the juridical conscience
(iv) natural law or natural reason

2.3 International law and its discontents

(v)   social necessity
(vi) the will of the international community (the "consensus" of the international community)
(vii) direct (or "stigmatic") intuition
(viii) common purposes of the participants
(ix) effectiveness
(x)   sanctions
(xi) "systemic" goals
(xii) shared expectations
(xiii) rules of recognition[9]

Schachter goes on to say,

> On looking at this . . . wide array of ideas concerning the "true" or "correct" basis of obligation in international law it may be wondered on the one hand, whether the choice of a "basis" has any great practical significance and, on the other, whether the diversity of opinion does not reveal a radical weakness in the conceptual structure of international law.[10]

Perhaps the real question is less that posed by the logicians and more a pragmatic question of what the policy objective (or policy objectives) of establishing international law norms is and how those objectives can be achieved. Certainly some of the policy objectives would be similar to those tied to domestic or other levels of legal systems. However, to dodge that question again and look in a more focused way to international norms or rules and their effects, might it not be possible to use empirical observation of the world as it is? This could suggest a policy objective that can roughly be characterized as a need for millions of operators/participants to benefit from a degree of predictability and stability which effective norms can supply. In Chapters 4 and 5 we see explicit expression of this policy in the WTO. The general thought of a rule-oriented system lowering the risk premium for entrepreneurs and investors is taken up also in many sections of this book (see 1.3, 4.2, 5.8, 5.12, 6.1, and Chapter 8).

Take a not-so-hypothetical case: assume that a London investor wishes to invest £1,000,000 in a way to maximize his/her return with a modicum of safety. Investing in a shoe plant in Costa Rica seems attractive to him and his advisors. It can produce a rate of return greater than in London (or elsewhere at similar risk). But such a plant to be competitive must produce a quantity of shoes which exceeds the likelihood of sales within the small country of Costa Rica, so that it will be necessary to export to other societies for the investment to be successful. Without any international law (treaty etc.) structure, such exporting can be very risky, since other importing countries (including the big market to the north) could, at a whim, close off such imports. By contrast, with a legal structure limiting in some ways (albeit not with perfection) the whims of import prevention, the risks of the investment are lowered. This means that the rate of return necessary for a successful investment can also be lower. In other words, the "risk premium" is reduced by the rule structure (if the rule is successful). Such a lowered risk premium may not only benefit the particular investor, but also (if the rule system is broadly general in the world) can benefit many investors and thus promote a much more efficient allocation of capital, leading to generally increased wealth in the world.

Clearly, the hypothetical depends on the devilish detail of how to create and implement an effective rule structure, a matter which will be a background theme throughout this book. An interesting question (not answered here) is whether similar analysis of the policy value of rule structures can also be made for a number of other societal subjects, such as control of weapons of mass destruction, responding to genocide or other mass violations of humanity, environmental controls, securing human rights, and of course the all important goal of preserving peace (avoiding war and armed conflict). The various impact factors of "globalization" outlined in section 2.2 all relate to these general questions of how to create and implement an effective rule structure.

So in this approach to sources for international rules (as for other rules also) observations of actual human behavior become crucial. Can we observe the reasonably satisfactory operations in some circumstances of a set of international law rules? If so, what are the characteristics of the set, and the circumstances in which they operate? Thus we ask (later in this book) if the WTO (and its predecessor GATT, and its affiliate institutions, if any) is one such set, and whether it is useful to consider its lessons for other "branches" of international law.

Professor Louis Henkin of Columbia University has made the following statement which is admirably famous in international law circles:

It is probably the case that almost all nations observe almost all principles of international law and almost all of their obligations almost all of the time.[11]

Apart from the four intriguing uses of the word "almost," one can ask whether empirical observation supports this statement (which Professor Henkin and this author would answer affirmatively), but also whether this observation breaks down in relation to many international law issues which have a real major significance, as compared with the myriad of rules which are relatively minor in impact and relatively costless for governments to follow. Even if the latter question is answered affirmatively, implying a negative view of compliance with IL rules with major impact, it can nevertheless be argued that the large amount of compliance for minor impact rules is tremendously useful in promoting policy goals which benefit from effective rule operation.

b. Customary international law

Careful observers of customary international law cannot help but be disconcerted by a number of evident characteristics of that subject which have attracted considerable criticism (and debate).[12] The basic idea for the formation of customary IL rules is usually described as requiring the practice of nations, accompanied by a willful element termed *opinio juris*, understood to mean a view that the particular practices occur partly because the nations responsible for a practice believe it to be required by an international legal obligation.[13] The ICJ Statute Article 38(1)(b) includes in the ICJ list of sources for its work, "international custom, as evidence of a general practice accepted as law." Critics of these concepts note (*inter alia*):[14]

(1) These concepts of customary IL contain enormous uncertainties, which can undermine their utility in a legal system. Some of these uncertainty problems include some of the items which follow in this list.
(2) As to "practice," what kinds of practice "count"? Are any of the following to be considered practice that "counts" for customary international law formation?[15]
    – verbal acts (statements of belief in a rule existence);
    – reports or actions including "adoptions" of rules by United Nations bodies or other international organization bodies, e.g., a "declaration," or resolution "finding" that a certain rule exists;
    – acquiescence in other practices;
    – new patterns of cooperation, including economic cooperation;
    – international tribunal decisions individually, or in aggregate;
    – repeated treaty clauses, but not embracing every single nation;
    – application of a rule to "holdout states," or those which declare opposition to the rule.
(3) *When* is a practice deemed to begin?
(4) *How long* must a practice go on?
(5) What is the effect of persistent violation of an older norm – does it change the customary IL rule?

(6) Partly because of uncertainties, there appear to be a number of situations where advocates of a customary IL rule are arguing that the rule already exists, even when some elements (such as those mentioned above) do not, in the view of many nation-states, adequately fulfill the criteria for customary IL. This over-reaching tends to cast doubts on customary IL generally.[16]

(7) Which nations count more than others? Is unanimity required? And if so, how often can that be ascertained? Or alternatively, if 90 percent of the nations manifest (practice?) acceptance of a rule, but the other 10 percent contain a majority of the world population, or a majority of the armed forces, or a majority of the economic activity, what is the effect?

(8) How can customary international law norms change? Does it require a breach (an action inconsistent with the norm) to lead to a change in the rule (absent treaty action)?

The flavor of the many critiques of customary international law (which often are rebutted in other works) can be seen in even a small number of examples, such as those which follow.

One of the most strident criticisms of customary international law is contained in a provocative article by J. Patrick Kelly.[17] In this article the author terms CIL as "indeterminate and manipulable" and therefore "should be eliminated as a source of international legal norms and replaced by consensual processes." His criticisms include the points that the CIL process "lacks procedural legitimacy," is a discourse that "varies from writer to writer and state to state," and is not properly "customary law." He opines that "CIL lacks all four of [Professor Thomas] Franck's indicators of legitimacy," arguing that the "CIL process is inconsistent with democratic values."[18] He further contends that "much of CIL is determined by the academic and judicial elites or by the practices of a minority of states without the participation or direct assent of the majority of states compromising the legitimacy of CIL norms" and is partly powered by the "claims of self-interested powerful states."

Several scholars have particularly criticized the use of customary international law in US courts, especially federal courts.[19]

The US Supreme Court has for decades wrestled with the problems of customary international law.[20] In the 1964 *Sabbatino* case, the Court declined to accept an argument relying on customary international law concerning the requirement of compensation by a nation which had expropriated property of an alien, partly because of reservations about the customary law validity of the rule in question.[21] In *United States v.*

2.3 International law and its discontents

Alvarez-Machain, a 1992 opinion denying relief to a Mexican citizen arrested by US drug officials after being abducted in US territory by Mexicans assisting the United States, the Court indicated that even if customary international law ruled against this arrest, in the United States (the Supreme Court felt) this matter is better left to the executive branch, and the processes of diplomacy.[22] These grounds touch on the questions of justiciability and political question, but can also be read to relate to uneasiness about the validity of the CIL norm being advanced.

Much more recently the US Supreme Court in a holding and opinion in 2004 denying the Mexican who had been abducted any monetary relief for improper arrest, struggled again with the CIL questions.[23] This case was brought under the US statute known as the Alien Tort Claims Act (ATC Act), a 1789 statute which has been used in recent decades by plaintiffs to assert claims for compensation due to violations of international law.[24] The US Supreme Court was asked by the defendant to hold that the ATC Act should not be available for a lawsuit unless that act or some other statute explicitly provided for a cause of action for the alleged wrong, arguing that the ATC Act only provided jurisdiction when such a right to sue was indicated. The Court rejected this approach after examining the origin and legislative history of the ATC Act. In doing so they recognized that the "international law" in that statute was not limited to "international law" as it existed at the time of enactment, but the Court said that it was "persuaded that federal courts should not recognize private claims under federal common law for violations of any international law norm with less definite content and acceptance among civilized nations than the historical paradigms familiar when '1350' was enacted." The Court felt that the brief period of arrest experienced by the plaintiff was not clearly covered by customary international law. This strong expression of the need in ATC Act cases for the international law rule to be "with . . . definite content and acceptance among civilized nations" can be read to suggest some skepticism by the US Court about the existence of international norms. Its rule for the ATC Act logically suggests a "sub-set" of international rules as eligible for ATC Act treatment, but it could also be a hint that the US Court is skeptical about the overreaching claims of advocates about the existence of customary international law.

With all this concern and criticism about customary international law, it can be and is sometimes argued that CIL should no longer be considered valid law. But even if one doesn't go that far, it can be and is sometimes argued that it is generally better in international affairs to utilize the treaty approach to developing norms of IL.[25] This indeed has much merit, and, particularly for international economic affairs, has been a preferred approach such that very few customary IL norms for international economic affairs appear to exist.[26] In Chapter 5 we see, however, some attempts at drawing on CIL to complement, embellish or extend certain elements of a case based on the WTO covered treaty texts.

In addition, there are strong arguments for many parts of customary international law (mostly the procedural and conduct of diplomacy parts) which benefit greatly from the many older rules governing conduct. Similarly, CIL is often recognized as the "background" or part of the "infrastructure" for treaty law, operating in some instances to provide fallback or "default" rules when treaties are silent or ambiguous. Furthermore it is recognized that CIL may indeed be a useful way for certain new universal norms to be developed.

However, even if one were able to argue to eliminate CIL, it certainly is not the case that the treaty approach is without problems, as we now see when we turn to the next sub-section. In some cases, the treaty problems might be solved or at least ameliorated by recourse to some CIL concepts. However, there is also a major risk (arising, e.g., in the WTO context) that certain advocacy interests will try to obtain from CIL what they failed to obtain from negotiating a treaty. Likewise, there is enormous ambiguity about the customary IL concept of *"jus cogens,"* with attending extravagant claims for this status for various CIL or treaty concepts.[27] If *jus cogens* is applied as an attribute to an international law rule, then that rule "trumps" even treaties, and could overrule even what the negotiators thought they had agreed.[28] Similarly concepts of *erga omnes* (usually referring to treaties) and universal jurisdiction seem fluid enough that temptation for recourse to customary international law regarding these concepts is likely, and could change some of the substance in the way treaties (and even some other CIL norms) are applied.[29]

c. Treaties

Two overwhelming characteristics of modern-day treaty operation jump out at an observer, namely (1) the incredibly large number of treaties in force, and newly made each year; and (2) the very large variety in scope, structure, and modes of application of treaties.

There are now 506 multilateral treaties deposited with the UN Secretary-General and more than 50,000 bilateral and multilateral treaties registered with the United Nations, not all currently operational of course.[30] It is probably not possible to ascertain overall how many

2.3 International law and its discontents

treaties are currently in force, but some governments issue a regular document listing the treaties to which they belong.[31] Of course, there is some ambiguity about the definition of "treaty,"[32] and indeed a large variety of international agreement "instruments" are utilized in different ways. Nevertheless, it is easy overall to conclude that treaties today are the core of most international law activity. Specific subjects such as the environment, investment, and taxation are estimated each to operate with more than a thousand treaties in force. [33]

The treaties also vary in type other than subject matter and scope. Some variation may result from differing national governmental constitutional requirements, such as distinctions like that in the United States between congressionally approved treaties, Senate-approved treaties, presidential agreements, and some less formal techniques. Some different types of agreement may for domestic purpose use different terminology, like "executive agreement" (used in some US procedures), even though they will technically have the status of "treaty" under international law.[34] Some agreements are explicitly "non-binding" and thus become what is sometimes termed "soft law."[35] Such agreements are sometimes used to avoid going through cumbersome national constitutional procedures for approval, often because avoiding parliamentary procedures seems politically necessary.

The methods of formation differ greatly also, in several dimensions. First, at the international negotiation level, the procedures for negotiation vary greatly. Often treaties are negotiated in the context of a particular international institution such as an organization, and thus the negotiation procedures may be particularized by specialized rules of that organization. The WTO is certainly an example of this. United Nations bodies have some variety of specific approaches, and other organizations also. The WTO tends to operate almost completely by "consensus" in treaty formation, and this has an enormous impact on the process, to be discussed in Chapter 4.[36] Voting procedures vary greatly in different contexts, and questions have been raised in particular by procedures which rely heavily on one-nation one-vote with simple majority rule or various enhanced majority processes. Questions can include whether these procedures are appropriate when, as in some cases, we have noted that, at least in theory, a majority of nations can claim to represent in their aggregate less than 5 percent of the population of the world. This can be particularly divisive when a treaty approved and brought into force by such procedure purports to impose binding obligations on nations which refuse to sign or ratify.[37] Even apart from formal legal obligations, some treaties can have an impact on non-acceptors that the holdouts can allege is unfair. There seems to have been virtually no overall systematic exploration of many of these worries.

A second dimension for treaty formation is the immense variety of national government procedures (usually constitutional), with some countries being ultra-democratic, with formal parliamentary approval required for treaty ratifications, while others may operate with a closed executive procedure which may or may not be subject to various techniques of democratic control.

Once in force, treaties are applied in a variety of manners. Indeed there are different "forms" of a treaty, at least in some views. Some treaties are "*erga omnes*," meaning that they have a broader lawgiving impact that engages the interest of all parties, not just those specifically harmed or immediately affected by breach of obligation. Likewise some treaties may call for "universal jurisdiction," which presumably gives the right (or even obligation) for all treaty parties to take "enforcement measures" against offending states (or individuals), such as cases related to international crimes such as genocide or torture.

A very big difference occurs between bilateral (or small group) treaties, when compared with multilateral treaties with large numbers of parties. Sometimes the latter form the basic "constitutional" framework or "charter" for an international institution.

Furthermore, sometimes treaties are termed "contractual" as compared with "non-contractual," which could occasionally mean "law-making treaty." The terminology "contractual" does not seem to have much support, but has been used by some diplomats to characterize treaties as being more attuned to "reciprocal" relationships, than to broader obligations of interest to all parties. An interesting discussion about varying legal implications of treaty text was focused on the 2004 draft treaty "constitution" proposed for the European Union. Viewpoints differ on what the legal instrument should be termed: a "constitution," a "treaty," a "constitutional treaty," or a "treaty-based constitution." These different viewpoints could potentially have different major operational effects in the way the legal instrument should be interpreted. (As this is written, in August 2005, the prospects for the proposed draft EU "constitution" seem to be fading in the light of the negative results of the referenda held in France on May 29, 2005, and in the Netherlands on June 1, 2005.[38]) Later in this book we come back to some of these issues in the context of the WTO and of other international organizations or institutions.[39]

Even as to similar or identical treaties, there is also a wide variety of modes of application, particularly as to differences in the domestic law

2.3 International law and its discontents

application of treaties. This issue has been very confusing, and subject to considerable discussion and literature. The WTO, for example, has a variety of domestic law impacts depending on which nation is involved. In the United States the WTO-covered treaty texts (basically the Uruguay Round agreement) do not have direct application in domestic US law but are applied by a 1994 statute which is the "Act of Transformation" of the treaty norms.[40]

With this type of number and variety, an important question arises whether the existing international rules about treaty application (including interpretation) are adequate to cope with this variety. Does "one size fits all" in IL rules (often customary IL rules) when in fact the actual characteristics of the instruments greatly vary? This is an important question (to be addressed in Chapter 5) about the appropriateness of using the Vienna Convention on the Law of Treaties as an embodiment of rules (customary or otherwise) which should apply to an institution such as the WTO.

A critical factor in treaty law is the institutional setting in which the treaty will operate, particularly as to the institutional structure for interpreting and applying the treaty. The existence in such a structure of a juridical body is extremely influential on various attributes of the treaty, including interpretation techniques, compliance effectiveness, evolutionary change, development of practice, filling of treaty gaps (ambiguities or lacunae), and so on. Sections 2.5 and 6.6 will return to this question of juridical institutions.

Combining a number of the various dimensions discussed above leads into questions of how a treaty application may change over time. If the membership is small, it may permit changes made fairly efficiently by amending or renegotiating the treaty. But if the membership is large, like the WTO or many other organizations with well over 100 parties, the amending clauses in the treaty structure are often not usable because of super-majority requirements and/or other political or practical constraints.[41] This can lead to "treaty rigidity" which can be recognized in a large number of important current international law institutions including the United Nations, the Bretton Woods group (the IMF and the World Bank), and of course the WTO. When there is treaty rigidity in organizations which have to cope with a constant and accelerating change of circumstances (such as the globalized economy), a very serious question arises as to how such institutions can or should cope with change. This becomes essentially a "constitutional" question, although many diplomats abhor (or are frightened by) the term "constitutional." We return to this question in section 2.5, and also in Chapters 4, 5 and 6.

2.4 International economic law

International economic law has now become a standard "sub-subject" of international law, like many other subjects.[1] But IEL may be the most (or at least one of the most) "populated" subjects of international law, meaning that in terms of the number of persons and hours spent working on IEL, as well as the amount of "practice" which occurs relating to IEL subjects, few if any sub-parts of IL generally exceed this "input or output."[2] Partly this is because of the very wide scope of the subject when denominated broadly as IEL. In that sense IEL covers virtually every economic activity which has a relationship that crosses national boundaries. Thus it can easily embrace international commerce and trade law, financial activity including exchange-rate questions and the Bretton Woods financial institutions and their "constitutions," investment activity (with thousands of bilateral treaties), tax activity,[3] environment issues, corporate activity and other business entity questions, movement of persons including immigration and emigration, sales of goods and services, government aids and subsidies, transport (air, sea, land, tourism), health matters, world poverty questions, and economic sanctions related to weapons, terrorism, and human rights.

All these subjects and more can raise important questions of international law generally, such as treaty and customary law; the relationship of the international norms to domestic laws and constitutions; and varieties of institutions including governmental and nongovernmental. An analysis of some widely used books for international law courses indicates that a high proportion of the cases and other content relate to "economic" activities.[4] Other literature relating to IEL is burgeoning[5] and new journals devoted to IEL or some sub-category of it are appearing,[6] while increasingly large numbers of articles within the scope of IEL are being published in journals with many years of publication.[7]

Certain attributes of international economic activity can have profound impacts on governments, including the asserted possible importance which extensive trade relations between countries can have in keeping peace among nations.[8] It is argued, for instance, that nations which trade with each other generally do not make war, or more allegorically stated, nations which have McDonald's fast food restaurant franchises generally do not go to war with each other.[9] Some assertions which explore this phenomenon argue that trade relations involve many individual persons and entities who, by doing business across borders, develop not only friendly personal relations but also encourage a growing economic interest in those trade

2.4 International economic law

participants to avoid activities which would interfere with trade.[10] Contrary views note historical examples wherein trade problems were a cause of war or exacerbated tensions among certain nations.[11] Thus the stakes for the rules which assist and promote cross-border economic activity are very high indeed.

Obviously IEL is intimately related to the facts and impacts of globalization. Indeed, it is IEL or at least some of the institutions of IEL which are called upon to facilitate and to "regulate" for the common good the trillions of cross-border activities which are constantly occurring. All of this activity adds to the general complexity of the subject, but also provides extensive and usually observable practice of a wide variety, which can inform the subjects of international law and IEL.

It should be noted, however, that IEL can have several different sub-activities. A rather sharp distinction can be made between "transactional" activity on the one hand, and "regulatory" activity (normally governmental) on the other hand. The transactional activity is mostly private (due to the prevalence of market economic systems) and therefore the law concerning transactions is also mostly denominated as "private." Contract laws or corporate laws are prime examples. "Regulatory" IEL, however, is primarily "public" or "governmental" in nature, and is therefore often a priority subject with much greater impact on and attention from governments and academic institutions, and also practitioners who find their clients' interests importantly engaged by governmental actions of various types and at various levels. (It is sometimes said that the international trade transaction is the most extensively regulated of all economic activity, because often every single activity requires at least a report to one or more governments.) Clearly, there are important relationships between the "transactional" subjects and the "regulatory" subjects, as is the case in domestic law systems.

Experienced legal practitioners have opined that failure to recognize issues of potential WTO rule impacts in advising clients should today border on malpractice. Other similarly experienced persons have indicated that major corporate clients with well-developed, long-range strategic planning activities are closely following the work and reports of the WTO Appellate Body.

IEL has several characteristics which at least partly differentiate it from general international law. First, IEL is very largely treaty law, at least as witnessed in recent decades. Almost always, when governments feel the need for a rule structure of some type to operate on a specific category of economic activity, governments prefer the precision, definition, tailoring, and timeliness to meet conditions which treaties can provide and customary international law cannot.

Secondly, IEL is inherently "multidisciplinary," in the sense that analysis of the underlying economic activity is often necessary both to understand the "regulatory" aspect of governmental IEL and to assist in designing and implementing new rules necessary to keep abreast of rapidly changing "global" economic circumstances.[12] This multidisciplinarity adds to the difficulty of understanding and studying the subject of IEL, and for that reason may in fact (as some anecdotal observation seems to confirm) have the effect of inhibiting or diminishing the amount of research (governmental and scholarly) devoted to IEL, despite the important need for such research. Other disciplines may also be involved.

A very important question, which will be also addressed later in this book,[13] is whether IEL or particular parts of IEL, such as the law of the WTO, are part of international law generally, as opposed to being "separate regimes" walled off from general IL. This author's view on this question strongly supports the position of IEL (and the WTO as seen in Chapter 5) as part of international law, and thus general IL norms not expressly embraced in the IEL (or WTO) treaty structure can have an impact on the application of IEL norms. Of course, as discussed in Chapter 5, there are serious and complicated issues about how great such an impact can appropriately be. Reciprocally, the practice of IEL activity can be highly relevant to general international law and its norm application.

The general relationship of IEL to IL arises in a variety of situations when it is argued that the IEL rule is interpreted in the light of the IL rule (e.g. a customary international law rule about "estoppel," or "fairness" or "good faith"[14]). Even more complex can be the hierarchy of norms when there appears to be a "conflict" between a general IL norm and a particular (usually treaty-based) IEL norm. Absent an assertion of *jus cogens* for the international norm (an assertion that often is challenged by the party opposing the norm application), it could be the case that the IEL treaty norm is sufficiently detailed and specific to give rise to a claim of "*lex specialis derogat legi generali*,"[15] so that the IEL treaty norm will trump the general international law. In the context of the WTO, these arguments have arisen, for example in at least one case wherein it was argued that the rather detailed remedies in the WTO texts regarding dispute settlement provided for a breach of obligation could be "enhanced" or subject to additional remedies provided (arguably) by customary international law.[16] Finally for this section, it can be noted that there is a view that IEL has not been adequately studied or appreciated by scholars and other professionals who concentrate on "general international law." One important professor of international and international economic law (Professor Donald McRae) has written (in his 1996 Hague lectures):

The study of international trade and of its regulation requires us to think more deeply about States, and about their roles, functions, and limitations in the regulation of economic matters. It requires that we think about the State and about international law in terms of national economies, or of an international economy, and this may throw new light on the way we think about international law.[17]

Such assessment, he argues, will "call into question some of the assumptions on which international law is based." He further asks, "why has the field of international trade law traditionally been regarded as outside the mainstream of international law?" and notes the failure of some widely utilized basic international law texts to have any reference to international trade law, even in the index. He also states that "it is difficult to see today how international law can be properly understood without considering the impact and implications of international trade and economic law."

In Chapters 4 and 5 of this work, the "case study" of the WTO will be explored and will elaborate some of the points made in this section and this chapter.

2.5 International institutional law

Increasingly, the older paradigm of international law as providing a framework for relationships between two or a small, relatively informal group of nation-states is giving way to international institutions of a wide variety. These institutions, mostly formal treaty-created international governmental organizations, are now the locus for most of the "heavy lifting" activities for a wide spectrum of international relations, many (but not all) of them with a major economic agenda. The treaties on which these institutions are based must often deal with what we can only call "constitutional" questions, despite the antagonism often seen towards the use of this word in the international context. These questions include the powers of the organization, the structure of its administration, the procedures for taking various types of decisions, and the degree to which these decisions are "binding" as "hard law" or, on the contrary, non-binding "soft law" (recommendations or generalized standards often subject to conditions under the control of the individual member states).

These multilateral institution treaties raise a number of evolving jurisprudential questions, many of which fundamentally differ from those which have traditionally engaged "international lawyers" working within a traditional diplomatic paradigm. Several of these can be mentioned here, partly to illustrate the differences from the older paradigms, differences at least in degree if not in kind.

A critical question concerning the decision-making legal capacity of various sub-bodies of an international organization is the structure of that procedure and, in particular, the question of voting. Here the fictional aspect of the "equality of nations" mantra is often apparent, particularly when binding decisions can require or constrain certain activities of the member states, something which they might not entirely appreciate. The basic dilemma often is that when equality of nations with a one-nation one-vote majority decision structure is applied, it is very unlikely that some of the most powerful states of the membership will tolerate being obligated by a majority which is less powerful. This is sometimes articulated with a phrase deprecating "the majority of mini-states." In reality, within some institutions the membership generally appreciates this informal constraint on its decision-making procedures no matter what the treaty language might say. One approach to a structure that fails to recognize real power is to follow an informal or "practice" reinforced system of "consensus" decision making. A clear example occurs in the WTO, as we shall explore in Chapter 4. Consensus is often defined as legitimating a decision based on a proposal to which no member present has objected (so neither absences nor abstentions operate as a consensus-blocking vote). This procedure, however, can have some important downsides in preventing progress and reducing the efficiency of the institution or its capability to carry out its mission.

Other approaches to the "equality fallacy" include weighted voting (which is used in some older institutions but now seems adamantly opposed by many smaller nations), various levels of super-majority (two-thirds, three-fourths, "critical mass" of population or economic power) and more complex procedures associated with more profound long-term decisions, such as amendment procedures of the "charter treaty," which make it very difficult to obtain a decision to amend.

Too often, it seems, these important structural problems result in "treaty rigidity" (discussed in 2.3), such that the institution is ostensibly incapable of adapting to the real, constantly changing world around it.

There is, however, an observable phenomenon of ad hoc or trial and error experimentation and practice that sometimes enables the essential "constitutional procedures" of the institution to evolve, even in some situations towards directions that seem inconsistent with its treaty language.

Tom Franck describes one such situation in the United Nations in relation to the veto power, where extensive consistent practice establishes that an abstention is not treated as a veto, even though the UN Charter language requires "the concurring votes of the permanent members."[1] The WTO also sometimes seems to utilize this "evolutionary" approach.[2] The European Union, at one point (at least) in its "constitutional evolution," utilized an approach to minimize the difficulties of a unanimous vote requirement, which called for restraint in casting a negative vote unless it was due to the "vital national interest" of the member casting such vote.[3] This has been recently recommended for the WTO also.[4]

These problems and practices thus point to several important "jurisprudential" points concerning international law, particularly as to the treatment of treaties. One such point is to ask whether the IL approach to treaties is too uniform, with "one size fits all," when in fact different sizes exist that are not always appropriate for a uniform solution. Thus, should not treaties be "disaggregated" for analysis purposes? Maybe there are a number of "sizes," such as short-term bilateral, long-term institutional, reciprocity-based, multilateral but regional with common heritage and societal values, broader worldwide treaties, and different subjects (economic, human rights, weapons, environment, etc.). Is it possible to think of different types of appropriate application procedures depending on the kind of treaty? Thus some treaties might be (and indeed "are" to some commentators) characterized as "constitutional" in nature. What does this mean? It could mean that the treaty instrument of such a type should receive treatment more analogous to the way in which national institutions (including courts) treat a "constitution," rather than the traditional way of treating treaties which could be seen as more rigidly "textual" (following the customary law rules as "reflected" in the Vienna Convention of the Law of Treaties).[5]

Again, the WTO becomes an interesting case study, as we shall see in later chapters. The phrase articulated in the early history of the US Constitution by Justice John Marshall saying "this is a constitution we are expounding" to differentiate that document's treatment from that of statutes or other "lesser" basic legal instruments is well known.[6] The United States even quoted this language in a World Court case in 1962 regarding the UN Charter application.[7] As noted in section 2.3.c, the extraordinarily interesting recent history of the European Union, with its 2004 draft proposed EU constitution, includes differences of opinion whether the new instrument would be a "treaty," or "constitution," or "treaty-based constitution," or "constitutional treaty."[8] Obviously these differences go beyond mere nomenclature and derive from a difference on substance as to how the subject text should be treated in the future.

The previous discussion raises the important issue of treaty interpretation. A key question in this regard is whether the "constitutional treaty," or even any large-membership multilateral treaty, should be interpreted by principles enunciated in the VCLT (Arts. 31 and 32). A strong argument could be made that the VCLT is too much weighed down by the older diplomatic bilateral treaty paradigm that seems to have influenced its drafting. Later chapters of this book return to this question. This also relates to the question of "state consent" as the legitimating source of international law. When a state consents to a treaty which creates an institution, has it not also consented to the procedures in that institution which may be used to interpret the relevant treaties and to fill gaps or resolve ambiguities which will inevitably occur? This surely must be answered in the affirmative, but clearly that is not the older "*Lotus*" type of international law thinking.[9]

A good portion of institution-creating treaty documents is usually devoted to distribution of powers within and among the bodies or entities of the organization. Furthermore such documents often have a mix of obligation and aspiration (hard law and soft law) and often some confusion, for example, "shall" versus "should," and when "should" becomes "shall."[10] Likewise, when large memberships negotiate a treaty instrument it is more likely than in other situations that the treaty text will have ambiguities and gaps inevitably created by the negotiating methodologies. Some of these are purposeful; others are a result of ignorance or of miscommunication between the members. Sometimes the ignorance is in regard to what rules of general international law might be the "fallback" or "default" rule which could be applied in a future case that raised the issue. Sometimes the gaps are due to time pressures on the negotiators, and/or a feeling that there will be many gaps and lacunae and most will not actually come to a dispute, and so may not be very important.

The constitutional treaty will also have, express or implied, a key question of "deference" which the institution should accord to member states in their related activity regarding governmental decisions and measures taken. This is often more formally called the "standard of review"[11] and in other similar contexts is termed "margin of appreciation."[12]

This issue relates to the distribution of power not within the organization, but as between the organization and its member states, in other words the allocation of power in the relinquishment of "slices of sovereignty," as will be discussed in Chapter 3. Governments have various ways to constrain or minimize the "power" of treaty institutions, and deference is one of them. But in addition there are examples of power constraints being inserted in the basic treaty itself (as severe voting constraints such as unanimity, or super majority requirements). In addition, and often much more hypocritically, governments constrain international institutions by depriving them of resources without which the organization cannot effectively carry out its mandated missions.[13]

Many of the various questions just discussed above are the kinds of questions with which judicial-type institutions struggle, particularly at the nation-state level, but also in various international institutions. Indeed, a distinct increase in the use of judicial or juridical institutions at the international level can be observed. The most notable in the minds of most observers of international affairs is the WTO dispute settlement mechanism, explored in greater depth in Chapter 5. Given the "constitutional"-type systemic issues now being persistently faced by international institutions, it seems likely that "going forward" from here, such juridical institutions will be deemed essential for an international organization to be reasonably able to carry out its tasks in a manner which comports with the elements of good governance, and which is consistent with the purposes for which such international organization is mandated in its charter.

And that last sentence is a good segue into a final point to be made in this section.[14] Much discussion has occurred about the principles of "good governance" which should guide national governments in their activities. Political scientists have written importantly about this.[15] Many of these ideas have also been applied to various levels of government, such as sub-federal units, and even to nongovernment entities, such as corporations. With the very great increase in the number, importance, and need for international institutions, it is increasingly becoming important to recognize that like all human institutions, some of the international institutions can fall far short of important and arguably general good principles of governance. Certainly corruption cannot be condoned and should not be allowed, and possibly some of the perquisites and immunities that have been traditional (such as tax-free status) should be reexamined.

In addition, other basic principles such as transparency, appropriate opportunities for civil society participation, principled methods of selecting officials, appropriate budgeting principles, can all be noticed. As important governmental decisions are made about the need to utilize international institutions to overcome systemic world problems that individual nation-states cannot solve, part of the determination of whether or how to proceed internationally must depend on an appraisal of the ability of existing or potential international institutions to do the necessary jobs, and this appraisal must include knowledge about the structure, power distribution, resources, and good governance "constitution" of the international institutions. It must also include evaluation of the checks and balances that are needed to prevent misuse of power (such as a self-perpetuating elite in a particular international organization).[16]

If the international institution is not trusted, or is seen to be a device for certain powerful private (or special public) interests to achieve an economic distributional goal by doing an end-run around national democratic procedures without an appropriate international substitute for those democratic procedures, then it will be natural for governments to refuse to "yield slices of sovereignty" to the international entity. There should be no general presumption that "international is better." Each case must be evaluated, hopefully with a meaningful analysis that eschews using unchallenged and unevaluated "mantras" such as "sovereignty" to tilt the analysis. But the legal and constitutional problems of international institutional law, including good governance, need serious attention, because it appears that world reality including "globalization" is increasingly depending on international governmental approaches to international problems.

2.6 Some conclusions: the international law system challenged

Chapter 2 is designed to outline the "landscape" of the international law system, and the challenges which that system has been facing for some time, as well as the additional layer of challenges which the current world reality of "globalization" poses.

The next chapter, Chapter 3, addresses more fully the problem of "sovereignty," and how that concept (or "mantra," labeled by some as "organized hypocrisy"[1]) relates to the international law system, and a section at the end of the chapter will more fully summarize the reflections which can be drawn from Chapters 1, 2 and 3 which comprise Part I of this book.

Several brief paragraphs here, however, can summarize the description of the existing international law system in the context of globalization as discussed in Chapter 2.

First, it can be seen that the globalization circumstances have an important relationship to the IL system in several different ways. Those circumstances clearly impact and challenge the traditional elements of the international law system. The circumstances include speed and lower cost of both transport and communication, and these and other factors lead to

2.6 Some conclusions: the international law system challenged

a series of phenomena that require the more traditional international law concepts to be rethought. As section 2.2 outlined, these phenomena include fragmentation of states as well as groupings of states into a variety of new multilevel state entities. They include increasing attention as to how nation-states govern internally, and an increasing amount of national activity that has an extraterritorial reach. Problems about the relationship of international law to domestic law pose considerable complexities. Procedures and governmental or diplomatic activity inside international organizations also add new layers of complexity and changing approaches, some of which are contrary to older diplomatic and international law ways of doing things. The very large growth of activities relating to international relations and institutions by nongovernmental organizations and entities clearly forces rethinking about international law and the conduct of international relations.[2]

Second, the brief overview of international law subjects and various important critiques of that subject note some important logical, structural, and operational problems. These problems pose serious impediments to the ability of international law to cope with the developments of "globalization," including difficulties about the perceived legitimacy of IL norms (customary or treaty), and problems of treaty rigidity and other difficulties relating to the need for changes in IL norms to keep abreast of world developments, including those conditions and circumstances outlined in section 2.2 (such as nongovernment actors, proliferation of IL relevant governmental entities, and difficulties embedded in decision making processes including voting). An important complementary suggestion to be noted in this regard is the importance of international "juridical" institutions. Also important is the notion that traditional IL concepts, such as "customary IL" and treaties, need to be more disaggregated or to be analyzed in greater depth, so as to better understand differences that occur in the real world which lead often to a sense that "one size does not fit all."

Third, the necessity of looking more particularly at international economic law, and international institutional ("constitutional") law, was stressed because of their importance for better understanding the challenges and potential remedies of the international legal and institutional system.

In particular it was noted that experience of international economic law practice of the past few decades contains a rich lode of jurisprudential material which is or should be highly relevant to that system. In addition, but not elaborately explored here, there exist important international institutional failures which also involve experiences that must be considered in relation to the international law system generally.

A major question, posed in other quarters but which must also be mentioned here, is whether there is a greater risk today than before that international law is becoming irrelevant (or perceived as such) because it is not suited for the newer conditions and premises of the globalized world we are now experiencing. The next few chapters are designed to shed further light on that question as well as on the other issues just mentioned.

3

Sovereignty-modern: a new approach to an outdated concept

However, for all the reasons mentioned already, the conditions under which sovereignty is exercised – and intervention is practised – have changed dramatically since 1945. Many new states have emerged and are still in the process of consolidating their identity. Evolving international law has set many constraints on what states can do, and not only in the realm of human rights. The emerging concept of human security has created additional demands and expectations in relation to the way states treat their own people. And many new actors are playing international roles previously more or less the exclusive preserve of the states.
International Commission on Intervention and State Sovereignty, 2001[1]

3.1 Sovereignty and the fundamental logic of international law[2]

Chapter 2 explored a number of puzzles and problems about international law and international economic law. Often related, indeed, axiomatically connected to these problems is the concept of "sovereignty," which, however, has many different meanings and implications.

Although much criticized, the concept of "sovereignty" is still very central to almost all thinking about international relations and particularly international law. The old "Westphalian" concept in the context of a nation-state's "right" to monopolize certain exercises of power with respect to its territory and citizens is in many ways discredited (as discussed below), but its main characteristics are still prized and harbored by those who maintain certain views, perhaps fairly characterized "realist," or who otherwise wish to avoid (sometimes with justification) interference in a national government's decisions and activities by foreign or international powers and authorities. Furthermore, when one begins to analyze and disaggregate the concept of sovereignty, it quickly becomes apparent that it has many dimensions, and is indeed very complex. Often, however, the term "sovereignty" is invoked in a context or manner designed to avoid and prevent analysis, sometimes with an advocate's purpose of fending off criticism or justifications of international "infringements" on the activities of a nation-state or its internal stake-holders and power operators.

In addition to the "power monopoly" function, sovereignty also plays other important roles. For example, the notion is quite central to the concept of "equality of nations," which can also be abused and sometimes is quite dysfunctional and unrealistic, such as in the context of decision making in international institutions and in inducing "consensus" as a way to avoid the "one nation, one vote" approach, which can sometimes seriously misdirect actions of international institutions. Consensus, in turn, can often lead to paralysis that is damaging to appropriate coordination and other decision-making at the international level.

The concept of equality of nations is linked to sovereignty concepts because sovereignty has fostered the idea that there is no higher power than the nation-state, so its "sovereignty" negates the idea that there is a higher power, internationally or foreign (unless consented to by the nation-state).

"Sovereignty" also plays a role in defining the status and rights of nation-states and their officials. Thus we know about "sovereign immunity" and the consequential immunity for various purposes of the officials of a nation-state.[3] Likewise "sovereignty" implies a right against interference or intervention from any foreign (or international) power. It can also play an anti-democratic role in enforcing extravagant concepts of special privilege of government officials.

To take these introductory thoughts even further, one can easily see the logical connection between the sovereignty concepts and the very foundations and sources of international law. If sovereignty implies that there is "no higher power" than the nation-state, then it is argued that no international law norm is valid when applied to such state unless that state has somehow "consented" to the norm. Of course, treaties (or "conventions") almost always imply, in a broader sense, satisfactory consent of the nation-states which accepted the treaty.[4] However, important questions are raised in connection with many treaty details, such as (for example) when a treaty-based international institution sees its practice and "jurisprudence" evolve over time and purports to obligate the nation members even when they opposed such evolution.[5]

In addition, the other major source of international law norms, "customary international law," is also theoretically based on the notion of

3.1 Sovereignty and the fundamental logic of international law

consent, through "practice of states" and "*opinio juris.*" For centuries, practitioners and scholars have debated the impact of customary international law on "holdout" states, and what constitutes a "holdout," but often in the context of rationalizing the notion that consent exists. The ambiguities of these notions are obvious, and, as noted in Chapter 2, part of a broader mosaic of criticism of the very existence of "customary international law norms."

The above remarks do not, by any means, exhaust the complexity of the "sovereignty" concept. There are other dimensions that could also be explored, and surely there are some dimensions that mostly have not even been considered yet. This chapter, however, does not try to cover all possible dimensions of sovereignty, but instead focuses primarily on what might be thought of as the core of sovereignty – the "monopoly of power" dimension – although it will be clear that even this focus inevitably entails certain linkages and "slop-over penumbra" at the borderlines of the other sovereignty dimensions. This chapter will examine this "core" dimension in the context of its roles with respect to international law and institutions generally, and international relations and other related disciplines such as economics.[6]

National government leaders and politicians as well as special interest representatives too often invoke the term "sovereignty" to mislead needed debate. Likewise, international elites often assume that "international is better," (thus downplaying the importance of sovereignty) and this, we can also say, is not always the better approach. What is needed is a close analysis of the policy framework that can get us away from these preconceived "mantras."[7] The objective here is to try to shed some light on these policy debates, or in some cases, policy dilemmas, and to describe some of the policy framework that needs to be addressed.

The subject has been extensively addressed in different kinds of frameworks, or academic disciplines. For example, there are a number of books from political science and international relations disciplines, many of which have important insights,[8] as well as many works by legal professionals.[9] However, in many of those works, the focus is on how to describe the concept of "sovereignty," how it operated in the past and operates in the present in international relations and how it can be criticized. This chapter is designed to address two somewhat different questions, namely, what, if any, are the valid issues raised in the so-called "sovereignty" debates, and how we can analyze those issues for future impact on policy.

The importance and need for this type of analytic activity (which hopefully will induce others to carry it further) should be obvious, but still merits mention. Much has been said and written about "globalization," which, as noted in Chapter 1, is a term of much ambiguity and controversial connotation, but which is usually reasonably well understood to at least apply to the exogenous world circumstances of economic and other forces[10] that have developed in recent decades as a result, in major part, of sharply reduced costs and time needs for transport of goods (and services) and likewise reductions in costs and time needs for communication.[11] These circumstances have led to very new structures of production,[12] which have, in turn, resulted in greatly enhanced (and sometimes dangerous) interdependency, about which there may not be much that we can do and which often renders the older concepts of "sovereignty" or "independence" fictional. As discussed in Chapter 2, these circumstances, particularly those of communication techniques heretofore unknown, are seen sometimes to affect dramatically the way in which governments can govern internally. These circumstances often demand actions that no single nation-state can satisfactorily carry out, and thus require some type of institutional "coordination" mechanism. In some of these circumstances, therefore, there is a powerful tension between traditional core "sovereignty" on the one hand, and the international institution on the other hand. This tension is manifest constantly, and addressed in numerous situations some of which are poignantly and elaborately verbalized in the work of international juridical institutions, such as the World Trade Organization (WTO) dispute settlement system.[13] Indeed, the now extraordinarily elaborate jurisprudence of the WTO[14] is a prime example of many of the tensions between internationalism and national government desires to govern and deliver to their democratic constituencies, and will be noted elsewhere in this book. This tension is, however, manifested in a large number of international law and international relations contexts. Some expressions of opposing approaches to "sovereignty" can easily be seen in the burgeoning literature and government documents on the subject, with examples such as the following:

One must not forget that some major factors remain much the same. . . . one of those major constant factors is surely still the sovereign State.[15] In the words of Kofi Annan: "[o]ur post-war institutions were built for an inter-national world, but now we live in a global world."[16] In a dangerous world marked by overwhelming inequalities of power and resources, sovereignty is for many states their best – and sometimes seemingly their only – line of defence.

However, for all the reasons mentioned already, the conditions under which sovereignty is exercised – and intervention is practised – have changed dramatically since 1945.[17]

3.1 Sovereignty and the fundamental logic of international law

The state will remain the single most important organizing unit of political, economic, and security affairs through 2015 but will confront fundamental tests of effective governance.[18]

America must stand firmly for the nonnegotiable demands of human dignity: the rule of law; limits on absolute power of the state; free speech; freedom of worship; equal justice; respect for women; religious and ethnic tolerance; and respect for private property.

History has not been kind to those nations which ignored or flouted the rights and aspirations of their people.

America is now threatened less by conquering states than we are by familiar ones. We must defeat these threats to our Nation, allies, and friends.[19]

Even a high government official of the current major great power perceptively recognized the multi-faceted complexity about "sovereignty" concepts when he used language including the following in a lecture he gave while still in government:

Sovereignty has been a source of stability for more than two centuries. It has fostered world order by establishing legal protections against external intervention and by offering a diplomatic foundation for the negotiation of international treaties, the formation of international organizations, and the development of international law. It has also provided a stable framework within which representative government and market economies could emerge in many nations. At the beginning of the twenty-first century, sovereignty remains an essential foundation for peace, democracy, and prosperity.

At the same time, sovereignty is being challenged from both within and without. Weak states struggle to exercise legitimate authority within their territories. Globalization makes it harder for all nations to control their frontiers. Governments trade freedom of action for the benefits of multilateral cooperation. And outlaw regimes jeopardize their sovereign status by pursuing reckless policies fraught with danger for their citizens and the international community. We need to adjust our thinking and our actions to these new realities.[20]

These considerations suggest further rethinking (or reshaping) of the core concept and roles of sovereignty, and to coin a new phrase to differentiate these directions from the old, some argue outmoded, "Westphalian" sovereignty concepts. We can replace the word "sovereignty" (which Professor Henkin wants us to do away with altogether)[21] with the phrase "sovereignty-modern." This new phrase could then indicate a newer approach, which is arguably more pragmatic and more empirically based and embraces a more "balanced and balancing" approach for "core sovereignty." However, it should be noted that there very well could be some dimensions of sovereignty other than what is above termed "core," which can continue to be benefited by more traditional approaches to sovereignty. But these are not the central subjects of this chapter, and it is likely that others will need to assume the heavy lifting of carrying the analysis into those other dimensions.

Consequently, this chapter will approach the subject of "sovereignty-modern" in three further sections, namely, sections 3.2 through 3.4.

These sections involve part of a connected logic which, in Chapter 1, noted the setting and "landscape" of the subject and, in Chapter 2, explored resulting impacts and challenges for various international law concepts. This chapter proceeds (in section 3.2) to outline and remind the reader about the older sovereignty concepts and to overview, with a brief survey of a tiny portion of a vast literature, the many criticisms of these older concepts. Section 3.3 then presents this author's views about which elements of the traditional sovereignty concepts may remain important in current global circumstances and how these "real policy values" need to be recognized and separated from the outmoded baggage of older Westphalian sovereignty concepts. This section suggests that one of the core policy values of sovereignty is power allocation, and explains what that means.

Section 3.4 then offers some perceptions and tentative conclusions. An important underlying theme of this chapter, articulated in this section 3.1 introduction, and reiterated again in section 3.4 is how the rethinking of "sovereignty" is not only necessary to escape the traps of use or misuse of older sovereignty thinking, but also challenges certain other key "fundamentals" of "general" international law thinking, such as the "nation-state consent" requirement of norm innovation, or the "equality of nations" ideas. Finally, some reflections summarize the broad implications of the three chapters in Part I.

3.2 Traditional Westphalian sovereignty concepts: outmoded and discredited?

The general perception is that the concept of sovereignty as many often think of it today, particularly as to its "core" of the monopoly of power for the highest authority of what evolved as the "nation-state," began with the 1648 Treaty of Westphalia. To read the 128 clauses of that document is to wade through dozens of provisions dealing with minute details of ending the Thirty Years War,[1] restoring properties to various feudal lordly owners, and solemnly promising not to interfere with the rule of certain rulers within their territories. Those read more like a "last will and testament"

3.2 Traditional Westphalian sovereignty concepts: outmoded and discredited?

than a treaty reshaping the world. It is not easy to surmise any general principle of "sovereignty" in these words, but the compact was a "Peace Treaty between the Holy Roman Emperor and the King of France and their respective Allies," and thus a passing of power from such emperor, with his claim of holy predominance, including choice of religion, to many kings and lords who then treasured their own local predominance, including choice of religion. As time passed, this developed into notions of the absolute right of the sovereign, and what we could call "Westphalian sovereignty," despite interesting criticism of the "myth" of Westphalia based on its historical antecedents and later evolution.[2]

As one recent academic work noted,
The classical concept of State Sovereignty . . . has increasingly become subject to criticism from different political quarters. [But] all seem to be unanimous in their expectation of the inevitable demise of the Westphalian State system . . .[3]

Ambassador Haass has also succinctly reviewed the criticism as follows:

Historically, sovereignty has been associated with four main characteristics: First, a sovereign state is one that enjoys supreme political authority and monopoly over the legitimate use of force within its territory. Second, it is capable of regulating movements across its borders. Third, it can make its foreign policy choices freely. Finally, it is recognized by other governments as an independent entity entitled to freedom from external intervention. These components of sovereignty were never absolute, but together they offered a predictable foundation for world order. What is significant today is that each of these components – internal authority, border control, policy autonomy, and non-intervention – is being challenged in unprecedented ways.[4]

As noted above, there has been a considerable amount of literature concerning the issue of "sovereignty," and various concepts to which it might refer. Most of this literature is very critical of the idea of "sovereignty," as it has generally been known. Some examples of this literature will give the reader a flavor of the variety of discontents with this idea.

One eminent scholar, Professor Stephen Krasner, has described the sovereignty concept as "organized hypocrisy."[5] This same author writes that there are at least four different meanings of sovereignty (some of which overlap). He describes:

domestic sovereignty, referring to the organization of public authority within a state and to the level of effective control exercised by those holding authority; interdependent sovereignty, referring to the ability of public authorities to control trans-border movement; international legal sovereignty, referring to the mutual

Sovereignty-modern: a new approach to an outdated concept

recognition of states or other entities; and Westphalian sovereignty, referring to the exclusion of external actors from domestic authority *configurations*.[6]

Some other authors have described sovereignty as being "of more value for purposes of oratory and persuasion than of science and law."[7]

Still other authors have explored sovereignty as a "social construct," saying "numerous practices participate in the social construction of a territorial state as sovereign, including the stabilization of state boundaries, the recognition of territorial states as sovereign, and the conferring of rights onto sovereign states."[8] The approach of these authors seems to be that there are no particularly inherent characteristics in the concept of sovereignty, but it depends very much on the custom and practices of nation-states and international systems.

In 1972, Professor Wolfgang Friedman wrote:
The growing interdependence of mankind has not so far significantly shaken the legal and political structure of international society. . . . But at the same time the stark realities of the contemporary world are pressing against the ramparts of the national state and the symbols of national sovereignty.[9]

More than thirty years later, one could now opine that passage of time has brought us to the no-man's land beyond these ramparts.

More recently, a different Friedman (Thomas Friedman, columnist for the *New York Times*) wrote how in circumstances of globalization, nation-states often found that they were subject to financial market forces which greatly constrain notions of independent "sovereign" action, saying,

Globalization isn't a choice. It's a reality. There is just one global market today, and the only way you can grow at the speed your people want to grow is by tapping into the global stock and bond markets, by seeking out multinationals to invest in your country and by selling into the global trading system what your factories produce.[10]

The global marketplace today is an Electronic Herd of often anonymous stock, bond, currency and multinational investors, connected by screens and networks.[11]

The Electronic Herd turns the whole world into a parliamentary system, in which every government lives under the fear of a no-confidence vote from the herd.[12]

A 2002 volume of twenty-five essays concerning sovereignty, from more than that number of different authors,[13] again with a wide variety of critical viewpoints about sovereignty, includes the view of another eminent senior international law scholar and professor, Henry Schermers, stating:

Sovereignty has many different aspects and none of these aspects is stable. The content of the notion of "sovereignty" is continuously changing, especially in recent years.

3.2 Traditional Westphalian sovereignty concepts: outmoded and discredited?

Under international law we are most often confronted with the idea that sovereignty of a State means that the State has unlimited power and is subjected to only those rules of international law which it has expressly accepted. Neither other States nor the United Nations have any right to intervene in matters which are essentially within the domestic jurisdiction of a State. This aspect of sovereignty has been seriously weakened during the second half of the twentieth century. . . . From the above we may conclude that under international law the sovereignty of States must be reduced. International co-operation requires that all States be bound by some minimum requirements of international law without being entitled to claim that their sovereignty allows them to reject basic international regulations.

Thirdly, we may conclude that the world community takes over sovereignty of territories where national governments completely fail and that therefore national sovereignty has disappeared in those territories. The world community by now has sufficient means to step in with the help of existing States and has therefore the obligation to rule those territories where the governments *fail.*[14]

Another symposium volume of twenty-one essays, published in 2003, contains a remarkable variety of ideas about sovereignty, ranging from defenses of the sovereignty concept to recent challenges to that concept, with some focus on the European Union. It also contains a series of essays appraising developments and attitudes in eight specific countries, which demonstrate quite striking differences.[15]

World leaders and diplomats have added their critical appraisals of older sovereignty ideas, albeit while often recognizing the importance of some attributes of the concept. In 1992 the then UN Secretary-General, Boutros Boutros-Ghali, said in his June 1992 report to the Security Council, "Respect for its [a state's] fundamental sovereignty and integrity are crucial to any common international progress. The time of absolute and exclusive sovereignty, however, has passed; its theory was never matched by reality."[16]

Almost a decade later, after some abject failures of the United Nations to meet apparent needs for action and intervention in Bosnia, Somalia, Rwanda, and Kosovo, the new UN Secretary-General, Kofi Annan said, in introducing his September 1999 Annual Report to the General Assembly:

If the new commitment to intervention in the face of extreme suffering is to retain the support of the world's peoples, it must be – and must be seen to be – fairly and consistently applied, irrespective of region or nation. Humanity, after all, is indivisible.[17]

Secretary-General Annan then expressed impatience with traditional notions of sovereignty, saying:

A global era requires global engagement. . . . If states bent on criminal behaviour know that frontiers are not the absolute defence; if they know that the Security Council will take action to halt crimes against humanity, then they will not embark on such a course of action in expectation of sovereign impunity.

. . .

If the collective conscience of humanity – a conscience which abhors cruelty, renounces injustice and seeks peace for all peoples – cannot find in the United Nations its greatest tribune, there is a grave danger that it will look elsewhere for peace and for justice. . . . Any such evolution in our understanding of State sovereignty and individual sovereignty will, in some quarters, be met with distrust, scepticism, even hostility. But it is an evolution that we should welcome.[18]

British Prime Minister Tony Blair has expressed similar sentiments, including in a 1999 speech in Chicago:

We live in a world where isolationism has ceased to have a reason to exist. By necessity we have to co-operate with each other across nations. Many of our domestic problems are caused on the other side of the world. Financial instability in Asia destroys jobs in Chicago and in my own constituency in County Durham. Poverty in the Caribbean means more drugs on the streets in Washington and London. Conflict in the Balkans causes more refugees in Germany and here in the US. These problems can only be addressed by international co-operation. We are all internationalists now, whether we like it or not. We cannot refuse to participate in global markets if we want to prosper. We cannot ignore new political ideas in other countries if we want to innovate. We cannot turn our backs on conflicts and the violation of human rights within other countries if we want still to be secure.

On the eve of a new Millennium we are now in a new world. We need new rules for international co-operation and new ways of organising our international institutions.

. . .

Today the impulse towards interdependence is immeasurably greater. We are witnessing the beginnings of a new doctrine of international community. By this I mean the explicit recognition that today, more than ever before, we are mutually dependent, that national interest is to a significant extent governed by international collaboration and that we need a clear and coherent debate as to the direction this doctrine takes us in each field of international endeavour. Just as within domestic politics, the notion of community – the belief that partnership and co-operation are essential to advance self-interest – is coming into its own; so it needs to find its international echo. Global financial markets, the global

3.2 Traditional Westphalian sovereignty concepts: outmoded and discredited?

environment, global security and disarmament issues: none of these can be solved without intense international co-operation.

. . .

> Any Government that thinks it can go it alone is wrong. If the markets don't like your policies they will punish you. The same is true of trade. Protectionism is the swiftest road to poverty. Only by competing internationally can our companies and our economics grow and succeed. But it has to be an international system based on rules. That means accepting the judgements of international organisations even when you do not like them.[19]

Situations of weapons of mass destruction, genocide, failed states, and rogue states, all pose extreme conceptual problems for doctrines of sovereignty. But, of course, an important dilemma develops when the international institutions do not have the capacity or the will to act to prevent or redress such extreme dangers to world peace and security or to particular regions and populations. In what circumstances, then, should other entities, including powerful sovereign states, have the right or duty to step into the breach? And to what degree is there a requirement before such action to exhaust international institutions? Or has the practice of nations replete with many such instances already begun to develop new norms condoning such conduct?[20]

In 2001 an International Commission on Intervention and State Sovereignty was formed under the initiative of the Canadian government to respond to some of these pronouncements and other debates within the United Nations. The Commission then produced an extensive report, *The Responsibility to Protect*, exploring the new trends in the doctrines of sovereignty. The report appended a large volume of research and commentary exploring many ramifications of "sovereignty." It is an extraordinary study of the subject, with an extensive bibliography. Several small extracts can capture some of the flavor of the larger work.[21] In a research essay appended to the report, the text (also quoting Kofi Annan) notes:

> Sovereignty has been eroded by contemporary economic, cultural, and environmental factors. Interference in what would previously have been regarded as internal affairs – by other states, the private sector, and nonstate actors – has become routine. However, the preoccupation here is not these routine matters but the potential tension when the norm of state sovereignty and egregious human suffering coexist. . . .
>
> The limits on sovereignty discussed above are widely accepted. They originate in the Charter itself, in authoritative legal interpretations of that document, and in the broader body of international law that has been agreed on by states. In

recent decades, and particularly since the end of the Cold War, four more radical challenges to the notion of state sovereignty have emerged: continuing demands for self-determination, a broadened conception of international peace and security, the collapse of state authority, and the increasing importance of popular sovereignty."[22]

The report itself bluntly comments with the statement quoted at the beginning of this chapter.

The burgeoning literature on this subject is yet more extensive and growing, and naturally draws attention to the important contribution of one of the previous editors-in-chief of the *American Journal of International Law*. Thomas Franck, in his seminal (and ahead of its time) 1992 article in that journal,[23] put forth his view as follows:

This newly emerging "law" – which requires democracy to validate governance – is not merely the law of a particular state that, like the United States under its Constitution, has imposed such a precondition on national governance. It is also becoming a requirement of international law, applicable to all and implemented through global standards, with the help of regional and international organizations.

He notes, however,

The question is not whether democracy has swept the boards, but whether global society is ready for an era in which only democracy and the rule of law will be capable of validating governance.

Yet he concludes:

The entitlement to democracy in international law has gone through both a normative and a customary evolution. It has evolved both as a system of rules and in the practice of states and organizations. This evolution has occurred in three phases. First came the normative entitlement to self-determination. Then came the normative entitlement to free expression as a human right. Now we see the emergence of a normative entitlement to a participatory electoral process.

Some of the discussion and practice about the role of "sovereignty" also focuses on the principle of "subsidiarity," which is variously defined, but roughly stands for the principle that governmental function should be allocated among hierarchical governmental institutions, to those as near as possible to the most concerned constituents, usually down the hierarchical scale. In the minds of some, therefore, an allocation to a higher level of government would require a special justification as to why a higher-level governmental institutional power was necessary to achieve the desired goals.[24]

In addition, most authors discussing "sovereignty" cite a very large number of "anomaly examples," mainly situations of governmental entities that simply do not fit into the normal concepts of sovereignty or

3.2 Traditional Westphalian sovereignty concepts: outmoded and discredited?

non-sovereignty.[25] Sovereignty is sometimes divided up or "fractionated," sometimes temporary, sometimes nominal, to facilitate a diplomatic compromise, and so on.[26]

Thus the concept of sovereignty seems quite often to be extremely, and perhaps purposefully, misleading, and a crutch to politicians and media to avoid the tough and very complex (as we see below) thinking that should be taken up about real policy issues that are involved.

In the area of trade policy, many specific instances can be cited as use of constructs to avoid some of the implications of "sovereignty concepts." Perhaps a striking example is the General Agreement on Tariffs and Trade (GATT) and now, WTO, criteria for membership, which is not limited to a "sovereign entity," but instead to a "State or separate customs territory possessing full autonomy in the conduct of its external commercial relations."[27]

Sometimes the principle of non-interference at nation-state level is closely linked to sovereignty, yet in the real world of today's "globalization," there are innumerable instances of how actions by one nation (particularly an economically powerful nation) can constrain and influence the internal affairs of other nations. In addition, there are examples of powerful nations influencing the domestic elections of other nations and also linking certain policies or advantages, such as aid, to domestic policies relating to subjects such as human rights. Likewise, international organizations partake in some of these linkages, such as the so-called IMF "conditionality."[28]

Professor Louis Henkin himself has written perceptively, "for legal purposes at least, we might do well to relegate the term sovereignty to the shelf of history as a relic from an earlier era."[29]

It would indeed be nice to get rid of the "s word" (as Henkin says in another work),[30] but it does not seem very likely that we will be rid of this nuisance, and even if we were, we would have to invent some other term to cover some of the concepts that the word "sovereignty" refers to. Somehow, it seems that to try to eliminate completely the word or the concepts associated with "sovereignty" would miss some important principles. This leads into the next section (3.3) of this chapter, discussing affirmative attributes of sovereign concepts, and to a subsequent section (3.4), which develops the concept of "sovereignty-modern."

Finally, it must be noted that the term "sovereignty" is sometimes used to describe subjects that are not international at all. For example, in the United States, discussions about reserved powers to the sub-federal states sometimes refer to the "sovereign powers" of those states, such as California or Michigan. Clearly this relates to the question of "division of powers" within a sovereign nation-state (the United States). It is an interesting parallel to some issues of nation-state international sovereignty "allocation of power" policies, but quite different from the Westphalian monopoly of power concept.[31]

Similar uses of the word "sovereignty" are also witnessed in the context of discussions about allocating powers between member states and the European Union.[32]

Also within the United States, the role of Native American tribes is often discussed, using the term sovereignty in an entirely different context. A book by Professor Alex Aleinikoff develops this context with a perceptive analysis of US Supreme Court cases that bear on the relationship under the US Constitution of powers of the US government concerning the tribes, and the degree to which such tribes can exercise governmental powers within their "reservation" territories.[33]

3.3 Potentially valid policy objectives of sovereignty concepts

a. Policy objectives of sovereignty concepts?

Apart from the politically misleading and debate-stifling use of "sovereignty" concepts and recognizing that almost no perceptive observer or practitioner is prepared today to sign on to the full import of the traditional Westphalian notion of sovereignty, what can be said in favor of modified or "evolving" sovereignty concepts?[1] Many if not most of the critics of the older sovereignty notions recognize with varying degrees of support some of the important and continuing contributions of the sovereignty concepts towards international discourse, stability, and peace. As indicated in section 3.1 of this chapter, sovereignty is deeply interwoven with the fabric of international law, and in order not to abandon the whole cloth very serious thought about the concept of "sovereignty" is required so that a substitute may be found efficiently to fill the gaps left by its absence.

Let us start with an interesting anecdote. Testifying before a US congressional committee in a hearing concerning the Uruguay Round massive trade agreement and the World Trade Organization (WTO)[2] was the well-known Ralph Nader, who opposed congressional approval of that agreement.[3] While not accepting some of the assumptions and some of the details of his statements, there are intriguing aspects that merit respect, including the following:

A major result of this transformation to a World Trade Organization would be to undermine citizen control and chill the ability of domestic democratic bodies

3.3 Potentially valid policy objectives of sovereignty concepts

to make decisions on a vast array of domestic policies from food safety to federal and state procurement to communications and foreign investment policies. Most simply, the Uruguay Round's provisions would preset the parameters for domestic policy-making of legislative bodies around the world by putting into place comprehensive international rules about what policy objectives a country may pursue and what means a country may use to obtain even GATT-legal objectives, all the while consistently subordinating non-commercial standards, such as health and safety, to the dictates of international trade imperatives.

Decision-making power now in the hands of citizens and their elected representatives, including the Congress, would be seriously constrained by a bureaucracy and a dispute resolution body located in Geneva, Switzerland, that would operate in secret and without the guarantees of due process and citizen participation found in domestic legislative bodies and courts.

. . . All over the country there is a bubbling up of citizen activity dealing with the environment and public health. People want solar energy instead of fossil fuels; they want recycling; they want to clean up toxic waste dumps; they want safer, biodegradable, environmentally benign materials instead of others that happen to be sold in greater numbers worldwide. And if local or state governments can make decisions to help achieve these goals, then people can really make a difference. But if existing or proposed local and state standards can be chilled by a foreign country's formal accusation (often in collaboration with domestic special corporate interests) that the standards are a non-tariff trade barrier, then the evolution of health and safety standards here and around the world will be stalled or degraded.

. . . This percolating-up process for advancing crucial non-commercial values that shape living standards will be stifled by the WTO, with bottom-up democratic impulses replaced by pull-down mercantile dictates.[4]

This and other worthy worries have led many persons to take a somewhat different tack in the analysis of sovereignty.

In broad brush, it is possible to see the "antiquated" definition of "sovereignty" that should be "relegated" as something like the notion of a nation-state's supreme absolute power and authority over its subjects and territory, unfettered by any higher law or rule (except perhaps ethical or religious standards) unless the nation-state consents in an individual and meaningful way. It could be characterized as the nation-state's power (embodied in the Prince?) to violate virgins, chop off heads, arbitrarily confiscate property, and indulge in all sorts of other excessive and inappropriate actions.

No sensible person would agree that such an antiquated version of sovereignty exists at all in today's world. A multitude of treaties and customary international law norms impose international legal constraints (at least) that circumscribe extreme forms of arbitrary actions on even a sovereign's own citizens.

But then, what does "sovereignty," as practically used today, signify? Here we can consider a tentative hypothesis: most (but not all) of the time when "sovereignty" is used in current policy debates it really refers to questions about the allocation of power; normally "government decision-making power." That is, when a party argues that the United States should not accept a treaty because to do so would take away US sovereignty, what the party most often really means is that he or she believes that a certain set of decisions should, as a matter of good government policy, be made at the nation-state (US) level and not at an international level.[5] Another way to put it is to ask whether a certain governmental decision should be made in Geneva, Washington DC, Sacramento, Berkeley, or an even smaller sub-national or sub-federal unit of government. Or, when focusing on Europe, should a decision be taken in Geneva, Brussels, Berlin, Bavaria, Munich, or a smaller unit?

There are also various other dimensions of the "power allocation" analysis. Those mentioned above could be designated as "vertical," whereas there are also "horizontal" allocations to consider, such as separation of powers within a government entity (legislature, executive, judiciary, etc.) and division of powers among various international organizations (WTO, ILO, WHO, FAO, IMF, IBRD, etc.). Indeed, one can go even further and note that power allocation could refer to the types of participants involved: government, non-government (which can embrace issues of government versus private enterprises), and so on. This is obviously a subject that could have very widespread relevance, but this chapter will focus on the "vertical" governmental choices of allocation of "power."

In all those dimensions, one can ask a number of questions that would affect the allocation issues. Questions of legitimacy loom large, and often today there is a focus on "democratic legitimization," which is frequently meant to challenge more traditional notions of sovereignty (as illustrated by Thomas Franck's views noted in the previous section), and is also related to part of some notions that sovereignty is gravitating from ideas of "sovereignty for the benefit of the nation-state" towards ideas of "sovereignty of the people."[6]

Other major topics relevant to vertical allocation issues include the capacity of the institution at each level to perform needed tasks for pursuing the fundamental policy goals motivating the choices (e.g. market economic efficiency principles, cultural identities, preserving peace, sub-

3.3 Potentially valid policy objectives of sovereignty concepts

sidiarity concepts, environment and externalities questions, environment and the global commons issues, etc.).

Clearly, the answer to the question of where decisions about a certain matter should be made will differ for many different subjects. There may be one approach to fixing potholes in streets or requiring sidewalks. There may be another approach for educational standards and budgets, yet another for food safety standards, and, of course, still another for rules that are necessary in order to have an integrated global market work efficiently in a way that creates more wealth for the whole world. Questions of culture and religion also pose important challenges.

When one reflects on these questions of allocation of power, it is easy to identify this issue arising in dozens of questions at various government levels. News reports almost daily recount activities related to these questions.[7]

b. Values involved in power allocation analysis

There are clearly many values or policy objectives that could influence consideration of the appropriate level or other (horizontal) distribution of power among a landscape of government and nongovernmental institutions. A small illustrative group of these policies are outlined below.

1. Reasons for preferring government action at an international level

A large number of reasons could be given for preferring an international-level power allocation. Some of these reasons relate to the need for what economists call "coordination benefits,"[8] and are sometimes analyzed in game theory as "the prisoner's dilemma."[9] This describes situations where, if governments each act in their own interest without any coordination, the result will be damaging to everyone. Whereas matters would be improved if they could make certain, presumably minimal, constraints, effective so as to avoid the dangers of separate action. Likewise, there is much discussion about the so-called "race to the bottom" in relation to necessary government regulation[10] and the worry that competition among nation-states could lead to a degradation of important socially needed economic regulation.

Sometimes economists suggest that upward placement of government decision-making is particularly needed where there is so-called "factor mobility," such as investment funds or personal migration. This is partly because governments find it more difficult either to tax or to regulate in an effective way when there is such factor mobility.[11] (We return to these concepts in Chapter 6.[12])

The subject area of the environment seems to be one that directly engages these issues of power allocation, and such issues as those involved in the so-called "global commons," or where actions that degrade the environment have "spill-over effects," are given as examples for a need for higher supervision.[13]

Many other issues can be listed, and many other arguments can be made. Many general subject matters are very controversial in this regard. For example, at what level should competition policy (monopoly policy) be handled? What about human rights? Democratic values and democratic institutions? Questions of local corruption or crony favoritism might seem to call for a higher level of supervision.

2. Values, goals or constraints that suggest allocating power more locally; the principle of "subsidiarity"

Advocates of subsidiarity (which is a concept much discussed in Europe) note the value of having government decisions made as far down the "power ladder" as possible. There are a number of policy values that are involved here,[14] and historically there has been reference to some Catholic philosophy of the nineteenth and early twentieth centuries.[15] One of the basic ideas is that by being closer to the constituents, a government decision can more reflect the subtleties and necessary complexity and detail that most benefits those constituents. Sometimes this is expressed as follows: "governments that know your name are more likely to know your needs."[16] Likewise, it is often said that the decision-making that is furthest down the ladder and closest to the constituent will be policed by a greater sense of accountability.

Indeed, there are many illustrations of the dangers of distant power, including, of course, the origins of the United States, in its rebellion in the eighteenth century against England. Similarly, colonialism, particularly twentieth-century colonialism,[17] and the move to decolonize raised a number of these issues. It is often found that decisions made remote from constituents become distorted to accommodate the decision-makers' goals, which are local to their own location and institution, not to accommodate the targeted "beneficiaries."[18]

In the United States there is an enormous amount of discussion about "federalism," which really engages these same issues. There is a worry that "inside the beltway" decisions often neglect the facts and details "on the ground" in local areas, remote from the center, partly to accommodate the particular, relatively selfish, goals of some senators or other members of the US Congress. Indeed, the US Supreme Court has, during the last decade, been paying a great deal of attention to the "constitutional

3.3 Potentially valid policy objectives of sovereignty concepts

federalism" questions, and one has to think about whether the Supreme Court's attitudes are totally based on an appropriate view of the US Constitution or are at least partly motivated by policy considerations (not necessarily inappropriate) about where power should reside.[19]

3. Some other policy goals and values – supporting both directions

Sometimes the controversy over what level to place a government decision is truly a controversy over the substance of an issue. Thus national leaders will sometimes use international norms to further policy that they feel is important to implement at their own level, but which is difficult to implement because of the structure of their national constitution or the political landscape. Likewise, other leaders may want to retain power over certain issues at the national or even sub-national level, because they feel they have more control at those levels to pursue those policies that they favor, in contrast to others who want the issue placed at another level of government because they have more control there. These issues do raise the question of power elites trying to bypass democratic procedures that annoy them.

Another policy that can cut both ways (up and down the ladder) is the policy of preventing a governmental institution from misusing power. Thus, those who wish to have governmental decisions made at a higher level, such as at the international level, must also consider the potential for misuse of the power that could occur in such international institutions. Since quite often the constraints on international institutions are less effective than on national institutions (e.g., lack of elections, etc.), this may be the core of an argument against placing power at the higher level. On the other hand, power can also clearly be misused at lower levels of government.

Likewise, there is generally a "separation of powers" principle (a "horizontal allocation") that could apply. Clearly the US Constitution has as its centerpiece the principles of the separation of powers, to avoid monopolies of power which then lead to misuse. Such separation can be as between various relatively "equal" levels of governmental action, or as between higher or lower levels of governmental action. Thus, in considering how governments should make certain decisions, it may be decided that only a portion of a power would be allocated to the higher level, retaining for a lower level some powers that would be used to check the higher level. To some extent the implementation of treaties, without having direct application in domestic legal systems, is potentially such a check against power at the higher level. But allocation of a greater power effect to the higher-level treaty may also check lower-level misuse of power.[20]

Another aspect of the decision involving values relating to the allocation of power is the policy goal of "rule orientation" in the matter concerned. Particularly for economic purposes, for example, a rule system that provides additional clarity, security, and predictability can be very significant, particularly when the subject matter involves millions of entrepreneurs ("decentralized decision making") as part of the market system. So part of the consideration regarding the level at which to place governmental power might deal with the question of whether different levels have different abilities to make an effective rule-oriented program. Of course, this raises a downside risk to internationalism in the minds of some, who may view with suspicion a rule system's method of interpreting treaty text. [21]

3.4 Perceptions and reflections for Part I: changing fundamentals of international law

a. Sovereignty and power allocation

Based on the analysis of the previous sections of this chapter, we can now see that one of several key questions is how to allocate power among different human institutions. It is probably not surprising that this question is a very complex one to answer. There are many factors to consider. To some extent, these all center on a common question of "power," and, therefore, in some ways this question relates to virtually all of government and political science studies, as well as international relations, economics, law, and so on. When one has to develop the landscape of this policy analysis, one recognizes that a huge number of specific substantive policies play a part, as well as what we might call "procedural" or "institutional" policies (how to design the appropriate institutions). Some of these policies are, typically, not congruent in the directions in which they would suggest allocation of power should occur. That is, differing policies often pose dilemmas for policy makers, where they must engage in a certain amount of "balancing," sometimes characterized as the principle of proportionality. When the need for such balancing occurs, a key question related to "allocation of power" is who or what institution should perform this balancing.

Indeed, the policy landscape is so complex that one can question whether it is possible to arrive at any worthwhile generalizations. It could be argued that the complexity is such that each case has to be decided *sui generis*, that is, on a "case by case" basis (to use a phrase often indulged in by juridical institutions).

3.4 Perceptions and reflections for Part I

However, the proposition being tentatively put forth in this chapter is that for the "core sovereignty" concepts mostly involving the monopoly of power for the nation-state and its logical derivative of state-consent requirements for new norms, the power allocation analysis, if taken more seriously and deeply than often presented, can help to overcome some of the "hypocrisy" and "thought destructive mantras," so that policy makers can focus on real problems rather than myths. This can thus help them weigh and balance the various factors to achieve better decisions on questions such as accepting treaty norms, dispute settlement mechanisms and results, necessary interpretative evolution of otherwise rigid treaty norms, and even, in some cases, new customary norms of international law.

But this analysis recognizes that there are desiderata in sovereignty concepts other than the "core" power allocation issues, and that even for the core issues there are clearly cases that the world must resolve by explicit (or well recognized implicit) departures from traditional sovereignty concepts. This is what can be labeled "sovereignty-modern" and it can be hoped that further analysis and discussion will help scholars and practitioners alike build some new "handholds on the slippery slopes" looming just ahead of certain issues not resolved by traditional sovereignty, in the face of major risks of uncertainty, miscalculations in diplomacy, and overreaching by certain nation-states.

The follow-up question becomes that of identifying some theories or principles that could reach beyond the traditional sovereignty parameters, but offer some principled constraints to avoid the risks just mentioned. Later chapters will take up this question.

b. Changing fundamentals of international law

To summarize briefly Part I of this book, we can see that chapters 1, 2, and 3 have outlined a "landscape of current circumstances" which profoundly impact the fundamental assumptions, or so called axioms, of international law (including international economic law). These circumstances, combined with an extraordinarily extensive literature of analysis and criticism, some of which is tied to the circumstances, provide a number of challenges to the underlying logic and legitimacy of international law norms. Responding to those challenges requires in-depth and extensive analysis, as yet only partly satisfactory. One way to carry forward the needed analysis is to examine empirically what is happening in the real world. One small part of that task is explored in the next two chapters (4 and 5), with an overview look at one of the most complex international institutions in existence today, namely the WTO. This exploration is enormously aided by the elaborate published reports constituting the developing and evolving jurisprudence of the unique dispute settlement "juridical" system which is central to the WTO and to the "rules-based" institutional structure deemed essential for economic coexistence in a globalized world, especially in the context of market-oriented features of that world.

PART II

The WTO

4

The WTO as international organization: institutional evolution, structure, and key problems

Anyone who reads GATT is likely to have his sanity impaired.
                              Senator Millikin, at 1951 US Senate Hearing[1]
I think your difficulty . . . is the inherent complexity of the subject. . . . I must admit I am thoroughly confused.
Winthrop Brown, one of the draftsmen of GATT, at 1951 US Senate Hearing[2]

4.1 The WTO as international economic law and its relationship to general international law

In this and the next chapter we examine the World Trade Organization (WTO) and its dispute settlement system (DSS). This remarkable international institution is one of the newest international economic organizations, but according to many opinions it is also the most important and the most controversial. It is in the specific cases and diplomatic and political problems of the WTO that one witnesses "the devilish detail" of the tensions between nation-state "sovereignty" and international legal norms.[3]

Also remarkable is the degree to which misunderstanding exists about the relationship of the WTO to general international law, and more specifically to international economic law. Indeed, as we have seen in Chapter 2, section 2.4, there is some observed tendency for those concerned with general international law to ignore, or at least overlook, the relevance for international law of the extensive practice which now exists in the IEL context with its young WTO intricate jurisprudence developed through decisions in specific cases.[4]

This and the next chapter will explore some of these developments and note how the practice of the WTO has much to say about many basic international law concepts, particularly those related to treaty implementation and interpretation. Conversely, we note that international law plays an uneasy role for WTO jurisprudence. This chapter will explore the general characteristics and evolution of the WTO as an organization, while Chapter 5 will focus on what has been described as the "centerpiece" or "jewel in the crown" of the WTO, namely its dispute settlement system.[5]

One general curiosity of this story of the WTO is the strange position of its predecessor, namely GATT (General Agreement on Tariffs and Trade.) GATT has often been described as the most important treaty for international trade relations, and the most important international organization for those relations. In a technical sense, neither of these descriptions was completely true. The GATT treaty as such never came fully into force, but was implemented in part by the "Protocol of Provisional Application" (forty-seven years of provisional application!).[6] GATT itself was also never intended to be an organization, as this chapter later describes, because the ill-fated International Trade Organization (ITO) was supposed to be the institutional and organizational framework for trade rules which would have included GATT. Yet when the 1948 ITO draft charter failed to come into effect, GATT had to fill the vacuum. This led to a strongly pragmatic element in GATT institutional evolution and considerable confusion for international trade relations. This pragmatism influenced a trial and error or ad hoc approach which promoted attitudes of "realism" and give and take that characterized the implementation of the trade rules. This undoubtedly had some causal relation to the spotty implementation for certain areas of economic endeavor such as agriculture and textiles. The fact that GATT had very few textual clauses relating to its institutional structure led to some makeshift arrangements, which, however, actually became quite powerful.

There are some important lessons in the GATT/WTO story which we explore in these chapters. Perhaps the most significant lesson is that human institutions inevitably evolve and change, and concepts which ignore that, such as concepts which try to cling to "original intent of the draftspersons," or some inclination to disparage or deny the validity of some of these evolutions and changes, could be damaging to the broader purposes of the institutions. Governments (or societies) which consent to become members of institutions must do so with the realization that institutional structures will not be frozen in time, and that such consent will certainly bring some surprises to the constituencies concerned.[7]

In the light of these broader observations, this chapter now proceeds along the following lines. Section 4.2 will open the story with an overview

4.1 The WTO as international economic law

and exposition of the logic of the policy objectives and preferences of the GATT and then the WTO system. This exploration will form the backdrop (or landscape) of the later sections which delve more deeply into the history and evolution of these institutions and the problems and tensions which were faced.

Section 4.3 will briefly overview the origins and history of GATT, the shifting emphasis over time (e.g. from tariffs, towards more attention to non-tariff "behind the border" national economic regulatory matters), and finally the enormous and profound achievement of the Uruguay Round of trade negotiations (1986–1994) resulting in a significant enlargement of the competence and responsibilities of the international trade rules, and the creation of the WTO and a reformed dispute settlement system (the particular story of the evolution of the dispute settlement system itself will be taken up in Chapter 5).

Section 4.4 will outline the current institutional structure of the WTO, with some focus on the decision-making processes (including "voting" and its avoidance) and the constraints explicitly and implicitly imposed by the negotiators of the WTO "Charter." Some of these issues have led to a worry that the decision-making processes are inhibiting the ability of the organization to achieve its goals and, some would say, may be leading to paralysis (a criticism particularly addressed to the "consensus" process of decision making). Obviously these circumstances reflect some of the policy tensions between outmoded ideas of international law (such as "sovereignty," "consent theory" and "equality of nations"), which have been raised in previous chapters.

Section 4.5 will then describe some of the institutional problems and tensions that became increasingly obvious in the last several decades of GATT existence and the first decade of the WTO. These problems include the consensus questions, the attitudes regarding nongovernment actors (and beneficiaries), questions of transparency and democratic legitimacy, the relationship of poorer countries to the WTO system, worries about inadequate resources of the organization, proliferation of discriminatory bilateral and small group trade agreements, and the evolving structures of power allocation within the organization and between the WTO and nation-states or other international organizations. Some of these problems were discussed in a January 2005 report of a "Consultative Board" of eminent persons, appointed in June 2003 by the WTO Director-General, Supachai Panitchpakdi,[8] as is also noted in section 4.5.

Section 4.6 will briefly take a look at the relationship of the WTO legal norms to the legal structure of its member states, again struggling with various aspects of treaty implementation, including those issues focused on procedures and jurisprudence in the domestic spheres of activity of member states.

Section 4.7 will examine some of the controversy about the appropriate scope of competency and activity for the WTO. This will require at least a brief peek at the varied and complex "trade and . . ." issues, to suggest directions for thinking about which among a large number of candidate subjects (e.g. competition policy, investment, human rights, environment, labor rules) should be eligible for inclusion under the WTO "umbrella."

Reflections and conclusions about the WTO as an institution will be deferred to section 5.12, at the end of the next chapter, after discussion of the WTO dispute settlement system.

4.2 The policy objectives and preferences for a WTO

A logical starting point for an analysis of the "constitution and jurisprudence"[1] of the WTO is to examine the goals or "policy objectives" of the organization. For such an examination it is appropriate to look at the text of the WTO "Charter"[2] itself and also the text of its predecessor, GATT. Also relevant is the preamble and other parts of the ITO "Havana Charter" which never came into formal effect but was the context for GATT.[3]

The GATT (1948) has a preamble which reads in part:
Recognizing that their relations in the field of trade and economic endeavour should be conducted with a view to raising standards of living, ensuring full employment and a large and steadily growing volume of real income and effective demand, developing the full use of the resources of the world and expanding the production and exchange of goods,

Being desirous of contributing to these objectives by entering into reciprocal and mutually advantageous arrangements directed to the substantial reduction of tariffs and other barriers to trade and to the elimination of discriminatory treatment in international commerce,

The WTO includes most of the GATT preamble language and also adds objectives as follows:

The Parties to this Agreement, Recognizing that their relations in the field of trade and economic endeavour should be conducted with a view to raising standards of living, ensuring full employment and a large and steadily growing volume of real income and effective demand, and expanding the production of and trade in goods and services, while allowing for the optimal use of the world's resources in accordance with the objective of sustainable development, seeking both to

4.2 The policy objectives and preferences for a WTO

protect and preserve the environment and to enhance the means for doing so in a manner consistent with their respective needs and concerns at different levels of economic development,

Recognizing further that there is need for positive efforts designed to ensure that developing countries, and especially the least developed among them, secure a share in the growth in international trade commensurate with the needs of their economic development,

. . .

Resolved, therefore, to develop an integrated, more viable and durable multilateral trading system encompassing the General Agreement on Tariffs and Trade, the results of past trade liberalization efforts, and all of the results of the Uruguay Round of Multilateral Trade Negotiations,

Determined to preserve the basic principles and to further the objectives underlying this multilateral trading system, . . .

Also related to these is Article 1 of the 1948 draft charter for the ITO, which is entitled "Purpose and Objectives." This language is a bit more detailed about the objectives, but covers essentially the same purposes as expressed in GATT. It speaks of the desire for a "growing volume of real income," "contributing to a balanced and expanding world economy," to "foster and assist . . . economic development . . . particularly of those countries . . . still in the early stages of industrial development" and to "encourage the international flow of capital." It also mentions "equal terms of access to . . . markets," "eliminat[ing] discriminatory treatment," and promotion of "mutual understanding, consultation and cooperation," in the "solution of problems relating to trade, economic development, commercial policy, business practices and commodity policy."

In short, the objectives of GATT, colored by the purposes mentioned in the 1948 ITO "Havana Charter," were to promote the economic welfare of the world. Some references in the Havana Charter were more pointedly aimed at aiding the poorest countries and also targeted some specific regulatory areas which needed cooperation (commercial policy, business practices, commodity policy). These related to the broader objective of improving welfare.

Although not explicitly highlighted in these trade texts, another underlying goal was extremely instrumental in expressions of policy by free world political leaders during World War II and after. This was the goal to "keep the peace" and avoid another world war.[4] So it is reasonable to believe that the principal original goals for GATT were broadly twofold: keeping the peace, and expanding world economic development and world welfare, and that these two were not unrelated to each other.

It is possible to see in the WTO preamble text some additional thoughts expressed, particularly the environmental goals of sustainable development, the renewed emphasis on reducing poverty in the world, and the institutional goal of developing a "more viable and durable multilateral trading system."

Furthermore, in the light of developments in the WTO since its January 1, 1995, beginning, it seems fair to focus further attention on the reduction of poverty, as well as concerns about financial crises that were inflamed by the Asian financial crisis of 1997–1998 and its ensuing spread to other parts of the world.

To summarize: one can see five prominent goals of the WTO system: keep the peace, promote world economic development and welfare, work towards sustainable development and environmental protection, reduce the poverty of the poorest part of the world, and manage economic crises that might erupt partly due to the circumstances of globalization and interdependence.

To focus particularly on the goal of promoting world economic welfare, what might this particular (and probably central) goal imply? Generally speaking, most experts (economists and other specialists) tend to accept the value of free markets as a societal mechanism to best achieve economic development which in turn increases the probability of individuals satisfactorily pursuing their own chosen goals (family, religious, career, contribution to society, etc.).

Whether economic policies which are based on market principles[5] are the best approach for maximizing human satisfaction is, of course, controversial. Various alternatives have been much debated, and many of those largely rejected, but substantial arguments are made in favor of some sort of mixture of policies, perhaps to temper the perceived negative effects of "too pure market approaches." Whatever mixture may appeal to certain societies, however, it seems reasonably clear that markets can be very beneficial,[6] and even when not beneficial, market forces demand respect and can cause great difficulties when not respected.[7]

While stressing the benefits of market economics, important thinkers note the importance of human institutions which guide and shape markets. Nobel Prize-winning economists have expressed this.

Ronald Coase has stated:[8]

It is evident that, for their operation, markets . . . require the establishment of legal rules governing the rights and duties of those carrying out transactions . . .

4.2 The policy objectives and preferences for a WTO

To realize all the gains from trade, . . . there has to be a legal system and political order . . . Economic policy consists of choosing those legal rules, procedures and administrative structures which will maximize the value of production.

Douglas North has written:[9]

That institutions affect the performance of economics is hardly controversial . . . Institutions reduce uncertainty by providing a structure to everyday life. . . Institutions affect the performance of the economy by their effect on the costs of exchange and production.

Joseph E. Stiglitz also has observed:[10]

The analytic propositions are clear: whenever there is imperfect information or markets (that is always), there are, in principle, interventions by the government – even a government that suffers from the same imperfections of information – which can increase the markets' efficiency.

Human institutions embrace many structures and take many forms, but it is clear that law and legal norms play the most important part of the institutions which are essential to make markets work. The notion that the "rule of law" (ambiguous as that phrase is) or a rule-based or rule-oriented system of human institutions is essential to a beneficial operation of markets, is a constantly recurring theme in many writings.[11]

With respect to international economics, the world is fortunate to have the advantage of institutions such as the Bretton Woods system (including GATT) established through the vision of statesmen, scholars, and diplomats at the end of World War II. At least some of the credit for the relative peace and economic growth of the past half-century goes to those institutions and their rules.[12] And now, of course, we have the World Trade Organization, with an extraordinarily elaborate set of rules.

A critical question often asked by those confronted with international law rules is "Why do they matter?" Put another way, there exists much cynicism about the importance or effectiveness of international law rules. Some of this was a central part of the "realist school" of international relations,[13] but there has been a noticeable shift in political science thinking in this regard, with views appreciating the role of "rules."[14] Still, the public can read news of violations of such rules by major and minor nations. In some cases such violations, even when admitted to be such (often there is bitter and inconclusive argument on this question), are rationalized or declared "just" by national leaders. Thus the fact that cynicism about international rules continues is not surprising.

A more careful examination of the role and effectiveness of international rules is necessary, however. First, it should be observed that not all domestic rules are always obeyed either. Yet there are many international rules which are remarkably well observed.[15] Why this is so has been the subject of much speculation[16] which will not be repeated here. Notions of reciprocity and a desire to depend on other nations' observance of rules lead many nations to observe rules even when they don't want to. There is even the thought that humans are not always motivated only by self-interest, contrary to some extreme views of "self-interest economics." There is a notion that the world is a better place when rules actually operate effectively, which notion may play a part in human motivation to follow the rules.

At least in the context of economic behavior, however, and particularly when that behavior is set in circumstances of decentralized decision-making, as in a market economy, rules can have important operational functions. As discussed in section 2.3, rules may provide the only predictability or stability to a potential investment or trade-development situation. Without such predictability or stability, trade or investment flows might be even more risky and therefore more inhibited than otherwise. If such "liberal trade" goals contribute to world welfare, then it follows that rules which assist such goals should also contribute to world welfare. To put it another way, the policies which tend to reduce some risks lower the "risk premium" required by entrepreneurs to enter into international transactions. This should result in a general increase in the efficiency of various economic activities, contributing to greater welfare for everyone.

Assuming then that institutions are important, and that law plays a significant role in those institutions, what legal principles can we identify that play such roles? Obviously this can be a vast subject, certainly ripe for scholarly and policy attention of various kinds for years to come. But perhaps one particular principle can here be mentioned, namely the value of a "rule-oriented" approach to the design of international institutions relating to economic activity.[17]

The "rule-oriented approach" focuses the disputing parties' attention on the *rule*, and on predicting what an impartial tribunal is likely to conclude about the application of a rule. This, in turn, will lead parties to pay closer attention to the rules of the treaty system, and this can lead to greater certainty and predictability which is essential in international affairs, particularly *economic* affairs driven by market-oriented principles of decentralized decision making, with participation by millions of entrepreneurs. As noted above, such entrepreneurs need a certain amount of predictability and guidance so that they can make the appropriate efficient investment and market development decisions.[18]

4.2 The policy objectives and preferences for a WTO

The phrase "rule orientation" is used here to contrast with phrases such as "rule of law," and "rule-based system." Rule orientation implies a less rigid adherence to "rule" and connotes some fluidity in rule approaches which seems to accord with reality (especially since it accommodates some bargaining or negotiation). Phrases that emphasize too strongly the strict application of rules sometimes scare policy makers, although in reality they may amount to the same thing. Any legal system must accommodate the inherent ambiguities of rules and the constant changes in the practical needs of human society. The key point is that the procedures of rule application, which often center on a dispute settlement procedure, should be designed so as to promote as much as possible the stability and predictability of the rule system. For this purpose the procedure must be creditable, "legitimate," and reasonably efficient (not easy criteria).

For example, suppose countries A and B have a trade dispute regarding B's treatment of imports from A to B of widgets. One technique for resolving it would involve a negotiation between A and B by which the more powerful of the two would have the advantage. Foreign aid, military maneuvers, or import restrictions on other key goods by way of retaliation would figure in the negotiation. A small country would hesitate to challenge a large one on whom its trade depends. Implicit or explicit threats (e.g., to impose quantitative restrictions on some other product) would be a major part of the technique employed. Domestic political influences would probably play a greater part in the approach of the respective negotiators in this system, particularly that of the negotiator for the more powerful party.

On the other hand, a second technique suggested – reference to agreed rules – would see the negotiators arguing about the application of the rule (e.g., was B obligated under a treaty to allow free entry of A's goods in question?). During the process of negotiating a settlement it would be necessary for the parties to understand that an unsettled dispute would ultimately be resolved by impartial third-party judgments based on the rules, so that the negotiators would be negotiating with reference to their respective predictions as to the outcome of those judgments and not with reference to potential retaliation or actions exercising power by one or more of the parties to the dispute.

In both techniques negotiation and settlement of disputes is the dominant mechanism for resolving differences; but the key is the perception of the participants as to what the bargaining chips are. Insofar as agreed rules for governing the economic relations between the parties exist, a system which predicates negotiation on the implementation of those rules would seem for a number of reasons to be preferred. The mere existence of the rules, however, is not enough. When the issue is the application or interpretation of those rules (rather than the formulation of new rules), it is necessary for the parties to believe that if their negotiations reach an impasse the settlement mechanisms which take over for the parties will be designed to apply or interpret the rules fairly. If no such system exists, then the parties are left basically to rely upon their respective "power positions," tempered (it is hoped) by the goodwill and good faith of the more powerful party (cognizant of its own long-range interests).

As the world becomes more economically interdependent, more and more private citizens find their jobs, their businesses, and their quality of life affected if not controlled by forces outside their country's boundaries. Thus they are more affected by the economic policy pursued by their own country on their behalf. In addition, the relationships become increasingly complex – to the point of being incomprehensible to even the brilliant human mind. As a result, citizens assert themselves, at least within a democracy, and require their representatives and government officials to respond to their needs and their perceived complaints. The result of this is increasing citizen participation, and more parliamentary or congressional participation in the processes of international economic policy, thus restricting the degree of power and discretion which the executive possesses.

This makes international negotiations and bargaining increasingly difficult. However, if citizens are going to make their demands heard and influential, a "power-oriented" negotiating process (often requiring secrecy and executive discretion so as to be able to formulate and implement the necessary compromises) becomes more difficult, if not impossible. Consequently, the only appropriate way to turn seems to be toward a rule-oriented system, whereby the various citizens, parliaments, executives, and international organizations will all have their inputs, arriving tortuously at a rule – which, however, when established will enable business and other decentralized decision makers to rely upon the reasonable stability and predictability of governmental activity in relation to the rule.[19]

The degree of desired flexibility for rules is a subject discussed by important writers. Sometimes these suggest that certain rules be raised to "constitutional status" and embedded in national legal systems,[20] but this approach has some serious policy problems of its own, including the risk of rule rigidity in the context of rapidly evolving economic circumstances.[21]

4.3 Historical background: from Bretton Woods to Cancún and Hong Kong

With these "policy building blocks" in mind, we can now turn to several other dimensions of the subject of international economic law in the WTO context.

4.3 Historical background: from Bretton Woods to Cancún and Hong Kong

a. Introduction: the conundrum of GATT

The previous section stressed the importance of institutions; and indeed, a response to the changing circumstances set forth in Chapter 2 can only point to the impact of institutions, both international and national, on the empirically observable effects of the international trade rules and policies.[1]

The WTO is now the principal institution for international trade, but to understand this institution it is necessary also to know something about its "predecessor," GATT. Indeed, the WTO Charter makes it clear that the GATT history is significant, prescribing (in Art. XVI) that "the WTO shall be guided by the decisions, procedures and customary practices followed by the CONTRACTING PARTIES [expressed in all caps to signify the Contracting Parties acting jointly under the GATT agreement] to GATT 1947 and the bodies established in the framework of GATT 1947." Given that the rules of international law are framed and interpreted by "customary practice," including practice of its treaty institutions,[2] in many cases the history and practice of institutions and international law are significantly more important than might be the case in some national legal jurisdictions. Thus, in this section we will briefly review the historical background of GATT, leading to the WTO Charter and its implementation[3] by the Uruguay Round negotiations, and developments since then.[4]

As briefly stated in the introduction (section 4.1), although for many years GATT has been featured in news headlines and those of major daily newspapers as the most important treaty governing international trade relations, the fact is that the GATT treaty, as such, never came into force. How could this be? What were the institutional and historical events that occurred during the formation years of GATT (1947–1950) that led to this state of affairs? How has this history affected the operation and the vigor of GATT? And how will this history affect the new WTO? These are some of the issues with which we struggle in this section. Although the GATT treaty as such never came into force, it is necessary to clarify that the obligations of GATT were (and are) clearly binding under international law, because of the historical circumstances that this section describes.

b. The flawed constitutional beginnings of GATT[5]

The 1944 Bretton Woods conference in the United States[6] established the charters for the World Bank and the International Monetary Fund, two pillars of the post-World War II international economic institutional system. Because the Bretton Woods conference was directed and organized by the financial ministers of the governments concerned, it was not there felt appropriate to address trade questions which generally belonged to other ministries. Yet the Bretton Woods conference explicitly recognized the necessity of an international trade organization to complement the responsibilities of the financial organizations. Indeed, in some ways the WTO, after many decades, has become the "missing leg" of the Bretton Woods system.

The major initiatives leading to the establishment of GATT were taken by the United States during World War II, in cooperation with its allies, particularly the United Kingdom. Two distinct strands of thought influenced these countries during the war. One strand concerned the program of trade agreements begun by the United States after the enactment of the 1934 Reciprocal Trade Agreements Act. Between 1934 and 1945 the United States entered into thirty-two bilateral reciprocal trade agreements,[7] many of which had clauses that foreshadowed those currently in GATT.

The various official records of the four preparatory conferences in 1946, 1947, and 1948 (Havana) total more than 27,000 pages in over 100 volumes, all publicly available.[8] Many of the preparatory documents have been used in interpreting GATT, as the GATT Analytical Index demonstrates.[9]

The second strand of thinking during the war period stemmed from the view that the mistakes made concerning economic policy during the interwar period (1920 to 1940) were a major cause of the disasters that led to World War II. The Great Depression has been partly blamed for this war, as has the harsh reparations policy toward Germany.[10] In the interwar period, particularly after the damaging 1930 US Tariff Act was signed, many other nations began enacting protectionist measures, including quota-type restrictions, which choked off international trade. Political leaders in the United States and elsewhere made statements about the importance of establishing postwar economic institutions that would prevent these mistakes from happening again.

The two strands of thinking about creating an organization for international trade began to merge in 1945. In the United States, Congress

4.3 From Bretton Woods to Cancún and Hong Kong

enacted the 1945 renewal of the reciprocal trade agreements legislation for a three-year period.[11] In December of that year, the US government invited a number of nations to enter into negotiations to conclude a multilateral agreement for the mutual reduction of tariffs. Also in 1945, the United Nations was formed; and in 1946 its subordinate body ECOSOC (the Economic and Social Council) began work to develop a draft charter for what was to be designated the International Trade Organization (ITO). The major work was undertaken at Geneva in 1947.

The history of the preparation of GATT is thus intertwined with that of the preparation of the ITO charter. The 1947 Geneva meeting was actually an elaborate conference divided into several major parts, including preparation of a charter for a major international trade institution, the ITO, and negotiating GATT as a multilateral agreement to reduce tariffs reciprocally.

The basic idea at Geneva in 1947 was that the ITO would be the organization and that GATT would be a specialized agreement as a part of the ITO and would depend on the ITO for institutional support such as decisions, dispute settlement, membership obligations, and so on. The US government knew that a treaty creating an organization such as the ITO would have to be submitted to the US Congress for approval. However the US executive branch was certain that the 1945 statute extending the president's authority for negotiating and implementing reciprocal trade agreements gave the US president the authority to sign and ratify the GATT. Some in Congress disagreed, but the executive branch prevailed.[12] However Congress made it very clear, in hearings with the US negotiators for the Geneva conference, that the president could not accept a GATT if it had attributes of an organization. Thus the negotiators returned to Geneva and scrubbed the then draft of GATT's "organizational" attributes. For example, the word "member" was taken out, and replaced by "contracting party."

The general clauses of the draft GATT imposed obligations on nations to refrain from a variety of trade-impeding measures. These clauses had evolved in the United States' bilateral trade agreements, and were seen as necessary to protect the value of any tariff-reducing obligations.[13]

One important implication of this preparatory history linking GATT to the ITO draft charter is that the ITO preparatory history, including in some instances the history of the Havana Conference (which occurred after some of the GATT obligations came into force), is relevant to the interpretation of GATT clauses,[14] and has been used extensively as important interpretive material throughout the history of GATT.

c. GATT and the Protocol of Provisional Application

At the end of the Geneva conference in November 1947, a complete draft of a GATT (with its many schedules of tariff "bindings"[15]) was basically complete, but the charter for a new organization needed more work. This added work was scheduled for a conference in Havana in March 1948, and only at that conference was the ITO Charter draft completed. Much of the GATT text was drawn from the ITO Charter's chapter on trade, and so there was a complex relationship between the GATT text and that of the ITO. GATT trade rules were designed to be changed later to conform to the comparable rules as they emerged in the ITO Charter after Havana, once the ITO came into effect. But although the ITO Charter was submitted to governments for ratification, and the US president submitted it to Congress (a two-house statutory procedure similar to that of the 1934 Reciprocal Trade Agreements Act and its extensions), Congress would not act. Finally, at the end of 1951, the US president's office announced that the attempt to obtain approval of the ITO was abandoned.

Although other countries could have gone ahead, at this time the United States was the preeminent economic power in the world, having emerged from the war largely unscathed. No country desired to enter an ITO that did not include the United States. The irony was that it had been the United States that had taken the principal initiative to develop the ITO charter in the first place.[16]

Since the GATT, including the various tariff obligations, was completed by October 1947 as the Geneva Conference drew to a close, many negotiators believed that it should be brought into force without waiting for the ITO. First, GATT consisted in part of thousands of individual tariff concessions. Although these concessions were still secret, the negotiators knew that it was inevitable that their contents would begin to creep into public knowledge and, as they did so, so traders would be influenced by them. Sellers might anticipate a forthcoming tariff reduction by holding back their product until the new tariff came into force. World trade patterns could thus be seriously disrupted if a prolonged delay occurred before the tariff concessions came into force.[17]

Another reason for early implementation of GATT influenced US negotiators in particular. They were negotiating under the delegated authority of the US trade legislation that had been renewed in 1945. Under this authority they would need to ratify GATT before the 1945 act expired in mid-1948.[18]

4.3 From Bretton Woods to Cancún and Hong Kong

On the other hand, there were several difficult problems in bringing GATT into force. Of course, some of the language of the general clauses of GATT had to be identical to the final ITO language, but this could be handled by amending GATT at a later date to bring it into conformity with the results of the Havana conference.

More troublesome was that some nations had constitutional procedures under which they could not accept parts of the GATT (particularly some of the general clauses) without submitting this agreement to their parliaments. Given that they anticipated the necessity of submitting the final draft of the ITO charter to their parliaments in late 1948 or later, they did not want to give their legislatures two bites at the apple. They feared that to spend the political capital and effort required to get the GATT through their legislatures might jeopardize their later efforts to get the ITO passed. Hence, they preferred to take both agreements to their legislatures as a package.[19]

The solution agreed upon was the adoption of the Protocol of Provisional Application (PPA),[20] to apply the GATT treaty "provisionally on and after 1 January 1948." The protocol contained two important clauses that altered the impact of GATT itself. The first reduced the time required for withdrawal. This, however, was not particularly meaningful, given that withdrawal from GATT was not a very viable option in practical terms, at least for any major participant.

The more important impact of the PPA, however, was its statement of the manner of implementing the GATT. Parts I and III of the GATT are fully implemented without a PPA exception, but the PPA called for implementation of Part II "to the fullest extent not inconsistent with existing legislation." Part I of the GATT contained the Most Favored Nation (MFN) and the tariff concession obligations, while Part III was mainly procedural. Part II (Arts. III–XXIII) contained most of the principal substantive obligations, including those relating to customs procedures, quotas, subsidies, antidumping duties, and national treatment. As to these important obligations, each GATT contracting party was entitled to "grandfather rights" for any provision of its legislation that existed when it became a party and was inconsistent with a GATT Part II obligation.

Many of these Part II obligations, especially those concerning national treatment, involved obligations which relate to domestic regulatory and other measures which reach deeply into national "sovereignty." These rules reflect the recognition by diplomatic negotiators that such internal measures could often be used to undermine the obligations relating to border measures (tariffs, quotas, customs procedures, etc.), and therefore must be subjected to rule disciplines to prevent such undermining. In later years of GATT, these internal "non-tariff barriers" (NTBs) increasingly became a more significant danger to trade liberalization than border measures.

This provisional and grandfather exception allowed most governments which would otherwise need to submit GATT for legislative approval to approve the PPA by executive or administrative authority without going to the legislature. It was understood that after the ITO charter was ready to be submitted to legislatures, the GATT would also be submitted for "definitive" application. In the meantime, the GATT contracting parties could deviate from those GATT Part II obligations to which they could not adhere without legislative authority. They must accept fully the MFN obligation of Article I of the GATT and the tariff cuts of Article II incorporating the tariff schedules, but in most cases the executives had authority to do this. Governments that later joined GATT did so on treaty terms that incorporated the same "existing legislation" exception.

Although attempts during subsequent GATT history were made to obtain "definitive application" of the GATT, none succeeded.[21] Thus, even until nearly the end of GATT's existence, one could witness the reliance on grandfather rights to justify certain national actions regarding international trade.[22] This legal context was an important part of the US bargaining position in the Tokyo Round (1973–1979) negotiation[23] and was also a central issue in some GATT panel proceedings.[24] Gradually many of the grandfather rights, however, became extinct. New legislation did not qualify for this PPA exception, and some of the old provisions passed out of existence, or for other reasons became non-operative or were superseded. One of the features of the WTO is the elimination of any generalized idea of grandfather rights, although one or two are probably represented by some specific new treaty clause obligations and exceptions.

d. *GATT fills the vacuum*

A major hole was left in the fabric intended for post-World War II international economic institutions, because the ITO did not come into being. It was only natural that the institution that did exist – GATT – would find its role changing dramatically as nations turned to it as the forum in which an increasing number of problems of their trading relationships would be handled. More countries became contracting parties, sometimes in groups (nine in 1949, four in 1951), sometimes individually.[25] Because of the fiction that GATT was not an "organization," there was considerable reluctance at first to delegate any activity even to a "committee." Gradually that

4.3 From Bretton Woods to Cancún and Hong Kong

reluctance faded, and soon there was even an "intercessional committee" that met between sessions of the contracting parties.[26]

No secretariat existed for GATT. After Havana, however, an Interim Commission for the International Trade Organization (ICITO) was set up, in the typical pattern of preparing the way for a new international organization. A small staff was assembled to prepare the ground for the ITO, and this staff serviced the needs of GATT.[27] As years passed and it became clear that the ITO was never to come into being, this staff found that all of its time was devoted to GATT, and as such it became de facto the GATT secretariat (technically as a kind of a "leased" group, whereby GATT "reimbursed" the ICITO for the costs of the secretariat).

By the mid 1950s, the GATT contracting parties began to prepare GATT to play better the role it was assuming as the central international institution for trade. They attempted to amend GATT (and only partly succeeded), and also drafted a new organizational charter for an "OTC" (Organization for Trade Cooperation).

This short treaty agreement was much less elaborate than the ITO Charter draft, but even this failed to get the approval of the US Congress, so that the OTC was also stillborn. (However, the OTC in some ways was a model for the initial thinking about a new WTO.)[28] The GATT contracting parties then cautiously took a decision in 1960[29] to establish a Council without any explicit treaty language and departing somewhat from the original political constraints against viewing GATT as an international organization. The Council became the principal permanent institution for GATT, and increasingly shouldered the burden of directing it.

Thus, GATT limped along for nearly fifty years with almost no basic constitution designed to regulate its organizational activities and procedures. Even so, GATT by any fair definition must be deemed to have been a de facto international organization. Through trial and error it evolved some fairly elaborate procedures for conducting its business. That it could do so, despite the flawed basic documents on which it had to build, is a tribute to the pragmatism and ingenuity of many of its leaders over the years.

In fact, GATT can be praised for its considerable success, certainly beyond what could be predicted by its flawed origins. Within several decades, by 1970, GATT, with its series of six major trade negotiations,[30] had succeeded in bringing about dramatic reductions in tariffs in the world, at least as to manufactured products imported into advanced industrial countries. By this time, however, it was apparent that tariffs were no longer the major problem for trade liberalization. A plethora (some say thousands[31]) of non-tariff barriers were creating many problems for trade. The seventh GATT trade negotiation, the Tokyo Round (1973–1979), was the first to focus on NTBs and resulted in a major expansion of the activity and competence of GATT. This was not, however, done by amendment to the GATT treaty text, because it was generally assumed that the treaty amendment requirements were too difficult to be practical. Instead the negotiators developed a series of separate instruments, sometimes called "codes," each of which was technically a stand-alone treaty. These codes addressed a number of non-tariff measures that distort international trade flows, such as government procurement regulations and the use of product standards to restrain imports.[32]

During the Kennedy Round period (1962–1967), the GATT contracting parties adopted an amendment to the GATT general clauses, which is the last such "true" GATT amendment. A protocol to add Part IV to the GATT, dealing with problems of developing countries, was approved in 1965 and came into force in 1966.[33] Articles 36, 37, and 38 of this part are primarily expressions of goals, and impose few if any concrete obligations. Nevertheless, this language has been relied on in legal and policy argumentation in GATT, and has had considerable influence.

One person in particular must be singled out for his influence on the evolution of GATT: Sir Eric Wyndham White, a British citizen (knighted in 1968) who was the chief administrative officer of the UN group that provided service for the drafting conferences of the ITO and GATT. He became the first GATT "executive secretary," a post he held (later embellished by the title of director-general) until he retired in 1968.[34] Although he was careful to give the appearance of playing the role of a typical international civil servant – that is, to be neutral among all parties and to avoid the appearance of taking initiatives that should be left to member states – Sir Eric nevertheless had a profound sense of the "possible" while continuously working toward achieving the basic goals of the GATT agreement. Some attribute important evolutionary steps of the GATT dispute settlement procedure to Sir Eric's actions behind the scenes.

Many other institutional innovations that enabled GATT to play its vacuum-filling role as the major international trade institution (some discussed in the next section 4.4, and in Chapter 5) were put in place without explicit treaty text authority, and Wyndham White's leadership was often critical to their success. In addition, during the Kennedy Round of world trade negotiations from 1963 to 1967, Sir Eric's role was reportedly crucial, particularly in the last few weeks of the negotiation, in helping nations break a stalemate and achieve a final agreement.[35]

4.3 From Bretton Woods to Cancún and Hong Kong

e. *The Uruguay Round*

The eighth and last of the major trade "rounds" under the GATT umbrella was the Uruguay Round (UR), launched at Punta del Este, Uruguay, in 1986, and finally concluded at a ministerial-level final negotiating conference in Marrakech, Morocco, in April 1994.[36] The UR was clearly the largest and most complex of all the GATT trade rounds, and probably the largest and most complex economic multilateral treaty negotiation in history. Its final text is approximately 26,000 pages long. Most of these pages are detailed schedules of concessions and obligation, but about 1,000 pages consist of reasonably dense and complex treaty general norms. The conclusion of the UR was several times delayed, but surprisingly (to some at least) ended on a very high note, with success for most of the subjects taken up. If half of the original aspirations for the UR agenda were successful, that itself would have been the largest conclusion of any of the GATT rounds. Many observers felt the UR was over 80 percent successful.

A key conclusion of the round was the establishment of a new international organization, the WTO (World Trade Organization), which in fact had not been included in the Punta declaration of the agenda, but only rose to a high priority late in the negotiation. This turn of attention clearly was partly a result of the views of the negotiators, who began to see that the UR results were so extensive and in some respects competence extending, that a new institutional framework would be essential for the successful implementation of the substance. The Marrakech text was submitted to governments for ratification, and a sufficient number of acceptances occurred for the treaty to enter into force on January 1, 1995.

Apart from the new WTO organization, the UR for the first time introduced intellectual property and services trade into the trade treaty system. Before that, GATT only applied to goods ("products"), but in the early 1980s groups interested in intellectual property (IP) and services trade, respectively, advocated to their governments that these subjects be included on the UR agenda. To some extent, this represented not only a view that these subjects were becoming increasingly important (services representing for some countries a larger share of GDP than products[37]) but also that that these were beginning to be affected by various troublesome governmental measures to limit competition from foreign sources. But another interesting motive for bringing IP and services under the GATT umbrella was a growing recognition by such groups that international treaty rules were needed, and that therefore a treaty application structure was essential for such rules to be worthwhile. The groups viewed the developing dispute settlement rules of GATT (see Chapter 5) as admirable in their assistance to the effectiveness of the trade rules.

Certain other features of the UR were also highly significant. For example, the negotiators established at Punta del Este that the new UR negotiation should result in a treaty that would be a "single undertaking," or "single package." By that they meant that all participants in the negotiation who wished at the end to become members of the new organization, and thus participants in the UR treaty norms, would be required to accept all the obligations of the massive treaty complex. This contrasted sharply with the approach of the Tokyo Round (1973–1979), which established a series of separate texts or "codes" on various key subjects (as noted above), which texts were each "stand-alone" treaties[38] and allowed each government (GATT contracting parties) to decide which (if any) it would accept. This has been referred to as "GATT à la carte." The UR results provide for a few exceptions to this single package approach, but mostly upheld the notion that all governments were required to accept almost all of the texts in the new treaty.[39]

Like the Tokyo Round, the UR negotiators felt that GATT was too difficult to amend, so an interesting feature in the transition from GATT to the WTO institutional structure was the technique of "getting from here to there." The WTO was constituted as an entirely new legal institution (this time a true "organization" with various treaty-based institutional clauses including "members" rather than "contracting parties"). GATT was therefore ended as such by the formal (or informal) withdrawal of all GATT contracting parties.[40] However the "GATT 1994" treaty text still exists, but now as an Annex to the WTO charter. The next section 4.4, will outline the WTO institutional structure as well as briefly overview the substantive obligations of the current WTO–GATT system.

The subject of trade in agricultural products was particularly troublesome, not only in the UR negotiation, but also throughout the history of GATT. There are a variety of causes for this difficulty, but among the most significant has been the long-run increase in productivity in the agriculture sector so that a steady migration from rural to urban jobs and living circumstances has occurred. In the United States, for instance, in 1880 approximately 44 percent of the population lived and worked on farmland, but as at 1995, this percentage was less than 2 percent.[41] This is somewhat similar to many other societies, particularly in Europe. Europeans also, in the immediate post-World War II period, had vivid memories of food shortages, and thus were determined to develop policies which ensured a sustainable supply of food.[42] These and other factors

4.3 From Bretton Woods to Cancún and Hong Kong

caused intense internal domestic support for protection against agriculture imports.

A US statute of 1951[43] established import barriers to some foodstuffs, particularly dairy and other farm products. These statutory barriers were quite clearly contrary to GATT rules prohibiting quantitative restrictions.[44] The US executive branch had been unable to prevent the congressional action, so the United States exercised its considerable diplomatic weight (at that time) to obtain a GATT waiver for its measures. The Europeans, on the other hand, developed its Common Agricultural Policy (CAP) as part of the newly formed European Economic Community.[45] Measures involved in the CAP were viewed by some as violations of GATT also, although there was some ambiguity. As time went on, Europeans implemented various measures to limit imports (and promote exports) of agriculture goods. The United States found itself in some difficulty over complaining, since it benefited from a waiver which the rest of the world felt was unfair. But, in addition, the United States clearly embraced a "geopolitical" policy largely to look the other way when it came to European agricultural measures. This was considerably true until the 1970s, partly because the United States felt that a united Europe was strongly desired as a cold war buttress against risks of Soviet dominance in Europe. This played a role in agriculture also, since the agricultural citizen vote in Europe was thought to be more conservative and thus assisted in preventing a "communist takeover" in some European countries.

Largely unsuccessful attempts were made in the Tokyo Round to develop a trade rule discipline for agriculture.[46] In the Uruguay Round some headway was made with rules and negotiating principles including some phase in provisions for norms which would discipline both barriers to "market access" and subsidies (including those on goods for export). These issues, however, are still quite central to plans for later negotiations.

A curious feature of the various GATT trade rounds after the mid-1950s is the absence of an official "preparatory" document set similar to the UN Document Series EPCT, for 1946–1948.[47] It appears from informal statements and interviews that the contracting parties at the time of these later rounds made a conscious but undocumented informal decision that there would be no "official preparatory records." Perhaps this reflects the sensitivity which negotiators felt about revealing some of the compromise decisions by various delegations. Of course, there were many documents produced during the rounds related to the negotiations, most of them "restricted." Informally, some of these documents have become available, and there have been some attempts to gather unofficial lists.[48] In addition, recent WTO actions have derestricted many of these older documents.[49]

f. Post-Uruguay Round – the ministerial conferences search for a new negotiation

Ever since the WTO came into force, members have realized the necessity for new negotiations on a wide spectrum of WTO rules, partly in order to fill gaps left by the UR, but also to tune the WTO system better to cope with rapid economic and other changes in the world. Whether the new negotiation should be a "round" or simply an "agenda" for further work has been disputed, but in effect the world is using the term "new round." This would then become the first "WTO round" or the ninth "WTO–GATT" round. But the route to this destination has been extraordinarily labored.

The highest level body of the WTO is its Ministerial Conference, which is mandated by the treaty to meet no less often than every two years. As of this writing there have been five Ministerial Conference meetings, with a sixth scheduled for December 2005 in Hong Kong. These conferences have become famous for troublesome protest activities in the streets and also for controversy about their policy directions.

The first WTO Ministerial Conference was at Singapore, on December 9–13, 1996.[50] At this meeting proposals were made to address some new issues (investment, labor, environment, competition policy),[51] resulting mostly in measures to coordinate with other international organizations (such as the International Labor Organization), or proposals to study further. Likewise, at the second Ministerial Conference in Geneva in 1998 further similar attention occurred. It was at the third Ministerial Conference at Seattle in December 1999 when the WTO organization faced a heavy dose of street protest. Dissonance, especially between the United States and the European Union, prevented the negotiators from reaching an agreement for future direction of the new organization. For some months thereafter the WTO embraced a work program designed to redress some of the Seattle problems and to move forward. The next conference was in Doha, Qatar,[52] which turned out to be taking place only a month or so after the 9/11 terrorist attack on New York City. Because of these circumstances the Doha conference, in November 2001, was heavily protected and consequently not as troubled by protest groups. In addition the diplomatic leadership organized the Doha Ministerial Conference with great attention to the inclusion of key diplomats from all parts of the WTO

4.3 From Bretton Woods to Cancún and Hong Kong

membership, especially the developing world. This was partly a response to the criticisms at Seattle about the WTO lack of transparency and inadequate participation by member diplomats who felt excluded. Prior GATT habits of often controlling "quad group" meetings (of the United States, the European Union, Japan, and Canada) and developing proposals which would then be "pushed" at GATT were resented. The so-called "green room" meetings (in a small conference room at the WTO headquarters which is adjacent to the Director General's office) were also resented as often allowing only selected members to participate in making some crucial decisions and negotiation preparations.

The Doha ministerial declarations[53] seemed very progressive to many. They established a work program toward more negotiations, struggled about whether to entertain new subjects now called "Singapore subjects," including investment and competition policy, and designated the ongoing activity to be a "development round" to address many demands from developing countries.

The Doha meeting contemplated a new set of negotiations which could result in a conclusion in 2005, but which would be "appraised" by an earlier ministerial conference held in Cancún, Mexico, in September 2003. This Cancún conference, like Seattle, essentially failed. A tense confrontation seemed to have developed, with the newly organized G-20[54] – a group of 20 developing countries making demands which challenged the richer WTO members – arguing against any Singapore issues and demanding action to redress the harm which rich country agriculture policies were inflicting on many developing countries.[55]

Shortly after Cancún, the principal EU diplomat termed the process and the WTO institution as "medieval" and in urgent need of reform, while the US diplomat criticized the "nay sayers" who prevented progress urged by the "yay sayers."[56] But tempers cooled, and considerable work has since gone forward to develop positions to be considered at the next scheduled ministerial conference (December 2005 in Hong Kong). Agriculture still seemed to be the most troublesome issue. It is clear that the culmination of a negotiation will be postponed, probably to sometime in 2007,[57] or perhaps later.

The next section of this book (section 4.4) will explore the institutional structure of the WTO, and following that section 4.5 will examine some of the particular institutional challenges and recommended reforms which have been put forward in various contexts. As previously noted, a "Consultative Board" of "eminent persons" was appointed by the WTO Director-General in June 2003, and this group issued its report in

January 2005 about some of these challenges.[58] More will be said about this in later sections, but the interplay of important challenges to the international legal and international economic law world institutions and the work of the WTO (and other international institutions) is clearly manifested in this history of GATT and the WTO. Even after only ten years of existence the WTO seems remarkably central to many of the dilemmas and policy arguments of the world situation, as outlined in Chapters 2 and 3.

4.4 The World Trade Organization: structure of the treaty and the institution

The WTO has a surprisingly complex institutional structure, no doubt influenced by the structure which was used for the negotiation of the Uruguay Round, but also responding to perceived problems of GATT, including its "birth defects." This section will only briefly overview this complex structure and the reader is referred to other works for detail.[1] In addition the all-important dispute settlement system is taken up in the next chapter, Chapter 5, so will not be detailed in this chapter.

a. The Uruguay Round treaty structure for the WTO

As explained in section 4.3, the Uruguay Round of GATT negotiations resulted in a massive treaty[2] which fundamentally overhauled the world trading institutional system. GATT was ended, and instead a new organization, the WTO, was established when the UR treaty came into force on January 1, 1995. A beginning portion of that 26,000-page treaty is a brief 14-page text which establishes the WTO as a proper (no longer provisional) organization. This portion of the long treaty is often informally called the "WTO Charter," but technically, as explained in section 4.3.e, the treaty is one entire unified document implementing the principle of a "single undertaking" to which all governments must agree in order to become members. Thus the major portion of the treaty pages are "annexes" to the "WTO Charter." An appendix to this book has an outline of this treaty structure.[3] The headings in this appendix also suggest the many subjects now covered by the WTO.

The full text of the Uruguay Round agreement is complex, and has many gaps as well as inconsistent provisions. This is partly the result of reluctance by the negotiators at late stages of the UR negotiation, to permit the lawyers to do a "legal scrub" to try to iron out such difficulties.

4.4 The WTO: structure of the treaty and the institution

There are four annexes to the WTO. Three of the annexes and their contents are mandatory. All members are bound by those. A fourth annex, however, contains some optional treaty text.

The outline of the annexes is as follows.

Annex 1 contains most of the treaty pages. This annex is termed the "Multilateral Agreements," which are mandatory substantive agreements. It is divided into three parts, A, B and C.

> Annex 1A consists of GATT 1994 (distinguished from GATT 1947) which includes the GATT treaty text (unchanged from when GATT existed) as amended until the end of GATT. It also contains a number of newer texts, some derived from Tokyo Round side-agreements (see section 4.3) which were revised and now become mandatory for every member. Certain other "understandings" and similar complementary documents are included, but the most extensive part of Annex 1A is the elaborate tariff schedules (called "bindings") which mostly set maximum tariff commitments for each member. Each member has its own schedule, which is the result of negotiation since it became a member (forty-seven years in some cases). Major schedules, such as those for the United States and the EU, each comprise a full volume and contain over 10,000 individual schedule items each. Since the GATT text was not changed when incorporated into the WTO, there are GATT provisions that are clearly superseded by other UR treaty text. A brief text at the end of the WTO "Charter" stipulates that if there is a conflict between GATT 1994 and the various other texts (numbering dozens) in Annex 1A, the later shall prevail. This can present important interpretation problems, such as "what is a conflict?"
>
> Annex 1B is the agreement on services (known as GATS – the General Agreement on Trade in Services), and the schedules (much shorter than those for goods) for Service commitments.
>
> Annex 1C is the agreement on TRIPS (Agreement on Trade-Related Aspects of Intellectual Property Rights).

Annex 2 contains the DSU (Dispute Settlement Understanding), a text of about twenty-four pages which governs the DS procedures in some detail (compared with the DS provisions of the original GATT which consisted of about three paragraphs).

Annex 3 contains the TPRM (Trade Policy Review Mechanism), a brief text designed to set up a structure of regularly scheduled institutional reviews of each member's trade policies. A schedule of such reviews is established[4] whereby the major trading countries have more frequent reviews (usually every two years), while others are less frequent. The review is not supposed to be limited to examining compliance with obligations, but to range broadly over all issues relevant to a member's international trade measures and policies.

Annex 4 contains agreements called "Plurilateral" which are supposedly optional. This is the major explicit departure from the "single undertaking" principle of the UR. At the end of the UR, there were four texts listed for Annex 4, but subsequently two relating to agriculture were terminated, so now there are two, namely a text on government procurement (which also has schedules of commitments), and a text on trade in civil aircraft. This annex could be a source of some dynamic flexibility for the WTO institution, but unfortunately the WTO Charter rules require a "consensus" of members to add any new agreements to Annex 4,[5] a requirement which so far has been assumed to be unobtainable. On the other hand, in some negotiations for the accession of new members, some existing members have conditioned their support for the new member on its willingness to accept a supposed "optional" text in Annex 4. This has particularly been the case where accession protocols, such as that of China, have stipulated that the government procurement text of Annex 4 be accepted by the new member.[6]

Unlike the General Agreement, the WTO Charter clearly establishes an international organization, endows it with legal personality, and supports it with the traditional treaty organizational clauses regarding "privileges and immunities," Secretariat, Director-General, budgetary measures, and explicit authority to develop relations with other intergovernmental organizations and – important to some interests – non government organizations. The Charter prohibits staff of the Secretariat from seeking or accepting instructions from any government "or any other authority external to the WTO." The secretariat "rented" by GATT 1947 (see section 4.3) became the WTO Secretariat.

There is strong indication in various parts of the WTO Charter to promote a sense of legal and practice continuity with GATT. Except as otherwise provided, the WTO and the Multilateral Trade Agreements shall "be guided by the decisions, procedures and customary practices followed by [GATT 1947]" (Art. XVI(1), as noted before in this chapter).

b. Institutional structure

The governing structure of the WTO follows some of the GATT 1947 model, but it also departs from it substantially. At the top there is a "Ministerial Conference," which meets not less often than every two years. Next there is not one but four councils. The General Council has overall supervisory authority, including responsibility for carrying out many of the functions of the Ministerial Conference between Ministerial Conference sessions. In addition, however, there is a council for each of the Annex 1 agreements, that is, for goods, services, and intellectual property. Some

4.4 The WTO: structure of the treaty and the institution

councils have established many committees for specific subjects. Overall there is some worry that the WTO structure is too ponderous, sometimes requiring draft documents or reports to work through various levels of attention.

A Dispute Settlement Body (DSB) is established to supervise and implement the dispute settlement rules in Annex 2. Likewise there is a TPRM Body for the Trade Policy Review Mechanism.

Each of these councils and bodies is open to membership of any WTO member[7] who chooses to take it on. A number of the poorer countries of the world do not feel that they have the resources to establish a mission in Geneva for WTO representation. Many WTO members conduct their WTO representation from a general Geneva-based mission for "International Organizations." With the enormous increase in WTO activity and meetings, such limited missions are clearly stretched, sometimes having only one or two persons who can devote attention to the WTO. The US mission has about sixteen officials and diplomats, and the mission of the EU Commission has about thirteen.

c. WTO decision making

Since GATT was not viewed as an organization, it is not surprising that the General Agreement had little in it about decision making. Article XXV called for one nation, one vote and decision by a majority of votes cast, unless otherwise provided.

The GATT treaty language about decisions (now superseded by WTO) is remarkably broad. Although cautiously utilized (at least in the early years), it was the basis for much GATT activity. For the United States, for instance, this language posed a danger. First, the United States could have been outvoted in a GATT with over 120 members, over two thirds of which were developing countries, and over half of which were formally associated in one status or another with the European Union. Second, a nation's vote is cast by the executive branch of its government, and for the United States (and possibly other countries as well) an executive decision to vote for a measure could result in its acceptance of a binding international obligation, without participation of its legislative branch. In practice, however, this was probably not a real danger, since the preparatory work, the failure of the ITO and OTC, the criticism of Congress, and the worry over voting strength led the contracting parties to be cautious in voting additional obligations. Moreover, a short withdrawal notice period and the relative ease of breaching obligations were also sources of caution.

Most efforts encompassed by GATT were accomplished through a process of negotiation and compromise, with varying degrees of formality and a tacit understanding that agreement was necessary among countries with important economic influence.

In fact, the "consensus" approach gradually began to be imperative for much of GATT activity, even though the word "consensus" does not occur in the GATT text. (This, too, is changed in the WTO, as we shall see later.)

The General Agreement also had measures specifying the procedure and votes for amending the agreement and for waivers. The WTO Charter substantially changes all of this and contains an elaborate matrix of decision-making procedures, with important constraints around them. Basically there are five different techniques for making decisions or formulating new or amended rules of trade policy in the WTO Charter: decisions on various matters, "interpretations," waivers, amendments to the agreements, and, finally, negotiation of new agreements. There are a variety of non-majority principles applied, including of course consensus, but also super-majority requirements such as that of WTO Charter Article IX for the members to make a "definitive interpretation" of some UR text: this requires a vote of three-fourths of the membership (not just those "present"). Amending also has difficult provisions, depending on text which normally requires a two-thirds vote which is not binding on those not voting to approve; however, a three-quarters vote is binding on all. Even in that case there is provision for a hold-out member to withdraw from the organization or negotiate a special dispensation. Since withdrawal by certain key members of the WTO would probably end the WTO's effectiveness, such key members probably effectively have a veto regarding amendments.

In addition, it is important to understand the potential which the dispute settlement procedures, and the panel and Appellate Body reports that result, have for the changing or evolution of the trade rules. This is explored in Chapter 5.

d. Accession and membership

GATT had several different modes for accepting contracting party status, but the WTO approach narrows procedures for membership to two, omitting a GATT provision that allowed colonial mother countries to "sponsor" GATT status for a colonial entity with independent customs territory status. The two WTO approaches are, first, the "original membership" which was conferred on any GATT contracting party that accepted both the UR treaty and negotiated schedules of concessions for goods and

4.4 The WTO: structure of the treaty and the institution

for services.[8] Second is the procedure for accepting new members. For this second approach, practice considerably embellishes the procedure, so that sometimes the accession process is very arduous indeed (requiring fifteen years for mainland China).[9] It requires the WTO's acceptance to begin the process, which is then followed by detailed reports on the applicant about its trade policy and legal structure, followed by elaborate questioning from the existing members (e.g. for China, over 500 questions were tabled at the working party stage). There is then further clarification, and existing members begin negotiating with the applicant, sometimes one on one, to develop over time an usually lengthy and elaborate draft protocol of accession. When this is approved, and the applicant notifies its ratification, then thirty days later the applicant becomes a member.

Three curious aspects of membership, mostly carried over from GATT, are worthy of mention, namely non-sovereign status of applicants, an opt-out provision against treaty relationship between certain parties, and the two-thirds membership vote provision for accepting a new member.

First, members of the WTO (and formerly contracting parties of GATT) do not have to be full sovereign nation-states. Instead they must be a customs territory that possess "full autonomy in the conduct of its external commercial relations" and other matters contained in the UR (WTO) agreement. Thus Hong Kong became a GATT contracting party by the now terminated "sponsorship" procedure of the United Kingdom, and continues as an original member in the WTO. A new member of this type is Chinese Taipei (Taiwan), which carefully crafted its application for GATT (and then WTO) status as such independent customs territory, so as not to offend mainland China.

Second, the WTO (as did GATT) has a special and somewhat complex provision (in Art. XIII) that allows either an existing member or an applicant member, at the time of accession only, to "opt out" of the treaty relationship between itself and any other member or applicant. This provision was in the original GATT (modified slightly for the WTO) to accommodate those countries or customs territories which for political or other reasons did not want any formal treaty relationship with another party. In GATT this was utilized by India to avoid treaty relations with South Africa. Later, when Japan acceded to GATT, there were many opt-outs, most of which were terminated in later years through bilateral negotiations between Japan and particular opt-outs.[10]

Third, the required two-thirds vote in favor for a new member seems in practice in the WTO already to have evolved into a consensus requirement[11] (arguably more restrictive than two-thirds).

Finally, the exceptional case of China's accession should be mentioned. It is clearly to the benefit of the WTO, the world, and China, for China to be a member of the WTO, and clearly both existing WTO members and the leadership of China thought this way. But the worry about the substantial differences in the economic institutional structure within China led to important worries as to how China's presence in the WTO would affect the existing members. A non-market economy can utilize certain techniques to avoid some of the disciplines of the WTO trade system. To the extent that the Chinese economy has attributes of non-market operation (government controls and subsidization, etc.), the existing members felt that they needed to negotiate certain assurances and "the phasing in" of privileges and obligations. Yet, remarkably, the Chinese protocol was negotiated and adopted. This protocol in some ways departs from the normal rules of the WTO by applying a somewhat more stringent set of rules to the China case. Over time, some (but not all) of these departures will disappear.

The basic policy underpinning the China accession is remarkably well expressed by the US economist deemed one of the most important experts on the Chinese economy.[12] China's accession, says Nick Lardy, is also of great importance to the United States and the world trading system in general.[13] For many years, China has been the single largest country outside the trading system. China's WTO membership will also greatly increase the possibilities for foreign direct investment in the Chinese market (telecommunications, distribution, financial services) and will increase market access and lead to the availability of lower cost imports for consumers in the United States. Further economic integration may also make China a "more constructive participant" in new trade negotiation rounds. The increased ability to achieve economic reform and liberalization will allow China to meet the needs and expectations of its population, will create greater stability, and will be beneficial to the rest of the world too. Better economic conditions may, in the long term, also lead to a more pluralistic political system, and will likely lead to stronger trade and investment ties between China and Taiwan that may contribute to a gradual reduction in tension between the two.

4.5 Institutional problems of the WTO

a. Introduction

From almost the beginning of the WTO, the new organization has been the target of major criticisms, some of them manifested through street

4.5 Institutional problems of the WTO

demonstrations (too often violent) and others through bitter communications by political and government leaders and the media. No organization facing the broad scope of responsibilities assumed by the WTO and established with an institutional framework negotiated with representatives of over 120 nation-states could be expected to please all interested parties and constituencies. And when the organization is newly endowed with some formidable powers (especially with regard to dispute settlement and treaty interpretation and implementation), it is not completely surprising that it would be the target of many expressions of disagreement. Much of the criticism relates to the substantive policies of trade liberalization and the management of the stresses and pains caused by adjustment requirements of globalization. These subjects are not the topic of this book (and are extensively explored by many, mostly non-legal, disciplines).[1] In this book, the focus instead is on the institutional structure (including legal norms) and important questions in that regard. These questions include: Is the institutional structure of the WTO as good for achieving its WTO goals as it should be? What are some of the developing problems and tensions regarding that institution that it seems currently necessary to explore? Needless to say, there are many more questions, only a few of which can be examined here.

The previous sections of this chapter, particularly section 4.4, have set forth the broad outlines of the institutional structure. These outlines substantially improved many of the difficulties of GATT (some of which we have termed "birth defects" stemming from the odd origin of GATT).

As the decades of GATT's history rolled by, many of the detailed problems of the trading system began to change, as greater "globalization" and interdependence often posed different kinds of problems from those uppermost in the minds of the draftspersons of the original GATT. These problems have already been touched upon in previous sections, but even since the WTO was established on January 1, 1995, it has become increasingly apparent to many observers and participants that the WTO also needs to evolve to accommodate circumstances that are constantly changing. It was partly for that reason than the WTO Director-General in June 2003 appointed a Consultative Board to prepare a report on institutional problems of the WTO, as mentioned in section 4.1.[2]

A theme that runs through many of the current institutional criticisms of the WTO is that of "good governance." In international institutions attention has quite often been paid to the need for good governance at the nation-state level. However, it is also the case that there are good governance principles that need to be important motivators of the structures and activities of international organizations. These principles can include some that have been articulated so well by important political science thinkers, as well as economists, lawyers, and diplomats.[3] To some extent, these principles focus on the importance of an appropriate mode of widespread participation by various constituencies to lend legitimacy to decisions and actions of governmental structures, and such participation, as well as the need for accountability, also emphasizes the necessity of transparency.[4]

b. Consensus: the knotty dilemma of the trading system

The decision-making process of the WTO must be reexamined in this context. The previous section outlined it, and it was noted that nation-state representatives rather explicitly imposed a series of constraints on the decision-making procedures of the WTO, particularly during the last six months or so of the effective negotiating process, which led to the text of the WTO Charter.[5] As the overview in section 4.4 demonstrated, the decision-making procedures are complex and relatively numerous. There are some special procedures with super-majority requirements. At the core, however, there is a relatively generic procedure of majority rule, with "one nation, one vote" operating.[6]

As we have also seen in the previous section, GATT, which also had a "one nation, one vote" majority rule for decisions that were very broadly and loosely described, had the well-established practice of avoiding decisions that would impose new substantive obligations upon its contracting parties. The situation was complex even in GATT, because there were a number of different ways in which decisions could be made, including waivers and, of course, the all-important negotiating rounds, during which new obligations could be imposed, subject to acceptance by each of the contracting parties. Basically, as noted before, the membership of both GATT and the WTO have consistently manifested strong skepticism about majority voting in the context of the "one nation, one vote" equality principle for nation-state members which varied enormously in population size, economic size, geography, and many other characteristics that effectively impact upon an appreciation of real power, as opposed to the nominal equality of the system.

Because of its skepticism, GATT gradually developed a practice of "consensus" decision making. The word "consensus" does not appear in the GATT text, but the practice in GATT developed over time such that a variety of decisions were deemed to require a consensus, and the consensus was defined by that practice, and is now defined more explicitly

4.5 Institutional problems of the WTO

in a clause in the WTO Charter[7] which states that a decision will be deemed accepted in any case where no party to the agreement (present at a meeting) objects. Thus consensus is not precisely the same as unanimity, since an abstaining position is not a negative and absence from a meeting or from a particular voting procedure is also not a negative.

In fact, although the rule normally imposes a heavy burden on decision making, in some contexts it is a lesser burden than some super-majority requirements because absences do not negate a decision. The consensus rule as defined above can thus be criticized as disenfranchising members that are absent but may have strong interests to protect.

Certain types of decisions require a super-majority of votes and, in some cases, require at least an attempt to achieve consensus (with a fallback to voting in some cases) or, in other cases, an absolute requirement of so-called "full consensus," with no fallback. A very prominent example of the latter is the requirement expressed in the Dispute Settlement Understanding[8] that decisions of the Dispute Settlement Body must be taken by consensus, unless otherwise stated. The "reverse consensus" procedure for the adoption of dispute settlement panel and Appellate Body reports is the most important "stated" exception. It is also clear in the text of the WTO and the DSU[9] that any change in the text of the DSU requires consensus.

This DSU example of a consensus requirement is, in some ways, particularly troubling, since so much of the DSU is procedural in a context where full consensus on changes to correct what have been discovered to be some drafting problems in the text cannot easily be achieved, since a consensus hold-out country can hold up the process, sometimes in order to bargain over matters unrelated to the instant subject being considered.

In general, experienced observers feel that the emphasis on consensus decision making in the WTO can sometimes lead to paralysis, and can be blamed for the perceived inability of the organization to achieve very much (except perhaps at the relatively infrequent trade negotiating rounds, where many new matters and new rules are negotiated in the context of a requirement that they be accepted by the governments concerned).

This problem in the decision-making process has been one of the sources of considerable tension between the dispute settlement system on the one hand, and the other parts of the organization on the other hand.[10] This is a matter that will be taken up in a more detail in Chapter 5, concerning the dispute settlement process.

One of the more prominent problematic developments in the recent history of the WTO was the great difficulty that occurred in selecting the

Director-General at the end of the term of the second WTO Director-General, Renato Ruggiero. The members of the WTO were considerably divided and perhaps even without a consensus rule motivation, the subject would have been very difficult. The end result, the split of the office into two three-year terms, the first to be held by Michael Moore, and the second by Supachai Panichpakdi, is generally perceived to have been unfortunate in terms of consistency and longer-term planning, particularly given the need to develop a new trade negotiation round. Fortunately the procedure was changed and the selection of the latest Director-General, Pascal Lamy, went relatively smoothly.[11]

The consensus rule is also likely to bear a fairly heavy responsibility for the failure of certain committees and working parties in the WTO to achieve any meaningful accomplishment in their work. Examples sometimes mentioned in this regard include lack of accomplishment by committees on regional and preferential agreements, rules of origin, and environmental agreements and their relation to trade rules.[12]

The rules for amending the agreement are also quite constrained, and indeed, while not absolutely equivalent to consensus, are often perceived to be effectively consensus-driven and therefore to make amendments virtually impossible. This was true under GATT, and was responsible for the seventh major trade round (the Tokyo Round under GATT) taking a rather convoluted approach to the development of needed new treaty norms for many non-tariff barrier areas, which, in the absence of amending the agreement, were placed in a series of specific "side agreements," which bound only those governments willing to accept them separately.[13]

What can be done about the consensus rule? Clearly, it has important values that need to be preserved. The rule forces the membership to achieve as wide an acceptance of new measures as possible, thus lending democratic legitimacy to measures that are finally adopted. It therefore forces the richer and more powerful members of the organization to take into consideration the needs and opinions of all parts of the organization, including the poorer and less powerful governments. The question is whether some slight modification in the consensus rule might provide some assurance of avoiding it resulting in "issue hostage taking," by one or a very few governments who use that technique to bargain or to be "paid" for certain actions of the organization.

There have been various suggestions put forward, such as an attempt to define a somewhat different process for procedural rules as opposed to substantive rules (the amendment provisions of the WTO Charter attempt to achieve this). In addition, there have been suggestions about having a rule

4.5 Institutional problems of the WTO

against one or just a few holdout votes defeating consensus. This gets very difficult to analyze, however, particularly when we have one very large and powerful block, the European Union, which now has twenty-five votes, and thus probably would be in a position to block a measure by lining up the votes of enough of its members to exceed the consensus change rule.

It is conceivable that a practice might be developed, perhaps beginning with a resolution adopted by consensus, that would strongly urge governments to refrain from blocking a consensus when there was an overwhelming majority (e.g., 90 or 95 percent), and such majority represented an overwhelming amount of trade interest or economic size (sometimes called a "critical mass"). Discussions about this, however, have met with objection from some countries even to that slight modification.[14]

There is also a concept partly embedded in the WTO Charter of "plurilateral agreements" (Annex 4 to the WTO Charter), which contemplates certain kinds of agreements or measures that might be adopted by a sub-group of the total membership, and then only applying to that sub-group. This raises important questions regarding the MFN clause (non-discrimination). In addition, and unfortunately (in the author's view), a consensus is required even to add an agreement negotiated by a subset of the total membership of the WTO to Annex 4 so that it would operate as a plurilateral agreement but still be under the umbrella of the WTO (and thus, for example, probably subject to the dispute settlement system).

In the practice of the WTO, there have been a few other ways to "end run" around the consensus problem. One of the more ingenious of such techniques is a "scheduling approach" (as in the Telecomms Agreement and the Financial Services Agreement[15]). In this procedure, the country which is willing to enter into an overall agreement that we would likely call "plurilateral," and which agreement would only bind those willing to accept it, would agree to put the essence of that agreement into its services schedule. Thus, you have multiple texts in a variety of schedules, and they bind only those countries that have accepted them. Presumably, they all continue to be subject to the MFN principles and rules. It is conceivable that something like this might actually be workable in some contexts of trade in products, as compared with the services trade. The problem of consensus, and the more general problem of voting, highlights the arguably dysfunctional effect of a general international law principle of equality of nation-states. But how to get around that, without taking on more baggage than it is worth, is a puzzle. Of course, the major financial institutions, such as the World Bank and the IMF, have an explicitly weighted voting system that certainly has strengthened those institutions through the decades of their existence, but has also given rise to considerable criticism about how the decision-making process is accomplished in those institutions.[16] In any event, it seems clear from various discussions that the concept of weighted voting is basically attractive to hardly any of the members of the WTO. Thus, it is a so-called "non-starter."

c. Resources to enable the WTO to pursue its goals effectively

Another important problem of the WTO, is the nitty-gritty, devilish detail of resources for the institution to operate in an appropriate manner that is both efficient and fair in relation to its very broad responsibilities and the goals of the organization. It is often noted how small the organization is compared with other major international economic organizations, such as the Bretton Woods financial institutions, and institutions such as the OECD. The WTO Secretariat has approximately 615 regular staff, including all support staff.[17] It has an annual budget of US$129,512,821.[18] This can be compared with the OECD, the World Bank, the IMF (see Table 4.1), and even some of the more specialized agencies of the United Nations which is devoted to particular subject such as health, agriculture, and intellectual property.[19]

Richard Blackhurst, former Chief Economist for the WTO (now retired), has written poignantly about some of these comparisons, noting the extraordinarily broad and heavy responsibilities that have been placed upon the WTO, while the governments have, partly through practices over time that imbed budgetary amounts allocated to various agreements.[20]

d. Steering group or other guidance institutions

Another important problem that has received much attention, criticism, and discussion, but no apparent movement towards any solution, is that of administrative guidance or control of the organization. With 148 members (which will increase during the next decade), the WTO has reached a point where it is virtually impossible to set up effective procedures for decision-making, negotiation, and so on when all members demand that they be present and active on such decisions (even when solely procedural). It is noted that virtually every other effective international organization has some kind of a smaller sub-group of the total membership that acts at least in an advisory or guidance capacity.

GATT for many years operated its "green room" approach, whereby the Director-General, in consultation with ambassadors of some of the

4.5 Institutional problems of the WTO

Table 4.1. *WTO, World Bank, IMF, and OECD: comparison of administrative budgets and staff size*

Organization	Administrative budget (US$ million)	Staff
WTO (2005)	130.0	630
World Bank	1,865.2[1]	9,300[2]
IMF	837.5[3]	2,700[4]
OECD	392.0[5]	2,000[6]

Notes:
[1] 2004 (US$2000.3 million approved for 2005). *World Bank Annual Report 2004,* Volume 1, Year in Review (World Bank, 2004), at 7, available at www.worldbank.org/annualreport/2004/download_report.html, last visited Jul. 7, 2005.
[2] In over 160 country offices. World Bank personnel information available at www.worldbank.org, visited 7 July 2005.
[3] 2004 (US$905.1 million approved for 2005). *Annual Report of the Executive Board for the Financial Year Ended April 30, 2004* (IMF, 2004), at 85–86, available at www.imf.org/external/pubs/ft/ar/2004/eng/index.htm, visited Jul. 7, 2005.
[4] In 141 countries. Staff information available at *The IMF At a Glance,* www.imf.org, visited Jul. 7, 2005.
[5] 2005 (total budget). OECD ANNUAL REPORT 2005: 45TH ANNIVERSAY (OECD Publications, 2005), at 11, available at http://www.oecd.org/dataoecd/34/6/34711139.pdf, visited Jul. 7, 2005.
[6] *Overview of the OECD,* available at www.oecd.org, visited Jul. 7, 2005.

most important and diverse members, would call together a group of principals (ambassadors only, perhaps) into the green room, which is a relatively small conference room in the WTO headquarters building. Unfortunately (or fortunately), the green room can only hold several dozen persons. The addition to the headquarters building of the WTO now has a very large auditorium, which can accommodate the entire membership, as well as ancillary staff support for the representatives, but, obviously, certain kinds of negotiation and decisions, including perhaps decisions about agenda and timetable, are very difficult to handle in such a large group.

For many years prior to the existence of the WTO and for a short time after it was established, there existed the "quad group," consisting of the United States, the European Union, Japan, and Canada. It would often meet separately, even at the Ministerial Conference level, and come up with various proposals, and then submit them to the larger membership, possibly initially in a green room setting, and subsequently to the total membership for approval. However, this process has fallen out of favor, starting with the Seattle 1999 Ministerial Conference which ended so disastrously. At the next Ministerial Conference (the Fourth) at Doha, Qatar, in 2001, a number of the important ambassadors, broadly defined so as to have representation from all continents and all levels of economic development, developed a system of "Consultants to the Chair," which seemed to work reasonably well in that atmosphere. At the Fifth Ministerial Conference at Cancún in September 2003, however, it was discovered that the procedures did not work, and that the Ministerial Conference is generally recognized to have been a failure.[21]

There is an ongoing process of trying to develop an appropriate way to have a sufficiently small steering group, working directly with the Director-General, so that decisions can be effectively and efficiently made, particularly as to procedures, timetables, and agenda. This group could also arrange for various proposals or options papers to be delegated and developed to avoid some of the problems of a decision being taken by either too large or too small a group. Unfortunately, every time such a group other than the total membership is suggested, governments that feel they would not be entitled to be part of that group oppose such a suggestion. Yet there continue to be various proposals to try to design a steering group that would be representative, and perhaps impose a system of transparency (possibly using computer documentation techniques) to keep all interested governments adequately appraised about what was happening, and to provide that certain members that were on the steering group (whether for limited periods of time, or on a more permanent basis) would have obligations to represent the views of a "constituency group" of members. These constituencies might be designed by reference to geography or other kinds of identities of interest.

e. Good governance: transparency and participation, internal and external

There are two particular subjects of "good governance" that are constantly being discussed in the context of the WTO, with some important criticism being aimed at the WTO with regard to them. These two subjects are transparency and participation. Often the word "transparency" is used in a broader sense, to include concepts of participation, but here we separate those terms, because they stand for quite different subjects.

Transparency, in the sense of providing a flow of information within an organization and to constituents and important "stakeholders" not necessarily within the organization, is, in many people's minds, very important.

4.5 Institutional problems of the WTO

It appears quite clear that the WTO is superior to GATT with respect to transparency. The WTO website is extraordinarily vast and full of information. The rules established for documentation try to enforce the presumption that documents should not be restricted (and, therefore, quickly available to the public on the web). To a large degree, this has already occurred. In particular, the dispute settlement reports are available on the website at least within a month or two of a decision (which some say is not quickly enough), and by the time of the adoption of a report, the public can view the official texts of these reports. That is a very great advance over the practice under GATT, which was a bit absurd, since these reports consistently leaked out to various media outlets, and were generally always available to special interests who had friends in the right places.

Nevertheless, there is still a "transparency deficit" in the WTO. Some governments and WTO officials avoid the transparency rules by producing "non-documents" (usually with very tentative proposals), or by using a document that is only referenced as "job number" and thus not in the official documentation nor even on the web. Also problematic is the fact that dispute settlement hearings are not open to the public, although many experienced diplomats and other participants in trade relations feel that the organization would be greatly aided by having those hearings open so that the public could see the seriousness and the high degree of expertise that goes into the deliberations about these specific legal dispute cases.[22] There is also some opinion that a good many of the committees and working groups of the WTO could make their meetings more transparent, either by having a public or press gallery, through Internet broadcasting, or at least through the provision of a transcript, available very quickly after a particular meeting.

There is also an *internal* transparency problem within the WTO, since sometimes some members do not have access to information that is known to other members. This is another problem with the dispute settlement system, since the hearings (both at the first-level panel and at the Appellate Body level) are not open to all members. Generally only the disputants themselves and the so-called "third parties" have the ability to attend the hearings, and even the third parties are not allowed to attend all portions of a procedure. It seems to many persons that, at the very least, all the hearings and documents, including the submittals by disputants in the dispute settlement process, should be made available to all the members. A small number of WTO members have followed a procedure to put their submittals on their government's website in every case in which they are disputants. More of this can be encouraged, but it does seem that at some point the transparency of these submittals should be mandatory, either through the governments themselves or through the Secretariat's placement of them online.

The question of participation is a somewhat separate one and, in many ways, is more difficult. Clearly the world is seeing an enormous amount of activity by nongovernment entities, and many of these entities, such as nongovernmental organizations (NGOs) or private businesses, are demanding some opportunity not only to learn about what is going on in decision-making quarters of the international institutions including the trade system, but also to have an opportunity to comment, make suggestions, or put forward various viewpoints that such entities have. This clearly is complex because the governments feel, and they are partly justified in so feeling, that they are the only legitimate entities that are participating in the WTO, and that they represent their constituents, and that is as it should be. The governments do not want the interference of non-governmental entities because they fear that economic power could alter the balance of the different interests that might demand participation.

As previously noted,[23] one of the problems with NGOs is that they are often single-issue entities, whereas governments have to balance a number of issues and a number of sometimes contradictory policy goals. A single-issue NGO may at times possess more resources than the WTO itself, and even perhaps more resources than a large number of the nation-state government members.[24] However, the experience of the last decade or two is showing that the NGOs and other nongovernmental entities cannot be ignored, cannot simply be excluded, and can also often make constructive additions to the general discourse of officials and diplomats.

Many international organizations, some of them in the UN complex, have made special accommodations regarding both the transparency and the participation of non-governmental entities, such as businesses, labor organizations, and NGOs.[25] One feature that seems to be fairly common among these various accommodations is a "credentialing process,"[26] by which the international organization receives applications from non-governmental entities to receive certain types of information, and also have an opportunity to make inputs into the decision-making processes of the organization. In the WTO context, credentialing is controversial, but there are calls for some sort of recognition for NGO contributions to policy debates.[27]

There is even a question of transparency and participation with respect to government entities other than the government participants at the WTO (or other international organizations). For example, in some areas of

4.5 Institutional problems of the WTO

international endeavor, parliamentarians from different governments are able to get together and to engage in discussions and perhaps prepare initiatives. In addition, perhaps judicial officers, or other specialized officers of governments should be encouraged to play a role that would give them input into some of the decisions being made, so as to improve the drafting of treaty language and to better avoid later interpretive problems.

f. Ministerial conferences

Finally, mention must again be made of the problems that have developed with the ministerial meetings of the WTO. As noted in section 4.3, as at January 2006, there have been six such meetings so far, Singapore in 1996, Geneva in 1998, Seattle in 1999, Doha in 2001, Cancún in 2003, and Hong Kong in 2005.[28] Most obvious were the difficulties in the procedural structure at the Seattle Ministerial. Doha seemed to be better, but then again at Cancún the process seemed to break down. Possibly it is better not to have ministerial meetings away from the headquarters in Geneva, because this means that a certain amount of the key leadership is provided by the host country, which may not always be the most appropriate approach for carrying out the requirements of the meeting. It is also, of course, much more expensive to have a ministerial meeting away from Geneva than in Geneva itself, although part of the WTO's motivation in having those meetings elsewhere is that most of the expenses are then covered by the host country (as opposed to the WTO Secretariat).[29] After the Cancún Ministerial there were some acerbic comments about the general institutional structure of the WTO. Some governments and the EU Commission have put forward proposals calling for extensive overhaul and reforms of the structure.[30]

Despite the many problems that have been raised in this section, and indeed, many other problems that we don't have room to cover here, these have to be analyzed in context, and with some deeper understanding of the total situation. It is certainly the observation of many that the WTO has been a remarkable new organization. It has attracted a very broad and powerful membership, now covering approximately 93 percent of world trade.[31] There is an extensive line of additional governments waiting to become members, and as at the date of this text, twenty-seven governments have begun the official application process for memberships.[32]

When questioned directly, a number of governments in the trading system would agree that, on the whole, the WTO is both necessary and desirable. The fact that there are a number of institutional problems and also a number of criticisms (some sound, others representing special interest or single interest advocacy) would likely be expected by any international institution, indeed, by nation-state governments as well. The WTO has a very difficult role to play, because it must address issues that are being generated in the world, with particular reference to economic issues, which constantly change and involve problems over which governments and the international organization have relatively little control. So the WTO's task is the unenviable one of assisting governments to achieve a better solution for managing the problems of globalization and interdependence than could be achieved without the coordination techniques that can be carried out under the umbrella of a WTO. In many ways, the organization needs to be recognized for its achievements in its very short history, more than it deserves criticism of its shortcomings. Nevertheless, the shortcomings exist, and they certainly merit attention.

The organization will evolve, as all human organizations do, and we can see other examples of such evolution, perhaps most particularly in recent decades with respect to the European Union and the United Nations. Writers on both of those institutions have noted how their evolution, including juridical and other decision-making bodies, have sometimes gone in directions that arguably would surprise the original supporters of the organization. For example, the European Union has been heavily influenced by the jurisprudence of its principal court,[33] and some of the positions that the court took have clearly been instrumental in shaping the direction of the EU institutions so as to be better able to achieve some of the goals of those institutions, such as the economic unification of Europe.

Likewise, as noted in Chapter 2, we have testimony of very important scholars on the United Nations, and particularly on Security Council activity and the question of the veto, that note that certain procedural practices do not seem to be entirely consistent with the language of the treaty, but nevertheless are now completely accepted as the correct direction for the organization.[34]

4.6 WTO rules and members' domestic legal systems

A subject that seems eternally perplexing and interconnected with the issues of this book is the relationship of international law (and international economic law) to member-state laws and even sub-federal laws. Already, we have noted the broad question of how to allocate power vertically from the multinational level through various intermediate-level governmental structures such as a regional organization like the European

4.6 WTO rules and members' domestic legal systems

Union, and of course, the nation-state federal government, all the way down to a very local unit.[1] The WTO and its predecessor, GATT, have had substantial concerns about a series of questions posed by this subject.

Most readers will be familiar with the questions of direct application of treaties in domestic or regional law, and the concepts of monism and dualism. As noted in section 2.2(d), monist legal systems generally apply treaties directly ("self-executing") into domestic law, at least in theory.[2] Dualist systems do not generally operate this way, but often require an "act of transformation" for international law norms to be given legal status (e.g., equivalent to statutes) in their domestic legal system. Often, the Netherlands is cited as one of the best examples of "monism," while the United Kingdom is recognized as utilizing a dualist approach (requiring an act of Parliament to implement an international norm into UK domestic law). The US system lies somewhere in between, but clearly, in some cases, treaties to which the United States has adhered have become "self-executing" in US law and are treated as roughly equivalent to a statute.

Actually, there are a number of legal issues about the relationship of international law to domestic law, and the broader landscape of these issues can be quite complex. For example, consider how a nation-state internally allocates its power regarding treaty-making, how it manages treaty implementing, and how it treats treaties in its domestic law.

The way in which many of these issues are addressed can profoundly affect the ongoing activities of an organization like the WTO. For example, some of the questions clearly will affect the way in which nations can effectively negotiate for new treaty rules in the context of the WTO. Since there are many different systems of legal application of international norms, these issues can be very complex, and sometimes have quite an impact on the structure of negotiations. In addition to the power to negotiate or even "sign" *ad referendum*, a critical step is the process by which a nation-state (or regional entity like the European Union) "accepts" an international law obligation as binding. This issue could also be complicated by the WTO members' constitutional processes for such treaty approval. In addition, the questions of the process for approval of treaties raise a number of broader, systemic political science and international relations issues, such as the democratic legitimacy of the procedures, the effect of domestic special advocacy interests on these processes, and the ability of governments to fulfill their obligations in some context where there is a disconnect between powerful domestic constituent interests, and the accepted international norms.

Apart from the negotiating process, there is also an impact on the decision-making processes within the WTO, under the applicable treaties. Different governments have different ways of controlling their approaches to those decisions. The United States generally approaches those decisions by policies and constraints (constitutional or statutory) on its presidential administration. For example, in the case of the World Bank and the International Monetary Fund, the US statute authorizing ratification of those charters provides that certain kinds of ongoing decisions within those organizations must be approved by Congress.[3]

Another important facet of this relationship, which will be taken up in Chapter 5, is the effect on domestic law of an adopted dispute settlement report under the dispute settlement procedures.

The negotiators of the Uruguay Round treaty were cognizant of some of these problems, and many countries in that negotiation were uneasy about the way in which the United States handles a number of these issues. Consequently, there are several different treaty clauses in the Uruguay Round agreements that were designed to address some of these issues, although, undoubtedly due to differing motivations and viewpoints of various negotiating entities, the language is not entirely clear. For example, in the text of the Agreement Establishing the World Trade Organization (the WTO Charter), Article XVI(4) requires each member to "ensure the conformity of its laws, regulations, and administrative procedures with its obligations as provided in the annexed Agreements." Another manifestation of this worry on the part of the negotiators can be found in the WTO Dispute Settlement Understanding (DSU), Article 23(2), stating that "members shall . . . not make a determination to the effect that a violation has occurred, that benefits have been nullified or impaired or that the attainment of any objective of the covered agreements has been impeded, except through recourse to dispute settlement in accordance with the rules and procedures of" the DSU. Certain disputes already brought in the WTO, particularly against the United States (for example in connection with the United States 301 procedure), have tested the meaning of this language, but such test has not resulted in very much clarification.[4]

Even when a government such as the UK government or, often, the US government does not directly apply a treaty in its domestic law, there may nevertheless be principles by which administrative or judicial application of the domestic law should, when the language of the statute or other law provides enough leeway to do so, be made consistent with the international obligations. In the United States, this is known as the "Charming Betsy" principle, named after a famous case very early in the history of

4.6 WTO rules and members' domestic legal systems

the US Constitution.[5] Even the degree to which this consistency principle shall be applied, however, is controversial and it is sometimes criticized or disregarded.[6] In addition, there are various legal effects of a treaty on a domestic legal system other than either direct application or the consistency principle, such as cases where a domestic law incorporates some treaty text by reference, or requires domestic officials to conform to a treaty norm or refer to policies articulated in treaty or customary international law as guiding principles for domestic agencies.[7]

The US legal structure, with respect to the many questions posed above, is extraordinarily complex and confusing. It is reasonably clear that the power to negotiate resides with the president, and that generally, the president has the power to "sign" *ad referendum*. What such signing means under international law and/or various domestic law cases is not, however, crystal clear, as one can see from examples where a country (e.g. the United States) has "unsigned" an agreement.[8] The tough part in US law comes when the president, after negotiating agreements, needs to ratify or "accept" the international obligations. Many people in the world are familiar with the "treaty clause" of the US Constitution, which provides that the Senate must give advice and consent by a two-thirds vote to the ratification of a treaty. However, there are at least four other ways by which the United States, as a government, accepts as binding an international treaty agreement. Two of these ways are by acts of Congress, and these are called congressional executive agreements. These are sometimes referred to as the "statutory" procedure for treaty ratification. In both of them, Congress approves a bill by simple majority of both houses (then sends it to the president for his signature). In one of these cases Congress has in front of it an already negotiated treaty, and by statute then delegates authority to the president to ratify. In the other case, Congress grants to the president advance authority to negotiate a treaty under certain parameters and policy guidelines, and if the president complies with the constraints and guidance, he is then presumed to have the delegated power to enter into the treaty. A fourth technique involves action solely by the president, under the president's constitutional powers. With respect to accepting international treaty obligations the president's powers are fairly limited, but they relate to his position as the executive authority of the United States and as Commander-in-Chief, his power to appoint and receive ambassadors, and to certain other clauses which have been "spun together" sometimes to suggest the existence of a "foreign affairs power" of the president.[9] There is also the possibility that a treaty that is valid in its own right can delegate authority to the president to act without further reference to Congress, usually referring to fairly detailed and mundane ministerial acts under a broader treaty umbrella.[10]

With respect to the major trade treaties of the United States, particularly those developed in the context of GATT and the WTO since the 1970s, and also regarding a number of free trade agreements (such as NAFTA, United States–Canada, United States–Israel), Congress has made it reasonably clear, in its reports and/or with statutory language (in the act delegating the authority to the president to accept the treaties), that the treaties themselves do not have a "self-executing" effect. This, of course, immediately raises the possibility (now seen probable in a large number of WTO dispute settlement cases, particularly in the "trade remedies" area) that the US statute delegating approval of the treaty itself, or administrative actions under that statute, will be challenged as inconsistent with US obligations under the international treaty. In this case, there is a disconnect between what the US is arguing should be the interpretation of the treaty and the international process of interpreting the treaty. This is why this situation would be called "dualist." The international law obligation still stands, and the United States is bound by it as a matter of international law. However, for domestic law purposes, the law is different, and in some cases, not consistent with the international obligations. The United States then has an international obligation to make its law conform to the international norms, and if it fails to do so, it must tolerate the actions that other nations are entitled to take in such circumstances. Quite a number of these situations have already occurred under the WTO and its dispute settlement process, as will be noted in the next chapter.[11]

Under US domestic law, when a statute and a treaty obligation (even if it is self-executing) clash, the latest in time will apply, at least as to domestic law. So even if a particular treaty is self-executing or, as some would say, "directly applicable," the US system (and that of many other nations in the world) is that Congress can effectively breach a treaty by adopting a statute that is inconsistent with it, but such breach prevails only within its own domestic law. This question of later in time having higher status poses a number of very important issues about the distribution of power in the international law landscape.[12] By contrast, for a directly applicable treaty to apply as domestic law, and also to have a higher status than subsequent legislation, essentially raises the status of a treaty to a position nearly equivalent to the nation's Constitution, but does so often without the usual normally required constitutional procedures for a constitutional amendment. Thus that situation can be criticized as being reasonably undemocratic and, of course, that would raise issues about legitimacy and ability to comply.[13]

4.6 WTO rules and members' domestic legal systems

These issues provide very interesting examples of the "devilish detail" of allocation of power principles, as between an international and multilateral treaty system, and nation-state or other level of government below the international. Again, when one analyzes these in depth, there can be a series of policy ideas that could affect how this allocation should be implemented. To some extent, a system that is "dualist" and does not automatically implement international norms in its domestic law, provides a sort of "check and balance" against possible or potential international institutional overreach of power, or misuse of power. It also raises the question about what a nation-state actually consented to when it agreed to become a member of an international organization and approved the treaties that such organization is designed to implement.

The European Union has some similar problems. It generally provides a structure for treaty negotiation, ratification, and implementation that is much more complex than that of many of its member states. Even as to the initial question of power to negotiate, the European Union has certain specified procedures.[14] When it comes to ratification, its procedures are also complex, have become more complex in recent years, and threatened to be even more complex under a proposed new EU constitution,[15] which currently has an uncertain future. With regard to some of the other issues, an interesting circumstance developed at the end of the Uruguay Round, whereby the resolution for approval of the Uruguay Round treaty that the EU Commission sent to the Council of Ministers contained a paragraph indicating the view of the Commission that the treaties themselves would not be directly applicable.[16] This has been criticized as attempting to regulate treaty application beyond the power of the commission to do so.[17] In addition, the European Court of Justice has struggled many times with the question of the direct applicability of the WTO or the GATT Agreements in European Community law.[18]

Japan also has very interesting procedures,[19] with a constitutional provision that seems to imply direct applicability, although actual cases have avoided some of the consequences of such a clause.

China is also an extraordinarily interesting situation, with many ambiguities about its own procedures, and the degree to which its international treaty obligations, most particularly the WTO, now that China is a member, apply in its domestic law, and how its domestic courts treat the WTO obligations.[20]

Finally, it must be noted that the WTO also affects and is affected by various domestic or "federalism" structures of a legal system. A question raised under GATT in several different cases[21] was whether, and to what degree, a rule of the GATT applied to sub-federal units, such as a state in the United States, or a province in Canada. Because of the use of particular language in Article XXIV(12) of the GATT (still applicable as part of WTO Annex 1A), there is the chance of some exception for subordinate government actions that could be a breach of international obligations. The language of Article XXIV(12) can provide for an exception in cases where, under the national or federal constitution, reasonable measures are not available to the highest level of national government to ensure observance of the international norms by regional and local governments and authorities within its territory. This in turn requires the international dispute bodies to evaluate the constitutional structure of the governments concerned. A declaration at the Ministerial Conference concluding the Uruguay Round negotiations makes reference to this provision, and tries to clarify the situation so that it is understood that the national or federal level government is nevertheless responsible for the breaches by lower-level government units.[22]

4.7 Scope of the subject matter agenda for the WTO: the question of competence

The question of competence for any human institution is often a major issue for them and the legal rules that pertain to them. This phenomenon may be particularly accentuated in the case of international institutions, partly because of the institutional and resource weaknesses of most, if not all, international organizations and institutions. There is also considerable debate and doubts about the legitimacy of activities of these institutions, since they are constantly juxtaposed to questions of power allocation and sovereignty (as discussed in Chapters 2 and 3).

But these same questions of competence and scope of activity may be especially accentuated for the international institutions in the economic realm, particularly in the trade area. This is partly so because the subjects of trade in particular, and economic activities in general, are so pervasive and have such a significant impact on individuals' daily lives and the many businesses and market participants that engage in economic activity. In a large number of these circumstances, the international institutions will have very strong competitors for power, such as huge international corporations that may have an economic activity exceeding the gross domestic product of many, if not most, nation-states, and also large constituency groups that have large political or other powers in various non-international contexts. Furthermore, the question of power competence

4.7 Scope of the subject matter agenda for the WTO

for international institutions has both a vertical and a horizontal dimension, as discussed in Chapter 3. The vertical dimension encompasses the questions as to how power or decision-making competence can be allocated between an international institution and a nation-state or other non-international governmental entity. The horizontal competence question is raised when there are other international organizations who could legitimately claim a role relating to a particular subject (such as the International Labor Organization, the World Health Organization, the Food and Agriculture Organization, the various financial institutions, etc.). Even within a particular international organization, there may be different parts of such organizations that would be competitors for power. For example, there may be questions relating to the different scope of competence of the UN Security Council, compared with the General Assembly, or, in the WTO context, the different power constraints and outlines that one finds in the dispute settlement system, as compared with the rest of that institution.

Historically, one can see tensions about the scope of competence that go back to the very beginning of GATT. Indeed, as indicated in previous sections, GATT was never intended to be an organization. The charter drafted for the International Trade Organization (ITO) (never in force) demonstrates how broad the subject matter for a trade system could well be. The list of subjects addressed by the ITO charter is considerable, including such matters as competition policy and commodity agreements.[1]

When the ITO failed to come into force, GATT evolved to fill the vacuum and, over time, it became a more sophisticated international institution, despite its birth defects and origin. This became attractive for various constituent groups with interests such as trade in services or intellectual property, as discussed earlier in this chapter. Partly, this developing interest in GATT related to the perceived success (particularly by the 1980s) of the dispute settlement system of GATT, despite the fact that this system had been developed through trial and error and was, in some ways, rather ad hoc, and certainly (as will be discussed in the next chapter) had some important defects, some of which were partly reformed by the Uruguay Round result.

In the context of the WTO, even after it was established in January 1995, the question of the appropriate scope of competence is still controversial. At the ministerial conference of April 1994, which completed the Uruguay Round negotiation, there was discussion of other potential subjects. One of these subjects was that of environmental controls, which had already proven to be related to GATT rules but created controversy about the relationship between GATT and the environmental measures of nation-states. At that April 1994 conference, therefore, the ministers created a committee on trade and environment, to explore these issues in more depth.[2]

The subsequent history of the WTO is full of discussions and proposals about additions to the subject matter competence of that institution. At its first Ministerial Conference in Singapore in 1996, the WTO representatives examined a number of issues and the way in which they might relate to the WTO, including labor regulation and rights, the environment, competition policy, and investment. This Ministerial Conference tended to defer those issues for further study, and suggested, in some cases, that the issues such as labor be taken up in other international institutions.[3]

Later in that same decade, the members of the WTO began seriously to consider the perceived need for a new round of negotiations (which would be the first for the WTO, or the ninth in the GATT/WTO system). The 1999 Ministerial Conference at Seattle grappled with the question of a new round launch, amid serious disagreements about the scope of a proposed agenda, as well as heated, strident, and even violent criticisms of the WTO, in relation to certain subject matters such as environment and labor. There was tension, particularly between the United States and the European Union, on the question of scope, with the United States leaning towards a very restricted scope that would focus largely on border measures and market access, while the European Union was very eager to include competition policy and investment, among other issues. The United States had considerable suspicions that the European Union was using these additional proposals partly to shield it from enhanced negotiating attention to the EU agricultural policies that had been heavily criticized and were arguably extremely harmful to world trade. At the same time, there was a substantial body of developing countries that had begun to question the inclusion of intellectual property in the mandate of the WTO, and proposals were made to strike it out of the WTO system (proposals that had very little chance of success as articulated in that context).[4]

These controversies have continued. At the 2001 Doha Ministerial, they were partly papered over with a "two track" approach, specifying that negotiations as to, for example, competition policy and investment would be decided at a later point in the Doha Round process. At the next Ministerial Conference at Cancún, in 2003, widely perceived to have been a failure, part of the cause of the impasse in the negotiation was a dispute about the scope of the new round, and attention in that regard

4.7 Scope of the subject matter agenda for the WTO

was focused on what were then termed the "Singapore issues," which included competition and investment (but also now included some issues of market access, and rules about corruption in the government procurement area).

With this history, and in the general context of human institutions suggested at the beginning of this section, it is not surprising that there have been a reasonably large number of views expressed about the scope of WTO competence, and a burgeoning literature in that regard.[5]

One of the viewpoints expressed is that the WTO should "return to its traditional GATT scope and focus," namely, restricting itself to concern about border measures (primarily tariffs and quotas). But this approach is clearly wrong, both as to the history of the GATT/WTO system, and, at least in the view of some (including this author), as to the general vision of where the WTO should evolve over time.

As to the historical expression of such a "restrict to the border measures" view, it is very clear that from the beginning the GATT language indicated major attention to internal governmental "behind the border" measures that would inevitably affect international trade. The most important provision of GATT in this regard is probably that of GATT Article III, regarding national treatment and the obligation not to discriminate against imported goods with regard to domestic tax and regulatory matters. But, in particular, the provisions of Article III(4) are very significant, since the text clearly has extremely broad implications affecting virtually all kinds of nation-state economic regulation.[6]

A key element of the creation of the WTO was to try to cope with growing problems of international interdependence and globalization, as well as to cope more successfully with what had become a shift from tariffs as the main focus towards attention to non-tariff barriers. Thus it was that GATT in the Tokyo Round (1974–1979) for the first time began seriously and extensively to address the non-tariff barrier questions. It then became clear that the mindset of traditional experienced negotiators in the GATT context, which tended to focus heavily on "reciprocity," and quantifiable measures (tariff numbers), could no longer be easily applicable to a major and growing part of the competence of GATT. The Uruguay Round treaty reinforces that expanded direction (and indeed this is what some of the critics oppose), with an enormous treaty text relating to a wide variety of subjects that essentially involved domestic internal economic regulatory activities. If one views the WTO as an essential and central element of the institutional structure for the "world market," which institutional structure, as we have seen, has been time and again said to be essential for the effective workings of the market structure, then this notion must color questions of what is likely to be the future evolution of the WTO. This suggests that in the future the WTO may need to cover an extraordinarily diverse and wide-ranging list of subjects. This development, however, is likely to occur only over time.

There are certainly pragmatic reasons for being hesitant to embrace the many potential new issues for the WTO, at least at the present. There is a consistent worry about "overloading" the WTO. Some view this as an inherent institutional problem of the WTO. On the other hand, others view this as more a short-term question of the resources and institutional capability of the organization. Given the extraordinarily tight resources of the WTO, it would appear wise that they not be stretched too thin and, therefore, some subjects that logically deserve attention by the WTO may have to be deferred for some future evolution in the institution.

Likewise, and closely related to the resources question, there may be issues which the WTO does not have adequate capacity to handle at the moment. This may be true for competition policy, for example. Experts in competition or antitrust law note that in many countries there is no national law framework for these subjects (although that is changing, with many countries adding this to their domestic legislation[7]). Even in those jurisdictions that now have elaborate competition and antitrust rules, the rules often stem from very sparse statutory texts and therefore have largely been designed, and the detail filled in, by judicial institutions. Some appropriately questioned whether the juridical institution of the WTO (particularly the Appellate Body) has adequate capacity and the appropriate expertise to be trusted with this extraordinary responsibility of developing competition policy rules over time. Consequently, as will be discussed in a later chapter,[8] some people who urge that competition policy be brought under the WTO umbrella are also in general agreement that the dispute settlement system should not apply to it. This train of thought clearly demonstrates the pragmatic limitations on the competence scope of the WTO.

A body of available literature includes discussion on subjects that have been mentioned above, including competition policy, investment, the environment, labor, taxes and taxation policy, human rights, and other issues. This literature suggests that institutional structures in a globalized financial market will not be immune to some sort of international attention and regulation, even down to the question of how societies structure their healthcare systems, which can have a major impact on the competitiveness of a particular society's industries.[9]

4.7 Scope of the subject matter agenda for the WTO

Another subject that will necessarily be engaged is the question of bankruptcy laws and how they relate to advancing globalization and international interdependence. Already, at least one WTO case has had to address issues in this regard.[10]

Indeed, even in the language of the Uruguay Round Agreements, particularly in the Services Agreement (GATS[11]), Article VI(4) appears to give extraordinarily broad powers to the WTO Council for Trade in Services. That article notes that the Council "shall, through appropriate bodies it may establish, develop any necessary disciplines" to ensure "that measures relating to qualification requirements and procedures, technical standards and licensing requirements do not constitute unnecessary barriers to trade in services." Already, negotiators are paying attention to the area of accountancy, and indicate also a need to look at the legal professions in this regard.[12]

So what conclusions can be drawn as to this question of competence scope? Arguably it appears that it is reasonably clear that there are no a priori or logically mandated limits on the economic regulatory measures with which governments or other entities in the interdependent and globalized world must cope. A very interesting grouping of articles in the *American Journal of International Law* addressed this question of scope and the "trade and . . ." linkage issues.[13] A conclusion that can be drawn from reading those articles, as well as the comments at the end (including one by this author), is that there is quite a diversity of opinion about what could or should be the constraints on new issues under the WTO umbrella. Consequently, this issue seems to not be one of logical imperatives, but rather one of pragmatic considerations, such as some already mentioned (the resources available, the skill and capacity of institutions and individuals). Perhaps in a broader sense, this relates intimately to the issues suggested in Chapter 3 and those to be pursued further in Chapters 6 and 7, about allocating decision-making power among institutions, both on vertical and horizontal scales.

Next we turn to the dispute settlement system, and at the end of Chapter 5 a final section of Part II of this book will outline some conclusions and perspectives which can be drawn from the elaborate "devilish detail" of the WTO–GATT system, as it attempts to cope productively with many facets of "globalization" as well as difficult challenges to the legal structure and axioms which are the context of the WTO–GATT system.

5

The WTO dispute settlement system

> This charter would deal with the subjects which the Preparatory Committee has assigned to its five working committees. It should deal with these subjects in precise detail so that the obligations of member governments would be clear and unambiguous. Most of these subjects readily lend themselves to such treatment. Provisions on such subjects, once agreed upon, would be self-executing and could be applied by the governments concerned without further elaboration or international action.
>
> Harry Hawkins, representing the US, speaking of the proposed ITO Charter, 1946.[1]

> We must never forget, that it is a *constitution* we are expounding,
> Chief Justice John Marshall, 1819.[2]

5.1 The WTO dispute settlement system – unique, a great achievement, controversial

Section 4.2 discussed the emphasis that eminent economists put on the essential role of institutions in ensuring that markets work satisfactorily. This principle can be expanded to apply to many contexts, such as keeping the peace, protecting human rights, and generally reforming "constitutional" structures. These thoughts inevitably lead to questions as to how (or whether) certain rules work. The WTO dispute settlement system then becomes a link in the chain of logic about these human affairs.

This thought process clearly plays a central role in the policy foundations of the world economic system. At the 1946 beginning UN conference, assembled to draft an ITO charter (described in section 4.3), a remarkably and directly relevant statement was made by one of the conference leaders, a US representative named Harry Hawkins. This statement is quoted above.

5.1 The WTO dispute settlement system

Chapter 5 continues to explore the WTO, but the focus is now turned on to its dispute settlement system (DSS), which is often described as the most significant activity of the WTO – the "jewel in its crown" – but in recent years has been the subject of some controversy.

This DSS is unique in international law and institutions, both at present and historically. It embraces mandatory exclusive jurisdiction and virtually automatic adoption of dispute settlement reports, extraordinary for an institution with such broad-ranging competence and responsibilities as the WTO – virtually every aspect of economic regulation and policy is touched upon at least potentially, if not actually, and it is already imposing obligations on 148 nations (out of 192 recognized[3]), comprising 93 percent of world trade, and 87 percent of world population[4]. The DSS has been described as the most important and most powerful of any international law tribunals, although some observers reserve that primary place to the World Court (International Court of Justice). Even some experienced World Court advocates, however, have been willing to concede that primacy under some criteria to the WTO DSS.

A quick overview of some statistics (section 5.5 will present more detail), will help in understanding the role of the WTO DSS. During its just over ten years of existence (January 1, 1995, to July 2005), 332 complaints have been received by the DSS.[5] For this period, the DSS has adopted 158 reports (97 first-level panel reports, and 61 Appellate Body reports).[6] The approximate total number of pages of this "adopted" jurisprudence is just under 28,000, or the rough equivalent of seventy 400-page volumes.[7] This is an average rate of thirty complaints and eight completed cases per year.

Any objective analysis and appraisal of this jurisprudence must conclude that, despite extremely tight deadlines for its work, the quality of this output is, on the whole, extraordinarily high. The reports are carefully crafted, extremely analytical, and very well reasoned, compared with the outputs of other excellent court systems – national and international. But this output has not escaped criticism and, reasonably, some of that criticism is deserved.

The body of jurisprudence reflects very difficult issues confronting the WTO, and a major part of these difficulties is directly related to questions discussed in the opening chapters of this book, especially chapters 2 and 3. The constant tension between the claims of authority and allocation of power by nation-state and other WTO members, on the one hand, and the assertions of the WTO as an international legitimate authority requiring control of some issues in order to carry out its responsibilities, on the other hand, is manifested repeatedly in this vast jurisprudence of the

WTO DSS. The "devil in the detail" is present in virtually every case. The characterization "boiler room of international relations," used by this author in a previous publication about GATT,[8] is surely appropriate. This jurisprudence contains many lessons with many "classical dilemma situations" that should instruct all participants and observers of international law in particular and international relations in general.[9]

This chapter will explore these issues of sovereignty and power allocation as illustrated in the WTO DSS jurisprudence, but can only do this for a small selected sub-set of the total issues now set forth in the publicly available documents. The many issues illustrated here include, *inter alia*, questions of deference owed to WTO members in their domestic governmental decisions and measures, the mode of compliance with WTO DSS findings and rulings and methods to encourage better compliance, questions about the structure of the DSS and how that affects sovereignty and deference, and details of the role of various techniques of treaty interpretation.

A basic question of international law "philosophy" regarding fundamental characteristics is the degree to which a government that accepts a treaty containing a dispute settlement process can be deemed to "consent" to the results of that process, and whether that extent of consent is really necessary or appropriate in a contemporary world of economic (and non-economic) interdependence in circumstances of globalization. Does consent in this regard include the inevitable "evolution" of practice and jurisprudence (always a characteristic of human institutions at all levels), which can result in "surprises" or unanticipated directions for the institution concerned, compared with understandings of nations and other members at the time of treaty ratification?

An interesting phenomenon in this regard is seen in the nomenclature used for WTO DSS bodies and processes. Certain words are never used formally for the DSS, for instance, "court," "tribunal," or "judicial." These words seem too threatening to some notions of sovereignty. Yet some informal or academic comments have explicitly used these or similar terms to describe the system. For some of these reasons, this book uses the slightly more ambiguous term of "juridical," to describe the WTO DSS.

This chapter proceeds as follows. The next four sections describe the history (5.2), the policy goals (5.3), the current DSS structure (5.4), and an overview of the DSS activity during its first ten years (5.5). The next five sections each take up certain groups of "key jurisprudential issues" manifested in the DSS. These deal respectively with the relationship and impact of the DSS to members and sovereignty (5.6), a short selection of basic

5.2 History of the GATT dispute settlement system

jurisprudential issues that affect the way in which the DSS bodies go about their work (5.7), a variety of methods of treaty interpretation (5.8), structural and procedural questions (5.9), and questions of compliance and implementation (5.10). Then section 5.11 will discuss some of the reform proposals that have been suggested for perceived structural and other problems of the WTO dispute settlement system.

Finally, section 5.12 will suggest some conclusions and perceptions, and overview the logic (and lessons?) of chapters 4 and 5, and how they relate to some of the themes of this book.

5.2 The bottom-up trial and error history of the GATT dispute settlement system and the Uruguay Round makeover

Looking back over the 1946–1994 history of the General Agreement on Tariffs and Trade (GATT) allows one to reflect on how surprising it was that this relatively feeble institution with many "birth defects" managed to play such a significant role for almost five decades. It certainly was far more successful than could have been fairly predicted in the late 1940s.[1] This success must surely be a consequence of a strong perception about the need for an international trade institution widely recognized among nation-states.

World economic developments pushed GATT to a central role during the period from 1950 to 1970. The growing economic interdependence of the world was increasingly commented upon. Events that occur in a particular location can have a powerful influence on the other side of the globe. Armed conflict and social unrest in the Middle East affect the farmers in Iowa and France and the auto workers in Michigan and Germany. Interest rate decisions in Washington have a profound influence on the external debt of many countries of the world, which, in turn, affects their ability to purchase goods made in industrial countries and their ability to provide economic advancement to their citizenry. Environmental problems have obvious cross-border effects. More and more frequently, government leaders find their freedom of action circumscribed because of the impact of external economic factors on their national economies.

In this context, GATT evolved and developed its dispute settlement mechanism. It is fair to say that this mechanism was quite successful. It was also flawed, due in part to the troubled beginnings of GATT. Yet these procedures worked better than expected, and arguably better than those of most other international dispute procedures. A number of interesting policy questions are raised by the experience of the procedure, not the least of which is the question as to what the fundamental objective of the system should be: to solve the instant dispute (by conciliation, obfuscation, power-threats, or otherwise), or to promote certain longer-term systemic goals such as predictability and stability of interpretations of treaty text.

Even though some argued that the purpose of the GATT dispute settlement mechanism was merely to facilitate negotiations designed to reach a settlement, the original intention was for GATT to be placed in the institutional setting of an ITO. The draft ITO charter called for a rigorous dispute-settlement procedure which contemplated effective use of arbitration (not always mandatory, however), and even appeal to the World Court in some circumstances.[2] Clair Wilcox, vice-chairman of the US delegation to the Havana Conference, noted that the possibility of suspending trade concessions under this procedure was "regarded as a method of restoring a balance of benefits and obligations that, for any reason, may have been disturbed. It is nowhere described as a penalty to be imposed on members who may violate their obligations or as a sanction to insure that these obligations will be observed. But even though it is not so regarded, it will operate in fact as a sanction and a penalty." He further notes the procedure for obtaining a World Court opinion on the law involved in a dispute, saying "a basis is thus provided for the development of a body of international law to govern trade relationships."

However, the ambition expressed in the 1946 quote of Harry Hawkins, set forth at the beginning of this chapter, was not fully achieved. Yet that language is strong evidence of the "rule orientation" principles which guided the diplomatic negotiators who drafted the ITO charter and GATT.

Although the ITO charter (which never came into force) would have established a rather elaborate dispute settlement procedure, GATT had only a few paragraphs devoted to this subject.[3]

GATT Article XXIII was the centerpiece for dispute settlement in GATT. It also provided for consultation as a prerequisite to invoke the multilateral GATT processes. Three features of these processes can be stressed: (i) they were usually able to be invoked on grounds of "nullification or impairment" of benefits expected under the Agreement, and did not depend on actual breach of legal obligation; (ii) they established the power of the contracting parties not only to investigate and recommend action, but to "give a ruling on the matter"; and (iii) they gave the contracting parties the power in appropriately serious cases to authorize "a contracting party or parties" to suspend GATT obligations to other contracting parties. Each of these features has important interpretations and implications.

5.2 History of the GATT dispute settlement system

Although Article XXIII does not say much about them, the procedures followed to implement these principles evolved over the four decades of practice into an elaborate process.[4]

Originally the key to invoking the GATT dispute-settlement mechanism was almost always "nullification or impairment,"[5] an unfortunately ambiguous phrase, and one that might connote a "power"- or "negotiation"-oriented approach. It was neither sufficient nor necessary to find a "breach of obligation" under this language, although later practice made doing so important. An early case in GATT[6] defined the nullification or impairment (N or I) phrase as including actions by a contracting party which harmed the trade of another, and which "could not reasonably have been anticipated" by the other at the time it negotiated for a concession. Thus the concept of "reasonable expectations" was introduced, which is almost a "contract"-type concept.[7] But even this elaboration is ambiguous, and perhaps faulty.

At the beginning of GATT's history, disputes were generally taken up by the diplomatic procedures. At first they were dealt with at semi-annual meetings of the contracting parties. Later they would be brought to an "intercessional committee" of the contracting parties, and even later were delegated to a working party set up to examine either all disputes or only particular disputes brought to GATT.[8]

However, around 1955 a major shift in the procedure occurred, largely because of the influence of the then Director-General, Eric Wyndham White.[9] It was decided that rather than use a "working party" composed of nations (so that each nation could designate the person who would represent it, subject to that government's instructions), a dispute would be referred to a "panel" of experts. The three or five experts would be specifically named and were to act in their own capacities and not as representatives of any government. This development, it can be argued, represented a major shift from primarily a "negotiating" atmosphere of multilateral diplomacy, to a more juridical procedure designed to arrive impartially at the truth of the facts and the best interpretation of the law. Almost all subsequent dispute procedures in GATT (and the new WTO) have contemplated the use of a panel in this fashion.[10]

Although under GATT Article XXIII the contracting parties were empowered (by majority vote) to authorize the suspension of obligations (by way of retorsion, retaliation, or "re-balancing" of benefits – a term which is not and never has been clear), such authorization occurred in only one case. That 1953 instance was the result of a complaint brought by the Netherlands against the United States for the latter's use, contrary to GATT, of import restraints on imported dairy products.[11] For seven years in a row, the Netherlands was authorized to utilize restraints against importation of US grain,[12] although it never acted on that authorization. This had no effect on US action, however. There have been other moves in GATT to seek authorization to suspend obligations.[13] Also, the United States has under GATT taken "retaliatory" measures without authorization.[14]

In 1962 an important case was brought by Uruguay, alleging that various practices of certain industrial countries were violations of the GATT obligations. The panel grappled with the language of Article XXIII, which called for "nullification or impairment" as the basis of a complaint, but the panel decided to push the jurisprudence beyond the language, and determined in its report that any "violation" of GATT would be considered a "prima facie nullification or impairment"[15] which required a defending contracting party to carry the burden of proving that nullification or impairment did *not* exist. This case, followed by many subsequent GATT dispute panels, reinforced a shift in the focus of GATT cases towards the treaty obligations of GATT, that is, in the direction of rule orientation. The panels still talked about the need to facilitate settlements and sometimes the panels acted like mediators. But in some cases occurring much later, panels which tried too much to "mediate" were criticized for compromising issues without developing more precise and analytical "legal" approaches.[16]

During the Tokyo Round negotiation (1993–1979), there was some initiative taken to improve the dispute settlement processes of GATT. The so-called "Group Framework Committee" of the negotiation was given this task, among others. However, partly because of the strong objection of the EC to any changes in the existing procedures, this effort did not get very far. The result was a document entitled "Understanding Regarding Notification, Consultation, Dispute Settlement and Surveillance," which was adopted by the contracting parties at their thirty-fifth session in Geneva, in November 1979.[17] Like the other "understandings" resulting from the Tokyo Round, the precise legal status of this Understanding is not clear. Unlike the Tokyo Round Codes and other Agreements, it is not a stand-alone treaty. It is also not a waiver under Article XXV of GATT, but is presumably adopted under the general powers of Article XXV to "facilitate the operation and further the objectives" of GATT. This document was, nevertheless, very interesting and was also very influential, since it, along with its annex, consisted of a detailed description of the dispute-settlement processes of GATT. It can be considered a "definitive"

5.2 History of the GATT dispute settlement system

interpretation of the GATT Agreement, binding on all parties by a decision taken by consensus. It thus formed a sort of "constitutional framework" for these processes in GATT after 1974 and prior to the WTO.

This Understanding described the procedures of GATT dispute settlement, noting the requirement of consultation as the first step, and providing explicit recognition of a conciliation role for the GATT Director General (almost never utilized). If these steps did not result in a settlement, then there was provision for a panel process on decision of the contracting parties usually acting through the Council of Representatives – GATT's standing body that met regularly and disposed of most of its business. (There was no provision for this body in the GATT text, and it arose through practice and the decision of the contracting parties.[18]) There was some ambiguity whether the complaining party had a right to a panel process. If the process went forward, there was provision for oral and written advocacy from the disputants, and a written report by the panel. The Understanding reinforced the concept of the prima facie nullification or impairment and permitted the use of non-government persons for panels while stating a preference for government persons.

The procedure under GATT was for the panel to make its report and deliver it to the "Council." The practice then became firmly established that if the Council approved the report by consensus, it became "binding." If it did not approve, then the report would not have a binding status. The problem was "consensus." In effect, the procedure which relied on consensus meant that the nation which "lost" in the panel, and might otherwise be obligated to follow the panel obligations, could "block" the Council action by raising objections to the consensus. Thus, the losing party to the dispute could avoid the consequences of its defeat. This "blocking" was deemed to be the most significant defect in the GATT DS process.

Subsequent to the 1979 Understanding, there was continued dissatisfaction in GATT about the dispute settlement procedures. At the 1982 Ministerial Meeting, a new attempt to improve them was made, again with modest success. The resulting resolution suggests the possibility of departing from the tradition of requiring a consensus to approve a panel report, so that the "losing" party could not block or delay that approval,[19] but subsequent practice did not seem much improved. Later, many GATT members continued to talk of the need for improving procedures, and this subject was included in the 1986 Punta del Este Declaration, establishing the framework for the eighth round of trade negotiations.[20]

In the 1980s, as the procedures became more legally precise and juridical in nature, there developed the idea that there were two types of case brought before GATT: the violation cases (based on the prima facie concept), and certain "non-violation cases," which were cases not involving a violation, but nevertheless alleging "nullification or impairment." In fact, the non-violation cases have been relatively few; one group of scholars has indicated that there were only about four cases of this type in the history of GATT (out of several hundred cases in total).[21] Nevertheless, some of these non-violation cases have been quite important.[22]

Many of the treaty agreements resulting from the Tokyo Round negotiations (the "side agreements") included special procedures devoted to the settlement of disputes relating to a particular agreement. Some of these closely followed the traditional GATT procedure, and unfortunately they utilized the language "nullification or impairment." In a few cases, special "expert" groups have been called into the process to handle highly technical problems involving such things as scientific judgments.[23]

A 1987 panel report pushed the prima facie concept even one step further. The case was a complaint (sometimes called the "superfund" case) by the European Community, Mexico and Canada against the United States for the effects of the US 1986 legislation which imposed a tax on imported petroleum products. Since the tax on imported products was admittedly higher than that for domestic products, the United States did not deny that the Article III national treatment obligation had been violated. But the United States then prepared to prove that the small tax had not caused nullification or impairment, by using trade flow statistics to show that no effects on the flow occurred because of the tax. The panel refused to examine this proof. It noted that "there was no case in the history of GATT in which a Contracting Party had successfully rebutted the presumption that a measure infringing obligations causes nullification and impairment." It then also noted that "although the contracting parties had not explicitly decided whether the presumption . . . could be rebutted, the presumption had in practice operated as an irrefutable presumption." The panel said that Article III(2), first sentence "obliges the contracting parties to establish certain competitive conditions for imported products in relation to domestic products. Unlike some other provisions in the General Agreement, it does not refer to trade effects. . . . A change in the competitive relationship contrary to that provision must consequently be regarded ipso facto as a nullification or impairment of benefits accruing under the General Agreement. . . . For these reasons, Article III:2, first sentence, cannot be interpreted to protect expectations on export volumes; it protects expectations on the competitive relationship between imported and domestic products." Therefore, the panel concluded, "a demonstration that a

5.2 History of the GATT dispute settlement system

measure which was inconsistent with Article III(2) first sentence has no or insignificant effects would... in the view of the panel not be a sufficient demonstration that the benefits accruing under that provision had not been nullified or impaired even if such a rebuttal were in principle permitted."

The *Oil Fee* case may perhaps be a high-water mark in this regard, since it arguably reverses the treaty language, because by stating that a "prima facie case" cannot be rebutted, it makes the "presumption" of nullification or impairment derive *ipso facto* from a violation, thus almost discarding the nullification or impairment concept in favor of a focus on whether or not a "violation" or "breach" of obligation exists.

The GATT jurisprudence was thus brought almost full circle by the evolutionary case-by-case process of the procedure. However, before one accepts completely this conclusion, it must be said that it is not clear that the implications of the *Oil Fee* case – irrefutability – will be pursued in the future. The language of the Uruguay Round text on dispute settlement procedures, the Dispute Settlement Understanding (DSU),[24] continues the phraseology of the 1979 Understanding,[25] stating that measures found inconsistent with GATT obligations are "prima facie" findings of nullification and impairment. "In cases where there is an infringement of the obligations assumed under a covered agreement, the action is considered prima facie to constitute a case of nullification or impairment. This means that there is normally a presumption that a breach of the rules has an adverse impact on other members parties to that covered agreement, and in such cases, it shall be up to the Member against whom the complaint has been brought to rebut the charge." This may lead panels to back away from some of the implications of the GATT *Oil Fee* panel.

The GATT DS process still had a number of problems, mostly due to the "birth defects" resulting from the flawed GATT origins described in a prior chapter. These flaws included the following:

The language was sparse, with little detail about goals or procedures.
The power of the contracting parties concerning supervision of the dispute settlement process was imprecise, leading to the practice of requiring consensus for many decisions, which gave rise to "blocking" defects.
The first blocking potential could occur at the time of request for a panel procedure by a complaining party; the defendant sometimes would block this decision, although by about the mid-1980s such a blocking vote became diplomatically very difficult to use.
The second and more serious blocking problem would occur at the time the GATT Council (or a committee for one of the Tokyo Round agreement procedures) would be asked to "adopt" a panel report. As mentioned above, the losing party

could object, defeat the consensus, and thus block the adoption of a report. During the 1980s various attempts to fix this problem were proposed, but none succeeded. Because there were separate dispute settlement procedures in various Tokyo Round specific "code" agreements, dispute settlement procedures were fragmented; also some disputes would occur over which procedure to use.

There had been several unfortunate instances of a contracting party government interfering with potential panel decisions by inappropriately pressuring a particular panelist.

When one reflects on the almost fifty years of pre-WTO history of the GATT dispute settlement process, some generalizations seem both apparent and quite remarkable. With very meager treaty language as a start, plus divergent alternative views about the policy goals of the system, GATT, like so many human institutions, took on a life of its own. Both as to the dispute procedures (a shift from "working parties" to "panels"), and as to the substantive focus of the system (a shift from general ambiguous ideas about "nullification or impairment," to more analytical or "legalistic" approaches to interpret rules of treaty obligation), the GATT panel procedure evolved toward more rule orientation.

The GATT dispute settlement process became sufficiently admired that various trade policy interests sought to bring their subjects under it. This was one of the motivations which led both the intellectual property interests and the services trade interests to urge those subjects to be included in the Uruguay Round. The Uruguay Round results, of course, apply the new DSU procedures to those subjects.

Not all of the GATT problems have been solved, but the DSU measurably improves the dispute procedures.

1. It establishes a unified dispute settlement system for all parts of the GATT/WTO system, including the new subjects of services and intellectual property. Thus, controversies over which procedure to use will not occur.
2. It clarifies that all parts of the Uruguay Round legal text relevant to the matter in issue and argued by the parties can be considered in a particular dispute case.
3. It reaffirms and clarifies the right of a complaining government to have a panel process initiated, preventing blocking at that stage.
4. It establishes a "reverse consensus" rule for adoption of a panel report, which results in almost automatic adoption with no chance for "blocking" (as described in section 5.4, *infra*).[26] However, an appeal can be made before adoption.

5. It establishes a unique new appellate procedure which will substitute for some of the former procedures of Council approval of a panel report. If appealed, the dispute will go to an appellate "division." After the Appellate Body has ruled, its report will go to the Dispute Settlement Body (DSB), but again in this case it will be deemed adopted unless there is a consensus against adoption, and that negative consensus can be defeated by any major objector. Thus the presumption is reversed, compared with the previous procedures, with the ultimate result that the appellate report will come into force as a matter of international law in virtually every case. The opportunity of a losing party to block adoption of a panel report will no longer be available.

The DSU is designed to provide a single unified dispute settlement procedure for almost all the Uruguay Round texts; however, there remain some potential disparities. Many of the separate documents entitled "agreements" including GATT in Annex 1A and certain other texts such as the subsidies "code," or the textiles text, have clauses in them relating to dispute settlement. But the DSU Article 1 provides that the DSU rules and procedures shall apply to all disputes concerning "covered agreements" listed in a DSU Appendix, so presumably these appendix procedures prevail over most of the other DSU procedures. However, even the DSU provisions allow for some disparity. For example, parties to each of the plurilateral agreements (Annex 4) may make a decision regarding dispute settlement procedures and how the DSU shall apply (or not apply). In addition another DSU appendix specifies exceptions for certain listed texts. Thus the goal of uniformity of dispute settlement procedures may not be 100 percent achieved. Actual practice will determine to what degree this may be a problem.

5.3 The multiple policy goals of international dispute settlement: dilemmas, balancing, and competing principles[1]

Although it may appear to some that the goal of any dispute settlement system should be relatively easy to articulate, as discussed in section 5.2 tensions already existed in the early years of GATT about competing policy objectives of its DS system. In fact, when more in-depth attention is focused on the policy goals of international dispute systems, "juridical" or otherwise, it quickly becomes apparent that there are potentially many such policy goals, and some of these policy objectives conflict with each other. Examination of the WTO DS jurisprudence as well as discussions with participants involved with this jurisprudence quickly leads to this realization, and provides numerous examples of real or potential "tensions" between various policy objectives. Some of this analysis clearly has important implications for broader aspects of general international law, challenging some traditional notions of treaty interpretation, for instance. Likewise, there are important implications for the WTO itself.

In particular, we can see some apparent conflict between some of the WTO DS goals and especially between the two explicit goals mentioned in Article 3 of the DSU.[2] One of these goals is to provide a jurisprudence that will bolster the predictability and security of the system, a characteristic extremely important in economic issues, where you have millions of entrepreneurs in need of a certain amount of risk reduction that is inherent in a predictable, stable, rule-oriented system. Another goal mentioned in the DSU is the efficient and relatively quick and amicable settlement of cases. Immediately obvious in the jurisprudence is a certain tension between these two goals. On the one hand, you want a thorough explication of the issues in a well-reasoned report written by impartial juridical participants (avoiding the word "judge"). On the other hand you want the process to move relatively quickly, to be amicable, and where feasible and appropriate, you want the parties to settle. Of course, a settlement in some cases could actually be detrimental to the broader goals of the DS system and jurisprudence because it could result in a deal agreed between two parties that disregards broader systemic interests of non-participant third parties.

Apart from these two *explicit* textual goals in the DSU, there are also *implicit* goals that lead to conflict. Indeed, some of the strong criticism that is emanating from various parts of the world, but most particularly from Washington, DC, and certain political interests there, centers on the goals which some think ought to be pursued by the dispute settlement system, but which are not so explicitly expressed in the DSU. It is therefore instructive to consider briefly what some of those goals could be.

A broad historical overview of GATT and the WTO demonstrates a gradual evolution from the beginning, when there was a different kind of tension between a rule-oriented system and a power-oriented system, changing gradually through historical precedents and world events, towards a rule-orientated system, as we have seen in section 5.2 (and outlined in 4.2). A power-oriented system might involve various power-oriented bargaining chips, and in even older days, military bargaining chips or military actions. Contrast this with today's notion (and certainly at least 50 percent of the notion of the original GATT DS system) of building jurisprudential predictability and leveling the playing field for parties of different wealth and power structures. To a great extent, the

5.3 The multiple policy goals of international dispute settlement

Uruguay Round and the DSU constitute another rather large step forward toward rule orientation.

Here we can examine twelve goals, although the list undoubtedly could be extended, and there may be some overlap. Not all these goals appear relevant to the WTO DS system, at least as so far established. Similar to the analysis of the two goals in tension in Article 3 of the DSU, mentioned above, we can also see conflicts between some of the following goals. These conflicts may arise not only in the case of the WTO, but in any international law system, as well as in nation-state domestic legal systems.

The following is a rather compressed list of the goals that need to be considered.

a. Undo harm done by the respondent, to redress the complainant's injury

A common goal in domestic jurisprudence systems is to undo a harm, to make the harm doer somehow pay back the harmed person, whether it is tort damages, criminal penalties, or another remedy. This goal does *not seem* to be part of the GATT–WTO system. There is some quarrel about the question of whether there should be reimbursement of antidumping duties or a repayment of subsidies, and some of the jurisprudence in that regard tends to be quite muddled, but, overall, the WTO system currently does not embrace the notion of retroactive, or backward-looking retribution, remedy, or compensation.

b. Settle differences amicably to restrict international tensions and avoid conflict or even war

Settling differences amicably was quite an important goal at the 1944 Bretton Woods Conference and during the three or four years following that, including the attempt at creating an International Trade Organization (an attempt which failed), and during the development of GATT. The foremost goal of those discussions was avoiding another world war, and indeed there has been quite a bit of success in that regard. This must remain an important goal of any international dispute settlement system to help prevent or control the use of force, war, etc.

c. Settle the differences efficiently ("promptly", see e.g. DSU 3.3).

If disputes drag on for a decade, it comes to a point where there really is no remedy, and the system is clearly not operating effectively. There is an argument now that, as tight as the schedules are in the WTO, they should be reduced even more, and that is going to create tension with the goal favoring the quality of the output.

d. Provide jurisprudence or "precedents" for predictability and security (DSU 3.2)

"Precedent" is a big subject, and cannot here be examined in depth. The basic ideas about predictability and stability mentioned above clearly underlie the policy goals of the DS system which are enhanced by the appropriate application of precedent techniques. A later section of this chapter will elaborate a bit.

e. Fill gaps and resolve ambiguities in the treaty text

Multilateral treaties always have ambiguities and gaps. Some of these gaps are necessary in order to get the consensus required to come to resolution. Many times the diplomats have to gloss over real differences with language that both sides can interpret the way they want to in order to reach a meeting of the minds as to language. Of course, when they do that, in a sense they are delegating power to a dispute settlement system to resolve conflicts of interpretation that will inevitably arise. Nevertheless, there may be some conflict between this and some of the other goals on this list.

f. Promote compliance with DS outcomes and with the norms of the treaty

A goal of a dispute settlement system is to promote compliance with the results so that the treaty norms can be effective and depended upon. The dispute settlement process itself (in fact, the mere existence of a dispute settlement process) has a strong component of assisting compliance in the international landscape, even without sanctions or "retaliation." Alternatives to sanctions and retaliation include shaming techniques, reciprocity notions, and other pressure techniques.

g. Redress asymmetries of power; fairness to weaker entities

A dispute settlement system helps redress asymmetries of power. Smaller or less developed countries can bring a case against larger, wealthier countries, and win at both the panel and Appellate Body levels. Costa Rica, for example won a case against the United States at the first-level

5.3 The multiple policy goals of international dispute settlement

and appellate stages in a case about underwear. The United States complied with the result.[3]

h. Reestablish balance of benefits, "rebalancing"

Rebalancing of benefits is an issue that has been central to some of the criticism of the WTO. Many argue that this should be a goal of the system. This is the reciprocity idea run wild, but it nevertheless has its origins in the preparatory work of GATT itself. Some argue that all we need to do is to rebalance so that the party that is the "wrongdoer" should give a new set of concessions equivalent to the value of what it seems to have taken away, and that should be the end of the matter. In other words, observance or performance of the international obligation takes a lesser role. This obviously creates an enormous tension with some of the goals, particularly the goals of predictability for the non-disputants in a particular case. For this reason, the reciprocity or rebalancing idea has virtually faded to nonexistence during the last twenty-five years or so of the GATT–WTO system, but nevertheless it is still advocated quite vociferously by particular interests in the United States.

i. Give the participating parties a sense of "day in court"; a right to fair procedure?

This immediately raises the question, "who is the real party?" Governments, their citizens, or international businesses (market participants)? The idea of a party's "day in court" is nothing new. If the parties battle it out in "court" (a term not used in the WTO system) or in a creditable process with genuine integrity that is non-corruptible, then the parties have a sense of having been treated fairly, and nation-state leaders, for example, can return to their constituents to report on their effort with the knowledge that they could win the next time.

j. Provide reasoned judgments to enhance broader public acceptance of the application and development of the rules

It is an important policy objective to be able to use the rulings in a dispute settlement proceeding to enhance broader public acceptance of the results. These rulings may tread on certain constituent toes in certain cases, particularly constituents who have benefited from some exception from international competition and now find that they must comply, but it is perhaps for this reason that the goal is important. This process is useful to governments to help them persuade their constituents to do the "right thing." This relates to item *i*, above.

k. Reasoned analysis of important policy implications of the rule application, so as to shed light on complex issues and dilemmas requiring a balancing approach (thus assisting other governmental processes)

This goal is subtler. The well-reasoned opinion can often alert rule makers and decision makers in the non-dispute settlement part of the system to particular intricacies of policy problems. In the *Shrimp–Turtle* case, for instance (one of the most important cases in the jurisprudence of the WTO so far), there is a deeper exploration in the analysis than may be necessary and really persuasive in the particular case. This goal can assist future negotiations.

l. Define and rationalize allocation of governmental powers, that is, to "repair" the constitution and provide for evolution

Finally, there is a sort of "constitutional" element of the dispute settlement process. It will, from time to time, be called upon essentially to allocate power among different parts of the same institution or different levels of the international landscape. That might call into question whether a certain kind of decision or regulatory norm, and so on, is best made in Geneva; Washington, DC; Sacramento, California; Berkeley, California; or a neighborhood in Berkeley. A similar scale or ladder of levels of governmental activity applies in Europe and elsewhere in the world. Chapter 3 discussed the issue of power allocation in more detail.

When appraising the list above, one can see that many of these goals can sometimes clash with other goals. Therefore, balancing is often necessary. There is not space here to go into the potential clashes between these various objectives, but the implications can be seen. It is also apparent that there is some overlap among some of these goals. There is probably a group of five or six that go together and do not necessarily clash, goals that indeed may complement each other. Most but not all of these goals apply in all legal systems, national or international, in varying importance.

Turning now to some of the "devilish detail," it is important to consider the factors that will affect the achievement of the dozen goals laid out above.

One factor is avoiding the monopoly of power, that is, avoiding too much power in any part of the system, including the dispute settlement

5.3 The multiple policy goals of international dispute settlement

system. It could be that there are checks and balances that have to be considered, but that is very worrisome because certain kinds of checks that are being advocated would undermine the credibility of the dispute settlement system. For instance, a political veto of a specific case should be avoided at all costs. On the other hand, a critique by the dispute settlement body looking forward to future cases could actually be healthy if it were done in a somewhat different atmosphere is now the case.

A number of other subjects are relevant in considering the goals listed. Some of these are also considered later in this chapter.

1. Is there an international law obligation to perform, that is, to comply with DS rulings (not just compensate or tolerate retaliation)? Such obligation promotes rule orientation, stability and predictability, and benefits all, including nongovernmental persons/entities, traders and so on. There is dispute on this (discussed further in section 5.6.b), but recognizing an IL obligation supports the goal of achieving compliance.[4]
2. Is it necessary to have some political oversight, such as an opportunity for political organs to redress juridical mistakes?
3. Use of precedent: there clearly is a precedent effect in the WTO DS system that is somewhat less stringent than the *stare decisis* one. The question is: how strong is that precedent effect? There is actually a whole range of different precedent effects, from a very soft effect all the way up to a very strong presumption (without being *stare decisis*). There is a very strong presumptive desire for the consistency idea to prevail so that what has been done before will be followed, but if there was a real reason for change, it could freely occur.[5]
4. The question of direct application or "self-executing" status, especially when coupled with higher legal status than national later legislation (such status tends to "constitutionalize" the treaty without the usual constitutional procedures).[6]
5. Deference to nation-state, or "margin of appreciation."
6. Techniques of "interpretation" affect the allocation of power and deference questions, for example:
   text, preparatory work, object and purpose, teleological;
   evolutionary, give effect to all clauses, not mechanical;
   accordion-like concepts, case-by-case, and so on.
7. Details of a DS system procedure and how the jurisprudence affects these issues:
   how judges are chosen, term length, renewal of terms;
   resources of the system.

5.4 The current structure and operation of the WTO dispute settlement system

The WTO Dispute Settlement Understanding,[1] which is Annex 2 to the WTO "Charter," provides the core treaty text of about twenty-five pages which govern the WTO DS process. This process consists primarily of four major stages, and the Dispute Settlement Body has the overall responsibility for supervising the process.

First, the parties must attempt to resolve their differences through consultations. Second, if that fails, the complaining party may demand that a panel of independent experts be established to rule on the dispute. Third, and new under the DSU, is the possibility of an appeal by any party to the dispute to the Appellate Body. Finally, if the complaining party succeeds, the DSB is charged with monitoring the implementation of its recommendations. If the recommendations are not implemented, the possibility of negotiated compensation or authorization to withdraw concessions arises. The DSU also provides for voluntary mediation[2] at any time (an option which is rarely used), and for an alternative procedure of arbitration,[3] also rarely used. The DSU provides for compulsory referral of all disputes regarding the "covered agreements" (WTO-related as listed or implied in the DSU text) to the procedures set forth.[4] This is obviously a very powerful measure of "compulsory jurisdiction," which, when combined with the virtually automatic adoption of a DS report (panel or appellate) is even more powerful.

A brief overview of the stages of the DS system follows.

a. Consultations

The requirement that disputing parties consult with a view towards satisfactorily adjusting the matter is contained in GATT Article XXIII itself, now carried forward in the DSU. The hope is that the parties will resolve their dispute without having to invoke the formal dispute settlement procedures. The manner in which the consultations are conducted is up to the disputing parties. The DSU only requires that consultations are to be entered into in good faith and are to be started within thirty days of a request. During the consultations both parties try to learn more about the facts and about the legal arguments of the other party. Despite the fact that the structure of consultations is undefined and there are no rules for conducting them, a significant number of cases end at the consultations stage (either through settlements or abandonment of a case). If consultations fail

5.4 The current structure and operation of the WTO dispute settlement system

to settle a dispute within sixty days after the request, the complaining party may request the establishment of a panel. In fact, consultations often go on for more than sixty days. There has been some criticism of the consultation process for not being very meaningful, and too often being a formal prerequisite with "canned speeches" and a lack of meaningful exchanges, but it is not clear how justified this criticism is.

b. Panel process

Under the DSU, the right of a party to have a panel established is clear and, unlike under GATT, cannot be blocked. If consultations fail to resolve a dispute within the sixty-day time frame specified a complainant may insist on the establishment of a panel and, at the meeting following that at which the request first appears on the DSB's agenda, the DSB is required to establish a panel unless there is a consensus in the DSB not to establish a panel. Since the complaining party may prevent the formation of this "reverse" consensus, there is effectively a right to have a panel established.

Once a panel is authorized, it is necessary to select the individuals (normally three) who will serve as panelists. The DSU provides that the Secretariat propose potential panel members to the parties, and that parties should not object except for compelling reasons. In practice, parties are relatively free to reject proposed panelists, but if the parties do not agree on panel members within twenty days of establishment, any party may request the WTO Director-General to appoint the panel on his or her own authority. In recent years, the Director-General has appointed some members of approximately one-half of the panels composed.

Article 8.1 of the DSU provides that panels shall be composed of well-qualified governmental and/or non-governmental individuals, including persons who have served on or presented a case to a panel, served as a representative of a Member or of a Contracting Party to GATT 1947 or as a representative to the Council or Committee of any covered agreement or its predecessor agreement, or in the Secretariat, taught or published on international trade law or policy, or served as a senior trade policy official of a Member.

These criteria suggest that there are three categories of panelists: government officials (current or former), former Secretariat officials, and trade academics or lawyers. The DSU provides that panelists shall not be nationals of parties or third parties, absent agreement of the parties. The DSU also specifies that in a case involving a developing country, one panelist must be from a developing country (if requested). It appears that the vast majority of panelists (80 percent) are current or former government officials.

Panelists serve in their individual capacities and the DSU requires that members should not give panelists instructions or seek to influence them. In addition, the DSB has adopted rules of conduct applicable to participants in the WTO dispute settlement system. These rules require that panelists "be independent and impartial, shall avoid direct or indirect conflicts of interest and shall respect the confidentiality of proceedings." The rules also require such persons to disclose "the existence or development of any interest, relationship or matter that person could reasonable be expected to know and that is likely to affect, or give rise to justifiable doubts as to, that person's independence or impartiality." Disputing parties may protest alleged material violations of the rules. If upheld, such protest could lead to the replacement of the challenged individual.[5]

The DSU provides for standard terms of reference (absent agreement to the contrary), which direct a panel "To examine, in the light of the relevant provisions in (name of the covered agreement/s cited by the parties to the dispute), the matter referred to the DSB by (name of party) in document DS/ . . . and to make such findings as will assist the DSB in making the recommendations or in giving the rulings provided for in that/those agreement/s." The Appellate Body has emphasized in its rulings that panels may not entertain issues outside their terms of reference. In practice, the panel request document, which must "specify the measures at issue and provide a brief summary of the legal basis of the complaint sufficient to present the problem clearly," will set the parameters for the panelists' attention. There are often lengthy arguments over whether specific issues have been adequately mentioned in the panel request.[6]

More generally, DSU Article 11 provides that a panel should make an objective assessment of the matter before it, including an objective assessment of the facts of the case and the applicability of and conformity with the relevant WTO agreements. In the *Beef Hormones* case,[7] the Appellate Body elaborated on this requirement as follows:

The duty to make an objective assessment of the facts is, among other things, an obligation to consider the evidence presented to a panel and to make factual findings on the basis of that evidence. The deliberate disregard of, or refusal to consider, the evidence submitted to a panel is incompatible with a panel's duty to make an objective assessment of the facts. The willful distortion or misrepresentation of the evidence put before a panel is similarly inconsistent with an objective assessment of the facts.[8]

5.4 The current structure and operation of the WTO dispute settlement system

The panel procedures are set forth in the DSU, but provide for some alteration by agreement between the panel and the disputants, so generally an agreed set of procedures (based on a template provided by the Secretariat which outlines the normal practice) is formulated. These provide for written submissions, and usually two or more oral proceedings (to allow for rebuttals, etc.). Panels confronted by intricate factual or scientific questions have sometimes innovated particular procedures to obtain outside information and expertise.[9] DSU Article 13 authorizes panels to "seek information and technical advice from any individual or body which it deems appropriate." The Appellate Body has made it clear that this authority can include receiving *amicus curiae* briefs (with the control of the panel) as well as other procedures, such as consulting key experts in a scientific field.

As at September 2005 all proceedings have been closed to the public, and indeed portions are closed even to WTO members that are not parties. Elaborate rules for "third party participation" are set forth, but parts of the proceedings may even be closed to such third parties. Needless to say, this degree of absence of transparency has been much criticized.[10] In an interesting case involving the *Beef Hormones* dispute, the three disputing parties (United States and Canada as complainants, European Communities as respondent) have agreed to open hearings. The panel agreed and, therefore, a WTO DS hearing was, for the first time, open for public viewing.[11]

Throughout GATT's history and at the beginning of the WTO's existence there were objections raised against governments bringing into the proceedings "outside counsel" who were not part of the government of the disputing member. This clearly disadvantaged those disputants who had very little "in-house" legal resources and experience for conducting DS cases. Early in the WTO history, however, the Appellate Body made it clear the sovereign prerogative of each member disputant enabled it to determine whom it would appoint to be part of its delegation to attend and speak at a DS proceeding.[12] Consequently for smaller countries and others without adequate legal staff or without prior experience in DS cases, it is common for disputant governments to retain private counsel to assist in cases, including presence in hearings and speaking when the client member country permits. It always was the case that private counsel were extensively used for preparation of written and oral submittals outside the hearing rooms.[13]

The panel deliberates and prepares a draft report. The fact description is generally shared with the disputants to assist in correcting any errors, and the panel then drafts a complete "interim report" containing its proposed findings and conclusions. The DSU rules provide that the interim report must be shared with the disputants (and otherwise kept confidential, although often it is leaked) for a period of two to four weeks to provide for comments to the panel from disputants. It is argued that this would give disputants a chance to urge the panel to correct any "errors," and it is also argued that this interim report might lead to a last-chance settlement of the case. Others now argue that this interim report stage is a waste of time and should be abandoned.

The DSU is elaborate and fairly specific on the timetable for the panel process,[14] although for certain complex cases the timetable will expand. The normal expectation is that panel final reports will be issued within six to eight months of the establishment of a panel, but often cases take more time.

Perhaps the most critical stage of the process, and one that dramatically changed the GATT process, is the stage of "adoption" of the panel final report in the WTO DS system. When the final report is complete, it is sent to the DSB for adoption. Under GATT the "Council" received such reports and used a consensus procedure for adoption, which meant that any contracting party could defeat the consensus, including that party that was the "losing" disputant. This was a critical defect in the system, as previously discussed. The Uruguay Round result prevents this blocking approach by providing that the final panel report (unless appealed) will be deemed adopted (at the second meeting at which the report is considered) unless there is "consensus" against adoption. This so-called "reverse consensus" thus would allow the winning party to block a negative consensus (against adoption), and this in turn means virtual automatic adoption (with some rare exceptions possibly involving settlement activity).[15]

c. The appellate process in the WTO

Partly because of the automatic adoption of panel reports with no blocking permitted, the negotiators in the Uruguay Round determined that it was necessary to have some appeal process from the panel determinations. Thus was born another one of the extraordinary and unique features of the WTO DS process, namely the appeal procedure.

Any disputant can appeal from a panel report on "issues of law." This WTO appeal is a very broad power, not limited to the narrow challenges in many international tribunals or arbitration bodies, such as exceeding terms of reference, or failure faithfully and honestly to carry out the duties expected of such bodies. Even a disputant that "wins" all or most issues

5.4 The current structure and operation of the WTO dispute settlement system

in its case can appeal. This has sometimes been the case when the language of the panel report displeases even a winner, such as using grounds for a determination that has long-range implications which bother the appealing disputant.[16]

An Appellate Body was created consisting of seven individual members, who sit in groups of three (termed a "division") on any particular case. The Appellate Body members serve terms of four years, once renewable. This group is served by a secretariat which together with the Appellate Body members is carefully kept separate from the general WTO Secretariat, to avoid any appearance of undue influence. The process of choosing which Appellate Body members will sit on a particular case is very secret so as to prevent any potential appellant disputant from anticipating who will be part of the division for its case. The choice is thus partly based on randomness, unpredictability, and a fair spread of the workload. Any member may sit on any case, regardless of national origin. In addition the practice of "collegiality" has developed so that all seven Appellate Body members will see the documents and submissions, and at a certain stage will meet together in Geneva to discuss the case, although the three chosen for the division will actually decide the case and prepare the Appellate Body report. The reports do not reveal which division members held which opinions, and generally do not reveal any measure of "dissent" or lack of full consensus, although there have been several Appellate Body reports in which explicit differences of view has been expressed (anonymously).

The appeal process is designed to be very speedy, so the normal timetable calls for a final report within sixty days of the appeal, sometimes extended to ninety days. In some cases even this is extended. This imposes enormous pressure on the Appellate Body members in a division, so very heavy work weeks (including working in the evenings and at weekends) are not unknown. Some conjecture has existed that this time pressure may have limited the quality of some reports, but that case seems hard to make, since overall the quality is quite high compared with most judicial institutions in the world.

The Appellate Body, unlike panels, is explicitly given the authority to develop (in consultation) its own rules, and this can be an important power. It was an issue in a troublesome question about the power of the Appellate Body to receive *amicus curiae* submissions, but the practice now seems to have settled down to recognize that that power exists for the Appellate Body.[17]

On the other hand the Appellate Body's authority appears somewhat limited. In addition to being confined to "issues of law" (and numerous questions about distinguishing between issues of law and of fact have arisen), the DSU provides that the Appellate Body may "uphold, modify, or reverse" legal findings of a panel. This has been taken to mean that there is no "remand" power. Thus when the Appellate Body finds a gap in the panel logic, it has faced a dilemma when its approach depends on facts or arguments which have not been addressed by the panel. The Appellate Body has in some cases "completed the analysis," but in other cases has indicated an inability to do so.[18]

When the Appellate Body's final report is completed, it is then sent to the DSB for adoption and, like the process for panel report adoption, the procedure is automatic adoption with the reverse consensus, thus there is virtually always an approved adoption. When the Appellate Body report is adopted, the ruling also adopts the panel report insofar as it is unchanged by the appeal report.

The Appellate Body has often referred to the language of the Vienna Convention on the Law of Treaties (VCLT), particularly Articles 31 and 32 for approved methods of interpretation. This has led the Appellate Body strongly to emphasize "text" and its ordinary meaning, in its determinations. This has been questioned in some of the comments about the Appellate Body jurisprudence, but has been defended (at least in the early years) as promoting objectivity and absence of bias or appearance thereof.[19]

A number of other major jurisprudential questions have captured the attention of the Appellate Body, including questions of standard of review of nation-state government measures, standard of review of panel reports, burdens of proof, degree of precedent value to be given to Appellate Body and panel rulings, and troublesome questions regarding compliance and international law obligation to implement the findings of DS reports. Some of these issues are discussed later in this chapter.

d. Implementation and compliance requirements

Important features of the DSU as negotiated in the Uruguay Round are the extensive provisions[20] relating to the "implementation" of recommendations in DS reports (panel and/or Appellate Body). There is a series of intricate steps, including a potential arbitration about the "reasonable period of time" within which implementation must occur (normally fifteen months), and provision for the winning complainant to demand compensatory trade liberalization measures (almost never provided) or to introduce trade restrictions as sort of "compensatory retaliation." There are provisions which have proved to be inadequately drafted and somewhat inconsistent, by which the "implementation" measures and or the compensatory trade restrictions can be "litigated" further. A large number of these "post-judgment" procedures have now been invoked, adding a considerable specialized jurisprudence concerning these steps. The DSU quite clearly (as discussed later in this chapter) requires full performance, explicitly stating that the various compensatory or "retaliation" measures are only temporary, pending full compliance. However, some governments have argued the contrary, that they are permitted to use compensatory measures or to tolerate retaliatory measures as a choice rather than comply. This latter position has major policy detriments as well as contravening the obligations as set forth in the DSU.

On the whole, observers suggest that compliance with the DS final reports has been quite good, but in recent years there have been a number of prominent cases, mostly findings against the United States or the European Union, which have not received adequate compliance, and these provide a troublesome backdrop to the general compliance situation. Nevertheless there is ample evidence that the compliance measures of the DSU are given considerable attention, and have been persuasive in some cases in leading national government political leaders to take steps to comply with rulings against their country.[21] In some cases the winning complainant governments have developed intricately calculated "retaliatory" measures which would cause the most distress to politically sensitive constituencies in the target nation, and this political pressure has led to legislative or other action in the direction of full compliance.[22]

5.5 A decade of WTO dispute settlement activity, 1995–2005

As already intimated in section 5.1, the WTO dispute settlement system proved remarkable from its beginning. The most important defect ("birth defect") under GATT, namely the power of a losing disputing party to block the adoption of a panel report, was corrected and this, plus other reforms and the fairly elaborate structure and procedure set out in the DSU, created a powerful juridical system. Indeed, this very fact made some diplomats and national political leaders worry that too much power resided in the DSS. Unlike national judicial systems, which may have considerable power, but are constrained by checks and balances of the legislature, which may "correct" errors of the judiciary, the WTO has no really effective check, in that sense, on the power exercised by the Appellate Body, except the possibility of major diplomatic efforts, such as negotiating amendments to the rules or a new procedure in the WTO Charter, Article IX, providing for "definitive interpretations," which many observers feel is not likely to be used.[1]

The first decade of DSS history is impressive from a number of viewpoints. All of the following attributes suggest reasonable success of the Uruguay Round DS reforms: the body of jurisprudence of cases with adopted reports; the care and intricacy of the text of these reports; their impact on international economic diplomacy;[2] the reasonably good (but lately troubled) record of compliance; and the sharper emphasis on the "rule-oriented" approach to enhance predictability and security (two goals mentioned in the DSU and particularly important for market participants and other non-governmental entities). Many diplomats and national political leaders seem well satisfied so far that the new WTO DSS is worthwhile, and should be maintained, despite some harsh criticism from certain national-level adversaries, who have found themselves, or their clients, on the wrong side of certain DSS determinations.

The statistics are interesting.[3] Of the total of 333 complaints brought (as of October 2005), only about half actually go on to a panel process,[4] suggesting the possibility that the jurisprudence is providing some predictability that promotes settlements or withdrawals of cases. The DS system has adopted 165 reports (95 first-level panel reports, and 70 Appellate Body reports), in a total of 102 cases[5] (although post-report procedures are increasing, usually related to compliance problems). Of the 102 first-level panel reports *circulated* (not all have yet been adopted as of this writing), 72 (or approximately 71 percent) have been appealed and the percentage of appeals has declined. This also suggests that the jurisprudence has enhanced predictability of outcome such that disputants may decide that an appeal is not likely to succeed (costs of the appeal influence this decision also). The number of complaints brought each year fluctuates, but overall, is sizable. There has been fear that the number would overwhelm the resources available in the WTO, but, so far, that does not seem to have happened.[6] As might be expected, the most complaints are brought by the United States (76, or 23 percent of the total) and the European Union (64, or 19 percent of the total). These members also defend the greatest number of cases, the United States 89, or 27 percent of the total, and the European Union 53, or 16 percent of the total. Thus the United States is a disputant in 165 complaints, or approximately 50 percent of the total, and the European Union, similarly, is a disputant in 117 complaints, which is 35 percent of the total.

Surprisingly, developing countries have been active participants, bringing 126 complaints, which is about 38 percent of the total, and defending

5.5 A decade of WTO dispute settlement activity, 1995–2005

139 cases, 42 percent of the total. Interesting is the fact that developing countries have been disputants in cases where both sides were developing countries. Until recently, however, no "least developed"[7] country had brought or defended a case, possibly because their trading abilities and opportunities did not make it worthwhile, but also probably because they did not have the expertise within their government to recognize or make a policy decision about whether to bring a case.

Of the many cases handled so far, a few have been particularly notable. The first case to be litigated (the second brought; the first was settled) was *US – Gasoline*,[8] which set part of the framework for future cases by, *inter alia*, clearly embracing a role for general international law in the WTO procedures (see section 5.6, *infra*), focusing on the Vienna Convention as expressing customary international law rules of treaty interpretation, emphasizing the role of text, correcting the first-level panel's logical approach, and indicating a measure of deference that should be accorded to the member of the WTO.

Another early case was *Japan – Alcoholic Beverages*,[9] which struggled with the national treatment clause of GATT Article III, mentioning a need for case-by-case working out of general rules (which often means retaining power to the juridical body), addressing the role of prior case reports as guidance, noting that identical language could have different meanings when set in different contexts.[10]

A later case, regarding *EC – Beef Hormones*,[11] struggled with the WTO Sanitary and Phytosanitary (SPS) Agreement (basically regarding foodstuffs),[12] and established some parameters for handling scientific information, and explored the burden of proof and other tricky issues.

It is interesting how prominent a role environment cases (including food safety and health) have had in the developing jurisprudence of the WTO DSS. Already mentioned above are *US – Gasoline* and *EC – Beef Hormones*. A slightly later case was the famous *US – Shrimp–Turtle*[13] case. This case is still, in this author's opinion, the most important "constitutional" case in all of the WTO jurisprudence so far. This is a very complex, intricately worded, and carefully nuanced case that essentially established a series of principles, some of major or even heroic importance. In section 5.8, we return to this case with a more complete description, but as a preview, the following is a brief list of some of the propositions articulated in this case,[14] some of which are described in section 5.8 in more detail:

unilateral measures for certain exceptions may be permissible;
instructing the first-level panel to follow prior Appellate Body reports, including the logical structure and its sequence relating to GATT Article XX;

the continued importance of the *text* of the treaty;
the degree of deference to the WTO member, nation-state or other;
the extra-territorial implications of a WTO member's regulation;
an evolutionary approach to some interpretations;
the power of the first-level panel to accept *amicus curiae* briefs or other communications of information or advocacy;
the use of international documents and activities from sources other than the WTO, to assist in interpreting WTO covered agreement texts;
recognizing the importance of non-trade policy goals, and articulating a need, therefore, to balance policy goals when interpreting treaty text;
subtly handling preparatory history;
the suggestion of a "good faith" generic international law requirement as part of treaty implementation; and
"judicial economy."

Many of these issues actually address some of the underlying jurisprudential problems explored in earlier chapters of this book. For example, many issues (e.g. deference, non-trade document sources) relate to the matters noted in Chapter 3 about the importance to a modern sovereignty concept of allocating power. Other issues relate to the methods of treaty interpreting which could be permissible, and treaty interpretation methodology clearly can affect the way in which certain international norms apply to or constrain nation-states in their governmental measures.

In recent years, however, the WTO DSS has been strongly criticized for its handling of a group of cases generically called "trade remedy" cases. This term embraces three different sets of cases, namely antidumping cases, subsidy and countervailing duty cases, and "safeguards" cases (meaning mostly "escape clause" cases).

The trade remedy cases against the United States (numbering twenty-five, with a finding of at least one violation in each of twenty of those[15]) have engendered within the United States (mostly by advocates located in Washington, DC) the most strident, persistent, and politically dangerous objections to the WTO DSS. Members of Congress have unfortunately entered the fray, often negatively pronouncing the view that the Appellate Body was exceeding its authority by "judicial activism," and slanted treaty interpretations that inappropriately impinge upon the sovereignty of the United States.[16]

More recently, several very important cases have been reported by the WTO DS system. One of those cases is the first to outline fully WTO obligations under the General Agreement on Trade in Services (GATS), thus involving trade in services as opposed to trade in goods. This case was

5.6 Key jurisprudential questions I

brought by Antigua and Barbuda against the United States, arguing that US federal and state regulations preventing or restricting Internet gambling provided by external suppliers was inconsistent with US treaty obligations in the GATS. The panel ruled that the United States was at fault, because it had included in its services schedule of commitments language regarding sporting activity that could be interpreted to cover gambling.[17] The United States argued to the contrary, but also that an exception in the GATS text regarding regulation of "public morals" should apply to the US case. The panel mostly ruled against the United States, but the Appellate Body reversed most of the panel's view on the public morals defense, giving the United States grounds to claim an appeal victory (the details are very complex!).[18] Although several prior WTO cases had dealt with services issues, some in the context of facts relating to goods, another case relating to special obligations regarding telecommunications, this gambling case was the first to walk though the logic of the GATS in a services-only situation.

Another important case is that brought by Brazil complaining against US agriculture subsidies regarding cotton (both export subsidies and domestic price support subsidies). A panel held in favor of Brazil, in an extraordinarily complex and intricate economics case which will undoubtedly have implications for the new Doha Round of trade negotiations (in which agriculture subsidies play the most crucial role), but also for the agriculture subsidy practices of major countries including not only the United States but also the European Union and Japan, Canada, and other countries. The Appellate Body has largely upheld the panel approach.[19] Already a similar case for sugar subsidies against Europe has created a similar panel result, a result which was essentially upheld by the Appellate Body.[20]

In the next five sections, this chapter will turn to several groups of "key jurisprudential developments" in the WTO DSS which will further explore how this dispute settlement system is handling the sovereignty and other "constitutional" issues that this book is about.

5.6 Key jurisprudential questions I: the relation of WTO law to international law – sovereignty tensions

This section is the first of five sections devoted to groups of selected "key jurisprudential issues," all of which illustrate, in differing degrees, the problem themes of this book, including the tensions derived from competing visions of the appropriate allocation of power between the international institutions and the nation-state or other government entities. Needless to say, these sections and the explorations included in them are only a brief overview of a now quite vast and exceedingly complex jurisprudential record based on the first decade of the new WTO dispute settlement system.

In this section, we examine issues that can be seen as part of an outline for the relationship of the DSS in particular, and the organization in general, to its member states and other entities. These issues are clearly relevant to some of the principles and problems discussed in chapters 2 and 3 of this book. This section will take up four such issues or issue groups: first, the relationship of international law generally to the WTO, noting how this relationship can affect some of the obligations of the WTO in ways possibly not anticipated by the members when they agreed to the Uruguay Round treaty. Second, this section will explore very briefly a rather perplexing jurisprudential issue that has emerged, both a bit in the discussion leading up to the implementation of the WTO and in developments after that. This issue concerns the question whether, where the DSS results in an adopted report, a member who is found to have measures in effect that are inconsistent with its obligations under the WTO covered agreements is then under an international law obligation to bring its measures into consistency. The alternative approach is to believe that the nation-state concerned has a right either to "compensate" or to bear the burden of compensatory measures against it, as an alternative to an obligation to perform. Third are the perplexing contours of the DSS's "standard of review" in appraising member state measures and actions which may be determined inconsistent with the obligations. Finally, this section will briefly appraise the question of whether there are available appropriate and practical measures that the Appellate Body or first-level panel would use to avoid addressing or answering certain questions that might be deemed political or non-justiciable, or basically just "too hot to handle."

a. General international law

The relationship of international law generally to GATT was commented on for a number of years, and was very prominently addressed at the very beginning of the existence of the WTO Appellate Body. The question in GATT times was sometimes stated to be whether GATT was a "separate legal regime" from international law, so that general international law norms would not necessarily be relevant or pervade the work of GATT. At

5.6 Key jurisprudential questions I

least in the literature, some advocates supported the view that GATT was a separate regime, and therefore had a totally stand-alone jurisprudence and legal structure. Many others, including this author, opposed that view, and there are relatively numerous examples throughout the history of GATT that would oppose the "separate regime" theory. There were several cases near the end of GATT, where a GATT panel directly and explicitly addressed the question of whether international law was relevant and intertwined with GATT law, and the conclusion of the panels was a distinct affirmative.[1]

The very first case in the WTO that went the entire route of the new DSS was a case brought by Venezuela and Brazil against the United States, with respect to US environmental regulations regarding gasoline (already briefly discussed).[2] The complainants argued and prevailed that US regulations on this matter discriminated against the importation of gasoline, as compared with its regulatory treatment of domestic producers. Most impartial observers felt that the United States would lose that case, and it did lose, both at the first-level panel stage, and then after the United States appealed these rulings. Basically, the DSS held that the US measure was inconsistent with US obligations, and required the United States to bring its actions into consistency. The case is quite curious on a number of counts. It was somehow symbolic that the very first case to result in adopted panel and Appellate Body reports[3] was against the largest, and arguably most powerful, trading member of the WTO. It was also interesting and symbolic that the case was brought by developing countries. Although the ruling against the United States was upheld by the Appellate Body, the latter disagreed with the logical structure of the first-level panel's case, and in that regard agreed with the United States' argument about the basis of the potential exception (under Article XX of GATT) which the United States was invoking. However, the next logical stage of the case resulted in the United States being held inconsistent with its obligations. Nevertheless, both the complainants and respondent could argue that they had won something. The United States had won a judgment about some specific treaty text that could be deemed more deferential to the nation-state sovereign (and particularly to the United States) than would otherwise be the case. The United States, however, did not meet the additional criteria of Article XX (in the Preamble) which were necessary for it to escape a ruling against it.

In this case, the Appellate Body immediately addressed the question of the relationship of international law to the WTO, and emphatically pronounced that, with respect to treaty interpretation, general principles of customary international law were binding on members of the WTO. The Appellate Body also noted that many countries deemed the text of the VCLT appropriately to articulate the customary international law of treaty interpretation, and the Appellate Body quoted Articles 31 and 32 of the Vienna Convention extensively. It then proceeded, at least in its view, to follow the principles set forth therein for treaty interpretation. In particular, the Appellate Body took the position in that first case, and in many later cases, that it would give prime significance to the *text* of the treaty. This textual emphasis became something of a determining characteristic for the Appellate Body, and actually has brought a certain amount of controversy to some of its opinions.

However, even though one can conclude that the WTO legal structure is part of general international law and therefore must, in appropriate circumstances, respond to international law principles, including customary international law and, in some situations, international treaty law, the question is: how far does that take you? One immediate question that comes up is: to what degree should "preparatory work"[4] be utilized for assisting in the interpretation of treaty language? It has been argued by some that the Vienna Convention gives a lower status to preparatory work, and that the mention of preparatory work in Article 32 seems to indicate that it would be an "ancillary" assistance to interpretation in those cases in which interpretation according to principles of Article 31 had not succeeded. The Appellate Body seems to favor that advice, and in a later (but also early in WTO history) case, *Japan – Alcoholic Beverages*,[5] the Appellate Body seemed to attempt to follow this notion of initially avoiding preparatory work. Nevertheless, when the Appellate Body examined the principles of Article 31 of the Vienna Convention that called for attention to the "object and purpose" of a treaty, it seemed to be influenced by preparatory work, since it cited some of the preparatory work of GATT in its footnotes.[6] Consequently, it is still not easy to judge how the customary international law principles of treaty interpretation related to preparatory work will be utilized in the WTO jurisprudential system. For many decades prior to the WTO, GATT panels had tended to embrace preparatory work in their interpretations of GATT, basically without any particular hesitation. One might even argue that there was a special rule of treaty interpretation law that had developed in GATT which might prevail over a more general international law proposition.[7]

Another situation that calls into question the relation of international law to WTO law is the concept of "good faith" called for in the Vienna Convention articulation of customary law. This can be construed to be an independent obligation of a treaty partner in the manner in which it applies and interprets the treaty obligations.[8] This has been noticed in several cases in the WTO jurisprudence, and it has given rise to some criticism that the concept of "good faith" is so general and open-ended that it is an invitation for any juridical body to "pour into that bottle" its own particular prejudices, tilts, and policy preferences, rather than to use more "objective" techniques for interpreting the treaty.[9]

In that line of thinking, there have also been arguments developed that the remedies provided to enhance and encourage compliance with the result of a dispute settlement adopted report could be complemented with reference to some of the general principles of customary international law regarding treaty remedies. These general principles might be those articulated in the Vienna Convention, but also might be derived from broader and more recent work relating to the development of customary international law, such as the report of the United Nations International Law Commission on "State Responsibility."[10] This suggestion has given rise to considerable concern. The opposing argument would be that since the remedial provisions of the WTO DSU seem to have an overall framework and completeness which suggest that the draftspersons did not anticipate or welcome other, ancillary notions of remedy, general international principles ought not to be read into the WTO DSU remedies. The argument could be taken further to say that even though there was customary international law that could be used, a treaty provision or set of provisions would trump the customary international law in the event of conflict, and would preempt the customary international law in situations where it appeared that the text was designed fully to exhaust the possibilities of remedies. This also raises the notion of *lex specialis*, so that it can be argued that it would be inappropriate to use this general argumentation based on customary international law remedies for treaty-inconsistent measures, in the context of the WTO, where the DSU seems to imply that it exhausts the possible remedies to be provided.

Another instance of the relationship of international law to the WTO law is raised in the *Japan – Alcoholic Beverages* case,[11] where the Appellate Body report is coming to grips with the impact of a prior opinion or report of either its own or a GATT dispute settlement panel, on a case then before the Appellate Body. Should it be "bound by" the ruling of a prior case in an adopted report? It seems quite clear, and will be discussed in a later section of this chapter, that there is not such a strict precedent requirement, but the Vienna Convention does speak of "practice under the agreement"[12] as important to interpreting a treaty.

Consequently, that raises the question of what is "practice under the agreement," and the Appellate Body report in the *Japan – Alcoholic Beverages* case, although not too clear on this point, seems to indicate that one single case is not to be deemed "practice under the agreement" in the Vienna Convention sense. That does not mean that such single case is irrelevant, and it is quite clear that, as we will discuss in a later section, there is broadly and generally a sense of a certain amount of "precedent value" in the cases.

b. Obligation to perform

A second important jurisprudential issue relating to the relationship of the WTO to its members in the DS system is the question of whether there arises an "obligation to perform" or comply upon the adoption of a first-level panel or Appellate Body report. This problem partly arises because the DSU does not have in it an explicit clause like Article 94 of the United Nations Charter, which imposes an international law obligation on each member state to "comply with the decision of the International Court of Justice in any case to which it is a party." Nevertheless, the DSU and the WTO Charter have about a dozen treaty clauses which when read together make a very strong case for such obligation to perform.[13]

For example, the DSU states that in case of a DS ruling, "the first objective . . . is usually to secure the withdrawal of the measures concerned if these are found to be inconsistent" with covered agreements.[14] Although the DSU specifies a number of counteractions which a winning complainant in a DS case can take, it explicitly states that these measures shall be "temporary and shall only be applied until such time as the measure found to be inconsistent with a covered agreement has been removed."[15] In addition, the DSU provides that the DSB shall "keep under surveillance the implementation of adopted recommendations"; that these matters shall "remain on the DSB's agenda until the issue is resolved"; and that "prompt compliance with recommendations . . . is essential."[16]

Likewise there are strong policy reasons for the existence of an international law obligation to carry out DS report "recommendations," including the importance expressed in the DSU for providing "security and predictability to the multilateral trading system," and the damage to credibility of the DS system that would occur if the richer WTO members were able to "buy out" of their obligations.

5.6 Key jurisprudential questions I

c. Standard of review

A third jurisprudential issue that is quite central to many of the cases in the WTO jurisprudence is the broad question of "standard of review." Of course, there are different standards of review in any system of jurisprudence, and in the WTO one could see that there is the standard of review as to what should be the degree of deference of the WTO DSS as a whole towards nation-states' or other members' interpretations of treaties or other measures in regard to consistency with international obligations. Another standard of review that is also present in the WTO system is the question of what should be the standard of review of the Appellate Body towards the report and holdings of a first-level panel in the same case. Here, we will discuss only the first of these two standards of review.

We can start with the proposition that there is no explicit language in the DSU, or elsewhere in the Uruguay Round texts, regarding what should be a generic standard of review applying to all the cases brought under the DSU. However, in one of the texts of the WTO, namely the antidumping agreement text,[17] there is an explicit reference and structured standard of review that is specified to apply to cases under that particular text.[18] This adds an additional complexity to the standard of review issue in the WTO DSS. The antidumping standard of review does not apply to any other than the antidumping cases, although there is language in a Ministerial Declaration/Understanding[19] that suggests that the antidumping standard of review might be considered for use, under a concept of parallelism, at least in subsidy/countervailing duty cases. Another such document suggests that after a period of time[20] the antidumping standard of review might be considered by the members of the WTO to be appropriately applied generally for all DSU cases. It seems quite clear that this latter proposition has not been accepted by any member of the WTO, although there are advocates for such position within certain member governments, including some within the US government and also certain special interest advocates to the US government. Likewise, the Appellate Body had indicated that there is no reason for it to assume that the antidumping standard of review applies in countervailing duty cases, because the language in the relevant Ministerial Declaration is not mandatory, but only raises the possibility.[21]

To look in depth at the antidumping standard of review reveals a rather curious situation. It is quite clear from various accounts of the drafting history that the antidumping standard or review was an attempt by certain US government negotiators to build into the international dispute

169

settlement law of the WTO the so-called "Chevron doctrine" of US federal law. Under this doctrine, the US Supreme Court has ruled[22] that when federal courts are reviewing a federal administrative agency's action, and the federal agency has based its action on a statutory interpretation, the federal court should defer to that agency's interpretation if it is a reasonably and permissibly possible one under the language of the statute. It also seems quite clear, in the accounts of the negotiators, that this Chevron doctrine would not meet with the approval of the other negotiators in the Uruguay Round, but that a compromise text was arrived at (possibly in the middle of the night, with deadlines approaching). The first paragraph of Article 17(6) deals with factual determinations, and that gives considerable deference to the nation-state, as needs to be the case, since the WTO DSS has very little capacity for much in the way of detailed factual determinations. Factual trials are basically not feasible under the resources currently available.

The second paragraph of 17(6), however, is more curious. The language is as follows:

(ii) the panel shall interpret the relevant provisions of the Agreement in accordance with customary rules of interpretation of public international law. Where the panel finds that a relevant provision of the Agreement admits of more than one permissible interpretation, the panel shall find the authorities' measure to be in conformity with the Agreement if it rests upon one of those permissible interpretations.[23]

It will be noted that there are two sentences. The first sentence calls for interpretation according to customary principles of international law treaty interpretation, and, as already indicated, that generally has been deemed to mean the articulation of that customary law in the VCLT. Since the VCLT has not been accepted by a number of prominent members of the WTO, including the United States, France, and Brazil, the negotiators decided that they could not simply specify the Vienna Convention in this text. It is nonetheless almost universally understood that the reference to "customary law of treaty interpretation" means, for the most part, the Vienna Convention, particularly as to treaty interpretation.[24]

The second sentence of Article 17(6)(ii) says that if there is more than one permissible interpretation under the principles of the first sentence, then the WTO DSS should defer to the nation-state's choice of which of those permissible interpretations it would utilize.

This brings the matter to a curious controversy between Europe and the United States. Many European jurisprudential scholars and practitioners

5.6 Key jurisprudential questions I

will argue that the first sentence of 17(6)(ii) would only allow *one* permissible interpretation of treaty text and, therefore, the system would never have to address the question of more than one permissible interpretation. To this author's mind, this seems a bit naïve. For example, we have many manifestations of courts being split (five to four, three to two, or two to one) regarding interpretations, and that could be taken as evidence of the existence of more than one permissible or, at least, more than one reasonable (and reasonable might mean permissible) interpretation.

Many US officials working on dispute settlement in the WTO, as well as a number of special interest advocates urging upon the United States various views, take the position that there are a number of situations where there is more than one permissible interpretation, and a number of those situations have occurred in the cases, and yet seemingly have been ignored by the Appellate Body. Indeed, the failure of the Appellate Body sometimes even to reference the special standard of review under the antidumping text[25] has been criticized as an indication that the Appellate Body is imposing its own view on the standard of interpretation, without giving adequate prominence to the text of Article 17(6). This issue, of course, only comes up frontally in the context of antidumping cases, but those cases have, in the later years of the WTO history so far, been extremely contentious, and have given rise to very strident criticism of the Appellate Body specifically, and of the WTO DSS generally. They have also been a major source of non-compliance by the United States.

Apart from the antidumping text, the dispute settlement panels and the Appellate Body have struggled with a broader question of standard of review. They indicate some attraction to the language of the DSU, Article 11, which calls for a panel to make an "objective assessment of the matter before it, including an objective assessment of the facts of the case and the applicability of and conformity with the relevant covered agreements." Panels and the Appellate Body have used this language to develop a generally applicable broader standard of review,[26] and possibly even one that gives some deference to nation-state members or other members, although probably not as much deference as the antidumping text or certain other standards of review that governments have in their domestic jurisprudence. The Appellate Body report on the *Beef Hormones*[27] case is the first to confront directly, in an elaborate way, the question of a generic standard of review for WTO disputes, and the Appellate Body opinion provides several parameters for the subject by saying that there is not a need for complete deference to the nation-state, nor is it appropriate to have a complete *de novo* determination by the DSS in cases before it. However, the Appellate Body report is not very specific about what in between those parameters would be appropriate, and the jurisprudence it articulates in various other cases could suggest that these standards of review would differ on a case-by-case basis, depending on the context of the provisions being looked at and, of course, other elements of interpretation, such as object and purpose. Needless to say, this is an area that is receiving some advanced and particular attention, including a book and a number of other publications devoted entirely to the standard of review issue.[28]

d. Issue avoidance

The fourth and final problem to be raised in this section has to do with issues that come before the dispute settlement system that have a political flavor, or are arguably "non-justiciable" in providing for measures that cannot readily be evaluated by a juridical-type body, or generally have a strong likelihood of considerably difficult political and diplomatic consequences of an interpretation in any of the possible directions of a textual measure. Some national judicial systems have a way in which their highest court or other courts can avoid taking on such issues, such as the political questions doctrine in the United States. There is no explicit provision for that concept in the WTO, of course, and therefore, arguably, it might not be appropriate to try to establish that doctrine.

There is also the concept of *non liquet* that is recognized as meaning a situation where a juridical body will simply, frankly, and explicitly decide not to decide an issue or case. Some legal systems seem to make a *non liquet* impossible or forbidden. It is not clear that a *non liquet* is totally inappropriate or forbidden in the WTO context, but there are those who feel that generally a juridical body should not be permitted that liberty. Nevertheless, there may be other ways in which the same result can be achieved. Occasionally in the WTO cases, the first-level panel or Appellate Body talks about "judicial economy" as leading it to avoid an issue when it is not essential to the determination of a case. Professor William Davey, who has had experience both as a US Supreme Court clerk, and as the director of the Legal Services Division of the WTO during its first five years, has written a very informative article about potential analogies from US Supreme Court jurisprudence that might be utilized in the WTO context.[29] He explores what he calls "techniques of issue avoidance," such as lack of standing or legal interest, mootness, ripeness (e.g. in the United

States a requirement of "case or controversy"), exhaustion of remedies, political judicial allocation of authority ("political question"), *non-liquet*, terms of reference, judicial economy, and scope of review.

5.7 Key jurisprudential questions II: structural doctrines channeling juridical techniques of decision

Continuing with our exploration at least briefly of some of the many jurisprudential issues of the WTO dispute settlement system, this section explores three basic structural approaches to the processes of deciding cases, which the Appellate Body has largely (at least tentatively) embraced. These three are: (i) precedent; (ii) whether an "effect" or "measure" has actually occurred; and (iii) fact-finding.

a. Precedent: many flavors of a complex concept

Too often some observers and commentators ("publicists") have tended to discuss the use of precedent in judicial decision-making as involving a dichotomous choice. They talk about it in terms of whether there is the principle of *stare decisis*, or not. Like many dichotomous analyses, this is deeply flawed.[1] Actually, when one begins to examine the real world, and looks at comparisons between various legal systems, it is quickly apparent that there are a number of different approaches to the underlying problem. That underlying problem is the question of how much influence a prior decision of a judicial body should have when considering new cases.

Stare decisis is a concept generally applied only in common law jurisdictions of the world, which is to say those jurisdictions that derive their legal system, at least in a major proportion, from that of England. *Stare decisis* is a rather strong form of "precedent," and sometimes the terms are used interchangeably. Nevertheless, there are many jurisdictions of the world, both at the nation-state level and above and below (including, generally, international law juridical systems), which use a degree of precedent in their deliberations. This degree of precedent can vary from one system to another, and sometimes can vary within the same system, depending on the nature of different groupings of cases. Often, it is said that European "continental" legal systems are not based on *stare decisis* and, some would even say, are not based on a precedent system, because, arguably, the courts are supposed to work from a statutory or codified set of norms directly, without being unduly tilted by prior cases. There is even some historical practice that tended to forbid judges from citing or relying on precedent.[2] Yet when, in today's world, contemporary court reports are examined, it is often the case that there is at least reference made to prior cases, and many people generally believe that the prior cases have a considerable impact. To some extent, observation of human behavior suggests a desire for consistency, and with respect to certain societal goals, particularly in the economic area, a degree of predictability and stability has important impacts on the success of economic and other societal structures.

But there are also clearly some legal institutions, perhaps more in the order of administrative agencies, that disdain recognition of prior cases and feel no inhibitions about doing so.

Thus it seems clear that the word "precedent" has a broad application which, in some contexts, could include the phrase *stare decisis*, but in many other contexts, such as in international tribunals, or in continental European law, does not mean *stare decisis*, but instead refers to a different form of utilization of prior cases in current case considerations. This distinction has been raised in discussions with respect to the European Court of Justice (ECJ), which sits in Luxembourg. Upon examination, it is quite clear that it is not *stare decisis* in the sense of court operations either in England, other common law countries, or the United States and its Supreme Court. There is, however, some commentary that there is something of a convergence going on in judicial affairs among these different legal systems.[3]

Nevertheless, there remains a distinction. It is not easy to get to the core of that distinction, but perhaps the discussion of the US Supreme Court in *Planned Parenthood v. Casey*,[4] is most revealing, when Justice Stevens indicates in his separate opinion that he feels constrained by the precedent of *Roe v. Wade*,[5] such that, although he might have preferred to vote differently in *Planned Parenthood*, he felt an obligation to follow the precedent that was established by *Roe v. Wade*. By way of contrast, in the ECJ one can see situations where, without any apparent constraint by precedent, the Court endeavors to undertake to change a conclusion that they have adopted in some previous cases. Recently, one of the Advocate Generals, in his presentation to the ECJ, explicitly urged the Court to take that approach and the Court, in its judgment, noted a need to reconsider the older judgment.[6] Consequently, there is some daylight between the concepts of *stare decisis* and the concept of even fairly strong use of precedent, as arguably occurs in the European Court of Justice, and probably elsewhere.

In addition, other legal systems in Europe may in fact have a somewhat softer approach to precedent than does the ECJ. It is also interesting to

5.7 Key jurisprudential questions II

note that the ECJ has been applying concepts of "judicial review," which enable them to declare void ("annul") legal documents deriving from the European Commission or Council, as violating the basic treaty structure. In short, they find some of those other legal measures "unconstitutional," even though, in the legal systems of many EU member states, there appears to be no doctrine of judicial review that strong.[7]

International tribunals surely do not follow *stare decisis*. The Statute of the International Court of Justice (ICJ) states, in Article 59: "The decision of the Court has no binding force except between the parties and in respect of that particular case."[8] Likewise, the general perception under international law is that, although there is a "precedential effect" that seems to be operating de facto and in practice, there is certainly not *stare decisis*, and in some cases, not a very strong precedent effect.

Taking all of this into account, as well as a number of other examples in the world and in the literature, it seems that a better approach to the word "precedent" is to view it as a multi-layered concept, or at least as having a number of different approaches of different flavors. Perhaps the most stringent "precedent" effect is *stare decisis*, although even that is, in some cases, perhaps arguably in the United States and in the United Kingdom, less stringent than it was some decades ago. The ECJ is clearly following an approach of considerable deference to its own prior cases. It thus might be considered the next level away from *stare decisis*. Likewise, the International Court of Justice appears to relish citations of its previous cases. One can identify other legal systems that actually give even less deference and, therefore, might be considered to be another step down the ladder of a "precedent rigor index." There could be a number of other gradations and, in particular towards the bottom, there could simply be an attitude that the juridical body or administrative tribunal would simply "look at" or "take into account" the reasoning of prior cases, but feel under no particular obligation to follow those cases or be very consistent with them. Of course, in the background of all of this is the extensive jurisprudential literature (particularly in the United States) that notes that courts have a number of different ways to get around, or avoid, the rigor of *stare decisis*, such as by "distinguishing a case," or other interpretive techniques.[9]

Turning then to the issue of precedent in the WTO (and GATT), we can detect a fairly strong use of precedent. First, as explored in section 5.2, the GATT "juridical process" has an interesting historical evolution, based on very little treaty text. In many ways, it gradually developed a practice within its dispute settlement procedures which, over time and with trial and error, gave more recognition and deference to prior cases. By the

1980s, the system was much more rigorously "legalistic" in that regard, and there was a rather persistent referencing of prior cases to guide the thinking of the panels (at that time, there was no appellate process). Consequently, it is fair to say that there was some precedent effect, that it was not *stare decisis*, and it was probably not as rigorous or constraining as even the ECJ. It may be argued, and was probably the case in the earlier decades of GATT, that the panels considered themselves more part of a "diplomatic process," with some responsibility to try to encourage a settlement between the disputants. Thus, they were less "legalistic," and less deferential to their prior cases. Of course, the panels then (as now) were ad hoc, and appointed only for a particular case, although certain individuals might find themselves, over time, having been a member of a number of panels. Since there was no single body that was permanently in session, there was probably less thinking about deferring to prior cases and, certainly until GATT set up a legal unit at the beginning of the 1980s, the panels often did not have much in the way of staff assistance to point out the existence of prior relevant GATT panel reports to a panel currently considering a new measure.

In light of the above, it is interesting to find in the WTO "Charter,"[10] Article XVI(1), the provision noted also in section 4.4.a of this book:

Except as otherwise provided under this Agreement or the Multilateral Trade Agreements, the WTO shall be guided by the decisions, procedures and customary practices followed by the CONTRACTING PARTIES to GATT 1947 and the bodies established in the framework of GATT 1947.

This "guidance clause" provides a treaty basis for the WTO DSS, giving deference to at least the GATT cases and, of course, if for the GATT cases, why not their own WTO cases? Thus it was articulated in a number of WTO cases that the prior cases were relevant and should be taken into consideration. As discussed before, one of the earliest cases, the *Japan – Alcoholic Beverages* case,[11] actually addressed the legal impact of prior cases, noting that one case alone did not constitute a "practice under the agreement," in the sense of the language of the VCLT. Nevertheless, the practice of relying on prior cases is very extensive now, and in a case in 2003, a panel report concerning steel safeguards[12] was 1,000 pages long, and included 5,800 footnotes, almost all of which were notes to prior WTO or GATT cases.

There is another interesting facet of this question under the WTO jurisprudence, which did not exist under GATT. The WTO Charter, for the first time, provides an explicit power for the Ministerial Conference and the General Council to "adopt interpretations of this agreement and of the multilateral trade agreements," such adoption requiring a three-fourths majority of all the members. In the case of GATT, there were some arguments towards the end of the GATT history that the panel reports became a sort of "new law," binding on all contracting parties for the future, although this was clearly not the implication of an adopted panel decision.[13] In the light of the new authority to adopt "interpretations" granted explicitly to the Ministerial Conference and the General Council, it would seem that the "precedential impact" of dispute settlement reports under the WTO is probably even less than under GATT. This is because, under GATT, at least there could be a plausible argument that the result of the process, including adoption by the contracting parties (ostensibly by majority vote, but actually in practice by consensus), was an adoption of a definitive interpretation. Under the WTO, however, it is clear that the power to issue a "definitive interpretation," binding on all members of the organization, is reserved to the special authority of the Ministerial Conference and the General Council and, therefore, is not available as part of the authority of the DSS.

In sum, it can be argued that there is quite a powerful precedent effect in the jurisprudence of the WTO, but that it is certainly not *stare decisis*, and it is not so powerful as to require panels or the Appellate Body considering new cases to follow prior cases, with the possible exception that once prior cases have been numerous regarding a particular issue and approach, and apparently accepted by all members of the WTO, then the language of the Vienna Convention about "practice under the agreement," may suggest a stronger impact. But short of that situation, it appears that the "flavor" of the precedent effect in the WTO is still somewhat fluid, and possibly will remain somewhat fluid for the time being.

The Appellate Body of the WTO has consistently made reference to its own prior cases. In *Shrimp–Turtle*, for example, it chastised the first-level panel for not paying close enough attention to the Appellate Body's logical approach in the prior case of *US – Gasoline* import measures.[14] Likewise, the Appellate Body has recently stated quite explicitly that prior Appellate Body reports have a precedent effect, at least upon panels.[15]

b. Effects or the need for a "measure"

An important and fascinating jurisprudential issue arose in the GATT jurisprudence, and is carried forward with considerable attention in the WTO DS practice. This is the question that arises when a statute or other legal instrument of a nation-state gives authority to an administrative body or other legal body to take measures which would be in violation (or at least nullification or impairment) of some of the many treaty obligations of the large WTO Uruguay Round agreement.

A question arises whether a complaint can be effective against a member nation because of the existence of the authority "as such," even though no action has been taken under that authority. Another question is how to evaluate whether an action can be complained against even if no actual "effect" has occurred.

This issue came up in GATT, as discussed in section 5.2, the *Oil Fee* case[16] as well as in some other cases, where it was decided that, at least with respect to the national treatment obligation under Article III, when a violation was noted by the panel, this became a "prima facie nullification or impairment," suggesting that the defending nation had the burden of refuting the presumption. However, as noted earlier, in the *Oil Fee* case, as in some other cases, the panel determined that no rebuttal information would be listened to. As such, their reasoning was that the particular effects of the particular measure were not relevant.[17]

There was also some development in GATT regarding the distinction between a statutory "mandatory provision," which would require action by another entity of the government, which action would be a violation, and, on the other hand, a "non-mandatory," or "discretionary" authority. In the latter case, there would not be found a "violation" until some particular measure under it had occurred.[18]

In the WTO, one of the most prominent cases facing this question was the case brought by the European Communities against the United States with respect to Section 301 of its Trade Act of 1974, outlining a procedure by which domestic interests could petition to the US Trade Representative (USTR) for study and possible action by USTR against foreign measures that were harming US trade.[19] The complainant argued that assistance of the statutory authority, particularly an authority that was not mandatory, was itself a violation of WTO obligations and therefore constituted presumptive nullification or impairment. The United States naturally argued that this was not the case, but went on to provide assurances to the WTO panel that its policy and authority on this matter was such that it would never take such action that would violate the WTO. The panel thus decided that the statute itself could be a violation, but decided in favor of the United States, that in the particular instance, and given the assurances of the US government advocates, there was not a violation, since even though there was an authority for measures that

5.7 Key jurisprudential questions II

would be a violation the United States had given strong assurances that it would never use it in this way. Thus, arguably, the "effects on the conditions of competition" were not in play so as to damage or have a "chilling effect" on the trade of the complainants. This panel opinion was not appealed. Observers noted that each side had won a point, and some, more cynical, observers referred to this panel report as "a diplomatic masterpiece, but a jurisprudential disaster."[20]

The language of the *Section 301* report is especially interesting. It stresses the importance of the recognition that non-government market participants in the world could be affected, and thus should be part of the considerations that go into whether there was a violation or nullification/impairment. For example, the panel stated,

It would be entirely wrong to consider that the position of individuals is of no relevance to the GATT/WTO legal matrix. Many of the benefits to Members which are meant to flow as a result of the acceptance of various disciplines under the GATT/WTO depend on the activity of individual economic operators in the national and global market places. The purpose of many of these disciplines, indeed one of the primary objects of the GATT/WTO as a whole, is to produce certain market conditions which would allow this individual activity to flourish.[21]

The panel listed in a footnote numerous prior GATT cases to support its view.

Subsequently, another case raising the same issue has occurred, namely the case brought by the European Communities against the United States 1916 Antidumping Act.[22] This is a curious US statute that authorizes a form of antidumping action by petition of private parties in the United States to the court for a procedure that is somewhat parallel to an antitrust, treble damage action, and particularly requires a specific intent. There has never been a successful case under the 1916 Act under which the a US court has awarded such treble damages, but the argument that was accepted by the WTO DSS (including the appeal), was that the mere existence of the statute had "an effect on competition," and would have a chilling effect on traders. Indeed, there is some evidence to that effect, since some cases have been brought, and have required extensive legal activity, with considerable cost to potential foreign defendant exporters to the US market.

One of the many perplexities of such a case is to figure out how the remedies under the DSU would apply. Although it should be assumed that there is an obligation on the United States to bring its law into conformity with the obligations of the WTO and, therefore, probably to repeal the statute, the question is what the complainants would be allowed to do by way of "retaliation" or other measures of "compensation," if the United States did not repeal the statute. Since such retaliatory-type measures are limited by the DSU to that which is "equivalent to the level of the nullification or impairment,"[23] and since there has been no measure under the 1916 Act, it becomes quite difficult to figure out what is the equivalent of the effect of the "nullification or impairment." One suggestion has been that the complaining member should be authorized to introduce into its own law a "mirror-image statute," which would only apply to the losing party's trade. Needless to say, these are messy concepts to implement.

Another case, commonly known as the *Byrd Amendment* case,[24] raises some similar problems, with the United States arguing that the complainant cannot go directly to "retaliatory" compensation measures, but must, instead, start a new case because it had not alleged any amount of nullification or impairment in the case already decided against the United States.

c. Fact-finding: a problem of resources as well as concept

Many legal systems face the tension over fact versus law. For example, in many common law jurisdictions there arise difficult line-drawing issues between fact and law, because juries generally are instructed as to the law by the court and then are asked to make findings of the fact under the legal principles of the court. In addition, an appeal can often only be based on questions or errors of law, and not of fact. In many of these jurisdictions, there is a fairly extensive experience with the difficulty of drawing a line between issues of fact and issues of law. For example, is the question of whether the facts actually fulfill a certain legal standard a question of fact or a question of law? In this author's view, this is a question of law, although it very much involves considerations of what the facts really are.

Focusing more specifically on fact-finding in the WTO DSS, clearly the system has been trying to find its way on some of these issues. The DSU is not very helpful. It provides some guidance in Article 11, when it states that a panel "should make an objective assessment of the matter before it, including an objective assessment of the facts of the case and the applicability of and conformity with the relevant covered agreements."[25] This suggests that the panels do indeed have responsibilities both as to fact-finding and to the applicable law. But appeals under DSU Article 17(6), are limited to "issues of law covered in the panel report and legal

5.7 Key jurisprudential questions II

interpretations developed by the panel."[26] Thus, it appears that the panel's findings on fact have to be given deference, if not finality. The Appellate Body has found itself in an odd situation occasionally, when it has decided that the panel's reasoning followed a path that the Appellate Body felt was incorrect. Therefore, as an exercise in "completing the analysis," the Appellate Body needed to pay attention to a different legal situation, which, however, had not been taken up by the first-level panel, so that the facts supporting that issue were therefore not available. This has led the Appellate Body to decline to take up the question that might otherwise have finished the analysis.[27]

In addition, there is an intense resource question with respect to fact-finding in the WTO DSS. This was brought out poignantly in the *Fuji Film* case,[28] which involved the presentation by the United States to the WTO panel of dozens of boxes of documents by which the United States was trying to show the impact of certain allegedly anti-competitive situations in Japan against the import of film from the United States (and particularly the Kodak company). Merely to evaluate such an extensive body of documentation itself stretched the resources of the legal services at the WTO (this case was not appealed when the panel ruled against the United States on its complaint). For the WTO DSS to have an extended fact hearing would be out of the question, simply because the budget or other resources for such do not exist. Thus, certain kinds of issues (possibly in future issues regarding competition) seem out of reach of the current WTO DSS. Indeed, there is a tendency for the DSS to rely very heavily on the fact statements of the parties, unless there is specific refutation.

Also to be noted is DSU Article 13, which gives the panel "the right to seek information and technical advice from any individual or body which it deems appropriate." This is a very broad authority, but, of course, its real limitation is the amount of resources available. Among other issues that this raises is whether facts could be elicited under the Article 13 right to seek information, or indeed, whether factual information could be offered by an *amicus curiae* brief to the panel. As noted earlier in this chapter, the Appellate Body has ruled that panels may accept such information.

The antidumping text, Article 17(6),[29] which expresses the antidumping standard of review, devotes its first paragraph to fact-finding, and in this text the panel is obligated to give great deference to the national government authority's establishment of the facts. If the establishment of the facts was "proper," and the evaluation was unbiased and objective, then, even though the panel might have reached a different conclusion, the evaluation shall not be overturned.[30] This great deference to the nation-state is probably necessitated anyway, because of the lack of resources mentioned above. The antidumping text language only applies, of course, to the antidumping cases, but it would not be surprising to find this same approach used by analogy by the DSS, perhaps under its interpretation of the Article 11 "objective assessment of the matter."

Finally, a very important consideration regarding this question of fact-finding is how the system will handle "scientific fact," when such scientific evidence is crucial to a determination of the DSS. This came up most prominently in the *Beef Hormones* case,[31] but also has been present in some other cases, and particularly will play a part in the potential genetically modified organisms (GMO) case, which is in process.[32] The panel in the *Beef Hormones* case ingeniously designed a system of getting advice from a certain small number of scientific experts. This procedure is not exactly congruent with the language in the DSU, but the procedure was approved by the Appellate Body.[33] Thus we have a good precedent for obtaining scientific information in the DSS cases.

5.8 Key jurisprudential questions III: treaty interpretation

Just as the question of precedent, discussed in section 5.7, has "many flavors," so too do techniques of treaty interpretation. Indeed, treaty interpretation techniques come in many more flavors, and they are not in a linear scale by any means. Furthermore, like many of the other principles discussed in this chapter, the choices by a juridical body for an international institution created by a treaty, as to what techniques will be used to interpret that treaty, can have profound effects on the "allocation of power," both vertical and horizontal. For example, as to vertical allocation of power, very important questions of treaty interpretation involve the appropriateness of "gap-filling," and the appropriateness of techniques such as "evolutionary" or "teleological." These different techniques of treaty interpretation each engage, to a different degree, the question of "consent" of the member or nation-state concerned, as we shall see. In addition, the techniques of interpretation, like many of the other jurisprudential principles of the WTO Dispute Settlement System (DSS), also involve an allocation of power between the juridical body of an institution and the other parts of the institution, which we could term diplomatic/legislative. As has already been mentioned in Chapter 4 and earlier in Chapter 5, certain tensions between a juridical body and other parts of an institution are not infrequent, because the juridical body can, by interpretation, constrain or enlarge various activities relating to goals

5.8 Key jurisprudential questions III

of the institution. It can also be noted that a number of the tension issues which occur in international law subjects also occur in domestic legal systems, perhaps even more often, and with more pronounced effect. Thus some of the commentary about issues at the national level, such as teleological interpretation or balancing, is highly relevant to the international scene, as noted in several places below.[1]

With respect to this dimension of the WTO, the DSU is obviously critical, and it contains evidence that the diplomats and negotiators who drafted the DSU were giving some thought to these allocation problems. As noted in section 5.3, the DSU itself sets forth several different goals concerning dispute settlement, and, as we have also noted, there are quite a large number of different goals, some of them conflicting, when it comes to dispute settlement in international bodies generally. Some of those goals are expressed in Article 3(2) of the DSU, including the phrase that a "central element" of the DSS is "providing security and predictability to the multilateral trading system." This goal of developing a jurisprudence that would enhance security and predictability in turn implies the use of precedent in some form as well as certain techniques of treaty interpretation.

Article 3(2) also specifies that "recommendation and rulings of the DSB cannot add to or diminish the rights and obligations provided in the covered agreements." The meaning of this language is certainly not clear, but it has sometimes been suggested that it was intended to inhibit too much "judicial activism" in the activity of the juridical body. In other words, some have thought that this is intended to constrain the techniques of interpretation that the DSS could use. Others doubt this. The DSU expresses a desire that the panel procedures result in "high-quality panel reports" (Art. 12(2)), and notes that panel procedures "should provide sufficient flexibility so as to ensure" that result, while not "unduly delaying the panel process."

In fact, as observers and practitioners of international law relating to treaties know well, there are a very large number of interpretive techniques. There is no attempt in this brief overview to inventory all of them, but most lists of treaty interpretive techniques would include the items set forth in the footnote.[2] Readers will certainly recognize that some, but not all, of these treaty interpretation techniques are embodied in the language of the VCLT, and they will recall that the VCLT is not applicable "as such" in many situations, particularly regarding large multilateral organizations, because the VCLT has not been ratified by many of the members. This is particularly true of the WTO.[3] Although not applicable as a treaty, the language of the VCLT nevertheless has been widely accepted as expressing the customary international law of treaties, at least as to interpretation, and, therefore, it is often referred to in contexts where it does not strictly apply as a treaty. This is certainly the case in the WTO (and in GATT before it), where panels have, on several important occasions, quoted extensively from the VCLT, particularly as to interpretation in Articles 31 and 32, as noted earlier in this chapter.

However, there is room for rethinking the application and adequacy of the VCLT regarding treaty interpretation. It can be questioned whether that treaty, in many instances, seems more suited to application to bilateral treaty situations (or at least small group situations) than to large on-going, multilateral treaties. These large multilateral treaties have aspects resembling more a "constitution" than a bilateral contract.

Among other considerations which would suggest a different treatment for large membership treaties is that often these cannot practically be amended or changed, and thus are subject to the problems of "treaty rigidity" noted in Chapter 2.

A critically important issue sometimes included in the subject of treaty interpretation can be roughly characterized as "gap-filling." In some cases, there are actual gaps in the treaty, in other words, the treaty is totally silent with regard to how it should apply in some circumstances. In other cases, there is treaty language that is applicable, but the treaty language is sufficiently ambiguous that it could reasonably be interpreted in several different ways. One could ask why there are such gaps or ambiguities. As noted in a previous section, experienced practitioners in international law and treaty making know full well that, quite often, it is necessary to leave some matters not discussed in a treaty or to leave some of the terms in a treaty ambiguous, rather than trying to define them precisely, with the purpose of actually achieving "closure," meaning, to obtain a finished agreement on paper, to which all necessary parties can consent. These "studied" gaps or ambiguities pose a conceptual problem for any institution, either at an international, national, or sub-federal level.

There are some opposed views on how to approach these gaps and ambiguities. On the one hand, one could argue that when the draftspersons have consciously left a gap or ambiguity, if they know that there is a juridical body as part of the institutional framework they have, in essence, "delegated" to that body the resolution of disputes about such interpretations when they arise. The opposing view is that such approach lacks consent and, under older views, the lack of consent should suggest that the treaty does not constrain nation-state behavior. Indeed, there is even a Latin phrase that relates to this issue, namely, *in dubio mitius*.

5.8 Key jurisprudential questions III

This phrase has been invoked in some situations in international law and, indeed, used in one footnote in a WTO appellate report and also in some panel reports and some national government WTO advocacy submissions.[4] It has not been demonstrated that *in dubio mitius* is part of the customary international law of treaty interpretation (and, indeed, there is some evidence that it was purposely left out of the language of the VCLT text[5]). Furthermore, such a notion, at least in the context of an important international institution with many nation-state members, is seriously damaging to the survivability and ongoing efficiency and the ability to achieve the goals of the organization. Among other things, to emphasize that principle in treaty interpretation is to tear the treaty apart, in the sense of making it apply in a different sense for different members in different situations. For the WTO, this defeats the very purpose of DSU Article 3(2), the need for providing security and predictability. In addition, it is a static view of international organizations, inhibiting such organization from being able to adapt to changing conditions in the world, particularly economic changes, in a way that it would allow it better to fulfill its mission.

Particularly in the case of large membership treaties which include a dispute settlement procedure, that procedure has to develop an appropriate and objective way to go about making determinations on ambiguous language and filling gaps (at least up to a point where it could be argued that the gap filling really becomes law-making, whatever that means). To provide that every case must tilt in favor of whatever a particular country has decided to do in its own unilateral view of gap filling or ambiguity resolution, could lead to great disparities among nations in the way in which they are carrying out what otherwise should be uniform obligations applying to them all. It would also appear to be a relatively extreme view of "state consent theory" of international legal norm making, as discussed in Chapter 2.

In short, it could be argued that an ambiguity or a gap is, in a sense, a delegation by the treaty participants to the process designed in the treaty for resolving the differences about ambiguities and gaps, that is, the dispute settlement system. For the broad multilateral treaty, particularly those establishing an international organization, to be viable over a long period of time, and to best carry out the goals of cooperation and joint application of activities of the organization so as to best achieve the underlying policy goals of the organization, it is necessary to understand that some situations will call for interpretations and "gap" filling which will not be entirely congruent with the views of one particular member, or a few members, of the organization, at the time of drafting the treaty or later. Indeed, since the large treaty members should be presumed to accept policies ("good faith"?) which favor activity that will assist the treaty-made institution in successfully achieving its mission, which mission was agreed, it can (and should) be argued that the treaty members have "consented" to the gap-filling which is necessary to fulfill that goal. An intriguing and important book concerning interpretation of various national law texts outlines important arguments relevant to the ideas expressed in this paragraph.[6]

There are other reasons why gaps and ambiguities occur, of course. Some of them may simply be errors or mistakes of the negotiators. In addition, the negotiators know full well that they cannot cover every conceivable problem that may arise as a matter of interpretation of the treaty, so they must, to some extent, rely upon the good faith and the effectiveness of a juridical-type institution to fill in the lacunae of the organization.

Another observable aspect of treaty interpretation, particularly in the context of an ongoing, important institution with many members, is the erroneous notion of some politicians, statesmen, and diplomats that treaty interpretation is essentially a near-mathematical exercise. This view sometimes results from a lack of legal training or experience with legal institutions on the part of the persons holding this view. In other cases, it is more an advocacy position adopted to achieve a particular outcome in the treaty interpretation that is desired by the advocate. But when one experiences in detail the problems of treaty interpretation, it becomes obvious both how complex treaty interpretation can be and how there may be different approaches.

The WTO Appellate Body, in *Japan – Alcoholic Beverages*,[7] considered the phrase "like product," which occurs in many places in the Uruguay Round text, either in the form just mentioned or in the similar form "like and competitive products."[8] The Appellate Body noted that the phrase "like product" requires that the Appellate Body examine that phrase on a "case by case basis," and that the context of the language was crucial. By that, it clearly meant that if the phrase occurs in a different context, the exact same words may be interpreted differently. The Appellate Body even used the analogy for the phrase "like product" of interpretations being "accordion-like" – stretching and contracting, depending on the context and other facets. In a later *Asbestos* case,[9] the Appellate Body made clear that interpretation of the "like product" phrase in Article III(4) of GATT should be approached differently than in the case of Article III(2).

5.8 Key jurisprudential questions III

A book devoted entirely to the WTO phrase "like product"[10] is a wonderful study of the process of interpretation of treaties, demonstrating the number of different interpretations of that phrase that might be valid. In the author's analysis, it is noted that various types of economic policy assumptions could well lead to quite different interpretations in particular and complex cases. The *Alcoholic Beverages* cases really touch on certain cultural attributes of consumers, and these can play a part in interpretation, as can the question of whether one is designing the rules to apply somewhat more advantageously to producers on the one hand, or to consumers on the other. In a world in which products move through several countries before developing their finished characteristics, the interpretive questions become even more complex.

The Appellate Body, at least in its first six or eight years, seemed to be taking a very "textual" approach to its interpretations, albeit in some particular cases manifesting departures from that. This textual approach was clearly motivated by the language of the VCLT. One of the former members of the Appellate Body, Dr. Claus-Dieter Ehlermann, has written a very revealing commentary about this process,[11] noting that the rationale of its strong textual bent was to establish the credibility of the Appellate Body as a new institution, by trying to be as objective as possible and avoiding circumstances and activities that would allow nation-state governments (members of the WTO or otherwise) to accuse the Appellate Body of tilting one way or another for bias reasons. This commentary raises the question whether the strong textualism of the Appellate Body needs to continue. However, there certainly are arguments in favor of such an approach that would motivate its continuing in that direction.

There are several treaty interpretation concepts, however, that do not necessarily square completely with the VCLT traditional approach, particularly in the context of an ongoing, permanent, and very important international institution with a large and growing membership. This may be particularly true in the case of economic organizations, since the structure of markets tends to give some premium to predictability and stability (which can, in turn, reduce the so-called "risk premium" described by economists).[12]

One of these principles that does not so easily square with the VCLT is the idea of "evolutionary" interpretation. This has been mentioned in the famous *Shrimp–Turtle* case, but also in several other cases.[13] This is analogous to some of the profound struggles in nation-state constitutional interpretation, particularly that of the United States, where on the one hand there are some authorities that wish to use a "static" or "originalist" interpretation of the constitution, clinging to interpretations that can be demonstrated from the contemporary evidence of the drafting of the constitution, and, on the other hand, those who view the constitution as a "living" document, which must evolve with the times and with changes in world and societal circumstances and mores.[14] The "originalist" view of document interpretation has been described, by one important judicial scholar and member of a court, as an interesting new version of "ancestor worship."[15]

Another concept that relates to treaty interpretation is the idea of "teleological" interpretation. The notion here seems to be to emphasize much more the basic goals of the organization, and to try to interpret its provisions in such a way as to enhance the long-term efficiency or ability to carry out those goals.[16] Again, this concept implies a somewhat more living and evolving notion about how at least the institutional structure, or "charter," of an important, ongoing, large-membership economic institution should be handled.

One of the most important, indeed, perhaps the single most important, case of the WTO jurisprudence so far, in the sense of fundamental and "constitutional" concepts, is the *Shrimp–Turtle* case.[17] This case touches on a number of the concepts mentioned earlier about interpreting the WTO's objectives and some other concepts outlined in section 5.5. The case was brought by four developing country members of the WTO against the United States, arguing that the United States was prohibiting the importation of shrimp into the United States on the basis of measures that were inconsistent with US obligations under the WTO. The rationale for the US action was that the harvesting of shrimp in certain ways tends to kill turtles, some of which are endangered species. Consequently the United States purported to regulate its importation of shrimp in such a manner as to require the exporting nation-state to take measures to ensure that turtle extruder devices, or other means to prevent harming the turtles, were utilized in the gathering of shrimp. The first-level panel ruled using quite strong language against the United States, based partly on its view that the unilateral measures were inappropriate in a multilateral organization. The Appellate Body dramatically modified the language of the first-level panel, but nevertheless concluded that, as applied, the US measures were not consistent with its obligations. After this report, the United States was able to change its practices by administrative changes (without seeking legislation from Congress) and argued that those changes brought its program into consistency with the WTO. One member of the original group of four complainants disagreed with that approach of the United

5.8 Key jurisprudential questions III

States, and brought another, follow-up case against the United States under the procedures of the DSU. This also went to a panel and then to the Appellate Body. This time, the Appellate Body upheld the US program, in light of the changes that it had made. This case is extraordinarily complex and nuanced, and cannot be thoroughly reported here, but a few broad ideas about the case can be briefly set forth.

One such idea is the explicit invocation of the Appellate Body of an "evolutionary" principle of interpretation, particularly relating to language speaking of "exhaustible natural resources" as an exception under Article XX(g) of GATT. The basic question there was whether a living animal could be considered an exhaustible natural resource, and the Appellate Body rendered its opinion that it could be, even though at the time of the origin of this language, it may have been primarily considered to apply to minerals and other fixed and non-living resources. The Appellate Body opinion was partly based on the idea of the developing international programs to save endangered species.

A second feature of the *Shrimp–Turtle* case is the idea that non-trade policies must be considered in connection with the trade policies of the WTO. This is a remarkable idea, with the effect of broadening the attention and priorities of the WTO. The Appellate Body gave a number of reasons for including environmental policies as part of the policy landscape of the WTO, particularly when interpreting the language of GATT Article XX "Chapeau" (the preamble to Article XX).[18] Part of the reasoning was drawn from the preamble to the WTO Charter itself, as well as from other international organizational activities for the protection of the environment. This was a striking jurisprudential development, and it led some observers to say that the Appellate Body had "saved the WTO," since a great deal of the criticism of the WTO was coming from the environmentalists. On the other hand, it engendered considerable opposition from other quarters, some of which were the developing countries that brought the case and felt that they were being made vulnerable to unilateral actions by the United States, based on policies to which they had not necessarily agreed. In this connection, the extraordinarily nuanced and qualified Appellate Body language, concerning the question of "unilateral actions," was intriguing. The Appellate Body stated in paragraph 121 of its report:

It appears to us, however, that conditioning access to a Member's domestic market on whether exporting Members comply with, or adopt, a policy or policies unilaterally prescribed by the importing Member may, to some degree, be a common aspect of measures falling within the scope of one or another of the exceptions (a) to (j) of Article XX. Paragraphs (a) to (j) comprise measures that are recognized as exceptions to substantive obligations established in GATT 1994, because the domestic policies embodied in such measures have been recognized as important and legitimate in character. It is not necessary to assume that requiring from exporting countries compliance with, or adoption of, certain policies (although covered in principle by one or another of the exceptions) prescribed by the importing country, renders a measure a priori incapable of justification under Article XX. Such an interpretation renders most, if not all, of the specific exceptions of Article XX inutile, a result abhorrent to the principles of interpretation we are bound to apply.[19]

The Appellate Body, in this, its first *Shrimp–Turtle* opinion, added to its consideration of "unilateralism" in paragraph 121, quoted above, a series of specific problems it saw in the US measure, as those would be considered in the interpretation of the Article XX Chapeau language, relating to "unjustifiable discrimination" and "arbitrary discrimination." The Appellate Body felt that it had to do this in a way that would take account of the environmental policies, and thus had to develop a "balancing approach" between competing norms. Again, this was quite profound and nuanced. Opponents to that would argue that the "balancing" in situations like this should be done by the nation-state. But of course, individual national balancing of that type could only result in large variations in different parts of the world, and in different circumstances, regarding the meaning of the language. The opposite approach, to be totally textual and not balancing any non-trade policies, could ultimately lead to the inability of the organization to maintain a degree of legitimacy that would enable it to carry out its broader objectives relating to trade liberalization.

Again, commentary about comparable national law concepts seem appropriate, since the tensions and thought processes are similar and relevant. One such commentary notes that "proportionality" (a term more often used in Europe) is virtually the same as balancing, and argues that "proportionality" is the "ultimate rule of law," and is an integral and indispensable part of every constitution which is essential to the legitimation of "judicial review."[20]

One final aspect of the *Shrimp–Turtle* case that does bear mentioning is the fact that the Appellate Body, in its determinations regarding the US measure, seems actually to have entertained what is called in GATT and WTO jurisprudence a process and production method (PPM).[21] PPMs had been involved in previous cases, particularly in the GATT cases involving the *Tuna–Dolphin* disputes,[22] which had some parallels to the *Shrimp–Turtle* facts. The *Tuna–Dolphin* cases were quite clear in establishing the idea,

5.8 Key jurisprudential questions III

relying on some older "precedents" of GATT, that the "like product" phrase in Article III should not involve matters occurring in the production of a product, but only matters that were involved in the characteristics of the product itself. The worry, clearly, is that of the "slippery slope," which could lead to a whole variety of governmental claims for exceptions for PPMs, including even a demand that imported products carry the same regulatory burdens and wage levels at the production phase as those of the importing country (which would result in a dramatic undermining of comparative advantage and trade liberalization). The Appellate Body, in the *Shrimp–Turtle* case, basically endorsed the possibility of a PPM, without ever mentioning the PPM problem or mentioning that it was shifting in emphasis, at least for that particular case, away from the more traditional attitudes towards PPMs in GATT.

There are, of course, other, very interesting facets of the *Shrimp–Turtle* case that cannot be dealt with here but were briefly listed in section 5.5.

Relevant to this discussion is the curious language in the Dispute Settlement Understanding mentioned at the beginning of this section. The DSU Article 3(2), last sentence, states that "Recommendations and rulings of the DSB cannot add to or diminish the rights and obligations provided in the covered agreements." Many observers have struggled with the meaning of this sentence, and indeed some who participated in negotiating that language do not pretend to know what it means, or whether it was intended to mean anything. Let us examine this language in the light of the total institution in which it is set. This institution includes the dispute settlement procedures. Thus what are the "rights and obligations" provided? They are set forth in the thousands of pages of the overall treaty, but that includes the dispute settlement procedures themselves as part of the DSU, which is Annex 2 of the WTO Charter. Thus it can be argued that any "right or obligation" is defined by the dispute settlement procedures, and thus any DSB recommendations or rulings are part of the "rights and obligations." To some extent there is thus circularity. If the DSU language means something more (or different), perhaps it is only an admonition to the individuals who must carry out the DS procedures to do so with caution and due regard to the traditions and established practices (and expectations?) of the disputing members. Who, then, will judge whether "caution and due regard" has been adequately supplied? It will probably be the DS system participants (DSB, panelists, Appellate Body members, etc.) themselves. Any other conclusion leads to difficulties which could diminish the ability of the institution to carry out its responsibilities, and that in turn would almost surely "diminish the rights and obligations" with respect to some members of the organization.

In summing up this section, it is easy to see that treaty interpretation is many times more complicated than many individuals involved in the processes of treaty interpretation have thought. It is extraordinarily varied, and it touches on a number of different institutional, or "constitutional" policies, as well as challenging the older, "consent" theory notions of Westphalian "sovereignty," depending on how the interpretive processes will relate to the ongoing viability and evolution of institutions. In many ways, treaty interpretation illustrates important implications of detailed aspects of modern tensions between "sovereignty" and "international institutionalism," as outlined in Chapter 2.

5.9 Key jurisprudential questions IV: dispute settlement reports and national law

In Chapter 4, at section 4.6, we discussed the relationship of the WTO and the Uruguay Round treaty to the legal systems of the member nation-states and the European Union. There we noted that an important related issue is the legal position of an adopted WTO DS report in the jurisprudence of national (or regional) legal systems. This section will provide an overview of this complex subject. In the next section, 5.10, the broader question of "compliance" or "implementation" generally, including some note about implementation of dispute reports, will be taken up. Here we focus on the national laws and legal structures which relate to these reports. Section 5.11 will discuss reform proposals for the WTO DS system, and there touch again on ideas for possible changes in that system which might affect the domestic national legal significance of a DS report.

A starting point to this discussion is the subject of section 4.6, mentioned above. It appears that four situations can be analyzed, based on whether the underlying treaty on which the WTO and its DS system is based is considered to be "directly applicable" (self-executing) or not, and whether the situation involves a WTO member that is a disputant to which the DS report applies, or not. This holds some key to the national law status of a DS report, although an analysis tends to show that the distinction may not always make much difference to that status.

If the treaty is self-executing, or directly applicable, then the domestic courts and legal system should normally implement the treaty in a manner similar to statutory law.[1] If the nation or regional unit concerned is a disputant to which the DS report is addressed, then presumably that nation

5.9 Key jurisprudential questions IV

or unit would be obligated as a matter of international law to carry out the report, although a question in this regard was taken up in section 5.6, and in addition there are a number of questions as to exactly what is the required implementation (usually to "bring [the nation's measures] . . . into conformity with its obligations under that agreement").[2] Thus there could be some "slippage" in the application of the treaty by a national or regional WTO member related to the techniques of interpreting such member's exact obligation either under the treaty or the wording of the "judgment" in the report.

If the situation involves a WTO member other than a DS report affected disputant, which member directly applies the treaty, then the interpretation would probably relate only to the treaty obligation, with the delicate question of interpreting the treaty provision in the light of the DS report. Since the report is not *stare decisis* (see section 5.7), it is not technically binding on such member, but that member's courts and legal institutions would nevertheless have to come to a judgment about the treaty's meaning, knowing that a certain fairly strong degree of "precedent" effect should influence that judgment. Of course, after a series of such "precedents," there may be a stronger sense of "practice in the application of the treaty" (VCLT language[3]) to lead to a conclusion on the meaning of the treaty.

If the situation involves a WTO member which *does not directly* apply the WTO treaty provisions (at least those provisions relevant to its case), then the matter is a bit different. Even in the case of a disputant member to which the DS report applies, that member's jurisprudence may be such that the member would not directly apply the treaty and therefore not directly apply the DS reports or "judgments." But this would not mean that the DS report is irrelevant any more than the treaty language is irrelevant (as discussed in section 4.6 concerning treaty status in members' domestic jurisprudence.) The appropriate approach here would be that as a matter of international law the treaty binds the member, and since the disputant member is bound under the treaty provisions of the DSU to carry out (in one way or another) the findings of the DS report, one question for that member is how to appraise the international law obligation of those findings. It would likely argue that the DS report does not have direct application any more than the treaty would. But as in the situation previously discussed above for directly applied treaty law of a non-disputant, there are other effects of the treaty even when it is not "directly" (statute-like) applied, including the "consistency principle" like that in the US *Charming Betsy* case.[4]

The fourth situation is the circumstance where a WTO member which does not apply the treaty directly also is not a disputant to which the DS report is addressed. Now this member is trying to ascertain its IL obligation under the treaty, and it must appraise the impact of the DS report on that question. Similarly to some of the situations discussed above, this member will understand that the DS report is not "binding" on it, but that there is a fairly strong "precedent effect" even if not "subsequent practice in the application of the treaty" as yet.[5] Yet this member may wish to argue that the report has no effect on it (absent enough cases to be "practice"), since it could argue for a contrary interpretation in a case involving it. Here we get into a delicate situation of the role and bona fides of this member while it tries to "predict" what the WTO (especially its Appellate Body) will decide about a particular interpretation of the relevant treaty text. Of course, like the other cases, even when the treaty is not directly applicable and the member is not a disputant addressed by the WTO DS report, there can be "effects" of the treaty obligation on its jurisprudence, and this may require a domestic court or other legal institution to make its judgment about the interpretation in a manner which will "take into account" the DS report. This would be done, however, in the light of general techniques of treaty interpretation, some (but not all, as we have seen in section 5.8) of which may be found in the VCLT.

The United States (and maybe other members) has taken a particularly troublesome position in some agency determinations relevant to WTO obligations.[6] Although an Appellate Body report for a case in which the United States is not a disputant may clearly state a ruling which interprets WTO obligations, the United States has argued that since the report is not "binding" on the United States as a matter of international law, the United States will proceed with measures that it argues are WTO-consistent. It does this knowing full well that any reasonable prediction of what the WTO DS system will decide would be inconsistent with the US view. The United States knows that a case will take several years to complete, and so the United States has a "free pass" for that time before it is obligated to change its approach. If the matter involves US restraints on imports, such as antidumping duties, US business interests will reap the protectionist benefit for the time it takes to complete a DS case against the United States This benefit will be the "monopoly rents" for those interests and could be many millions of dollars, to the detriment of the complainants. Since the WTO DS system is designed only to change future practice, it has no provision to redress past harm with monetary or other compensation. The foreign exporting interests will suffer without redress, even when it is very clear that the US action will be found WTO-inconsistent.

In fact, this situation can go even a step further. Even when a case against the United States has already interpreted a WTO treaty provision, the United States has argued that it is only "ruling" in that case, and so the United States can in another case follow its own contrary view of the same legal principle until a new case is brought against it. And this could be repeated, over and over again.

So this moves the analysis into the concept of "precedent," even if a "soft precedent." A way is needed that will better help achieve "security and predictability," especially for entrepreneurs dependent upon the rules. Perhaps arguments about "good faith" will be useful, or perhaps the meaning of "treaty obligation" needs to embrace more clearly the interpretations (not waiting for "practice under the agreement"), at least to the extent that governments have an obligation to refrain from action reasonably understood as WTO-inconsistent. It could *still* be deemed appropriate for governments to argue later in the DS system that a prior case is wrong and will not be followed.

This analysis clearly relates to the subject of compliance taken up next, in section 5.10.

5.10 Key jurisprudential questions V: compliance and implementation

The question of compliance or implementation is always very important when related to international law norms, since unlike most nation-state legal systems, international legal systems do not have a monopoly on the use of force, and generally have very few forceful means of inducing compliance. International relations literature extensively explores the problems raised by these circumstances, and in recent decades[1] there has been increased attention to the effect of legal norms on international relations. Some of the problems in this regard were discussed in chapters 1 and 2 of this book. The literature concerning compliance and the WTO dispute settlement system activity is already very extensive.[2]

With respect to international economic law, which is most often governed by treaty norms, these questions loom large. Some international law institutions have inducements such as subsidies or lending facilities to induce compliance.[3] Much has also been written in the treaty literature, including that literature concerning the Vienna Convention on the Law of Treaties (VCLT), about implementation inducements that might be

The WTO dispute settlement system

available by reaction measures taken by harmed parties. Such inducements include reciprocal deviations from treaty norms, or even without treaty measures themselves, certain customary law ideas including retorsion and other sanctions.[4]

The GATT had some possibilities for reciprocal and other measures to "encourage" compliance with the GATT treaty obligations, but they were relatively weak. In the WTO and its DSU, however, we now have an elaborate set of possibilities for reacting to measures by WTO members which harm others. Indeed, and almost unique, GATT through practice development and the WTO through explicit clauses in the DSU recognize two types of measures which could result in countermeasures, namely a "breach" or violation of the treaty norms, and in a few circumstances a "non-violation" situation.

The GATT language concerning dispute settlement proceedings is centered in GATT Article XXIII, which is now mostly superceded by the DSU.[5] As outlined in section 5.2 of this chapter, this language did not originally focus on "violation," but instead is expressed in terms of "nullification or impairment."[6] Gradually, however, there developed the doctrine that a violation when proven, amounted to a prima facie nullification or impairment, and therefore could create a possibility of countermeasures (or demand for reciprocal "compensations").

The WTO DSU now explicitly recognizes a distinction drawn from the GATT practice between "violation cases" and "non-violation" cases. For the former it sets up an elaborate set of "remedy measures" usually resulting in a requirement for a violator to bring its measures into conformity with the WTO rules. For non-violation cases, however, the requirement is softer, with no obligation to bring measures into conformity (because no finding of non-conformity has occurred). Instead the party responsible for the nullification or impairment non-violation measures is required to enter into negotiations with the harmed parties, with a view to restoring some measure of fair reciprocity or equilibrium. Since the definition of "nullification or impairment" has never been too clear, the concept is, in some ways, in tension with warnings expressed in the DSU that "the panel and Appellate Body cannot add to or diminish the rights and obligations" of the parties concerned;[7] sometimes, as noted before, this warning is referred to informally as a warning against "judicial activism." In the rest of this section, however, focus will be on violation cases which comprise the overwhelming percentage of all cases, especially since the WTO came into existence.[8]

5.10 Key jurisprudential questions V

GATT Article XXIII provided that on hearing a complaint and making findings, the GATT contracting parties could authorize "a contracting party or parties to suspend the application to any other contracting party or parties of such concessions or other obligations under this Agreement as they determine to be appropriate in the circumstances." This appears potentially very powerful, and might even suggest "penalizing" actions, or virtual expulsion (all parties suspend all obligations?). In fact, as previously discussed, there was only one case of such authorized suspension, when the Netherlands was authorized (repeatedly) to suspend obligations towards the United States.[9]

Turning then to the WTO and the remedies portions of the DSU, we learn that a panel, buttressed in some cases by the Appellate Body, can make a finding in its report that a respondent member of the WTO should bring its measures into conformity with its obligations:

Where a panel or the Appellate Body concludes that a measure is inconsistent with a covered agreement, it shall recommend that the Member concerned bring the measure into conformity with that agreement. In addition to its recommendations, the panel or Appellate Body may suggest ways in which the Member concerned could implement the recommendations.[10]

Technically this is a finding of violation, which is thus a prima facie nullification or impairment[11] which could be rebutted by the responding disputant, but in some cases at least the jurisprudence (as noted in section 5.2) may not permit such rebuttal.

When these findings occur, then a series of follow-on steps may take place, as outlined in section 5.4. In addition the aggrieved (winning) disputant can take "compensatory measures," that is, retaliatory trade limiting measures (but not called that) upon submittal and virtually automatic "reverse consensus" procedures of the DSB.[12] There is a limit on the compensatory measures: they must be "equivalent" to the nullification or impairment, and this can be tested by another procedure.[13] Until now, "compensation" has almost never meant a "check in the mail," but instead indicates trade measures that may be taken. But various ideas for changes to those "compensatory" or "compliance-inducing" actions have been proposed.[14]

In international law terms, this set of countermeasures and their procedures are unique. They also, coupled with the "automaticity" of adoption of the DS reports, are comparatively very powerful. The system is probably still too new to be able to draw very assured conclusions about its effectiveness, but it has indeed been used with increasing frequency, with countermeasures constructed in ways to deliver the most political pain possible to noncomplying disputants. An interesting and prominent example was the action by the European Communities against the United States in the *Steel Safeguards* case, which resulted in a demand by the European Union for the United States to conform to its obligations (as found by the DS system)[15] with the threat of a retaliatory increase in tariffs against US goods targeted to certain politically sensitive US states and areas which would be most affected. Soon thereafter the US President announced withdrawal of the "condemned" safeguard measures (claiming no connection to the WTO case). The *New York Times* had the following fascinating comment on this case:

For the organization that conservatives, and some liberals, once denounced as an unelected bureaucracy that should never be given power over American jobs, [the *Steel Safeguards*] case was the rough equivalent of *Marbury* v. *Madison*, the 1803 decision that established the Supreme Court as the final arbiter of the constitution, able to force Congress and the executive branch to comply with its rulings.[16]

A major problem with the current system of WTO DS-approved countermeasures is that since they almost always involve trade restrictions, they are directly contrary to the broader WTO policy of encouraging liberalization of trade. Furthermore, in economic terms, the restrictions actually hurt the nation imposing them, so that the winning complainant is "shooting itself in the foot." In today's interdependent and globalized world, such restriction can hurt specific businesses in the winning complainant nation which are intertwined with businesses in the losing, respondent country. To restrain the flow of parts, for example, harms the downstream businesses, which need those parts. In addition, the restrictions often harm the losing respondent's businesses that wish to export to the winning complainant, and rarely are these businesses related to the proponents of the WTO inconsistent measure. Thus, when the European Union restricts imports of bananas, and the United States counters with restrictions on sweaters or cognac, the businesses harmed by the retaliation are innocent "bystanders." The same is true when the United States restricts steel imports, so that the Europeans impose higher tariffs on dozens of products normally shipped by US businesses to Europe.

These and other practical problems lead some to favor an overhaul of the WTO compliance system. But many proposals have various flaws also.[17] Despite these problems with the current details of the WTO DS compliance system, the overall record of compliance is seen as quite good, and often held out as considerably better than most treaty compliance mechanisms.[18] Perhaps improvement, however, will depend on non-legal, or soft law techniques embracing concepts examined by political scientists and others.[19]

5.11 Dispute settlement structural problems and proposed reforms

At the final GATT Ministerial Conference for Uruguay Round negotiation, when the GATT ministers adopted the vast UR treaty for submittal to nations for signing and/or ratification, one of the "Decisions" of the Ministers related to the dispute settlement system and its review. This decision "invited" the WTO Ministerial Conference to "complete a full review" of the DS rules and procedures within four years after the entry into force of the WTO, and to "take a decision on the occasion of its first meeting after the completion of the review, whether to continue, modify or terminate such dispute settlement rules and procedures."[1]

The four-year period ended on December 31, 1998, after the WTO had come into being on January 1, 1995. Prior to that date, the WTO members started work on such a review, and many governments put forward many ideas for reform. However, there never was a formal completion of this work. The ideas were often embodied in "non-papers" from governments, sometimes widely available to government persons or even private persons knowledgeable and proficient in DS practice, but otherwise not very transparent. The number of individual proposals when totaled up by some observers exceeded 250,[2] but many of the proposals were for small-detail problems of the DS procedures. There was some mumbling about whether, in the event of failure of the WTO members to fulfill the Marrekesh decision, the DS system must end, but this mumbling had no "traction" and the WTO DS procedure continued on its course. From time to time further attention was given to the "review," and at Doha, the Fourth Ministerial Conference, the ministers decided to reinvigorate the review process and set out some procedures designed to accomplish this. A notable feature of those procedures was the intention to separate the DS review process from the normal trade "round" diplomacy, and to put it on a separate track.[3] The idea seemed to stem from notions that the dispute settlement rules should not be influenced by ideas of reciprocity, since improvement of the rules should be advantageous as a systemic matter, beneficial to all members. As this is written (August 2005) not much progress on DS review has been made, and it is unclear to what degree there will be any reform and whether the idea of keeping DS review separate from the other "round" bargaining will actually be implemented.

Even apart from the review process, there has been occasional discussion of various problems and the need for change in the DS procedures. However, there has also been a number of expressions by experienced diplomats and DS practitioners that the WTO DS procedures have on the whole been working quite well, so that some thought that no reform as yet was seen to be necessary and others felt that the risk of doing damage to the DS system through certain reform ideas was great enough to suggest that it was better not to touch the system. Thus some persons said that the most important goal for any review of the DS system was similar to the renowned physicians' ethic of "do no harm." The WTO Consultative Board report of January 2005 includes a chapter on the DS system making this point.[4]

There will be no attempt in this short section to develop much detail about the dozens and hundreds of reform proposals, but we will here examine (briefly at least) several of the more important or more frequently mentioned DS reforms proposed.

a. Appellate Body

Some persons feel that the appeals procedural addition of the UR texts has been a great success, and that the Appellate Body has developed an amazingly analytical and elaborate jurisprudence in its short ten years.[5] Others have criticized the Appellate Body as "overreaching its mandate" and engaging in "judicial activism" outside its competence and transgressing the allocated powers of the diplomatic process. Some proposed changes have, however, suggested that the Appellate Body members should be full-time rather than part-time and on call, as they are now. During some years of the Appellate Body's busy existence, its workload required Appellate Body members to devote more than two-thirds of their professional time in a year to the Appellate Body tasks, even though they are retained on a part-time basis. This was more than many had anticipated and put some strain on the time of those Appellate Body members who had other active professional positions (even though already retired from another long-term position), such as teaching or private practice. This burden led some Appellate Body members, whose four-year terms ended, to refrain from seeking renewal of their appointment. It has also been calculated that the pay and travel costs for part-time members were likely to have been larger than the cost of a full-time salaried Appellate

5.11 Dispute settlement structural problems and proposed reforms

Body.[6] On the other hand, in other years the caseload has not been so demanding.

Furthermore, there has been some thought that the Appellate Body should be enlarged, from seven to nine. Since they "sit" in panels ("divisions") of three, a total of nine might result in spreading the burden more, but Appellate Body members for any particular case are selected in such a way as to prevent outsiders from predicting who will be on a division and also to avoid the same composition for repeated divisions. Although these have been discussed, there does not seem to be much impetus to introduce these (or any other) changes to the Appellate Body. Certain relatively minor adjustments to the Appellate Body rules of procedures (which they have the power, as a body, to determine, subject to consultation), can be and are being implemented.[7] One possibility is to authorize the DSB, under certain circumstances, to enlarge the Appellate Body membership.

A much more significant and, in the view of many, potentially dangerous group of proposals has been put forward to address the perception in some parts that the Appellate Body has "overreached its mandate" and exceeded its competence, or has otherwise unfairly tilted decisions or been engaged in "judicial activism." One of these proposals has been put forward by the United States, along with Chile. It would provide a new procedure that would enable the DSB, after a DS report was circulated, to decide by consensus not to adopt a finding in the report or the basic rationale behind a finding.[8] Another proposal would give the DSB or the General Council the option in effect to veto a DS adopted report with a two-thirds (or similar super-majority) vote.[9]

Any such proposal would reintroduce a fundamental weakness that was present in the GATT DS procedures, politicizing the DS process and encouraging diplomats and their governments to divert their attention away from the reasoned argumentation and process of a juridical procedure towards lobbying and diplomatic bargaining that would lead to the ultimate decision in a particular case. In short, this would greatly reduce the "rule-oriented" integrity of the existing procedures.

The existence of a worrisome disparity of power between the DS process and the diplomatic or "rule making" negotiation process, has already been noted in this book.[10] This disparity results from the relative effectiveness of the DS process, while the other WTO procedures tend to be much more constrained, limited, and frail, even to the point of paralysis.[11] The WTO Consultative Board also made this point. These "reform" proposals would, however, weaken the DS procedures to bring them "down to" the diplomatic/negotiating level. Much better would be to seek ways to enhance the procedures of the latter, to improve the decision-making and rule-making processes and to weaken the consensus risk of paralysis by some modest modifications of those processes.

There could well be an appropriate additional role and responsibility for the diplomatic/negotiation side of the WTO through establishing procedures, possibly within the DSB,[12] to provide a reasoned critique of some DS final adopted reports (Appellate Body or first-level) which would then be "adopted" or otherwise made public with a view to influencing the DS process in future cases. As we have seen in our discussion[13] of "precedent," there is certainly the power and sense of appropriateness for the DS bodies including the Appellate Body to "change their mind" or to rule differently from prior cases, when good reason (or changing circumstances) would warrant that. Other international and national tribunals have found ways to do this. In addition, some observers, including former Appellate Body members, are convinced that such a well-formed and reasoned critique would very likely be followed by the Appellate Body (and thus the panels).

b. Panels

Considerable attention has been given to ideas for changing the structure of first-level panel appointments. The most prominent of these ideas would encourage the establishment of a permanent roster of persons to be part of such panels, emulating somewhat the current Appellate Body structure. There are many permutations to these ideas. Some would call for a roster large enough (and possibly full-time) so that all panel members would be drawn from it. The argument in favor of a permanent roster hopes that the panel members' experience and longevity would enhance the expertise and quality of the panels. It would also provide a more consistent set of findings and for a body of panelists to be available for various possible ancillary procedures which would enhance the DS system, such as remand opportunities and handling of preliminary questions before a panel was even appointed for a specific case.

These considerations are worthy, but there are some advantages to the existing system of drawing on experts and experienced (sometimes retired) persons with considerable knowledge of trade rules and policies, or sometimes persons with great expertise in a subject that will be central to a dispute (such as food safety, or intellectual property). In addition, there are advantages to drawing on young or middle-level diplomats from WTO members, who can bring a practical knowledge of national government

5.11 Dispute settlement structural problems and proposed reforms

concerns to the deliberations and when completing their service as a panelist will have witnessed from the inside the DS process, giving them a valuable perspective on that process to inform their own or other governments, or their public.

But clearly, a first-level roster proposal need not be all or nothing. A roster just large enough to provide at least one roster person for each panel, could capture the benefits of both the roster system and the ad hoc current system.

c. Good governance and transparency

A major consideration concerning "good governance" ideas of transparency has been often discussed also. Many persons have advocated that the panel and Appellate Body hearings (but not deliberations) should be open to the public or that at least the public should be able to view them in some form, possibly only through transcripts or tapes. Many have observed that the WTO is harming itself through its restricted non-transparent procedures, especially in regard to the DS system. These persons feel that the public would find the procedures very admirable, and very much as high-quality as most national juridical procedures (many of which have open hearings and great transparency).

d. Remedies

The remedies part of the DS system has also attracted considerable attention and expressions of need for reform. A well-known fault in the drafting of the DSU has been perplexing. This has to do with the relationship of the provisions of DSU Article 21(5), which authorizes a brief follow-on procedure after a DS report is adopted and promulgated, to challenge whether the "losing" party is adequately implementing the obligations found neglected by the report. On the other hand, provisions of Article 22 offer the "winning" party a short period in which it can propose near-automatically approved "retaliatory measures" called "compensatory." DSU Article 22(6) provides a procedure to challenge those measures. But these two sets of procedures are virtually impossible to operate together, under the time frames and other procedures set out. This has been termed the "sequencing" problem, since it would seem more sensible to have a third-party (panel?) determination of the appropriateness of the proposed measures *before* they are "adopted."[14] Many disputing parties have agreed in particular cases to an ad hoc understanding how to resolve the dilemma through changes in the rules of the DSU for a specific case only. Some therefore say that no further reform is necessary. But others note the instability of these ad hoc measures and the risk that in a particular case one side might find some advantage in refusing to agree to sensible understandings. It is also noted that the procedure of ad hoc agreements can engage "other diplomatic considerations" or "bargaining chips," and therefore is not very transparent, since the DSU rules are affirmatively misleading. Most observers feel that this situation is an example of "consensus paralysis," since the way to resolve the issue through changes in the DSU language seems apparent, but such change requires "consensus" and thus diplomats despair of trying to get such change accomplished.

5.12 Perspectives and conclusions for Part II: the lessons of the GATT/WTO system

Chapters 4 and 5 – Part II of this book – present a brief overview of the history and practice of the GATT/WTO system with a focus on how that history and practice relates to the broader context of international law generally. These chapters followed Part I (Chapters 1, 2 and 3), which described the landscape of forces in world affairs which affected international law concepts and international relations, including technological innovations of the last fifty years which diminished "natural barriers" to trade such as transport and communications. Part I also explored various sources of tension and challenge to the fundamental assumptions of the international legal order, including the concept of "sovereignty."

Pursuing the logical structure of this book, the two chapters of Part II have used the GATT/WTO history to explore detail of how the practice of one particular but very important subject of international relations related to and affected international law concepts which were part of that history. Part III – chapters 6, 7 and 8 – then moves back to a more general frame of reference to explore some potential and practical implications (with focus on economic affairs) of the "lessons" of Part II. At the end of Part III, Chapter 8 will discuss some broader perspectives about problems posed in Part I and elaborated in Parts II and III.

Thus in this Part II, Chapter 4 explored mainly the "non dispute settlement" portion of the WTO and its history, while Chapter 5 emphasized an examination of the dispute settlement procedures and their practice and its implications. Several broad generalizations supported by this GATT/WTO history are mentioned here, after which this section will look at implications arising from the subjects of each of the two chapters.

5.12 Perspectives and conclusions for Part II

The original contracting parties for GATT, which came into force (provisionally) in January 1948, probably could not have predicted how that institution would evolve over many decades, nor could they know what exactly they were consenting to in the longer term. Indeed, the negotiators were focused on a charter for a full-fledged legal international organization, the ITO (International Trade Organization), which in fact did not come into force. The GATT was to be subordinate to the ITO and to depend on it for its organizational characteristics. When the ITO's failure to come into being became apparent, it is doubtful that more than a few national representatives would have expected very much from the troubled "birth defected" GATT. Yet, in fact, GATT soon became the most important international institution for international trade subjects (de facto?), and continued to be so until it evolved into an even more definitive organization, the WTO. This situation, whereby a human institution evolves into a structure and practice which were not predicted by most of the originating participants, arguably is not uncommon in world history. Which of the draftspersons for the US Constitution could have predicted the form of government of that nation today? Which of the draftspersons for the European Economic Community (and the European Union) could have predicted the form of that remarkable institution which is now established?

Throughout GATT's history it was the umbrella for eight major rounds of negotiation designed to liberalize world trade and to inhibit protectionist nation state practices which could seriously damage world trade and the world economy, as the lessons of the 1930s had demonstrated. These negotiations in retrospect and in a broader context perspective, have established an amazing "rule-oriented" institutional landscape which has vital importance to millions of entrepreneurs and "market participants." Such landscape is important for a market system to work, and its predictability and security are major contributions to lowering the "risk premium" and otherwise promoting at least aggregate world economic welfare.

But for such institutional developments to occur, certain notions of international law, such as state consent, or equality of nations, or "sovereign" immunity from international measures which affect internal or "domestic" governmental activities, must not be over emphasized to the extent of preventing the evolving institution to carry out its mandated mission. Of course, the delicate problem is balancing these international goals with other important goals which may be better enhanced by more traditional "nation-state sovereignty" thinking, such as protection of democracy, or in some cases protection of human rights.

For example, "consent" should not be considered as a requirement for every small detail, or for every resolution of ambiguity or gap-filling by a dispute settlement institution. The mere fact that the original consent of nation-states included consent to a dispute settlement system, suggests a measure of deference to the results of that system, at least to the extent that such deference is necessary for the institution to be able to keep pace with rapidly changing global characteristics and therefore to be reasonably able to carry out its responsibilities in light of its mission.

So the history and practice of the GATT/WTO system, outlined in chapters 4 and 5, are the practical detail of how an international institution can fulfill its mandate. Regarding the subject of Chapter 4, addressing the diplomatic/political side of the institution, one can see a number of interesting and possibly crucial elements. For example, despite the failure of a more definitive and traditional organization to come into force shortly after 1948, clearly the world had such a strong need for the functions of discourse, cooperation, and coordination in matters of international trade that the national representatives experimented and innovated with a defective "provisional" treaty such that it in fact was able to make progress on issues within its purview. Clearly particular individuals, such as Eric Wyndham White, were important parts of that history. Their broad and innovative perspective and ability to improvise and bring pragmatic attention to specific facts as they developed are what sustained and embellished GATT.

It is also clear that governments felt a need for a "rule-oriented" dispute settlement procedure. Innovations which could be argued to have exceeded the permissible implications of the limited GATT treaty text, such as development of the "prima facie nullification or impairment" concept,[1] were not only tolerated by the national representatives, but were later more formally adopted. Over time the procedures became more "rule-oriented" in the sense of relying increasingly on "precedent," and also with greater reference to general international law concepts.

Likewise, it is reasonably clear that one nation, one vote decision making was not realistic. Thus the "consensus" principles began to govern almost every activity of GATT, carried over to a great extent into the WTO. Also it can be seen that "treaty rigidity" and the difficulty it created in amending the treaty, played a role in the desire of the nation-states finally in the Uruguay Round negotiation to establish a new "constitution" for the trading system, namely the WTO. It is also true, however, that the new organization has been somewhat jeopardized by a lack of resources commensurate with its responsibilities, and by the attitudes of

5.12 Perspectives and conclusions for Part II

some national representatives which undermine the needed leadership role for the Director-General and for the Secretariat officials generally.[2] Thus the member states have other ways to constrain the power of the international organization.

It can also be seen that there is need for considerably more thought about the relationship of the international trade institution in the form of the WTO to nation-state governments and their own institutions, whether constitutional, parliamentary, judicial, or culture and societal norms.

More particularly with respect to the dispute settlement system as explored in Chapter 5, it can be seen how a remarkable number of details of that system can play important roles regarding tensions between concepts of sovereignty and international rule needs. The WTO dispute settlement system takes a major leap in the direction of greater rule orientation, to the chagrin of some nation-state representatives. The "reverse consensus" automatic adoption of panel reports, coupled with the appeal system, is extraordinary but also seems to be receiving much support. Other seemingly technical issues, such as rules of treaty interpretation, methods of promoting compliance with DS reports, the method of selecting panelists and Appellate Body members, burden of proof rules, ability of disputant governments to appoint outside counsel to assist them even inside hearings, the role of *amicus* briefs, all have implications for the distribution of power between the international and national legal/governmental systems.

Indeed the relative success of the DS system, when compared sometimes with the apparent paralysis of the diplomatic/political side of the WTO, has led to some concern that this power imbalance could be detrimental to the systemic longevity of the WTO and the trade institutions. In reports of some WTO meetings, this concern has been manifested by strident statements, such as in a situation involving the validity of *amicus curiae* briefs for the Appellate Body.[3] The report of one meeting described as no less than a "temper tantrum" the conduct of the diplomats. In some cases, statements reflect a profound misunderstanding about the nature of an effective juridical institution (and the necessity that such institution be reasonably independent in order to be effective). Some diplomats at the WTO and some academic or special interest advocacy groups have proposed some reforms which, however, run a great risk of undermining the WTO juridical institution by establishing a political veto which would refocus diplomatic energies towards lobbying rather than rational rule argumentation.[4]

However, the criticism that the WTO system does not have a counterweight or checking and balancing procedure, such as those found in nation-states (such as a legislature), has some merit. This critique should imply that it is necessary to seek ways to make the diplomatic or political decision-making process more effective than it currently is (rather than try to cut back on the effectiveness of the DS process).

In sum, once again the current problems challenging the international law system as it has been traditionally understood seem to force attention more and more in the direction of international institutions or, in other words, towards "constitutional law."

PART III

The search for solutions

6

Policy analytical approaches and thought experiments

What are the objects and purposes of the DSU, and the WTO more generally, that are relevant . . .? The most relevant in our view are those which relate to the creation of market conditions conducive to individual economic activity in national and global markets and to the provision of a secure and predictable multilateral trading system.

. . . [I]t would be entirely wrong to consider that the position of individuals is of no relevance to the GATT/WTO legal matrix.

WTO first-level panel, *Section 301* case (2000)[1]

6.1 Introduction to Part III and Chapter 6

Part I (consisting of chapters 1, 2 and 3) explored the problems and challenges which are impacting the fundamentals of international law and international economic law. Part II (Chapters 4 and 5) explored the GATT/WTO institution partly as a case study, to provide detail of actual practices affecting the questions raised in Part I.

This last part (Part III, containing chapters 6, 7, and 8), now shifts the viewpoint from the past and the present, more towards the future. The objective is to present a few ideas about how the international law system generally, and the economic part of it in particular, may respond to the many challenges which they face. Needless to say, these ideas are neither a full inventory of possible suggestions, nor do they comprise any particularly elaborate all-embracing simple theory as a definitive road map for the future. As noted in Chapter 1, this book is about "queries rather than theories." There are many complex problems facing the IL subject, and no "one size fits all" will likely be found to address the myriad of sub-subjects of international law and the many extraordinarily complex situations which those subjects have faced or will face. If anything, the most generic proposition which is put forward here is to reinforce the importance of analysis in depth which will often include disaggregating older subjects and assumptions, and putting aside older predilections and tired premises. For example, the "treaty" can be seen as a broad term covering many differing instruments of international law, such that a single set of rules or one framework for treaty operation may embrace elements undermining the effective and efficient operation of an instrument. Thus the Vienna Convention on the Law of Treaties, probably designed more for the older prototypical bilateral or small membership instruments based on habitual techniques of diplomacy, may not be well designed to enhance the effectiveness of institutions embracing many dozens of members, in some cases encompassing an extreme variety of cultural and governmental circumstances. Likewise, the enormous operational difficulties of relying on what some observers consider to be customary international law (which is often contradicted by other observers, or alternatively phrased so generally as to pose many troublesome interpretative ambiguities) may lead to suggestions that put a high priority on treaty-making rather than attempts to "tease out from complexities in a variety of circumstances" imprecise notions of customary international law.[2]

In this part, Chapter 6 explores some approaches to analysis with attention to several particular institutional characteristics that have broad implications for the subject of this book. Chapter 7 then briefly puts forward some specific real examples of situations which involve such analysis and embrace substantial struggles about some of the questions raised in the analysis. Finally, Chapter 8 completes the book with some summary observations, perceptions, and conclusions.

Turning to the subject of Chapter 6, a very important number of the analytical problems which confront world leaders and international relations participants today deal with the question (discussed in Chapter 3) of allocating "decision-making authority" among various human institutions, some of which may reside in different contexts and levels of human structure, such as the nation-state compared with an international institution. This puzzle of how to make those allocations which will best enhance the opportunity to achieve certain human goals in a world context that makes older institutional structures less likely to be able to succeed is extremely pervasive, as any analysis of daily news media can show.[3]

Perhaps one of the broader general propositions which can be put forward, however, is the need to avoid a presumption in favor of either international institutions or other human structures such as the nation-state

6.1 Introduction to Part III and Chapter 6

as the appropriate locus of "power." Furthermore, an appropriate answer will often be mixed, suggesting that (if we retain the use of the term "sovereignty") a disaggregated analysis is necessary that speaks not about "transfer of sovereignty," but rather allocating "slices" of sovereignty. The key question often is: how thick is a slice?

This chapter is designed to overview some of the elements of analysis that will almost inevitably be part of the "slicing of sovereignty," in the light of the experience of the WTO, and also in the context of other challenges (some of them not as new as globalization) to the subject of international law. Thus section 6.2 will explore the "sovereignty conundrum" as a logical continuation of the discussion in Chapter 3 (and other chapters), section 6.3 will suggest an overall (but not too detailed) "policy analysis matrix" which will be a sort of "starting template" of methods of thinking about the problems of this book, suggesting that more careful attention be given both to the goals of any proposed or actual program (whether it involves trade, human rights, environmental policy, use of force, democratic norms, good governance ideas, or one of many other programs) as well as to the constraints affecting the probability of goals being enhanced due to empirically observable characteristics of the available or planned institutions at various levels which offer options for service needed to achieve the goals.

The remaining sections of this chapter will then take up several illustrative broad approaches or techniques which might apply to a variety of specific situations (leaving Chapter 7 to explore a few such specific situations). Section 6.4 will be a thought experiment "walk-through" illustration using traditional economic thinking about "market failure" as a jump-off for examining the impact of globalization on such thinking.

Section 6.5 will further explore the subject (or subjects) of "constitutionalization" as it might relate to international law and international economic law in the context of problems raised in Parts I and II of this book.

Section 6.6 will then build on the preceding sections and on Parts I and II, to look particularly at the growing central importance of "juridical" institutions at the international level, including attention to the stresses which such institutions impose on situations more embedded in older international and diplomatic structures.

Finally, section 6.7 will offer another thought experiment, here entitled the "interface theory," which illustrates how even relatively modest differences in the economic structures of two societies can be the source of unintended aggravations and unanticipated tensions between such societies. This suggests the need for appropriate international institutions which can provide an interface mechanism.

Policy analytical approaches and thought experiments

Needless to say, there are many more approaches from various disciplines which could be considered in this chapter, especially the enormous economic literature about international economics and trade. The basic concepts of comparative advantage and the prisoner's dilemma model are important considerations bearing on the role of markets in a globalized policy landscape. These subjects and the evolving thinking about them are better left to economists, and will only be touched on here. But it is important to remind the reader to examine the thinking found in that and other disciplines in relation to the problems raised in this book.

Another reminder to be noted here is the relevance of discussions in Chapters 4 and 5 regarding the necessity of institutional structures for markets to work effectively, and expressing the importance of rule orientation structures to reduce the "risk premium" of market activity (so as to increase world welfare).

6.2 The sovereignty conundrum: slicing the concept

Chapter 3 explored the concept of sovereignty and many of its criticisms in some depth. The literature sampled in that chapter manifested a variety of views about the meaning of sovereignty and how the word "sovereignty" was often used to obscure rather than illuminate the functions and meanings of the term. Embraced by the term are notions (*inter alia*) of monopoly of power within a nation-state, equality of nations, freedom of the nation from external interference (force or otherwise), theory of consent as basis of any higher (international) norm, source of stability in world international relations, enhanced opportunity for market economies, controls over movement across borders, freedom to make foreign policy choices. Many of these notions are criticized, and others are described as fictional ("hypocrisy"). Thus some scholars suggest the word should be "relegated to the dustbin of history," and others suggest that its implications are damaging to world peace and order (e.g. in situations of "rogue states," especially those causing humanitarian crises). Furthermore, there are various complex dimensions for the application of "sovereignty" ideas, including a vertical (international, regional, national, sub-national, etc.) and horizontal (different international or national institutions on the same level). Likewise there are third dimensions, of "type," for example, "economic" or other, or government or nongovernment (and among the latter, profit or non-profit). All of these institutions can, in a "globalized world," compete for allocation of power, which can be called "sovereignty" or "sovereignty yielding" or "sovereignty displacement."

6.2 The sovereignty conundrum: slicing the concept

If one explores the suggestion of Chapter 3 and focuses for the most part on "allocation of power," then one can easily see that most of the allocation problems are not black or white, but involve some gradation of "ceding of sovereignty" as a matter of degree, not kind. Thus we can speak of "sovereignty" as involving "slices," for example slices of power. Should a subject be turned over to international entity X or should just some sub-part of the subject be handled that way? Even for the part of a subject turned over, should it be subject to international decisions regarding its evolution in the future (to face changing science or economics, for example)? In addition, should the internationalization of a subject matter be strengthened by an international juridical system which will fill gaps and make findings on ambiguities? These and many more problems are embedded in the loose word "sovereignty," and often when it is used mantra-like these subtleties are not examined. Yet they clearly should be, and that is part of the message of this chapter. In Chapter 3 some of the policies which should motivate such an analysis were suggested, including reasons for moving a slice upward into international institutions, and also reasons for moving such slice (or power allocation) downward (subsidiarity).

The argument of Chapter 3 opposes the wholesale rejection of the term or concept of sovereignty, but even a partial slicing of the concept does pose some logical problems for the general subject of international law. As noted in Chapter 3, it can be argued that several other characteristics often attributed to the operation of international relations and international law today, depend on (or have been justified by) sovereignty, namely equality of nations, non-interference from outside a nation, and above all, the consent theory as the basis of any international legal norm. A disaggregation ("slicing") of the sovereignty concept opens the door at least a crack to claims that these other characteristics are no longer valid fundamentals for the international system. And yet many persons (including this author) would argue that, at least to a certain extent, these other characteristics have significant advantages for the operational success of international law in the context of international relations. So an important inquiry should involve an examination of how other policy arguments supporting these characteristics could be developed. Some of this examination will have to be undertaken in other places and probably by other persons, but a few thoughts can be mentioned here.

In particular, the consent theory for international law norms will certainly need rethinking, and many writers have been doing just that, including some noted in Chapter 3. But if "consent" is no longer to be the basis for the legitimation of international norms, what is? Several approaches could be suggested. One would pursue a line of logic that begins with a notion that international government must be based on "democratic" and other "good governance" fundamental axioms, just as should also be the case within nation-states. Then a calculus (or procedure) needs to be worked out about how individual citizens apart from their nation-states can have a participatory role in the rule formulation process. This moves in the direction of nongovernment actors on the international scene, as noted in chapters 2 and 3.

Among the items on Schachter's list described in section 2.3 is "natural law" or "natural reason," which could also be related to more recently developed concepts of deontological axioms inherent or innately present in human beings, sometimes analogized to Noam Chomsky's "universal grammar" ideas. Both the general idea of "natural law" (or "natural reason") and the notions of an innately present in humans "universal moral grammar," when used to justify international axiomatic norms, raise great analytical problems of belief and empirical study, which are left for discussion in other works.[1] Another approach would also note the Schachter list of concepts[2] which contribute to international law norms, probably emphasizing a juridical-type institutional embracing of such concepts. This could be elitist to the extent of diminishing the governance values suggested in the prior paragraph, or it could be set up to coexist (in varying recipes) under some institutional structures. If this begins to sound like "constitutionalism," that should not be surprising, and a later section of this chapter will return to this subject.

Clearly the often hypocritically treated concept of "equality of nations" should be the object of careful rethinking. Indeed, in various international institutions (as we could see from the explorations of the WTO in Chapters 4 and 5) there has been an effective departure from "one nation, one vote" decision making, and in virtually all major international institutions which have some "hard law" powers which go beyond recommendations (and even in some of those) there have been various departures from the equality of nations theory. But there still may be some important elements formerly captured by the equality theory, most particularly (again) democratic ideas of meaningful participation as essential for good governance. The equality theory can encourage the institution-making process to bear those ideas in mind. The consensus idea certainly does assist in achieving some of the good governance ideals, but of course it also runs a high risk of going so far as to undermine the opportunity for even a vast majority of nations to proceed with measures they feel are needed to cope with the changing world of globalization. Likewise, some characteristics necessary for the successful protection of human rights are anti-majoritarian, and that must be factored into this discussion.

The non-interference ("non-intervention") ideal also has important advantages for international relations in the imperfect world as it currently is, probably adding stability and predictability to those relations and prohibiting egregious international interference activities which should be condemned. It might be feasible to base such norm on reasons which do not depend on "sovereignty," and therefore even to extend ideas beyond the sovereign notions, to suggest some measures to inhibit undue interference by international bodies, and into sub-national bodies. But these notions are certainly uncharted (but recall the twentieth-century ideas of "self-determination" of peoples and how that has resonated occasionally).[3] One basic problem is the need to break away from a non-interference norm in those circumstances of rogue nations and drastic anti-humanitarian activity. This is a direction that the Commission on International State Sovereignty took in its 2001 report, emphasizing the "responsibility to protect" in some circumstances, rather than the "national sovereignty" rights.[4] Several thinkers, such as Anne-Marie Slaughter[5] and British Prime Minister Tony Blair[6] have articulated some preliminary ideas about when departures from a norm of non-interference (such as grounds for "regime change") might be justified.

When one has wended one's way through the logic of these prior few paragraphs, it is possible to conclude that the sovereignty concepts should not be completely abandoned, at least at this juncture of human history. So the alternative is to try to maintain sovereignty concepts (at least slices) perhaps as the "prima facie" norm for which exceptions can now be devised (by careful analysis and good governance techniques of participation and transparency, and with checks and balances built in). This, as suggested in Chapter 3, could be termed "sovereignty-modern."

6.3 Towards a policy analysis matrix: a three-dimensional puzzle (at least)

If traditional policy road maps including the sovereignty concept become disconnected, how should one proceed to develop a new framework for thinking about the many problems raised in this book? Assuming some of the guidelines previously mentioned, such as rejecting a "presumption" for or against power allocations towards an international level,[1] and focusing for a moment on the vast set of issues raised by power allocations, it can be seen that there are at least three dimensions to the array of possibilities

Policy analytical approaches and thought experiments

in which to locate a particular societal decision.[2] First, a vertical dimension comes to mind as expressed in Chapter 3 as the problem of allocating a decision at the broadest international level (e.g. Geneva and the WTO), or to an international regional institution (European Union), a nation-state (Germany), or a sub-federal unit such as a state or province, or even lower to a city or a neighborhood therein.

But a second dimension suggests that at each level there are often multiple governmental units which could be utilized: internationally, with a variety of international organizations (or new ones to be created); nationally, among various governmental segments including some designed for principles of checks and balances (executive, legislative, judicial) or allocated various degrees of "independence" such as certain commissions; and sub-national ("regional") entities with similar options.

Yet a third dimension, as expressed earlier,[3] could be available at each level or horizontal option, namely different *types of institutions*: government compared with non-government (and mixtures thereof), and within the non-government category, profit compared with non-profit structures (and many more variations such as religious or tribal units). Within the governmental category, "separation of powers" and checks and balances often need to be examined. This can lead to consideration of allocation of decision-making among a variety of entities, such as executive, legislative, and judicial.

A starting point to analysis would likely be to define the goal or objective being undertaken. Even this is complex, with there often being multiple goals for a particular undertaking. For example, regarding road safety there is a goal of protecting human life, yet there are opposing goals of economic necessity and of freedom of movement. Thus, multiple goals require "balancing" or "proportionality" concepts. Human rights goals are prime examples of elaborate and complex decisions regarding balancing or proportionality. They can also engage major issues about the level or horizontal choices regarding the allocation of decision-making authority.

As a thought experiment, assume that a policy question occurs regarding food safety for citizens, something which might arise in the light of very new technologies. Think of an example such as questions about genetically modified foodstuffs. These "GMOs" could provide new strains of grain which arguably hold out a promise of greatly reduced hunger and malnutrition in the world. On the other hand such new strains create some important risks, both as to the effects on human or animal/plant health and as to the competitive effects on producers of more traditional foodstuffs. There are thus a series of questions which are likely to be considered.

6.3 Towards a policy analysis matrix

1. An initial question could be whether governments should do anything about this, or should they (third dimension) leave it to nongovernment actors such as consumers or producers in a market system? But there may be market failure, for example, in instances where there are asymmetries of information. In that case should the government step in with prohibitions or labeling/information requirements?
2. What should be the basis of such action, and what level or choice of government entity should be allocated the appropriate decision? Would very local authorities have the information and resources to regulate appropriately? Would there be conflicts of interest at that level (e.g. protection of local producers of competing products?) Would national authorities do better? Or would such authorities have conflicts of interest or other governmental systemic problems (such as election finance defects) that would bias any decision?
3. In addition, is the configuration of world markets such as to make it impossible in practice for nations to regulate effectively? Would regulation in one country be ignored in another in situations where both are competing to sell in a third country? Or in the light of covert importing possibilities (often depending on geography and societal makeup) could a country even find it practical to regulate its own market? If so, should this suggest that an international level should have at least some of the decision making authority?
4. But then questions must be asked about the caliber and characteristics of existing or proposed international institutions. Would they have the structure for making educated and timely decisions? Would they have the resources? Might they also have conflicts of interests?
5. These questions also must consider the effects on principles of good governance of moving a decision far away from those affected. Subsidiarity would call for restraint in that direction. The degree to which a particular society might have cultural preferences dramatically different from the rest of the world (or from a world with a dizzyingly elaborate set of cultural preferences) would have to be taken into account.[4]
6. In evaluating these institutional allocation questions, a large number of issues regarding the structure or "constitution" of the institutions are often raised, such as whether there is an impartial "rule orientation" approach, and whether an "impartial" juridical institution exists which enhances the "rule orientation" concepts. But then issues arise about the effective and efficient operation of such institutions (such as are discussed in Chapters 4 and 5 regarding the WTO).

Thus it could happen that some of the questions would point towards the need for international control, while others relating to the international institutions would lean towards relying entirely or heavily on less international institutional approaches.

To begin to elaborate such a chain of "matrix issues" is to begin to think that national sovereignty solutions could be attractive after all, since they appear so much simpler, requiring less thought. The problem is that to tilt systemically towards the lower levels of decision making have been historically found to be disastrous in too many realms of endeavor. Add the circumstances of "globalization" to the mix, and one can readily find that we are doomed to the complexity of this policy analysis matrix.

If, however, so many answers to the questions above point towards an international approach, this makes it all the more vital that the international system be carefully appraised and forced to evolve in constructive directions which help it beneficially to resolve the myriad of questions being raised.

In many situations, balancing or proportionality[5] will be central to the resolution of questions like those above. But this simply adds another dimension to the matrix, namely who and what institutional structure should do the balancing. For example, should it be a relatively impartial juridical-type institution which, however, would probably of necessity be "elitist," or should it be more "democratically representative" and accountable to democratic political/diplomatic entities (if they exist in the particular case being examined)?

6.4 Economics and markets: a thought experiment about market failure in the era of globalization

As a "thought experiment," consider the following.[1]

Advocates for market economics argue that the most efficient process for decision making in an economy is to rely on the private sector to handle most of the choices, and to keep the government out. However, there are well-recognized exceptions of "market failure,"[2] and thus it becomes necessary to analyze what market failure is – when does it occur, and what are the possible responses?

Often, lists of market failures include monopolies and competition problems, asymmetries of information or lack of information, public goods and free rider problems, and "externalities." In each of those cases, one can have a look at how the economics of a globalized economically interdependent world operates. It is quite likely that in some

6.4 Economics and markets: a thought experiment

cases, if it is appraised only at the nation-state level, one could make one kind of judgment about the existence of market failure, but one could come to a different conclusion when one is looking at a broader, global or international level. Monopoly judgments will depend somewhat on how one defines the "relevant market." Are borders really open, and thus does a single producer within a nation-state really have to face competition and not have monopoly power? Asymmetries of information are found across national borders, particularly in different cultures and different languages.

Then, even if there is a judgment as to the existence of market failure that should lead to a government response, the kinds of government responses possible at the nation-state level differ dramatically from those at the international level. Most often, the international-level institutions do not have powers to effectively tax, subsidize, or in a major way alter market mechanisms (such as setting up tradable permits). Another governmental response is to have rules and prohibitions. Often at the international level this is almost the only available government response, and even it raises a very important realistic question as to whether a particular rule or prohibition will in fact be effective, that is, followed, and therefore operate efficiently to correct the market failure.

For example, there has been a lot of bitter fighting, at least in discourse, on the question of whether there should be an international competition policy or set of rules, an international competition policy for subjects such as monopoly and antitrust, and so on. There is some disconnect between the United States and the European Union on this. And for Europe, at least, in the Brussels institutions, there is quite a desire to have this subject integrated into international level institutions. The EU member states might be less interested actually. In the United States, there has been considerable opposition to the idea. After originally saying that there was no real need for it, it now, however, appears to be softening a bit. A US special commission, the International Competition Policy Advisory Committee (ICPAC), was constituted several years ago to study the idea and it issued a nuanced report.[3] The one thing it did say clearly was that more and more US antitrust cases involved an international aspect. Therefore, some argue for a need for at least some minimal coordination. We are beginning to see a trend that suggests that there is a needed response to market failure. That happens often at the nation-state level, but there are situations that are now a little beyond that level, and call for something at the international level.[4] It has been noted, however, that, to a rather large extent, competition policy is already "in the WTO," because a computer search shows over three dozen UR treaty text clauses dealing with competition, monopolies, and similar matters.[5]

But there are also major "constitutional" or procedural constraints which prevent or inhibit the addition of subjects to the WTO. For example, when there is discussion about placing a major responsibility regarding competition policy under a WTO umbrella, it is noted that competition policy cases can be extremely fact intensive, involving elaborate study of the way in which markets perform. Such study is not likely soon to be within the capability of the WTO processes. Thus, hesitation to put competition policy explicitly in the WTO is understandable, although a possible solution is to exempt competition policy from the DSU (similar to what was temporarily done concerning agricultural subsidies).[6] Such exemption, however, may detract from the desirability of putting more of this matter under the WTO umbrella.

Many more examples could be given to illustrate the policy analysis and landscape described above.

6.5 Thinking constitutional

There are at least four different definitions or types of "constitutionalism" concepts, and related to each of them is the question: what is a "constitution"? To some observers "constitution" is a term strictly reserved to the government of a nation-state. Clearly it implies more than just a single document, because for centuries persons have spoken of an "unwritten" constitution (especially in the case of the United Kingdom), and often the term will be used in a situation to embrace the fundamental structure of a nation or other entity which embraces not only written words, but a plethora of practices and evolutionary interpretations which can be said to include "custom" and implicit "understandings" sometimes termed the "*acquis*" of a governmental system.[1]

To this author, the idea that the word "constitution" is exclusively reserved to a single "sovereign" which observes no higher power does not adequately account for many uses of the word,[2] including uses for non-governmental entities. It is in this book used to embrace a variety of "constitution" authorities, using a variety (and often a large number) of instruments and traditional practices and experiences which have some impact on the views of constituents of an entity concerning the permissible procedures and behaviors involved in the process of governing. Some interesting, much debated questions include whether there are particular attributes in the instruments and traditional practices which must be

6.5 Thinking constitutional

observed for those instruments and practices to use the nomenclature "constitution." For example, should not a "constitution" imply a certain degree of stability involving constraints on the methods of change to the constitution, which constraints make it more difficult to change a constitution than a process that can occur with frequent referenda? Is an element of "rigidity" therefore likely to be a characteristic of a "constitution?"

Constitutionalism therefore would naturally seem to be a term used for the practice of being guided by and restrained from easy change of structure and purpose. In the broad sense this could apply to various levels of government, or even non-government societies.

The four different types of "constitutionalism" mentioned above can be seen in discussions of the following situations.

First, the term most often would apply to a nation-state which enjoys a "constitution," and as noted some would argue that this should be the exclusive use of the term.

Second, the term is sometimes used to put a normative meaning on the content of a constitution, that is, to argue that a "true constitution" which creates the practice of "constitutionalism" must have certain attributes, sometimes related to democratic practices or human rights.

Third, "constitutionalism" is used sometimes to describe the development of a particular "international" (or "transnational," meaning crossing borders) governmental institution or international organization. Thus developments in the United Nations under its 1945 Charter are described as having "constitutional significance," or reinforcing a spirit of "constitutionalism." In relation to the recent legal developments which propose changes in the legal structure of the European Union, there has been a large amount of discussion about whether proposed new treaties would be "only treaties" or whether they would constitute a "constitution." Straddling this approach are the uses of terms in the EU context of "treaty-based constitution," or "constitutional treaty."[3] The use of the term "constitution" or "constitutional" in this and similar contexts can in fact have some major consequences, particularly in the process of interpreting and construing the basic legal norms and the way in which such process might result in evolution of the institution itself.[4] There is also an intriguing conundrum embedded in these developing constitutional processes, namely how in the modern European context the participants in these processes should develop and appropriate a mode for establishing a new "constitution" which is recognized to have legitimacy. Is the treaty route adequate? Or would procedures more analogous to that of the United States and other nations, relying heavily on

Policy analytical approaches and thought experiments

broad participation in referenda-type voting rather than elite negotiators, be more appropriate?[5]

Fourth, a perhaps more nebulous and less regular use of the term "constitutionalism" is the situation in which it describes the processes of norm creation (and evolutionary application) of the entire international law system as a whole. In this sense, it represents the subject of this book and many other studies which struggle with the issues of concepts like "sovereignty," or international customary law, or treaty formation.[6]

Part of the issue of constitutionalism or the application of a constitution deals with a variety of power allocation issues, even within a particular nation-state. Of course the US Constitution deals extensively with the partition of authority between the US federal government and its sub-federal states. The framers and commentators often use the term "sovereign" to describe those sub-federal states. It also deals with such partition among the three branches of the federal government (executive, legislative, judicial) and stresses the importance of "separation of powers" and "checks and balances."[7] In addition, a curious feature of US constitutional law (depending primarily on the US Supreme Court for development) is the "sovereign" status accorded to various Indian tribes in the United States. This use of the term "sovereign" clearly is different from the use of that term in international terms as described in this book and in the vast literature on sovereignty partly described in Chapter 3.[8] Here the meaning is not to provide for the tribes a theory of their monopoly on power even within their territories, but rather to recognize the overriding power of the US government while carving out certain allocations of power to those tribes for particular purposes.

Likewise the evolution of the European Union from 1957 (and even before, i.e., since 1952) onward has seen a huge number of elaborate negotiations and struggles over power allocation among the various entities of the European Union and over its relationships to other branches of EU governance (Council, Parliament, Commission, Court of Justice) and with its member nation-states.[9]

For international law and the law of international institutions, the term "constitutionalism" can have very great importance. As to the fourth definition type mentioned above, the term could signify and endorse an overall approach to "redesigning" the fundamentals of international law (including international economic law and international institutional law). It could be the rubric with a flavor of approval and promise, to cover present and further necessary study and activity designed to examine the "gestalt" of the international legal system. "Constitutionalism" thus may

6.5 Thinking constitutional

be a good approach to developing replacements or substitutes for the many existing perplexities and challenges to the overall international system. "Constitutionalism" could, if evolved appropriately with considerable careful thinking and discussion combined with practical experiments blending eventually into general practice, substitute for the problematic concepts of "sovereignty" and their corollaries such as the troubled "consent theory" of international norm making, the dilemmas of the concept of equality of nations, the desperate need to redress the atrocities of failed and rogue nation-states, the sometimes unrepresentative modes of treaty making, and other out-dated theories. Practice of international law in certain subject areas, such as international economic law and the WTO, can sometimes contribute to such new approaches for the international legal system, as chapters 4 and 5 sometimes suggest explicitly or implicitly.

Also for international law, however, is the importance of "constitutional" thinking about specific institutions. The "treaty versus constitution" conundrum exists here also,[10] but arguably a treaty "charter" signals the intent of the treaty adherents to create a "constitutional" entity (such as the United Nations, many other international organizations including the World Trade Organization, and the Bretton Woods institutions[11]). If the world begins to view the foundation documents of international organizations, and their interpretation and application, in the sense of "constitutionalism," this could be more constructive than the relatively blind adherence to the mantra of "sovereignty" when facing some of the issues discussed in the previous chapters of this book. Professor Thomas Franck's Lauterpacht lectures[12] describe some of this new process in connection with the United Nations charter, and chapters 4 and 5 in this book also suggest some movement in the "constitutional" direction for the WTO.[13]

Such careful thinking should not presume a tilt in juridical application of the constituent (better to say "constitutional"?) documents, either in favor of internationalizing results or the contrary. Nevertheless, some serious thought is warranted to explore issues such as decision making (and problems of consensus), "treaty" (now "constitutional") interpretation techniques and the shortcomings of the Vienna Convention on the Law of Treaties, tensions between a juridical body and the diplomatic/political processes of an organization, the role and possible importance in at least some contexts of "rule orientation" procedures including the existence of a juridical type body, and many issues of "good governance" including transparency (information available to the public and to non-government entities), appropriate participation of various actors (but not such as to distort the legitimate democratic representation of duly elected officials), and true accountability.[14]

It may be that globalization will require more support for international governmental activity in the context of certain activities, such as those related to economic market developments, or human rights, or a myriad of other issues. But factored in should be the necessary opportunity for a variety of societies to choose certain characteristics for their governments to carry out constituent mandates. For example, tolerance for variety in economic structures and in distribution or redistribution of wealth within a society, arguably should have a stronger "subsidiarity" component than might be considered appropriate for human rights, or use of armed force. Indeed, even for human rights the history and experience of the European Convention on Human Rights (clearly the most successful international endeavor for the protection of human rights the world has seen) contains the remarkable, nuanced idea of "margin of appreciation," which makes the Convention sensitive to diverse and evolving societal appreciation of certain specific (and arguably newly developing) human rights.[15]

Interface concepts (as discussed in relation to one example in section 6.7) are relevant to these thoughts.

Additional considerations in these "constitutionalism" developments should recognize the fact that international organizations sometimes can go astray or be faulted for corrupt, inefficient, or inappropriately elitist privileges and immunities.[16] Thus care should be given to build into the international "constitutional" system (in the third and fourth definitions mentioned above) strong checks and balances. Indeed, some would argue that the continuing importance and strength of the nation-state system lies in just such important checks and balances.[17] This is based on the not inappropriate observation that in many respects it is still often the nation-state which best protects democratic principles, including, in some cases, human rights. The international system is strongly criticized, with some justification, for its lack of "democratic legitimacy," including the deficiencies mentioned in paragraphs above. One example of a check and balance in this context is the structure of some nation-state constitutions and governments that do not provide that treaties "apply directly." Although there is considerable academic criticism of this perceived domestic mistreatment of treaties, it has also been noted that treaties in some contexts are not democratically arrived at, even within many nation-states, so the requirement of legislative attention and action to apply a treaty in domestic law helps preserve the democratic principles for international norm making, recognizing that in today's globalized world many international norms have very profound effects on various constituencies and individual citizens. Another way to think about some of these matters is to worry a bit about "rogue international organizations" as well as "rogue states."[18]

6.6 The growing importance of juridical institutions

One of the more important implications of the WTO experience so far is the rapidly developing importance of the WTO Dispute Settlement system. This system has been described as the "jewel in the crown" of the WTO, and Chapter 5 explored that system in some detail. Chapter 4, section 4.2, explained the basic importance of "rule orientation" to the WTO and the world trading system. Chapter 5 noted the developments in WTO jurisprudence including the history of the dispute settlement system under GATT, which then evolved into the WTO with the Uruguay Round enhancements. As noted in section 5.2, even under GATT the DS system with all its defects had become attractive to various interests because of its perceived effect in promoting compliance and therefore effectiveness of treaty norms. (Why negotiate treaty norms if they are not effective?[1]) The WTO system greatly strengthened that system, so that now the WTO DS system is described as the most powerful and therefore "significant" international broad multilateral juridical system which exists, and probably the most impressive in many respects which the world has ever seen.[2]

In a number of other treaty and institutional contexts, it is possible to observe greater importance being attached to a dispute settlement system. The European Community[3] established at its beginning a strong judicial branch of its "governance," which has had a profound effect on the "constitutional development" of that international organization.[4]

Of course the Law of Sea Tribunal and its multiple "tracks" approach broke some new ground (but is still getting established, with a small number of cases so far completed, or brought).[5] The World Intellectual Property Organization (WIPO) developed a set of new rules for dispute settlement, possibly stimulated to do so by the Uruguay Round negotiation and conclusion of the TRIPs agreement.[6]

NAFTA established a multi-track dispute settlement system which in many respects emulates that of the GATT and WTO.[7] Several bilateral or small-group free trade area agreements are incorporating DS systems,[8] and Mercosur, the customs union of four southernmost Latin American nations[9] includes an important institutional treaty framework for dispute settlement, still not too much used.[10] It has even been said by some in connection with Mercosur and other trade treaty developments that unless there is a meaningful dispute settlement procedure for treaty application, which can resolve ambiguities and gaps, the market participants (multinational business entities, etc.) will not take the treaty norms seriously enough to build them into their strategic business plans.[11] In private discussions with this author, officials in other international organizations, including long-standing ones, have indicated an inclination to develop *de novo* some specialized procedures for dispute settlement or mediation.[12] There is a developing worry (expressed in some literature and ongoing research) about "fragmentation of international juridical institutions." However, there are numerous counterarguments, including the important views of Jonathan Charney expressed in his 1998 Hague lectures.[13]

As noted in section 5.1, diplomats and national political leaders are still uneasy about dispute settlement, such that at least in GATT/WTO there is hesitation in using terms such as "court," or "tribunal" or even other similar terms suggesting a strong court-like procedure. Thus this author has utilized a "softer" or more ambiguous term, that of "juridical." The hesitations sometimes represent a fear of the unknown. Some national diplomatic services have not included "positions" denominated for law trained persons, instead appointing persons with such expertise as "economists" for which "slots" do exist. Older diplomats may feel threatened by their (often much younger) lawyers' expertise. Likewise there has been much criticism of the alleged "extreme legalization" brought on by the dispute settlement systems, which some argue (not without some truth) sometimes gets in the way of appropriate diplomatic settlements and accommodation.[14] The WTO DS system has gradually embraced elements found in many domestic legal systems, such as the right to utilize and retain private lawyers of a disputant's choosing, considerable argumentation on procedural points (testing uncharted waters, and not unexpected at the start-up of a new procedural system), and very long reports (sometimes possibly excessively long).[15]

Yet, as also noted in Chapter 5, there seems to be widespread support for the WTO DS system, with considerable utilization including by many developing countries (even *between* developing countries), and some relatively spectacular rulings favoring small and/or developing nations in litigation against giant industrial trading nations.[16] The support leads some to conclude that the WTO members should be cautious about reforms or changes, so as to "do no harm."[17]

The dynamics of a dispute settlement system can also extend very broadly beyond the particular disputants. Several recent cases regarding

6.6 The growing importance of juridical institutions

agricultural subsidies and trade restraints of the principal WTO membership (the United States and the European Union) resulted in findings in favor of the developing country complainants[18] which clearly will have an effect on the ongoing trade negotiations in the current Doha Round.[19] The difficulties of the WTO regarding norm change may have led to a stronger motive for using the DS system to achieve goals seemingly blocked in the diplomatic negotiations. Furthermore, these cases may be seen to "crack open" a subject that has perplexed and stymied the world trading system at least for a half century (if not for a century).[20] It can also be argued that the curious case brought by the European Union[21] on taxation reductions on export goods, resulting in a finding against the United States, may have led the US Congress to address some tax measures which some members of that body wanted to change anyway.[22]

The importance of "rule orientation" in international affairs (particularly in the context of treaties), which generally is intended to emphasize rule security and predictability, strongly underscores the desirability of an effective dispute settlement system. As noted in Chapter 4,[23] such policy objective is strongly supported by need of market systems for "institutional structure." Furthermore, as outlined in Chapter 5,[24] there is a substantial number of policy goals relating to the desirability of dispute settlement systems in various international contexts (as also noted, some of these goals are not always mutually consistent, so there are policy objective tensions that sometimes require "balancing"). However, these policy objectives, and the now considerable experience in international institutions including the WTO, strongly suggest that an important role for a juridical institutional framework exists in many contexts of international relations, and such institutions can often be considered as important prerequisites for changes in the international systems including institutions and "constitutionalism," that are necessary in the light of globalization and other problems troubling the existing international law system. In the context of a broad scope of subject matter competence (which, although addressing economic issues, is not confined to more specialized or technical international law subjects),[25] the WTO offers the most elaborate broad multilateral international juridical system and the most detailed reported jurisprudence evidencing how that system is operating in existence today. The caseload and report statistics noted in Chapter 5[26] and the tens of thousands of pages of what is generally accepted as high quality jurisprudence (albeit not without debate on some particular points) confirm this importance of the WTO. Many issues addressed in those pages will necessarily be part of almost any international juridical institution, including such subjects as burden of proof, prima facie case, procedures for fact finding, standard of review and deference to national governments (and "margin of appreciation"), precedent, interpretation techniques, and so on.[27]

6.7 Interface theory: managing globalization in a world of wide variation

Policies which suggest the need for international institutional structures to enhance cooperation and coordination benefits constantly come into tension with opposing policies urging "subsidiarity" or institutional structures which benefit various local interests. Such subsidiarity policies clearly have many values which need consideration, as discussed in Chapter 3.[1] Nevertheless, too much stress on local needs can be costly to broader policies for enhancing world (and local!) welfare and other international policies designed to keep the peace or protect human rights. Economic concepts of comparative advantage, and the risks demonstrated by the prisoner's dilemma mentioned in section 6.1 provide incentives for structures which will diminish those risks and build on comparative advantage or other policies which point towards disciplines provided at levels "higher than" the nation-state. Consequently a difficult analytical and balancing process is often called for to accommodate these opposing approaches.

Sometimes such policies lead to extensive "harmonization" or international structures encouraging measures of uniformity in national regulation to conform to international disciplines, and indeed the history and landscape of current international institutions is replete with examples. The "global market" itself can be an important force for greater uniformity, for example with respect to accounting rules or corporate governance standards, as well as many product or service standards,[2] to which market participants will respond.

When a global institution such as the WTO develops such disciplines, however, the enormous variety of governmental, political, economic, cultural and other societal institutions imposes constraints on the international disciplines, and sometimes meets with extreme countermeasures. This is true for a variety of subject matters. An important example particularly relevant to international economic law is the existence of important differences among a variety of national economic structures, ranging from market-oriented systems, to non-market economics to transition economies, from rich to poor, from agricultural to industrial to service-oriented, and so on. A question which arises (and arose in the history of GATT) is to what extent a more comprehensive membership provides

6.7 Interface theory: managing globalization

advantages which outweigh economic structure differences. If part of the objective of the system is to preserve peace, it can be argued that global membership is more important than uniformity of economic systems. Clearly the new membership of China, as well as other applicant countries, involves important policy choices and balances. Also it was clearly difficult for GATT and now the WTO to develop a mechanism which can accommodate such differences.

What is not always realized, however, is the degree to which relatively minor cultural differences or differences in economic structures can come into tension with policies of trade liberalization. Differences in internal (and sometimes ancient) economic practices can have substantial trade-inhibiting effects.

An illustration of these problems can be seen in a hypothetical situation which has been analyzed in relation to antidumping laws and the GATT/WTO rules regarding them. The "dumping" concept can be defined in many ways, and import tariffs to counter "dumping" (because dumping is termed "unfair") create considerable tensions. As described in a recent casebook on international trade law,

> As the subject of unfair practices develops, however, it becomes clear that it reaches deeply into matters of domestic concern to governments, and the question of unfairness becomes more controversial. In many cases of subsidies, for example, the government providing such subsidies feels that they are an essential and praiseworthy tool of government, sometimes useful to correct disparities of income, or to help disadvantaged groups or regions. With respect to dumping, for example, it is argued that such a practice, a form of price discrimination, actually has beneficial effects on world and national prosperity, encouraging competition. The rules for responding to some unfair trade practices allow use of import restrictions, such as added duties, which can be anticompetitive and can reduce world welfare. In some cases, exporting nations feel bitterness towards these import restrictions on their trade, and argue that the rules on unfair trade are being manipulated by special interests for effectively protectionist reasons.[3]

Consider the following hypothetical economic situation of two societies, both of which are strong market-oriented economies, but which have relatively modest structural differences. As this case demonstrates, the impact of "variable" costs compared with "fixed" costs can give rise to differences in the way in which respective economies operate over the course of a business cycle, such as to create tensions about the fairness of governmental actions designed to offset some of the differences. These tensions arise even though neither economy operates consciously unfair policies. To accommodate these problems it is suggested that the international structures

Policy analytical approaches and thought experiments

need to provide an "interface mechanism" which allows such different economies to trade in a friendly and sustained manner.

Consider then the following, as described in the International Economic Relations casebook mentioned above:

Take an industrial sector (such as steel) in two economies (such as the United States and Japan) with the following characteristics:

Society A: Worker tenure (no layoffs of workers); capitalization with a high debt-equity ratio (e.g. 90 percent debt).

Society B: No worker tenure (wages for workers are therefore variable costs); capitalization with low debt-equity ratio (e.g. less than 50 percent) (dividends can be skipped).

In time of slack demand, economists note that it is rational for a firm to continue to produce as long as it can sell its product at or above its short-term variable costs. This is true because it must in any event pay its fixed costs. Of course, this is true only for limited periods; presumably over the regular full course of the business cycle, the firm can only incur losses which will harm the firm in the long term.

An analysis of the short-term variable costs of firms in societies A and B can be done as shown in table 6.1.

As noted above, it will be rational for producers in Society A to continue production so long as they can obtain a price equivalent to 250 units of production, while producers in Society B need to receive a price of 530. Thus, in a period of falling prices and demand, the producers in Society A can be expected to garner, through exports to Society B, an increasing share of the Society B market. Suppose this happens, and the firms in Society B close. Are Society A's exports to Society B unfair?

Table 6.1. *Analysis of the short-term variable costs of firms in societies A and B*

	Society A	Society B
	(costs expressed as units of production)	
Plant upkeep	20 fixed	20 fixed
Debt service	90 fixed	50 fixed
Dividends (cost of capital)	10 variable	50 variable
Worker costs	240 fixed	240 variable
Costs of materials	240 variable	240 variable
Total costs	600	600
of which		
Fixed	350	70
Variable	250	530

232

6.7 Interface theory: managing globalization

There are no easy answers to the questions raised above. Indeed, they are in fact probably more complicated than the foregoing would indicate because whatever general rules exist, it is argued that special considerations should apply to developing countries, and to "emerging" or transition economies.

Often the response engendered by the above hypothetical situation is to apply antidumping duties. Thus this awkward response becomes a sort of interface mechanism. Likewise, "safeguard" measures or rules against subsidies can be similarly justified. An important question is whether these existing mechanisms are too blunt or are subject to too much manipulation for protectionist goals. The broader subject raised by these circumstances is the need, in a complex and varied world, for measures that can appropriately reconcile, or at least balance, the competing goals of desirable coordination and competition, while providing "policy space" to individual national economic (and cultural) systems, possibly through rule structures which also engage "variable geometry."[4]

7

Illustrative applications

> In the context of a globalizing world in which states acting alone cannot achieve important performance goals, only the processes of treaty-based cooperative action can overcome this growing inability to achieve those goals. This is particularly the case when it comes to economic affairs, which are often driven by global economic structures – global companies, global markets and global distribution networks – which individual states acting alone cannot effectively manage or regulate. Cooperation through a treaty institution may be the only way out.
>
> WTO Consultative Board Report, 2005[1]

7.1 Illustrative applications – grappling with detail and diversity

In order to make more concrete some of the ideas put forward in the previous chapters of this book, Chapter 7 touches on a few illustrative applications, thus to "round out" the logic and descriptions elsewhere presented.

If anything, these short presentations illustrate the complexity of the various subjects, as well as their diversity. Clearly no single size fits all, but if the thrust of this book is understood to demystify and "de-mantra-ize" some of the older and traditional concepts of international law including those of sovereignty and the consent theory of norm legitimization, so as to reduce some of the restraints on thinking imposed by those concepts, this could be taken as at least limited success.

These applications are not selected to be comprehensive, nor to represent any judgment about relative importance. They are partly drawn from the particular expertise of this author (international economic law), but also to illustrate again that the experience of international economic law can and should assist thinking about international law in general, as well as to illustrate the reciprocal relationships of IEL and IL.

7.1 Illustrative applications – grappling with detail and diversity

In particular, questions that arise with each of these different application situations include the following: Is any resort to international law or institutions necessary? If it is necessary, what factors should enter into a decision whether to embrace international law and extend the competence of international law institutions to the situation? These factors must include not only whether the independent private or governmental measures involved require some international dimensions, but also whether the available or potentially available international rules and institutions have the capability of enhancing those measures in terms of achieving the desired policy goals, and in addition whether they have the possibility or potential of checks and balances against abuse and misuse and provide for the elements of "good governance" and accountability which are important at the international level as well as at the nation-state level.

In addition, the analysis must go further and consider what "portions" of nation-state competence ("sovereignty slice"?) would need to be granted to the international institutions, and whether such grants could be reversed if need be, or modified over time to keep abreast of rapidly changing circumstances affecting the operation of the international institutions.

Often, different societies may have different views on these questions, sometimes because a particular society and its officials draw analogies about governing activities from their domestic experiences. Sometimes these analogies are fallacious, because the international context differs from that of the domestic situations.

For example, when it comes to international activity affecting the operation of a particular market circumstance, national societies may have vastly different views about the efficacy and fairness of the way in which markets work. These views are often conditioned by the specifics of market operation in a particular legal (e.g. regulatory) context. Thus to transport a corporate securities market system from a national structure that involves elaborate and effective legal institutions in order to prevent fraud or ensure fairness, into an international framework where those institutions are lacking can indeed be unsatisfactory.

These policy and institutional questions differ dramatically from subject to subject, as well as from society to society. When they focus on the operation of markets for economic productivity and efficiency they may lead to certain conclusions, whereas in the context of such subjects as health or human rights, or even environmental goals, they could lead to opposite conclusions. Failures of certain regulatory measures in some societies may lead such societies to seek external controls or parameters, while other societies would feel much more comfortable in retaining all aspects of such measures under their own national government controls. Indeed, in some cases certain interests in a particular society may find it impossible to achieve certain particular regulatory goals (which may or may not be in the broader best interest of society) and therefore would like to obtain their specific (and even anti-social) goals by seeking international-level activities that would enhance those particular goals. Special interest advocacy is not a monopoly of nation-states; it also exists at the international level.

Some of the prior sections of this book also include ideas relevant to this chapter, such as section 4.7, which deals with how the scope or mandate for WTO competence could be limited or expanded, and also section 6.4, which uses competition policy as the basis of a thought experiment using "market failure" ideas.

After this introduction this chapter continues with several sections which focus on the operation of markets. These can be read in conjunction with section 4.7, and section 6.4 noted above. Section 7.2 revisits the WTO, to pursue the discussion of "scope of competence" which was outlined in 4.7, this time exploring the WTO jurisprudence (including Chapter 5) which could affect decisions about that scope. Section 7.3 then takes the story to another current economic policy issue, namely investment.

Next, another grouping of sections turns to questions less dominated by market operation (but not always excluding market considerations), namely environment (section 7. 4), health (section 7.5) and human rights (section 7.6). These issues obviously engage more strongly many societal cultural and moral choices, and thus it would not be surprising if national attitudes varied a great deal.

Section 7.7 then briefly looks at and compares the fascinating struggles of both the European Union and the United States to develop or evolve their "constitutions" and the allocation of power within those entities.

Section 7.8 concludes the chapter with a brief note about the relevance of many parts of this book to problems of the United Nations and its rules regarding the use of force.

Conclusions and perspectives will be reserved to the last chapter of this book, Chapter 8.

7.2 The WTO and its "constitution": institutional detail and dynamic evolution

Section 4.7 outlined some of the controversy about the scope of competence of the WTO, but this section explores that subject as it relates to

7.2 The WTO and its "constitution"

some of the detailed structure and jurisprudence aspects of the institution. Can it cope with the needs of the world community?

With respect to the development of new rules, through a negotiating procedure, or possibly as amendments to the treaties, or by certain decisions of WTO members, the negotiating nation-states in late 1993 clearly recast the proposals for the development of the WTO Charter text, so as to restrain the power in that part of the WTO. Thus the original text proposals were amended to develop new and more constraining rules of procedure for various decisions. Super-majority requirements were added, including the relatively extreme "super-majority" requirement of "consensus." Specific other constraining elements were introduced into various, already fairly weak, powers that were granted to the WTO diplomatic/negotiating part of the organization. For example, "definitive interpretations" of the WTO Agreements included in the expansive Annexes, were made possible by an explicit delegation of authority for such action to a super-voting structure of the WTO. As noted in Chapter 4, this action requires a three-fourths vote of the entire membership of the organization, which many observers feel can probably not be achieved.[1] Likewise, the amending clauses of the WTO are quite severe,[2] albeit somewhat similar to the pattern of its predecessor GATT, which, towards the end of its life, was deemed not to be amendable. Many of these features have resulted in what, in earlier publications and earlier parts of this book, this author has described as "treaty rigidity."[3]

The WTO has a number of systemic or "constitutional" problems, which clearly are affecting, and will continue to affect, its place in the overall landscape of power allocation. The WTO foundations are deeply embedded in the historical context of its "constitution," which is to say, embedded in the past century of trade policy and negotiation, much of which was influenced by nineteenth-century concepts. These concepts may imply too much emphasis on "reciprocity," which seems strongly related to mercantilist concepts so much criticized by many international economists. These concepts also involve a higher degree of emphasis on "sovereignty," including many of its fictions, than may be appropriate for today's globalized system. For example, a number of the measures embedded in the treaty language of the WTO, especially GATT, are exceptions that were formulated in the past for national or nation-state special political needs, namely the escape clause, antidumping, countervailing duties, and so on.

In addition, and related to the previous statements, it can be argued that the WTO is weighted too much overall, in its rules and decision-making processes, in favor of a tilt towards producer-oriented approaches. This emphasis on "market access" – for diplomats' home producers to gain markets abroad while at the same time limiting that producing market when it comes to imports of goods from other producer countries – creates a constant tension in the procedures, negotiations, and even in the dispute settlement system of the WTO.

Likewise, the WTO has a number of institutional difficulties, including decision-making that is too dependent on a "consensus" approach, and decision-making authorities in the WTO Charter that have been extremely constrained to protect "nation-state sovereignty." Some of these institutional problems run the risk of pushing important decision activities into the dispute settlement system, where that system is called upon to play a "law making" rather than a "law applying" role.[4]

In addition, the WTO has a number of serious institutional or "constitutional" faults and problems. It is appropriately criticized for its relative lack of openness (although much progress over this has been achieved). It is also vulnerable to criticism about its antiquated, sloppy, and inefficient relationships to nongovernment organizations. Some of these problems stem from outdated attitudes to modes of diplomacy and an exaggerated sense of privilege for nation-state diplomats who claim legitimacy (whether the legitimacy purportedly stems from democratic governance or some other source). On the other hand, some opposition to any changes comes from Third World fears that the changes could be implemented in a way that could be abused by some of the great trading powers, fears that have considerable basis in experience.

Nevertheless, the analysis regarding allocating power, particularly in the face of needs of international cooperative mechanisms for the globalized market, cannot stop at the WTO. It must also look at alternatives. These alternatives can include institutions other than multilateral institutions, such as regional institutions, bilateral treaties, and even unilateral actions. They can include dependence on nation-state decisions, ad hoc diplomacy, and quite a number of other possibilities. This power allocation analysis thus becomes a very complex landscape. This means that the agenda for that analysis, and therefore the agenda for consideration of the evolutionary needs of the WTO, is quite long.

The question is not whether the WTO, as now constituted, should be the location of additional inter-nation coordinating power, but whether, given the alternatives, the WTO is capable of being, or at least of evolving into, the best available location for such power allocation. Clearly, many of these issues require further thought and research, but the complexities (and uncertainties) are so great that one should not expect a definitive road map that is very detailed.

7.2 The WTO and its "constitution"

Contrast the problems outlined above with the dispute settlement part of the WTO, which, as indicated earlier, is extraordinarily powerful. The members of the WTO are beginning to see and, in some cases, resent and fear that power. Part of the reason that the power is so great is the relative weakness of the other part – the non-dispute settlement part – of the institution. In theory, that negotiating/diplomatic part of the organization should be able to ameliorate or, to a certain extent, overrule the dispute settlement part, possibly through the process of a definitive interpretation. But as the organization has evolved so far in its short history, this has not occurred. Therefore the results of a dispute settlement process that goes all the way through the many steps including the appeal are binding[5] and obligatory as a matter of international law, and have the effect of being the final word that is available to disputing parties.

To a great degree the dispute settlement system has been quite effective, and a very elaborate jurisprudence has already developed during its short existence. There does seem to be a modicum of greater predictability and possibly stability, but, on the other hand, powerful nation-state governmental participants are beginning to appear restless and sometimes unwilling to implement fully the results of the dispute settlement process.

Another thing that becomes interesting in regard to our power analysis in this book is the impact of various details of the institutional structure of the WTO on the degree of power that it exercises. For example, with particular reference to the dispute settlement process, one can now see the importance of the selection of the members of the Appellate Body. In addition, certain procedural rules and interpretive methodologies obviously have an impact on the degree of power that can be located in the WTO dispute settlement system. One question that has been raised, although not prominently put forward, is the degree to which precedent should result from the reports of the dispute settlement system. The stronger the degree of precedent (for example, if *stare decisis* were to be a correct characterization of the level of precedent), the more power the dispute settlement system would seem to have. This is undoubtedly one of the reasons why, under general international law, *stare decisis* is *not* the prevailing approach, and is opposed by some experienced WTO dispute settlement officials.[6] However, as we have seen in section 5.7.a, there are a number of different levels of precedent impact, short of *stare decisis*, which can have different degrees of influence on the power of the dispute settlement system in developing reports and interpretations.

Another example is what is sometimes called the "standard of review," or the "degree of deference," which the dispute settlement system should

239

extend to nation-state governmental decisions that it is reviewing (see section 5.6). If the deference is very great, then the power of the dispute settlement system is more constrained. On the other hand, if the deference is minimal, the converse can be seen to be operative. There are many other such relatively detailed and often unassuming characteristics of the dispute settlement system, which can, however, at least in the aggregate, have an enormous impact on the extent of its power. This is a lesson to be learned by diplomats and treaty negotiators in the future. Such enhanced or additional power of a dispute settlement system may actually work to the overall advantage of some of the policy goals that are the fundamental foundation of the institution itself. Without such rigor and power in the dispute settlement system, many of the policy objectives, such as predictability and security, may be lost. On the other hand, nation-states desire and deserve a certain degree of "policy space" or "margin of appreciation" to be able to take actions that work on behalf of their constituents. Thus ideas of "subsidiarity" could apply to even some of these relatively minute details of the procedures of a dispute settlement system. One could go on at great length in this regard about many other details of both parts of the WTO, and how they affect the allocation of power, but for the purposes of this chapter these illustrations and examples should suffice as examples.

However, as noted in section 6.4, one of the characteristics of the WTO dispute settlement system that constrain its ability to take on new subjects is the weakness of its fact-finding mechanism. Government measures regarding competition policy have often been accomplished by elaborate fact-finding in a juridical setting, so that the absence of this capability is clearly a constraint on allocation of subject matter to the WTO.

7.3 Investments and international rules

Investment flows which cross national borders are part of an economic subject which has attracted an enormous amount of discussion, writing, and advocacy relating to international law. A brief overview of that subject can remind readers of this book that it often engages the tensions between nation-state sovereignty and international norms.[1] Some of the older elaborations of the subject relate to the issues involved in national government expropriation (seizure) of foreign investment.[2] Other discussions as well as negotiations deal with bilateral and multilateral investment treaties, sometimes stimulated by the renowned difficulty with and arguably unsatisfactory (read "controversial") status of customary international law norms concerning expropriation and adequate compensation.[3]

7.3 Investments and international rules

In addition to the expropriation questions, other issues have increasingly been addressed concerning cross-border investment and the effect of the presence in a society of foreign-based multinational corporations (MNCs). Questions include the conduct of such entities, and the worries that some of them have such enormous power that they can undertake activities which may undermine nation-state policy goals, such as those relating to worker safety and health, adequate pay, the right of labor unions to organize, and taxes.[4] Some of this thinking leads economists and other professionals in the subject area to feel that nation-state governments acting unilaterally or even in small groups simply do not have the capability to regulate appropriately these various activities in such a way as to carry out legitimate (and democratically endorsed) policy objectives established for such nations. It seems to be a classic situation requiring coordination and cooperation activity enhanced by international measures.

Most commentators with expertise in economics or related subjects note the great contribution which foreign investment, and the MNCs (which often go with it), can make to a particular economy's development, and also to world welfare. This can come about as a result of transfers of technology (including workers learning through employment with the foreign subsidiaries), higher pay than local standards, and higher productivity because of investment in machinery and techniques of production.[5]

This subject, like so many in this chapter, is clearly multidimensional, involving a number of different policy issues and different tensions between such policies. Thus it is not surprising that international norms are sought and proposed to try to ameliorate some of the perceived difficulties. Often governments of richer societies with the ability to send investment resources, enter into negotiations with the hosting countries to try to establish norms which will protect the investment-sending citizens at least from the most arbitrary and unfair host country government measures relating to the foreign economic activity in its territory. A series of bilateral agreements known as "BITS" (bilateral investment treaties) have come into force since the end of the 1950s,[6] so that they now number more than 2,200, encompassing 176 countries.[7] Earlier treaties known as "FCN" (friendship, commerce, and navigation) agreements were numerous also, although the combination of new forms of treaty such as the BIT and the GATT/WTO have largely taken over most of the subjects of the FCN agreements (although many still exist on the books).[8]

In sum, internationalization is now and has been for centuries an important part of the world economic picture concerning investment flows. Nevertheless, in the last few decades a very contentious issue has been whether the world should develop an "MIA" (multilateral investment agreement). The Organization for Economic Cooperation and Development (OECD)[9] began in 1995 a negotiation designed to achieve an MIA,[10] but this ended unsuccessfully in 1998, partly because the OECD membership[11] lacked the effective participation of most developing countries (which is essential to the success of a MIA). Subsequently, the question has been prominently raised whether the WTO should take on this task. Some WTO members, including Japan and the European Community,[12] have pushed hard for opening a negotiation for an MIA, starting at the Seattle WTO Ministerial in late 1999 which failed to reach agreement.[13] After a hiatus, a new WTO Ministerial occurred at Doha, Qatar,[14] which resulted in the Doha Ministerial Declaration calling for preparations for a new round of trade negotiations, but contained equivocal and contentious language as to whether the agenda would include negotiation for an MIA.[15] At the follow-up Ministerial in September 2003[16] several nations again pushed hard for inclusion of several issues (called the "Singapore Issues")[17] including the MIA, and again an impasse occurred, partly because of adamant developing country opposition, especially to the MIA. Following that event, a long and arduous negotiation occurred to restart the Doha process and launch a new negotiation. Because US elections were to take place in 2004, it was perceived that not much concrete could occur until 2005, but the WTO members did achieve in August 2004 a framework agreement for further advancing the Doha negotiation process.[18] This agreement, however, makes it quite clear that the MIA will not be on the agenda (absent some unforeseeable developments).

Why should this be such an issue? For one thing, many observers note the existence of the many BITs, and argue there is no need for an MIA. However, the fragmented nature of the multiplicity of the BITS is deemed by others to be inefficient, putting greater administrative burdens on developing countries with minimal capacity to administer many BITS, and probably adding to the transaction costs for investment of the treaty system, a cost to be born by both investors and the host country beneficiaries of the investment.[19] Furthermore, it is noted that the current WTO agreements contain many references to investment matters, particularly in the GATS (General Agreement on Trade in Services – this WTO text deals *inter alia* with "business presence" within a host country, which presence is necessary to facilitate trade and often needs an investment component (local facilities, finishing premises, after-sale service, etc.)). There are also a few other norms in the WTO treaty system relevant to treatment of foreign investment, including some imposing a national treatment obligation on the host country government regulatory measures. Furthermore, it is generally recognized by observers and scholars that rules affecting investment are logically closely associated with the policy goals of trade. These goals include policies mentioned in preceding chapters,[20] such as keeping the peace, enhancing world welfare, alleviating poverty (in poor nations), and generally managing risks created or exacerbated by globalization.

This is a brief overview of the very complex and contentious subject of economic regulation, which many feel needs a more careful and appropriate relationship to the trading system and to international economic institutions generally. Some predict that eventually an MIA or something nearly the same, will take its place under the WTO umbrella, or if blocked there, will be established in some other institutional structure, perhaps one yet to be created. This overview also demonstrates the complexity of some of the decisions about "internationalization" of subjects, since here the issue arguably is not alone or even prominently the question of establishing international norms, but more about the question of which types of norms and which types of institutions should be the best way to proceed. Much is at stake, because the reliance and further development of bilateral activity may have the effect of lessening the bargaining power of weaker nations, including most of the poorer countries. A multilateral forum may be better able to protect the interests of the poorer countries most needing inward investment. It may also have a "signaling" effect, encouraging increased investment for participants in the system. Yet, paradoxically, it seems that much (but not all) of the opposition to a multilateral approach is currently concentrated in developing countries.[21]

7.4 Environmental policies

The previous sections focus on activities relating to markets and their relation to the WTO. The next three sections examine subjects somewhat less concerned with economics, and more related to social and cultural norms of societies, as follows: this section, 7.4, concerns environment policies, section 7.5 concerns health, and section 7.6 concerns human rights. Each of these subjects and sections raises important issues which have strong central ties to the nation-state, so questions about international attention to the policies concerned inevitably involve a somewhat greater tension between the ideas tending towards national control and those which would lead to international measures.

Illustrative applications

The environment is a subject which has a number of different dimensions. For one, when the question asked is whether there should be international action, there certainly is a wide prevalence of opinion and worldwide recognition that there does need to be some international action on a variety of environmental subjects. However, there are a number of incentives for a nation-state government to protect the environment, at least as applies to its own citizens, and so, arguably, it is not necessary to go very far internationally. But on the other hand environmental protection at the nation-state level depends heavily on the capacity and resources of a country. It is argued that the richer the countries are or become, the more they will turn to environmental protection, and there is some empirical evidence in the economic literature to that effect.[1] Therefore, some believe that in order to protect the environment you should make countries richer, and you can do that through trade. Then you can let them control their own environmental activities.

On the other hand, however, there are externalities, situations where the pricing of goods does not build in environmental damage or costs that may be incurred outside the border of the acting state. There is also the question of public goods, the global commons, the atmosphere, the seas, and so on. So there seems to be a considerable view that there must be, and that there already is, in fact, quite a bit of international activity. There are dozens of treaties – some estimate 300 multilateral – on environmental matters.[2] But this raises a series of other questions: where? which institutions? which treaties?

A big question debated in recent years is whether there should be an international organization for environmental policy that would in some way be the complement and counterpart of the WTO. This idea partly has the goal of getting the WTO out of the questions of environment, which some people would like to do. But on that, apparently, there is no agreement. There are various arguments. Would a single institution be counterproductive because it would be too monopolistic of the subject? Is what we need competition between a dozen different organizations, even though they conflict? At the Johannesburg Summit, held at the end of August 2002, it is interesting that a recommendation to have a new environmental coordinating or central organization of some type did not come out of that conference, even though it was apparently sought.[3] As described in section 2.2, at that summit, we had a manifestation of another issue related to international "governance" questions, namely, the extraordinary statistics regarding the huge presence of NGOs, far outnumbering official delegates and even the press.

7.5 Health, globalization, and international institutions

Similarly to the previous section, the subject of health turns the attention of political leaders and constituents towards domestic measures, often considered to be a core part of any national government's responsibilities and thus its sovereignty. Protecting the health of a nation's citizens relates to a large number of policy goals, including consumer protection, food safety, product safety, adequate health facilities, questions about the costs and coverage of medical services, the licensing and quality control of health professionals, and so on. But beyond those, many other (sometimes conflicting) goals are often involved, such as the desire to provide for the poor and the sense of a society's general responsibility for those handicapped in various ways including having inadequate financial means. Aid for poorer parts of the world plays a role, and questions even within the nation-state often involve some aspect of redistribution of wealth and regard to problems of great inequality among citizens (or among nations). Many of these issues are most prominently identified as components of national government control and power, and thus sovereignty.[1] Health policy is often central to these issues.

But in addition to the profound national government responsibilities and functions, the subject of health clearly demands attention at an international level, for several reasons. First, as recognized at least a century and a half ago,[2] various health issues transgress national borders, and by at least 1920[3] it was recognized that increased world trade created added dangers of transmittal of communicable diseases.[4] Much more recently the scourge of HIV-AIDS, and the scare caused by the possible SARS (severe acute respiratory syndrome) epidemic, as well as the current potential disaster of avian influenza[5] demonstrated poignantly the importance of the WHO (World Health Organization) and actually led that organization to begin work on revising its International Health Regulations (IHRs) to better accommodate international activity.[6] In addition some sources recognize the potential important relationship between health measures and the attainment of peace and security for all peoples.[7]

Thus international attention is warranted for assisting poorer nations and developing research and gathering statistics to assist all nations in their respective endeavors to establish quality health services for their citizens.

This perceived need for international attention caused the United Nations and its Economic and Social Committee (ECOSOC) to adopt a resolution[8] to negotiate and bring into force a charter for a World Health Organization. The Charter was signed in 1946 and entered into force on

April 7, 1948,[9] partly to bring together several international health organizations and to continue the work of some health organizations which actually date back to 1839.[10] Clearly this centuries-old history of international endeavors colored the thinking of the creators of the WHO, and paved the way for its establishment. The Charter, however, is an interesting example of an international institutional structure which gives great deference to the concept of sovereignty and the nation-state, while establishing a very broad competence and authorizing a wide assortment of functions. In addition to providing for research, recommendations, conferences, public education, and so on, the WHO Constitution[11] authorizes the organization to establish "conventions" (i.e. treaties) by a two-thirds vote; however, these come into force for a member only when it accepts it.[12] An interesting recent example is the Framework Convention on Tobacco Control.[13] It also authorizes "regulations" to be adopted after "due notice" by the WHO Health Assembly (majority decision on a one nation, one vote basis),[14] which come into force for all members except those which notify rejection or reservations within a stated period of time.[15] In addition the Constitution explicitly provides for relationships not only with member governments, but also with other intergovernmental organizations, nongovernmental organizations, and the private sector, although some express the opinion that these provisions are not adequate for twenty-first-century activities.[16] In addition the WHO Constitution seems to give some recognition to "subsidiarity" by providing for regional entities with a large degree of autonomy concerning regional health policies[17] (in six established regions), and providing as well for WHO offices or other facilities in a number of member countries.[18]

The WHO Constitution, however, is not necessarily rigid or unchangeable. Even without explicit amendments or other legal actions (regulations and conventions, etc.), persons with deep experience in WHO matters have commented that WHO constitutional grants of authority develop through the practice of the organization, and that international organizations are "living and dynamic organisms, which adapt and evolve."[19] Indeed, although voting is the constitutional technique of decision making, knowledgeable individuals note that in fact a practice of seeking consensus for decisions has developed (albeit with voting as a fallback).[20] In addition the WHO Constitution establishes a method of dispute resolution under which the Health Assembly attempts to settle the matter, but if that does not succeed, reference can be made to the International Court of Justice.[21] There is some internal thinking about establishing some sort of mediation or other more refined dispute settlement system. The new IHRs reflect this.[22]

7.5 Health, globalization, and international institutions

WHO activity, however, does not exhaust the international activities relating to health (as suggested by subjects mentioned at the beginning of this section). Other organizations which play some role include the UN Food and Agriculture Organization (FAO), the World Intellectual Property Organization (WIPO), the Codex Alimentarius Commission (a Joint FAO/WHO food standards program),[23] and of course the WTO.[24] In particular, the WTO, with its competence well established over trade in products and services, has considerable relevance to health issues.[25] The WTO Sanitary and Phytosanitary (SPS) Agreement deals with product safety and health related to foodstuffs and animal health,[26] and its text on Technical Barriers to Trade (TBT)[27] creates norms relating to product standards in other types of goods.

An interesting "sovereignty" aspect of the SPS Agreement is the language relating to "risk" when products can cause certain health dangers, such as taken up in the WTO *Beef Hormones* case (evaluating the risk of artificial growth hormones causing cancer) and the *Asbestos* case (relating to GATT Article III national treatment, and implicating but not deciding about the TBT Agreement). The SPS Agreement contains tortured negotiated language trying to reconcile international goals of liberalizing trade and thus requiring scientific evidence of potential harm (to avoid barriers that are really due to protectionist motives), while still giving each member the "sovereign" right to determine the level of risk which should be tolerated in its society. Since science often declares that there is no such thing as totally risk-free circumstances, to allow a society to determine that only risk-free products can be imported is to deliver a blow to trade liberalization.[28] This is clearly one of the most interesting (and perplexing) issues in the perpetual tug-of-war between national and international authority and the question of which government level will have the authority to make the determination of acceptable science and some minimal threshold of the risk requirement.

Also quite controversial, however, is the WTO text on Trade-Related Aspects of Intellectual Property Rights (TRIPS)[29] and particularly the relationship of TRIPS to pharmaceutical products and their costs, which has stirred enmity from many countries, those of the Third World included. Many such countries are distressed by the costs arguably imposed by TRIPS intellectual property norms on drugs which are crucial to many government health plans and insurance provisions, including poignantly those in poor countries with major endemic disease problems such as HIV-AIDS, cholera, and malaria.[30]

Many of these matters pose directly conflicting policy directions for different international regimes. They also sometimes pose some interesting aspects of heavy-handed activity of special profit-oriented business groups which are enabled by one or more affluent industrial nations. WHO officials, recognizing the complexity of these problems, have recently established an exercise to try to explore carefully the potentials for legal conflict between its own activity and the measures it takes and the norms of other international treaties and institutions.[31] Consequently it can be seen that the subject area of health engages most of the difficult policy tensions of concepts of sovereignty – subsidiary, nongovernment relations, scientific data, norm legitimacy, power of juridical institutions, allocation of authority and competence, both vertical and horizontal, and many other issues. These issues will likely forever be part of the international relations landscape, and societies (civil and governments) will need to experiment with ways to reconcile these many dilemmas. One of the most in-depth elaborate sites of such experimentation is the still short history (fewer than fifty years) of the European Union, which has been forced to address many of these issues. This is one of the reasons why the evolving "constitution" and regulatory system of that multi-nation government is so interesting and can be instructive for considerations concerning worldwide institutions.

7.6 Human rights and nation-state sovereignty

Like the subjects of the two previous sections, that of human rights also involves important national domestic policy views, as well as perceptions of the necessity of international involvement. However, for certain parts of the world the international component becomes crucial. This is partly because to a certain extent human rights are a challenge to the nation-state itself. Human rights are often seen as a protection *against* states, and states are often viewed as the perpetrators of violations of human rights, so that particularly in the decades after World War II protection of such rights has been perceived as necessitating a force outside the nation. In short, it is perceived that in many contexts, nation-states have a conflict of interest when it comes to protecting human rights. Thus there is arguably a compelling reason why international attention and protection of human rights is necessary.

Clearly this is not a universal view. In addition, there has been philosophical contention over the question whether human rights are "universal" and thus equally applicable to every nation, or whether, on the contrary, such rights are deeply culture-bound and thus must be applied

7.6 Human rights and nation-state sovereignty

in different manners to different nations and their societies. These views are deeply felt,[1] but to a large degree such international attention to human rights as is witnessed today seems to lean in the direction of universality, although some argue that some differences as to particular human rights continue to exist, as can be observed in matters such as the death penalty, gender discrimination, sexual preference, and so on.[2]

Even within the Western tradition we see some powerful differences in attitudes as to the best ways to protect human rights (even assuming the universality of a core set of such rights). Such differences are noticeably apparent between the United States and Europe, and can probably be attributed to very different historical experiences of those two societies. For Europe, the first half of the twentieth century was surely a disaster, with two "European civil wars," and the experience of the Holocaust (and indeed other gross departures from human rights as understood by most impartial observers). Thus it is understandable why Europe was so inclined towards international institutions as a means of protecting or helping to protect individual citizen human rights. Citizens in many countries did not trust their national government to protect them. After the Soviet Union fell apart and many central European nations drew up new constitutions, often those constitutions emphasized human rights, giving special status to treaties for added protection. Europe developed the remarkable Convention on Human Rights which came into force in 1953,[3] and through other international institutions such as the Council of Europe compelled acceptance of the European Convention on Human Rights as a condition of membership in the Council. As of this writing, that Council and that Convention count forty-five European countries (including Russia) as members and thus bound by the norms and the Convention's court procedure for applying those human rights norms. The jurisprudence of that court procedure is extraordinarily rich, involving over 4,800 judgments delivered so far in forty-five years.[4] An intriguing "deference to national sovereignty" concept, the "margin of appreciation," has contributed to the broad acceptance of the human rights norms in Europe, partly through the process of viewing rights as "evolving" as acceptance or definition of the norms evolves in the societies concerned.[5]

More recently perceptions that the European Union (European Communities) needed similar international institutional protections for human rights to become part of the EU legal system has led to the formulation of a "Charter of Human Rights" with somewhat informal status;[6] this document has been included, however, in proposals for a new "European Constitution" drafted by European summit procedures culminating in Brussels in June 2004, and sent to the member states for ratification[7] (with considerable uncertainty as to whether the draft will ultimately come into force).[8]

But observe the different views in the United States. For citizens there, the original constitutional Bill of Rights (the first ten Amendments to the Constitution of 1789)[9] and the court procedures which have evolved to apply those rights, are in their perception far more meaningful for protection of their rights than any international system existing. Thus, to the average citizen in the United States interested in protecting his or her quality of life and family welfare, the nation-state is the most meaningful. In Europe, by contrast, it is understandable that individuals interested in such goals of life and family welfare would in many places be very skeptical of the ability of the nation-state to protect those goals, given the history of Europe during the first half of the twentieth century.

In the United States, therefore, it is not totally surprising that there is a certain amount of political hostility to the application of human rights norms by treaty,[10] sometimes because it is perceived that the treaty norms many diminish the strength of the US legal human rights protection, but also, candidly, because some of the international norms differ from understandings of similar norms in the US system. To some extent, although understandable, this transatlantic divergence is unfortunate, because given the prominence of the United States and the resources available to it which could potentially assist in better world application of human rights, the United States seems too often to stand aside, and at least not to undertake the role of being an example. Another potential downside to the more juridical US approach is the focus on language which is more than 216 years old, and the consequent necessity sometimes to force current applications into linguistic formulae that probably were not designed to accommodate some situations. On the other hand, the court processes in the United States with their powerful judicial review results, may be more protective of the rights than other institutions could likely achieve.[11]

Another problem for the international application of human rights, however, is the difficulties regarding "customary international law" discussed in section 2.3. Some scholarship and some observers with direct experience observe that in some cases advocates of human rights go very far in claiming the development of customary human rights rules, without the benefit of treaty. They also try to apply some treaty norms to non-consenting nations. In some cases such advocacy claims that norms are *jus cogens*, which then are claimed to trump even treaties. Yet the evidence of

7.6 Human rights and nation-state sovereignty

the essential prerequisites for developing such customary norms may be equivocal at best.[12]

Likewise, even in treaty law, there tends to be a vast array of human rights, many relatively "new." Human rights advocates have been noticeably reluctant to "prioritize" or emphasize a "hierarchy" of importance for human rights, thus the plethora of such rights claims, perhaps particularly those in the economic, social, and cultural subject realms, may dilute the degree of support which society in general is willing to marshal for protection. In the United States, the experience of Supreme Court attitudes in the 1930s, favoring strong protection of economic rights which led to potential blocking of economic reforms of the Roosevelt administration in the face of economic crisis, has soured many astute observers of human rights jurisprudence about ideas of absolute economic rights. Some views support strongly the separation of economic rights from the strong enforcement measures of "civil and political" rights.[13] Views from other quarters which would like to reinforce economic rights by strong judicial and constitutional enforcement are thus deemed contrary to the rights system as it is known in the United States (and in some other countries with similar approaches.)

In many ways it is clear that international attention to human rights is important, and well accepted, even in the United States. Thus there is relatively little quarrel with the view that the United Nations should play an important role. But there is considerable controversy about whether the United Nations has been, or is likely to be, very effective, and worries about "politicization" or "diplomacy compromises" concerning rights that are observed or likely in the United Nations.[14] Thus in appraising the "allocation of power" or competence regarding rights, these concerns about the nature of the institutions concerned will inevitably play an important role.

Finally it must be noted that there are a number of strong logical and practice links between human rights and international trade institutions and norms. Several broad categories of thought include the desire by human rights advocates to utilize trade measures as sanctions to encourage compliance with human rights norms and, second, the idea that for markets to work well the effectiveness of certain rights are important.[15]

Regarding the sanction linkage, many commentators have puzzled over the history of the use of such sanctions.[16] Some of these actions can be deemed inconsistent with trade or economic international norms, and thus advocates urge that the norms be changed or interpreted in a manner which would avoid such conflict.[17]

By contrast, the second category mentioned above suggests that there is a complementarity or at least symbiosis between certain rights and the good operation of markets. Markets depend on information, so freedom of speech or the press may be critical. Market participants must travel, so the protection of individual freedom from arrest or other barriers to travel is important. Ownership rights for property (including foreign investments) are obviously important. Due process type procedures (right of appeal), as well as fair notice and transparency (and other "good governance" norms), are likely to be relevant. Other rights might also be added to this list.[18] A question thus is raised as to whether international institutions and norms for trade and economic transactions should explicitly recognize some of this necessary function of rights. And that could lead to issues about how the nation-state might recognize that complementarity and whether if it did so it would be consistent with existing or prospective treaties in the realm of trade, finance, and other economic activity.

7.7 Federalism examples: US and EU struggles with the allocation of power

In Chapter 3 we noted that one of the more valid issues of "sovereignty" was the question of the allocation of power. That chapter also noted that this question can be set in a broader context than that of international versus nation-state power. Section 3.3 noted that many issues involved decision-making authority in the vertical array of locations including Geneva, Washington, DC, and Sacramento and Berkeley, California. Likewise, for Europe, one would insert the European Union just after Geneva, and before the locations at nation-state or subordinate levels.

It is interesting how the two greatest "subdivided" (dare we say "federal?") governmental entities are extensively, and arguably perpetually, immersed in controversy over allocation of power. They are both also struggling with "horizontal" allocation. A note on each will illustrate the point:

a. United States

Very recently we have seen a remarkable debate with many strident overtones concerning power allocation, both horizontal and vertical, within the United States. This debate is poignantly represented in the December 12,

7.7 Federalism examples: the US and the EU

2000, opinion of the US Supreme Court in the case of *George W. Bush, et al. v. Albert Gore, Jr., et al.*[1] In this case we can see words directly raising some of the issues of this chapter. For example, the majority *per curiam* opinion includes the following paragraph:

> None are more conscious of the vital limits on judicial authority than are the members of this Court, and none stand more in admiration of the Constitution's design to leave the selection of the President to the people, through their legislatures, and to the political sphere. When contending parties invoke the process of the courts, however, it becomes our unsought responsibility to resolve the federal and constitutional issues the judicial system has been forced to confront.[2]

In addition, in the concurring opinion by Chief Justice Rehnquist, in which Justice Scalia and Justice Thomas join him, we see the following sentences:

> Of course, in ordinary cases, the distribution of powers among the branches of a State's government raises no questions of federal constitutional law, subject to the requirement that the government be republican in character. See U.S. Const., Art. IV, "4. But there are a few exceptional cases in which the Constitution imposes a duty or confers a power on a particular branch of the State's government. This is one of them. Article II, 'Section 1, cl. 2.[3]

On the other side of some of these issues, we see language in the dissenting opinions, including some very pointed language in the dissent by Justice Ginsburg, in which she is joined (as to this part) by Justices Stephens, Souter, and Breyer.

The Chief Justice contradicts the basic principle that a State may organize itself as it sees fit.[4]

Quoting an earlier case by the Supreme Court:

> The Framers split the atom of sovereignty. It was the genius of their idea that our citizens would have two political capacities, one state and one federal, each protected from incursion by the other.[5]

Other issues that are the basis of considerable debate about allocating decision-making authority at different levels of government include many environmental policy issues, as well as food safety issues (perhaps going to the core of "sovereignty").

b. Europe

Another example is provided by the fascinating developments in the European Community other than regarding human rights, which is going through a potentially significant constitutional evolution, partly inevitably given the vast subject matter of the Community but also accentuated by the prospects of additions to the EU membership. Many of the issues it is discussing have, as the "central perplexity," questions about how to allocate power between the EU institutions and member state governments on the one hand, and between different parts of the EU institutions (e.g., the Luxembourg court compared with the Commission, or with the Council) on the other hand (some of this was mentioned in sections 2.3.c, 2.5, and 6.5).[6]

The proposed draft new EU constitution, now troubled by the 2005 referenda results, contains much concerning allocation of powers both between EU institutions and between the EU institutions and the government institutions of the member states. It also contains much concerning decision making (e.g. voting), but in addition has some ingenious proposals to facilitate "variable geometry" which would allow some smaller groups of EU member states to undertake measures and activities which could not be approved by the usual EU decision-making authority because of a lack of consensus or significant majority.[7]

c. Federal states or other nation-state groups, and their power relating to conduct of foreign affairs

A key question for international juridical institutions is the appropriate approach by those international institutions in relation to the deference (or "margin of appreciation") to be given by them to the nation-state or nation-group and their officials, diplomats, and negotiators. (This is often a "standard of review" question, as discussed in section 5.6.c.) The deference issue arises as to many decisions and measures taken by nations or nation groups in the normal course of their governmental activity, most often without any domestic law question about the domestic power to do so. But an additional dimension to the interplay of national government competence and its international affairs activities can be seen. Both in the United States and in the European Union there is much debate and consideration about the extent of "foreign affairs" powers. These can include dimensions, constraints, and distribution among national government institutions, regarding the power to enter into treaties, the powers involved in applying treaties (direct application etc.), participation in international organizations (as members or with different status), the role of customary international law, various questions about regulating economic activity and protection of property (and foreign investments), the allocation of powers relating to these and other international issues such as control of citizen activities abroad, immigration, many taxation issues, and so on. It is interesting sometimes to compare how different national or regional (e.g. European Union) governmental institutions approach some similar questions. For instance, the issue of treaty domestic application differs considerably in different countries. The US approach differs greatly from that of the European Union (including the question of which governmental institutions can control the approach). There has been concern expressed that such differences have unfair effects on some parties, compared with advantages which appear to accrue to others. Thus EU Commission officials felt that the approval of the Uruguay Round treaty text should not result in the direct application of that text, partly because the European Union would not benefit reciprocally from US direct application (see section 4.6, *supra*). These considerations raise a broader, reasonably profound issue about the degree to which the constitutional/legal institutions of a nation-state or grouping of nations affect the ability of such national or group of nations effectively to operate an efficient and satisfactory "foreign policy." Could some national-level constitutional restraints prevent a nation or group from bargaining effectively in certain types of treaty (or other international) negotiations? Would constraints requiring referendum for treaty approval handicap a nation or group? Or, by contrast, do some countries have a distribution of internal powers that could pose dangers to the world or international systems, for example, where excessive power has been granted to one person or to an unrepresentative elite within a nation or nation-group? Related to these issues is the question whether nations or nation-groups could effectively accept treaty obligations (such as some in the European Union treaties) which would limit existing national institutional powers? Could an international treaty require nations to give treaties direct application? Could an international treaty effectively oblige certain nations or nation-groups to refrain from entering certain types of treaties or treaties with certain other states?[8]

7.8 The United Nations and the use of force: constitutionalism evolving[1]

The current (as of August 2005) most strikingly significant issue of sovereignty and allocation of power is clearly the situation regarding Iraq and the United Nations. Since this situation is extremely complex and as this is being written, very much in flux, it is not feasible to draw many important conclusions, except perhaps to note the obvious, which is that the analysis presented in this chapter is exceedingly relevant (but probably not determinative in most cases). There is already extensive comment on this subject by reputable authorities, both governmental and nongovernmental. One troubling feature of this commentary is how varied and contradictory it is. The situation and its commentary do not reflect well on the concepts of international law, either in the traditional sense, or the evolutionary sense, for the general public understanding.[2] Hopefully, when the facts become clearer and the dust settles, some potential international law principles will emerge.

Much of the contested commentary has been about the legality under international law of the use of force by the United States, the United Kingdom, and the "coalition of the willing" to effectuate "regime change." Much of that focuses on UN law, which is very controverted. Actually, there are probably at least four bases for legal analysis of the situation (none of which command general or unequivocal support). These four are (i) the United Nations, especially Chapter VII of the Charter and the Security Council resolutions over more than a decade; (ii) self-defense and Article 51 of the UN Charter; (iii) humanitarian intervention and human rights norms (including those under the UN "umbrella"); and (iv) an idea expressed by some that the obligation to avoid the use of force under Article 2(4) of the UN Charter does not encompass all possible uses of force, some of which may remain untouched by the UN Charter.

If it were possible to conclude that the UN Charter authorized the regime change/humanitarian/self-defense use of force, it could be argued that the defending nation-state (Iraq), as a member, has "consented" to that force, and thus preserve the international law "consent theory." However, it is a long stretch even then to argue that consent to be the object of force for regime change would be implied by accepting the UN Charter, since state survival is, itself, a pillar of international law. Would ratifying nation-states have thought they were giving consent to that?

The only thing reasonably possible in this short space is to suggest some of the "power allocation" questions, which the situation clearly implicates. Varied answers, some contradictory, can elsewhere undoubtedly be suggested for each question.

First, is there a need for international action of some sort in the circumstances?

Second, is the United Nations the place to go for such international action? What legal competence does it have? What capacity does it have to make its actions effective?

7.8 The United Nations and the use of force: constitutionalism evolving

Third, if not the United Nations, then where to go? NATO? Ad hoc coalitions? Hegemonic power state (sometimes called "empire")? Regional arrangements?

Fourth, what are the conditions and prerequisites that should be applied to our international force action in the circumstances? It is this question that, with very few exceptions, has been ignored or has gone unanswered.[3]

The Iraq situation demonstrates, with extraordinarily poignant realism, the enormous risks of use of force, but has also raised many risks of non-action when diplomacy or other non-force actions fail. These failures occurred in this situation with plenty of blame to go around.

Many of the thoughts expressed in Chapter 3 are relevant, including suggestions to change "sovereignty" concepts to a "responsibility to protect"[4] and Professor Henry Schermers' statement that a "failed state" loses its sovereignty, which passes to the United Nations.[5]

8

Perspectives and implications: some conclusions

Globalization, by increasing the interdependence among the people of the world, has enhanced the need for global collective action and the importance of global public goods. That the global institutions which have been created in response have not worked perfectly is not a surprise: the problems are complex and collective action at any level is difficult.

Joseph E. Stiglitz, 2002[1]

This book, which has been purposefully kept relatively short, has nevertheless covered a lot of conceptual territory, more than this author expected when he accepted the challenge of the lecture series on which this book is based. As stated early in this work, however, this book is more about queries than theories.[2] The goal has been to raise a series of questions about some of the traditional views concerning the foundations and logic of the general subject of international law, and to relate those views to the subject of international economic law, particularly as represented by the history and practice of the GATT/WTO system.

The complexity of this task is manifest. Although others have tried to develop a "unified theory" of international law and/or international economic law, it is not the desire here to so disguise the complexity and variability of the subject. Rather it is the task of this work to pursue the logic and the empirical observations concerning the subjects to point in directions further along the path towards fulfillment of the important goals for international institutions today, even though this involves "devilish detail." These goals include, most importantly, the objectives of preserving and enhancing peace, preventing all but essential uses of armed force, reducing poverty in the world, and promoting democracy and human rights so that more people in the world can enjoy their lives with human dignity and without infringing on such dignity of others. The path is uncertain, and hard to predict. It passes through a landscape fraught with perils and often without handrails or road signs or even roads. But the effort here has been to outline some guidelines based on the empirical analysis and logical connections of the major phenomena facing the world of international legal systems, including the history and practice of the major international economic institution.

The logic of this book has been explained throughout. It is divided into three parts. First, the three initial chapters describe the current context for international law and international economic law, noting the profound circumstances of the last half century (following the catastrophic half century preceding that). These circumstances include three or more major technological developments which have reduced the cost and time for transport and for communications, plus the developments of weapons of appalling "efficiency." The circumstances also include changes in patterns of human organization and institutions, with an astonishing increase and effectiveness of nongovernment actors in the world, and a fast-paced trend towards economic interdependence. These circumstances are obviously related to and colored by the technological developments mentioned. These (and other similar phenomena) create situations where traditional nation-state governments find it more difficult to "govern" and to satisfy constituents' desires and needs, including preserving peace and prosperity and protecting citizens from violence and degradation.

The first part of this book continues in Chapters 2 and 3, where it looks closely at the traditional "legal concept landscape" concerning international affairs, and surveys the now elaborate literature criticizing those legal concepts. These concepts include sovereignty and its logical progeny such as notions of equality of nations, non-interference, consent as basis of any international norm, and monopoly of all power within the sovereign "borders."

Part II of this book, in two chapters, then explores the WTO as a crucial international institution with an elaborate history and practice which has many lessons to offer concerning its own subject and situation, but also for general international law. In particular, the large and remarkable "jurisprudence" that has developed, first in GATT, and later more prominently in the WTO, poignantly demonstrates the conceptual tensions and struggles of international law and institutions, including problems of sovereignty and its progeny mentioned above.

Finally Part III takes a very selective and brief look at some ideas about modes of analysis which might be pursued for better future understanding of the world's legal system (Chapter 6), and then briefly examines

Perspectives and implications: some conclusions

several specific institutional and policy questions in the light of potential newer ways to approach such questions, modifying (but not necessarily discarding) some of the traditional perceptions about the logic and fundamentals of international law (Chapter 7).

Now it is the task of this final Chapter 8 to help the reader integrate the above described parts of this book, and to suggest some broader implications of the logic and historical practice in those parts.

The most basic criticisms of the international law fundamentals are demonstrated in the overview survey of the vast literature on this subject, literature which is found mostly in the discipline of political science (international relations), as well as law. This survey is included in portions of Chapters 2 and 3. The start of the critical trail is the basic concept of "sovereignty," which is widely described as faulty or out of date, or even as "organized hypocrisy." Older "Westphalian sovereignty" is fully embraced by almost no thoughtful scholar or practitioner (government or private). But even versions of sovereignty which discard attributes of the original Westphalian version of absolute monopoly of power within the contours of the "sovereign state" still often cling to notions or "mantras" about sovereignty that are severely dysfunctional in the modern world. Yet, as Chapter 3 demonstrates, there are aspects of "sovereignty concepts" which arguably contain ideas which are relevant and important even today, such as the important policy tensions about "allocating power" at various levels of government, or horizontally among various different institutions of government. It also makes the important point that "sovereignty-modern" demands a disaggregated analysis of the concept(s) of sovereignty, which means that the concept (and its implementation) can be and often is divided into parts, or "slices."

However, more troublesome perhaps, are some of the "logical corollaries" of older sovereignty concepts, which Chapter 2 explores. If the nation-state with sovereignty is considered to be the highest level of authority so that no other higher level can mandate it, this suggests several attributes often repeated in relation to international law fundamentals, including four listed above: the "equality of nations," the theory that all international norms must be based on consent of the affected nation-states, the rule against outside interference with the nation-state, and the belief that the sovereign has absolute and unaccountable authority over its subjects and all matters of internal government control. Each of these propositions has some merit, but also must be constrained in some way by norms not under each sovereign's control. For example, few today believe that a sovereign government can do what it wishes to its own citizens without limits on arbitrary and degrading governmental behavior. The constraints can, of course, be treaty based and therefore justified ("legitimated"?) by nation-state consent, but it is widely accepted that some norms apply even when no consent can be demonstrated.

Furthermore Chapter 2 describes ways in which traditional subjects of international law have weaknesses in their fundamentals or basic propositions which create problems in the challenging world of today's circumstances. Treaty rigidity and the basic difficulties and defects of developing customary international law are examples. In addition, consent theory often does not adequately assist in the process of resolving differences about the extent of legitimation for international norms. Treaty interpretation often becomes situated in the cross fire of tensions between objectives aimed at enhancing the efficiency and capability of necessary international action on the one hand, and on the other hand the desire of national government officials or constituents to preserve prerogatives, privileges, economic or other benefits, or even meritorious "policy space" to carry out measures designed to implement a society's chosen policy preferences. Many more complexities of the "devilish detail" of the operation of international law norms are described in this book, but also in many other books and writings.

Because of the broad extent and growing abundance of practice and jurisprudence in the areas of international economic activity, international economic law is a worthy subject of study in connection with the broader policy and theoretical tensions outlined in the previous paragraph and in this book. The WTO is the most elaborate repository of IEL practice and jurisprudence in the world today, and many of the challenges and criticisms of international law are manifested in that practice and jurisprudence. Section 5.12 is a summary of some of these, and partially lists a series of "lessons" which can be drawn from IEL. It can easily be seen that a number of those "lessons" are relevant to particular logical corollaries mentioned above and in Part I of the book. To some extent these practices provide empirical evidence to support criticisms of some of the traditional foundations of international law generally.

Consider, for example, some matters mentioned in section 5.12:

The evolution of GATT after the ITO failure, and the change of GATT into the WTO, manifested a sense of many nations that an institutional structure was needed for international trade discourse and disciplining constraints on national behavior. Pragmatic accommodation, good practical sense, and important leadership led a weak "birth defected" GATT to become an important part of the world's international economic institutional landscape.

Full "sovereignty" was never a prerequisite for participation in GATT or the WTO.

Equality of nations seemed mandated by the GATT treaty text, but in fact the practice veered away from voting and its dilemmas, to a "consensus approach" to decision making developed by practice, and was carried more formally into the WTO, although such approach has a potential for impeding progress on a number of important issues.

Consensus has important value in promoting full participation and greater transparency at all levels and in all types of participating nations in the institution.

Problems of treaty rigidity clearly diminished the ability of GATT to evolve satisfactorily with the rapidly changing economic environment of the world.

With regard to rule orientation, the objectives of predictability and stability (reducing the risk premium of economic decisions of millions of entrepreneurs) are important, and lead to support for a rule-oriented system, with dispute settlement procedures in a "juridical system." Even without explicit treaty rules about this, the GATT DS system evolved and was accepted by the nation-state participants (contracting parties).

Nongovernment entities (including individuals) are major beneficiaries of the international institutions, particularly in the context of economic subjects, as well as human rights. The practice and jurisprudence has begun explicitly to recognize this, and to reflect understanding of this principle. Important attention to questions about the role of NGOs is also needed, including careful consideration of better procedures for transparency and participation.

Treaty interpretation becomes an important part of the system, and requires an important juridical approach. Questions are developing about whether the traditional "customary" international law approaches to treaty interpretation, such as those embodied in the Vienna Convention of the Law of Treaties, are adequate for use with treaties which have large membership and are of long duration and thus are more like "constitutions" than a simpler paradigm of bilateral or mini-lateral treaties.

Some treaty interpretation concepts, such as *in dubio mitius* (which is not in the VCLT, but has been urged in some of the advocacy in the WTO), are absurd and destructive of the purposes of institutions like the GATT and WTO. This treaty concept represents "consent theory gone amok," and also evokes thoughts about criticism of the famous international law *Lotus Case* as being "extreme positivism."[3]

There is clearly an important conceptual and juridical relationship between international economic law and general international law. But the relationship is complex, and if misapplied could be destructive. Among the problems is the broad ambiguity of some international law norms, such as "good faith." When juxtaposed with elaborate and reasonably precise sets of procedural norms such as are found in parts of the WTO, a broad or ambiguous rule can offer dangerous latitude to a juridical institution.

Good governance principles need to be applied to international institutions as well as to nation-states. These principles include issues raised above, such as transparency and participation, but also need to include checks and balances, and recognition of "subsidiarity" ideas relating to the importance of local accountability.

The principle of non-interference in the domestic affairs of "sovereign" nations must be balanced with needed international norms to prevent internal government measures from causing harm to other nations, particularly with reference to economic measures which could seriously inhibit economic development and progress in welfare.

A major question relevant to the discussion above and most of the exploration in this book is what happens if we downgrade the importance of the traditional fundamental propositions of international law. What can replace them, or how should they be modified?

One possibility would be to recognize certain international institutions as the legitimate entities to decide some of these fundamentals. This would require such institutions seriously to discuss these limits and modes of activity (without a tilt favoring that institution's "turf"), and to develop these limits with enough precision for them to be useful to national and international decision makers. This seems to be more carefully done in juridical institutions, which might well be an argument for more reliance on such institutions. However, caution requires that there are "checks and balances" regarding those institutions, lest they go wrong through faulty analysis, lack of adequate empirical information, remoteness from the real world activities that are relevant to reasoned and just opinions, or generally from lack of adequate resources.

Another possibility is to follow a chain of argument developed by some scholarly analysis to the effect that "sovereignty" concepts themselves must evolve and be redefined. This might also be done by juridical-type institutions, with the same caveats of the preceding paragraph and of prior sections of this chapter.

Another and probably more heroic possibility is to develop a general theory of sources of international law based on what some authors have called the "international community." To some this implies a sort of *acquis communautaire*. It could well imply participation by nongovernment persons and entities, and it could embellish the more traditional concepts of "practice" under agreements or with *opinio juris*, to stretch those frontiers. The risk and problem is the imprecision and thus the controversy that can develop about the use of this approach in specific instances. It has been referred to in some situations, such as the Kosovo crisis,[4] using the phrase "overwhelming humanitarian catastrophe." These thoughts relate to one of the four definitions of "constitutionalism" described in section 6.5.

Yet another approach is to use the concept of "interdependence," often most associated with economic policy and activity, to justify certain new norms. In many of these cases it is likely that this concept can be used in tandem with more traditional sovereignty and nation-state consent approaches to persuade nations to give such consent. A key question often, however, is the holdout state, which in some economic circumstances is given added incentives to hold out when other states are constraining their reach for policy and economic advantages. This is relevant to the problems of "consensus" discussed in several sections in this book.

One of the approaches of this book is to respond to the many extensive challenges and criticisms of the concept of "sovereignty" by urging a pause for reflection about the consequences of discarding that concept in broad measure. Since that concept is fundamental to the logical foundations of traditional international law, to discard it risks undermining international law and certain other principles of the international relations system. This could challenge the legitimacy and moral force of international law, part of what Professor Thomas Franck terms the "compliance pull"[5] of norms backed by characteristics of legitimization. It seems clear that the international relations system (including, but not limited to the international legal system) is being forced to reconsider certain sovereignty concepts. But this must be done carefully, because to bury all the sovereignty concepts without adequate replacements could lead to a situation of pure power prevailing, which, in turn, could encourage chaos, misunderstanding, and conflict, almost like Hobbes' state of nature, where life is "nasty, brutish, and short."[6] In the alternative, this vacuum of legitimization principles could lead to greater aggregations of hegemonic, monopolistic, or "imperial" power that might not always be handled with appropriate principles of good governance or subsidiarity.

As noted in section 2.3, the search for a Kelsonian *Grundnorm* or some other axiomatic legitimation does not seem too productive and can lead to circular logic. So perhaps the best approach is a pragmatic one of observing real-life circumstances and events to see what "works," in the sense of the American pragmatist philosophers Charles Sanders Peirce, William James, and John Dewey. This could lead logically to the view that such empirical appraisal might produce varied results for different international law subject matters. It is also a difficult endeavor to undertake the observations required for generalization, although the opinions and testimony of persons experienced in international relations endeavors can be a short-cut, whether through authored works, interviews, or testimony on similar evidence. Henkin's famous phrase quoted in section 2.3 is an example. This process, while derived from varied circumstances, could be viewed as developing some uniform generalizations for international law generally, and if cautiously applied can be seen as similar (but not necessarily congruent) to IL concepts such as *opinio juris*, and "practice under the agreement" (for treaties).

Reflecting on some of these thought currents, one of the recommendations of this book is to disaggregate and to analyze, to break down the complex array of "sovereignty" concepts and examine particular aspects in detail and with precision to understand what is really at play. A major part of this approach would be to understand the pragmatic functionalism of allocation of power as between different levels of governance entities in the world. To the extent that it is feasible, this should be done in a manner not tilted either in favor or against international approaches.

Indeed, as time moves on and the world trends of interdependence and agreement on the need for cooperative institutions that can also enhance peace and security continue, it is likely that the substitute for portions of nation-state sovereignty will be international institutions which embrace a series of legitimizing "good governance" characteristics such as some recommended by Robert Keohane[7] and other thinkers and philosophers. Those characteristics will likely include a broader set of participants than just nation-states, looking also to non-state and nongovernmental actors and individuals, including economic (business); moral, religious, and scholarly entities; and international organizations. They will likely include elements of "democratic legitimization" and some notions of "democratic entitlement," not only for nation-states, but also for international institutions. Validating characterizations will also likely include elements of efficiency and capacity to carry out appropriately developed institutional goals and to build in techniques for overcoming "treaty rigidity," so that the institutions can evolve to keep up with the changing world. It is increasingly likely that a juridical institutional structure of some kind will be seen as a necessary part of any such international institution, and that the use of force or other concrete actions impinging on local societies will be constrained by the institutional and juridical structures.

In order for the world to cope with the challenges of instant communication and fast and cheap transportation, combined with weapons of vast and/or mass destruction, that world will have to develop something considerably better than either the historical and discredited Westphalian concept of sovereignty, or even the current, but highly criticized, versions of sovereignty still often articulated. That "something" is not yet well defined, but it can be called "sovereignty-modern," which is currently more an analytic and dynamic process of disaggregation and redefinition than a "frozen-in-time" concept or technique.

Finally we come to some of this author's personal perspective on all this. A key lesson of the last 100 years is that international institutions are critical and are here to stay and increasingly to play a larger role in world and local affairs. This lesson is even more strongly reinforced by the events of September 11, 2001, and the period immediately following that event. Clearly a fragmented nation-state sovereignty emphasis will not be able to cope with the world reality which has been imposed on this globe, and a desire for hegemonic supremacy is myopic and will not be workable. The hegemon, or "empire," model contains internal inconsistencies (e.g. parochial favoritism) which undermine the very purposes of the model; the model confronts the reality of constraints on even great power in an interdependent world with added "asymmetries" which can favor terrorism as well as nongovernment network activities that can operate without accountability.

Constraints on great power are also apparent in democratic societies which must balance and reconcile many conflicting policy goals, most of which are mundanely constrained by budgets and the messiness of democratic institutions. Constraints even apply to a nation with twelve aircraft carrier task forces, each with awesome power and many capabilities, each costing more than two billion dollars per year to maintain,[8] and existing in a world where no other nation has even one such force that matches these capabilities. Such a richly endowed nation learns that it cannot accomplish all it wishes without a very large measure of international cooperation.

Likewise related to these observations, the balance of power ("balance of terror" ??) model fails to address some of the awesomely difficult problems of a landscape of new technological challenges and "shifting borderlines of nationhood."

The only sensible solution thus appears to be international institutional development, in a context of norms of varying strength from soft law norms (and soft power) to hard law norms and juridical institutions to effectuate them.

Clearly, however, the international institutions which exist today have many problems. Other works have chronicled some of these problems in great detail, and the media is full of stories about them, including reform ideas for the United Nations, failures of certain peacekeeping responsibilities, the limited effectiveness of some (but not all) human rights institutions, and criticism of various economic institutions including the Bretton Woods institutions (the "Washington Consensus")[9] and of course the WTO.

Many of the worries about some international organizations include arguments that they lack credibility, legitimacy, transparency, participatory mechanism, check and balances, effective but fair methods of decision making, and more. In sum, many of the criticisms about international institutions relate to the lack of "good governance" attributes. Thus some critics strongly favor the nation-state and stridently demand that decision making be confined to the nations and not gravitate to international institutions. It is at this point that the hypocrisy and misanalysis regarding sovereignty and the concepts that are its logical progeny (consent, equality, etc.) cause major damage to better mechanisms for achieving certain broad world societal goals. All too often close and careful analysis of the problems and where they could best be tackled requires considerable attention to the institutions (at various levels) which are available or could be available, and all too often this attention is never given. Mantras are used to avoid thinking, and to promote special interest advocacy.

All of this has led this author to use the term "constitutionalism" to apply to a set of institutional concepts such as those mentioned above. This term has been defined by some in a way substantially different from its use in the previous sentence and as used elsewhere in this book.[10] Indeed, as mentioned in section 6.5, the term can have at least four different major meanings. Some also use a definition which is based on a series of characteristics which are described as being necessary for a human institution to fulfill before such institution can be called "constitutional." These are worthwhile endeavors, and have the function of promoting good ideas of "governance," or sometimes ideas related to "management," such as ideas of transparency and participation. But "constitution" can also be used more broadly (and more ambiguously) to refer to a human institutional framework somewhat more stable and substantial than that implied by the term "institutional," but still broadly embracing empirically observable entities which need features which enable the institution to carry out its responsibilities and objectives effectively over a long time period. That is an implicit sub-text theme of this book.

International lawyers must begin to stress the importance of the attributes of "good governance" for international institutions as much as others would stress such attributes for a nation-state. This must include not only transparency and participation, but also checks and balances to protect against monopolies of power and misuse of power. It must also protect other levels of government in the world including the nation-state, sub-national entities and even individuals (human rights). It must provide for realistic decision making not too disconnected from real power in the world so that propositions followed by an organization can actually achieve goals rather than merely provide words. It must provide enough flexibility in the constitutional structure of the institution so that the institution can evolve to keep up with fast changing characteristics of the world. Therefore attention needs to be given to addressing the risks of treaty rigidity.[11] The processes of interpretation need to be rethought, and attention paid to methods of interpretation which may be necessary but which current applications of the Vienna Convention on the Law of Treaties tend to inhibit.

These ideas may seem to pose unsolvable problems, particularly given democratic processes and public attitudes in various parts of the world. However, at least concerning the most powerful trading nation, the United States, a recent, extremely interesting poll carefully carried out by the Chicago Council of Foreign Relations[12] demonstrates a remarkable degree of public acceptance for international institutions including the WTO and its dispute settlement system. Sometimes it appears that there is a disconnect between general public attitudes and the assertions by political leaders and members of legislatures in the United States (but also in other parts of the world).

What is described above is, in essence, a "constitutional" approach to international law, using the term "constitutional" in a broad sense. Thus "international lawyers" must "morph" into constitutional lawyers.

As a closing note, reference can be made to two interesting propositions made by two very knowledgeable thinkers. One is the title of a book by a former US congressman, a former Speaker of the House of Representatives, named Tip O'Neill. The title is "All Politics Is Local." The other proposition was made by a well-regarded economist and author, Peter Drucker, who states in an article, "all economics is international."[13] The tension between these two propositions and the implications of such tension are a major challenge for the wisdom needed by practitioners and scholars to enhance the policy goals for a world full of risks going forward into the twenty-first century. It is also a challenge to democratic governance.

In sum, the problems explored in this book require much more thinking than has yet been done. Hopefully this book at least demonstrates how important it is for the world that such thinking does occur, and what are some of the directions necessary to pursue.

Appendix: Outline of the Uruguay Round treaty agreement establishing the World Trade Organization[1]

ANNEX 1
ANNEX 1A: Multilateral Agreements on Trade in Goods
General Agreement on Tariffs and Trade 1947, as amended
    General Agreement on Tariffs and Trade 1994
    Understanding on Article II:1(b)
    Understanding on Article XVII
    Understanding on Balance-of-Payments Provisions (including 1979 Declaration)
    Understanding on Article XXIV
    Understanding in Respect of Waivers
    Understanding on Article XXVIII
    Marrakesh Protocol
Agreement on Agriculture
Agreement on the Application of Sanitary and Phytosanitary Measures
Agreement on Textiles and Clothing
Agreement on Technical Barriers to Trade
Agreement on Trade-Related Investment Measures
Agreement on Implementation of Article VI
Agreement on Implementation of Article VII
Agreement on Preshipment Inspection
Agreement on Rules of Origin
Agreement on Import Licensing Procedures
Agreement on Subsidies and Countervailing Measures
Agreement on Safeguards
ANNEX 1B: General Agreement on Trade in Services and Annexes

Appendix

ANNEX 1C: Agreement on Trade-Related Aspects of Intellectual Property Rights
ANNEX 2: Understanding on Rules and Procedures Governing the Settlement of Disputes
ANNEX 3: Trade Policy Review Mechanism
ANNEX 4: Plurilateral Trade Agreements
Agreement on Trade in Civil Aircraft
Agreement on Government Procurement
International Dairy Agreement
International Bovine Meat Agreement

MINISTERIAL DECISIONS AND DECLARATIONS

  Decision on Measures in Favour of Least-Developed Countries
  Declaration on the Contribution of the World Trade Organization to Achieving Greater Coherence in Global Economic Policymaking
  Decision on Notification Procedures
  Declaration on the Relationship of the World Trade Organization with the International Monetary Fund
  Decision on Measures Concerning the Possible Negative Effects of the Reform Programme on Least-Developed and Net Food-Importing Developing Countries
  Decision on Notification of First Integration under Article 2.6 of the Agreement on Textiles and Clothing
  Decisions Relating to the Agreement on Technical Barriers to Trade
  Decisions and Declaration Relating to the Agreement on Implementation of Article VI of the General Agreement on Tariffs and Trade 1994
  Decisions Relating to the Agreement on Implementation of Article VII of the General Agreement on Tariffs and Trade 1994
  Decisions Relating to the General Agreement on Trade in Services
  Decision on Accession to the Agreement on Government Procurement
  Decision on the Application and Review of the Understanding on Rules and Procedures Governing the Settlement of Disputes

Notes

Abbreviations used in notes

AJIL	AMERICAN JOURNAL OF INTERNATIONAL LAW, AMERICAN SOCIETY OF INTERNATIONAL LAW
DSU	Understanding on Rules and Procedures Governing the Settlement of Disputes, Art, 3.2, Marrakesh Agreement Establishing the World Trade Organization, Apr. 15, 1994, Annex 2, in WORLD TRADE ORGANIZATION, THE LEGAL TEXTS: THE RESULTS OF THE URUGUAY ROUND OF MULTILATERAL TRADE NEGOTIATIONS (Cambridge University Press, 1999)
GATT ANALYTICAL INDEX	GUIDE TO GATT LAW & PRACTICE – ANALYTICAL INDEX, 6th ed. (Geneva, 1994)
JACKSON ET AL., CASEBOOK	JOHN H. JACKSON, WILLIAM J. DAVEY, AND ALAN O. SYKES, LEGAL PROBLEMS OF INTERNATIONAL ECONOMIC RELATIONS: CASES, MATERIALS AND TEXT ON THE NATIONAL AND INTERNATIONAL REGULATION OF TRANSNATIONAL ECONOMIC RELATIONS, 4th ed. (West Group, 2002)
JACKSON, JURISPRUDENCE	JOHN H. JACKSON, THE JURISPRUDENCE OF GATT AND THE WTO: INSIGHTS ON TREATY LAW AND ECONOMIC RELATIONS (Cambridge University Press, 2000)
JACKSON, WTLG	JOHN H. JACKSON, WORLD TRADE AND THE LAW OF GATT (Bobbs-Merrill, 1969)

JIEL	JOURNAL of INTERNATIONAL ECONOMIC LAW
Marrakesh Agreement	Marrakesh Agreement Establishing the World Trade Organization, Annex 2, in WORLD TRADE ORGANIZATION, THE LEGAL TEXTS: THE RESULTS OF THE URUGUAY ROUND OF MULTILATERAL TRADE NEGOTIATIONS (Cambridge University Press, 1999)
NAFTA	North American Free Trade Agreement, Dec. 17, 1992. Can.–Mex.–U.S., 32 ILM 289 & 605 (1993) (entered into force Jan. 1, 1994), at Chapters 19 and 20
Sutherland, The Future of the WTO	Peter Sutherland et. al., The Future of the WTO: Addressing Institutional Challenges in the New Millennium, Report by the Consultative Board to the Director-General Supachai Panitchpakdi (WTO, January 2005) available at www.wto.org/english/thewto_e/10anniv_e/10anniv_e.htm#future, visited March 18, 2005. The Consultative Board comprised Peter Sutherland (Chairman of the Consultative Board), Professor Jagdish Bhagwati, Dr. Kwesi Botchwey, Niall W. A. FitzGerald, Professor Koichi Hamada, Professor John Jackson, Professor Celso Lafer, and Professor Thierry de Montbrial. Brief biographical information for each is available at http://www.wto.org/english/news_e/pres03_e/pr345_e.htm, last visited March 18, 2005
UR Texts	Texts which are part of the Marrakesh Agreement Establishing the World Trade Organization, such as the Anti-Dumping Agreement
VCLT	The Vienna Convention on the Law of Treaties, 1155 UNTS 331, opened for signature May 23, 1969, entered into force Jan. 27, 1970, repr. 8 ILM 679 (1969)
WTO Charter	Marrakesh Agreement Establishing the World Trade Organization, in WTO LEGAL TEXTS. "Charter" is an informal term, referring to the fifteen pages of Marrakesh text which create the WTO

WTO Legal   World Trade Organization, The Legal Texts:
The Texts   Results of the Uruguay Round of
             Multilateral Trade Negotiations (Cambridge
             University Press, 1999)

1 Introduction: international law and international economic law in the interdependent world of the twenty-first century

1 Thomas L. Friedman, The Lexus and the Olive Tree: Understanding Globalization (Farrar, Straus, Giroux, 1999), at xviii.

1.1 A time of challenge and changing assumptions

2 This book derives from and expands on the author's Hersch Lauterpacht Memorial Lectures delivered on November 5, 6, and 7, 2002, at Cambridge University. This book also builds on prior published works of this author, including World Trade and the Law of GATT (Bobbs-Merrill Company, Inc., 1969); The World Trading System: Law and Policy of International Economic Relations, 2d ed. (MIT Press, 1997); The Jurisprudence of the GATT and the WTO: Insights on Treaty Law and Economic Relations (Cambridge University Press, 2000); The World Trade Organization: Constitution and Jurisprudence (Chatham House Papers, Royal Institute of International Affairs,1998); John H. Jackson, William J. Davey, & Alan O. Sykes, Legal Problems of International Economic Relations: Cases, Materials and Text on the National and International Regulation of Transnational Economic Relations, 4th ed. (West Group, 2002).

3 Counterparts to the ASIL include the International Law Association (ILA), the British Institute of International and Comparative Law (BIICL), and various bar associations, such as the American Bar Associations (ABA–International Section) and International Bar Association, associations of the individual EU member states and the European Bar Association CCBE (Council of Bars and Law Societies of Europe).

4 The literature for these debates and other commentary is voluminous. The pages of the American Journal of International Law illustrate some of the commentary, such as the agora on the Iraq invasion: *Agora: Future Implications of the Iraq Conflict*, AJIL 97 (2003): 553.

5 Chapters 2 and 3, in particular, have many references to the literature embodying criticisms and concerns of this type. Prior lectures in the Lauterpacht Lecture series also include thoughtful analyses, e.g., Francisco Orrego Vicuña, International Dispute Settlement in an Evolving Global Society: Constitutionalization, Accessibility, Privatization (Cambridge University Press, 2004); Thomas M. Franck, Recourse to Force: State Action against Threats and Armed Attacks (Cambridge University Press, 2002); Martti Koskenniemi, The Gentle

CIVILIZER OF NATIONS: THE RISE AND FALL OF INTERNATIONAL LAW 1870–1960 (Cambridge University Press, 2001); and others, *see* http://lcil.law.cam.ac.uk/publications/hersch.php for more complete series listing, visited Apr. 20, 2005.

6 *See, e.g.*, works cited *supra* note 5 and Chapter 2, *infra*.

7 A few other important examples include LOUIS HENKIN, INTERNATIONAL LAW: POLITICS AND VALUES (Martinus Nijhoff Publishers, 1995); OSCAR SCHACTER, INTERNATIONAL LAW IN THEORY AND PRACTICE (Martinus Nijhoff Publishers, 1991); and ANNE-MARIE SLAUGHTER, A NEW WORLD ORDER (Princeton University Press, 2004).

8 *See* WALTER VAN GERVEN, THE EUROPEAN UNION: A POLITY OF STATES AND PEOPLES (Stanford University Press, 2005); KAREN J. ALTER, ESTABLISHING THE SUPREMACY OF EUROPEAN LAW: THE MAKING OF AN INTERNATIONAL RULE OF LAW IN EUROPE (Oxford University Press, 2001). *See also* brief discussions at sections 2.3.c, 2.5, and 6.5 *infra*. *See also* Treaty on European Union, July 29, 1992, O.J. (C 191) 1 (1992); Treaty of Amsterdam Amending the Treaty on European Union, The Treaties Establishing the European Communities and Related Acts, Nov. 10, 1997, O.J. (C 340) 1 (1997); Treaty of Nice Amending the Treaty on European Union, The Treaties Establishing the European Communities and Related Acts, Mar. 10, 2001, O.J. (C 80) 1 (2001). *See also* GRÁINNE DE BÚRCA & JOANNE SCOTT, EDS., CONSTITUTIONAL CHANGE IN THE EU: FROM UNIFORMITY TO FLEXIBILITY? (Hart Publishing, 2000).

9 *The Bretton Woods Agreements Act of 1945.* This conference resulted in the Charters for the World Bank and the International Monetary Fund. The "Bretton Woods Conference," officially called "The United Nations Monetary and Financial Conference," held July 1–22, 1944. Forty-four nations met to negotiate the establishment of the International Monetary Fund (IMF) and the World Bank. *See* United Nations Monetary and Financial Conference (Bretton Woods, N.H., July 1–22, 1944), Proceedings and Documents 941 (U.S. Dep't of State Pub. No. 2866, 1948).

10 *See* sections 5.2 and 5.4, *infra*.

11 A simple search (done in March 2005) of online booksellers such as Amazon.com, disclosed the number of available titles for "WTO" and "World Trade Organization" to be almost 1,000. For "globalization," the number is 2,881, for "sovereignty," 1,273 (touching on a variety of uses of that term). "International law" generally disclosed 8,065 titles, 161 of which date from January 1, 2005 (including forthcoming publications), and "international trade law" brought forth a list of 367 results, with 30 dating from January 1, 2004. Elsewhere in the world there may be similar results, and this author has been told (several years ago) that the number of published books on the WTO in Chinese (published in China) exceeds 3,000. In addition to books, of course, the journal literature is also exceptionally numerous.

12 *See supra* note 2. Many other books are cited in later relevant chapters.

Notes to pages 8–11

1.2 Facts on the ground: the world situation landscape – change, interdependence, globalization, adjustment

1. In Chapter 2, section 2.2, the discussion of circumstances will be extended with particular reference to law.
2. *See*, in particular, Martin Wolf, Why Globalization Works (Yale University Press, 2004). The literature on globalization is also extremely extensive. Special mention should be made of the following: C. Fred Bergsten, ed., The United States and the World Economy: Foreign Economic Policy for the Next Decade (Institute of International Economics, 2005); Brink Lindsey, Against the Dead Hand: The Uncertain Struggle for Global Capitalism (CATO, 2001); Jagdish Bhagwati, In Defense of Globalization (Oxford University Press, 2004); Thomas L. Friedman, The Lexus and the Olive Tree: Understanding Globalization (Farrar, Straus, Giroux, 1999); Joseph E. Stiglitz, Globalization and Its Discontents (Norton, 2002).
3. *See* section 2.2, *infra*, at text and note 55, for references expressing this observation. *See also* the interesting discussion of different definitions of globalization in Lindsey, Against the Dead Hand, *Id.*
4. Wolf, Why Globalization Works, *supra* note 2, at 109; Niall Ferguson, *Sinking Globalization*, Foreign Affairs 84 (Mar/Apr 2005). *See also* Jeffrey Frankel, *Globalization of the Economy, in* Governance in a Globalizing World, Joseph S. Nye Jr. & John D. Donahue, eds. (Brookings Institution Press, 2000): 45.
5. *See supra* note 2.
6. *See* Stephen C. Fehr, *More Than Just Pie in the Sky; Cargo From Roses to Red Peppers Helps Lift Dulles's Soaring Economy*, Washington Post, Aug. 22, 1995, at B01; Dina ElBoghdady, *Moving off the Docks*, The Washington Post, Jan. 10, 2005, at E01.
7. *See, e.g.*, James N. Rosenau & J.P. Singh, Information Technologies and Global Politics: The Changing Scope of Power and Governance (SUNY Press, 2002); Jeffrey James, Technology, Globalization and Poverty (E. Elgar Publishers, 2002), at 11–22.
8. Examples include trade rules on dumping, safeguards, and subsidies. Also "origin" is a question for both national treatment (GATT Art. III) and Most Favored Nation treatment (GATT Art. I). *See, e.g.*, John H. Jackson, The World Trading System: Law and Policy of International Economic Relations, 2d ed. (MIT Press, 1997), section 6.4. Production supply chains are described in (e.g.) Thomas L. Friedman, The World Is Flat: A Brief History of the Twenty-First Century (Farrar, Straus and Giroux, 2005), at ch. 12; and Pietra Rivoli, The Travels of a T-Shirt in the Global Economy (John Wiley & Sons, 2005).
9. Thomas M. Franck, Recourse to Force: State Action against Threats and Armed Attacks (Cambridge University Press, 2002), at 4.

10 United Nations, *Report of the World Summit on Sustainable Development*, Johannesburg, South Africa, 2002. UN Doc. A/CONF.199/20, available at www.johannesburgsummit.org/html/documents/documents.html, visited Apr. 9, 2003. *See also* section 2.2.f, *infra*.
11 Edith Brown Weiss, *The Rise or the Fall of International Law?*, FORDHAM LAW REVIEW 69 (2000): 345, 357–60.
12 VICTOR BULMER-THOMAS & ALAN KNIGHT, THE ECONOMIC HISTORY OF LATIN AMERICA SINCE INDEPENDENCE, 2d ed. (Cambridge University Press, 2003), at ch. 11.
13 AMY CHUA, WORLD ON FIRE: HOW EXPORTING FREE MARKET DEMOCRACY BREEDS ETHNIC HATRED AND GLOBAL INSTABILITY (Doubleday, 2003).
14 *See, e.g.*, Paul Kennedy, *The Eagle Has Landed*, FINANCIAL TIMES (London), Feb. 2, 2002, at 1; and Gregg Easterbrook, *The World: Out on the Edge; American Power Moves Beyond the Mere Super*, NEW YORK TIMES, Apr. 27, 2003, at 1.
15 *See* JOSEPH S. NYE, SOFT POWER: THE MEANS TO SUCCESS IN WORLD POLITICS, (Public Affairs, 2004); J. F. RISCHARD, HIGH NOON: 20 GLOBAL PROBLEMS, 20 YEARS TO SOLVE THEM (The Perseus Press, 2002).
16 In his book, THE LEXUS AND THE OLIVE TREE, Thomas Friedman describes the "electronic herd" (a combination of institutions and millions of individuals), whose investment decisions, carried out by the click of a mouse, affect the fortunes of nations, having impacts as significant as triggering the downfall of governments. FRIEDMAN, *supra* note 2, at 93–119.

1.3 Implications for international law and its role for international relations: challenges to the fundamental logic and axioms of international law (a brief overview of things to come)

1 *See particularly* MARTIN WOLF, WHY GLOBALIZATION WORKS (Yale University Press, 2004), at 288–95.
2 *See* discussion in Chapter 5, *infra*. A prime example is the WTO *Shrimp-Turtle* case, *US – Import Prohibition of Certain Shrimp and Shrimp Products*, WTO Doc. WT/DS58/AB/R, adopted 6 Nov. 1998, discussed in sections 5.5 and 5.8, *infra*.
3 *See* Chapter 4 (especially 4.2), and Chapter 5 (especially 5.7), *infra*.

2 The real world impinges on international law: exploring the challenges to the fundamental assumptions of international law and institutions

1 UN Secretary-General, Kofi Annan, *We the Peoples – The Role of the United Nations in the 21st Century*, quoted *in* Marcel Brus, *The Authority of Law*, *in* STATE, SOVEREIGNTY, AND INTERNATIONAL GOVERNANCE, Gerald

Kreijen et al. eds. (Oxford University Press, 2002): 3, 19. Full UN report available at http://www.un.org/millennium/sg/report/full.htm, visited Jun. 22, 2005 (emphasis in original).

2.1 Introduction to exploring the challenges and their impacts on international law
2 Although the birth of the law of nations can be traced back to 2100 B.C., when a territorial limitation treaty was concluded between two states in Mesopotamia, Hugo Grotius is generally considered as the "founding father" of international law, along with some other philosophers such as Vitoria and Gentili. *See* ARTHUR NUSSBAUM, A CONCISE HISTORY OF THE LAW OF NATIONS, rev. ed. (Macmillan, 1954); W. S. M. KNIGHT, THE LIFE AND WORKS OF HUGO GROTIUS (Oceana Publications, 1965).
3 *See* ANTHONY CLARK AREND, LEGAL RULES AND INTERNATIONAL SOCIETY (Oxford University Press, 1999); GEORGE F. KENNAN, AMERICAN DIPLOMACY, exp. ed. (University of Chicago Press, 1984); HANS J. MORGENTHAU, POLITICS AMONG NATIONS: THE STRUGGLE FOR POWER AND PEACE, 5th ed. (A.A. Knopf, 1978); KENNETH N. WALTZ, THEORY OF INTERNATIONAL POLITICS (Addison-Wesley, 1983).

2.2 Circumstances and conditions
1 *See* books cited in Chapter 1, *supra*, for definition of "globalization." *See* BRINK LINDSEY, AGAINST THE DEAD HAND: THE UNCERTAIN STRUGGLE FOR GLOBAL CAPITALISM (CATO, 2001) (explaining several different definitions).
2 Mercado del Sur (Mercosur) or the Southern Cone Common Market (1991) is a customs union, consisting of Argentina, Brazil, Paraguay, and Uruguay, with currently a common external tariff up to 23 percent. *See Treaty Establishing a Common Market Between the Argentine Republic, the Federal Republic of Brazil, the Republic of Paraguay and the Republic of Uruguay*, Mar. 26, 1991, 30 ILM 1041.
3 The North American Free Trade Agreement between the United States, Canada, and Mexico, entered into force Jan. 1, 2004. *See North American Free Trade Agreement*, Dec. 17, 1992, Can.–Mex.–U.S., 32 ILM 289 & 605 (1993) (entered into force Jan. 1, 1994), at Chs. 19 and 20, available at: www.nafta-sec-alena.org, visited Apr. 21, 2005.
4 THE WORLD BANK, GLOBAL ECONOMIC PROSPECTS 2005: TRADE, REGIONALISM AND DEVELOPMENT (World Bank 2004).
5 E.g., the South Asian Association for Regional Cooperation (SAARC) – India, Pakistan, Bangladesh, Nepal, Bhutan, Sri Lanka, and the Maldives – signed in January 2004. Japan is currently negotiating free trade and economic partnership agreements with Malaysia, South Korea, the Philippines, ASEAN, and Thailand. As recently as April 2004, ASEAN foreign ministers reaffirmed their commitment to create a single market by 2020. China and ASEAN are currently discussing a free trade agreement by 2010, and China is exploring

the idea of a network of bilateral and regional free trade agreements in the region.

6 Belgium has, in the past fifty years, experienced a parallel complex process of upward integration in the now European Union and continuous inward federalization. Regarding the latter, *see* BARRY TURNER, ED., THE STATESMAN'S YEARBOOK 2005, 141st ed. (Palgrave Macmillan, 2004), at entry for Belgium.

7 Research by Georgetown University Law Center librarians, Marylin Raisch and Amy Berchfield, has revealed that there are currently fifty-four human rights treaties in force (excluding amendments and protocols), of which thirty are UN treaties and twenty-four are regional human rights treaties. Although the count of total human rights treaties is less than expected, it should be noted that human rights are increasingly included in non-human rights treaties (for example, the EU human rights clauses).

8 Thomas M. Franck, *The Emerging Right to Democratic Governance*, AJIL 86 (1992): 46.

9 Henry G. Schermers, *Different Aspects of Sovereignty*, *in* STATE, SOVEREIGNTY, AND INTERNATIONAL GOVERNANCE, Gerard Kreijen et al. eds. (Oxford University Press, 2002): 185, at 192. *See also* Chapter 3, *infra*.

10 The International Competition Policy Advisory Committee (ICPAC), a distinguished panel of antitrust specialists from various backgrounds appointed by the US Dept. Of Justice, reported in February 2000 that around eighty countries had adopted antitrust laws.

11 *Public Company Accounting Reform and Investor Protection Act of 2002*, PUB. L. No. 107–204, 116 STAT. 745 (2002); *Rules of Professional Responsibility for Attorneys* (Sarbanes-Oxley Act), 15 U.S.C.S. 7201 (2003).

12 There are over 2,200 bilateral investment treaties in existence; *see* section 7.3, *infra*, at note 7.

13 Derek S. Whitman, *Barclays Bank v. Franchise Tax Board of California: Worldwide Combined Reporting Survives for State Taxation of Multinational Enterprises*, TULANE JOURNAL OF INTERNATIONAL & COMPARATIVE LAW 3 (1995): 265; Keith Highet, *Barclays Bank PLC v. Franchise Tax Board of California*, 114 S.Ct. 2268, AJIL 88 (1994): 766.

14 *See especially US – Restrictions on Imports of Tuna* ("Tuna I and II"), GATT BISD 39 S/155 (Sept. 3, 1991, not adopted), DS29/R (June 10, 1994, not adopted); *US – Standards for Reformulated and Conventional Gasoline*, WTO Doc. WT/DS2/AB/R, WT/DS4/AB/R (adopted May 20, 1996); *US – Import Prohibition of Certain Shrimp and Shrimp Products*, WTO Doc. WT/DS58/AB/R, adopted Nov. 6, 1998.

15 *See* FRANCIS G. JACOBS AND SHELLEY ROBERTS, EDS., THE EFFECT OF TREATIES IN DOMESTIC LAW: THE UNITED KINGDOM NATIONAL COMMITTEE OF COMPARATIVE LAW 7 (Sweet & Maxwell, 1987), at XXIV; John H. Jackson, *Status of Treaties in Domestic Legal Systems: A Policy Analysis*, AJIL 86

(1992): 310; Curtis A. Bradley, *International Delegations, The Structural Constitution, and Non-Self-Executing*, STANFORD LAW REVIEW 55 (2003): 1557, 1587–94.

16 Other examples of countries often designated as monist include Belgium, Cyprus, France, Greece, Luxembourg, the Netherlands, Portugal, Spain, Switzerland, and the United States. *See* J.H.A. van Loon, *The Hague Conventions on Private International Law*, in THE EFFECT OF TREATIES IN DOMESTIC LAW, Jacobs & Roberts, *supra* note 15, at 221 & 229.

17 Various gradations of "dualism" exist, however, ranging from a mere formal legislative requirement to a substantive transformation of the treaty into domestic law.

18 *See* JOHN H. JACKSON, WILLIAM J. DAVEY, & ALAN O. SYKES, LEGAL PROBLEMS OF INTERNATIONAL ECONOMIC RELATIONS: CASES, MATERIALS AND TEXT ON THE NATIONAL AND INTERNATIONAL REGULATION OF TRANSNATIONAL ECONOMIC RELATIONS, 4th ed. (West Group, 2002), at 90–105. *See also* sections 4.6 and 5.9, *infra*. *See also* BARRY E. CARTER ET. AL., INTERNATIONAL LAW, 4th ed. (Aspen, 2003); Jackson, *Status of Treaties*, *supra* note 15.

19 TREVOR C. HARTLEY, EUROPEAN UNION LAW IN A GLOBAL CONTEXT (Cambridge University Press, 2004), at 239-261; PIET EECKHOUT, EXTERNAL RELATIONS OF THE EUROPEAN UNION (Oxford University Press, 2004), at 281–300.

20 *See North American Free Trade Agreement Act*, PUB. L. No. 103-182, 102, 107 Stat. 2057, 2062 (1993), 19 U.S.C.A. sec. 3312 (a) (1): "No provision of the Agreement, nor the application of any such provision to any person or circumstance, which is inconsistent with any law of the United States shall have effect." Similar language can be found in the *Uruguay Round Agreements Act*, PUB. L. No. 103-465, 102, 108 Stat. 4815, 19 U.S.C.A. sec. 3512(a)(1). *See also* Commission of the European Communities, *Proposal for a Council Decision Concerning the Conclusion of the Uruguay Round of Multilateral Trade Negotiations* (1986–94) Com(94), 143 Final of 15 Apr. 1994, at Preface.

21 *See* sections 5.9 and 5.10, *infra*.

22 *See* Chapter 3 and section 5.9, *infra*.

23 *SOSA v. Alvarez-Machain*, No 03-339 and 03-485, June 29, 2004, 124 S.Ct. 2739 (Opinion of Justice Souter). *See also* section 2.3.b, *infra*.

24 In *Murray v. Schooner Charming Betsy*, the US Supreme Court said that if a court is confronted with the interpretation of an ambiguity in a statute and one possible interpretation is consistent with international obligations and other options are not, the court should choose the interpretation that makes the US statute consistent with the US international obligations. Chief Justice Marshall wrote that "an act of Congress ought never to be construed to violate the law of nations if any other possible construction remains." *Murray v. Schooner Charming Betsy*, 6 U.S. 64, at 118, 2 L.Ed. 208 (1804). The Restatement reads that "where fairly possible, a United States statute is to be

construed so as not to conflict with international law or with an international agreement of the United States." *Restatement (Third) of the Foreign Relations Law of the United States sections 114* (1987).
25 *See* section 2.5 and section 7.2, *infra*.
26 When my assistant and I examined a list of all the United Nations nation-states and ranked them from those with the smallest population to those with the largest population, and then counted from small upward until we passed the midpoint, so that we had a majority of the UN nation-states, we learned that the total population of that majority (ranked from the smallest upward) amounted to less than 5% of the total population of all of the nation-states that are UN members. Likewise, when we do this with a slightly larger list of all nation-states and include some that are not UN members, we get the same result. I wish to acknowledge the able assistance of Ms. Woojung Kim, J.D., for the study relating to this footnote.
27 The European Union signed the Cotonou Agreement on June 23, 2000, with seventy-nine African, Caribbean, and Pacific countries ("ACP countries"). *See Cotonou Agreement*, 2000 OJ L317/3 (Dec. 15, 2000).
28 Multiple intergovernmental organizations and international agreements prescribe formal decision-making by consensus, while providing default mechanisms in case no consensus can be reached. Examples include: UNCTAD (UN Doc. A/5479); UNCLOS III (Third UN Conference on the Law of the Sea, Rule 37, UN Doc. A/Conf/62/30/Rev.1; 13 ILM 1205 (1974); MERCOSUR, *supra* note 2; UPU (Art. 19.1 of the Rules of Procedures of UPU Congresses). For an overview of decision-making by consensus *see* HENRY G. SCHERMERS & NIELS M. BLOKKER, INTERNATIONAL INSTITUTIONAL LAW: UNITY WITHIN DIVERSITY, 3d. ed. (Martinus Nijhoff, 1995), at sections 771–786; HENRY G. SCHERMERS, INTERNATIONAL INSTITUTIONAL LAW: UNITY WITHIN DIVERSITY, 4th ed. (Brill, 2004).
29 *See* discussion of accountability of international organizations (including recommendations), in ILA Committee on Accountability of International Organizations, *Final Report* (Berlin Conference, 2004), available at www.ilahq.org/html/layout_committee.htm, visited Aug. 29, 2004.
30 *See* Robert O. Keohane, *The Concept of Accountability in World Politics and the Use of Force*, MICHIGAN JOURNAL OF INTERNATIONAL LAW 24 (2003): 1130; Robert O. Keohane, *Governance in a Partially Globalized World* (Presidential Address, American Political Science Association, 2000), AMERICAN POLITICAL SCIENCE REVIEW 95 (2001):1.
31 Rosalyn Higgins, *The Concept of "The State": Variable Geometry and Dualist Perceptions*, in THE INTERNATIONAL LEGAL SYSTEM IN QUEST OF EQUITY AND UNIVERSALITY: LIBER AMICORUM GEORGES ABI-SAAB, Laurence Boisson de Chazournes and Vera Gowlland-Debbas, eds. (Martinus Nijhoff Publishers, 2001): 547; Christopher D. Stone, *Common but Differentiated Responsibilities in International Law*, AJIL 98 (2004): 276.
32 *See also* Sutherland, *The Future of the WTO*, at paras. 291–300.

Notes to pages 25–27

33 The enlarged European Union of 25 member states is increasingly relying on the principle of "enhanced cooperation" for the further development of the Union. The concept was introduced in the 1997 Amsterdam Treaty and has since then been reinforced in subsequent treaties. Art. I-43 of the proposed draft 2004 European "Constitution" sets outs strengthened procedures and requirements for the use of the "enhanced cooperation" mechanism.

34 Reports of alleged corruption in international organizations, referred to by World Bank president James Wolfensohn as the "cancer of corruption" in his speech during the Bank's 1996 Annual Meeting, led major multilateral intergovernmental organizations, such as the World Bank group and the United Nations, to develop specialized units focusing on professional ethics and internal fraud. The UN General Assembly established in 1994, by resolution 42/218 B of July 29, 1994, the independent Office of Internal Oversight Services (OIOS) to enhance oversight functions in the UN system through the use of intensified evaluation, audit, inspection, investigation, and compliance monitoring; and to promote responsible administration of resources, accountability, transparency, and enhanced program performance. The IMF Executive Board in 2001 established, after a deliberation process of almost ten years, the Independent Evaluation Office (IEO) to enhance transparency and accountability in the IMF. *Independent Evaluation Office Annual Report 2003*, available at www.imf.org/ieo, visited Aug. 24, 2004.

Kimberley Ann Scott, *Combatting Corruption in Multilateral Development Banks*, Testimony before the US Senate Foreign Relations Committee, July 21, 2004, available at www.iie.com, visited Aug. 24, 2004.

35 For an excellent discussion of this development in international trade, see STEVE CHARNOVITZ, TRADE AND GLOBAL GOVERNANCE (Cameron May, 2002).

36 *See* United Nations, Report of the World Summit on Sustainable Development, Johannesburg, South Africa, 2002. UN Doc. A/CONF.199/20, available at: www.johannesburgsummit.org/html/documents/documents.html, visited 9 Apr. 2003. Readers will note that no organization was established. *See also* Steve Charnovitz, *A World Environment Organization*, COLUMBIA JOURNAL OF ENVIRONMENTAL LAW 27(2002): 323.

37 United Nations, *Report of the International Conference on Financing for Development*, UN Doc. A/CONF.198/11, at 100.

38 *See* WTO SECRETARIAT, WTO ANNUAL REPORT 2004 (Geneva: WTO, 2004), 76, Table II.8. Since 1999 the WTO has also organized an annual public symposium to offer civil society representatives a forum to discuss contentious issues with diplomats, academics, and other civil society representatives. The 2003 symposium, entitled "Challenges ahead on the Road to Cancún," was attended by approximately 700 participants. The 2004 symposium, "Multilateralism at a Crossroads," was held on May 25–27, 2004. The 2005 annual Public Symposium was held under the title "WTO After 10 Years: Global Problems and Multilateral Solutions," on 20–22 April 2005.

39 Sutherland, *The Future of the WTO*, at Ch. V.
40 Since the formation of the first registered international NGO in 1839 (the Anti-Slavery Society) the number of international NGOs has grown to more than 40,000. *See* WILLIAM KOREY, NGOs AND THE UNIVERSAL DECLARATION OF HUMAN RIGHTS: A CURIOUS GRAPEVINE (St. Martin's Press, 1998).
41 In 2003, One World Trust (a UK charity) released a report, *Global Accountability Report 2003*, that assessed the accountability of five intergovernmental organizations (IGOs), six transnational companies (TNCs), and seven international nongovernmental organizations (NGOs). One World Trust cooperated with a group of experts from NGOs, universities, and international institutions to guarantee the accountability and transparency of the report. The report focused on the availability of online information, using it as a proxy for an organization's overall transparency. The study concludes that NGOs provide less online information about their activities than IGOs and TNCs, and that all of the organizations studied limit access to information about their decision-making processes.
42 The "quasi-governmental" function of the increasing number of NGOs has spurred initiatives such as NGOWatch.org (www.NGOWatch.org). This project is a collaboration of the American Enterprise Institute for Public Policy Research and the Federalist Society for Law and Public Policy Studies that monitors NGO activities and aims to "without prejudice, compile factual data about nongovernmental organizations." *See also* Alison Maitland, *Accountability "Vital" if NGOs Are to Retain Trust*, FINANCIAL TIMES (London), June 25, 2003.
43 *See also* Steve Charnovitz, *The Emergence of Democratic Participation in Global Governance (Paris, 1919)*, INDIANA JOURNAL OF GLOBAL LEGAL STUDIES 10 (2003): 45.
44 The ILA Committee on International Securities Regulation noted in its recent report that "international securities regulation serves as a paradigm of a new forum of international 'law' creation by market actors" other than states or international organizations. ILA Committee on International Securities Regulation, 6th Interim Report (Berlin Conference, 2004), available at www.ila-hq.org/html/layout_committee.htm, visited Aug. 30, 2004.
45 During the 1999 World Economic Forum UN Secretary-General Kofi Annan urged UN agencies, the business community, the civil sector, trade unions, and other actors to form a strategic international partnership aimed at protecting and supporting nine (now ten, including anti-corruption) core principles in the areas of human rights, labor, and the environment. Since the official launch of the Global Compact in 2000, this voluntary, non-regulatory partnership has grown towards a network of more than 100 partners and has taken positive steps in promoting global responsible corporate citizenship and a more sustainable and inclusive global economy. For more information, *see* www.unglobalcompact.org, visited Jul. 20, 2005.

46 *See* Dale D. Murphy, The Structure of Regulatory Competition: Corporations and Public Policies in a Global Economy (Oxford University Press, 2004).
47 *See* Eleanor M. Fox, *Antitrust Law on a Global Scale: Races Up, Down, and Sideways*, in Regulatory Competition and Economic Integration: Comparative Perspectives, Daniel C. Esty & Damien Geradin, eds. (Oxford University Press, 2001), at 348; Steven Vogel, Freer Markets, More Rules (Cornell University Press, 1996); Garry P. Simpson, Trade, Environment and the WTO (Johns Hopkins University Press, 2000).
48 *See* section 3.3, *infra*.
49 For example, the economic reality of global sourcing and multinational manufacturing probably makes the application of the "last substantial transformation" standard, as recommended by Art. 3, WTO Agreement on Rules of Origin, increasingly complex and inappropriate for contemporary global production processes.
50 The financial crisis of the Asian tiger economies (January 1997–98) has led to many controversies and much debate among diplomats, economists, academia, journalists, lawyers, politicians, etc. on the true economic causes of this crisis and its impact on the future development of the international financial system in a more and more globalized world. The two most common referred rationales for the Asian financial crisis are the sudden shift in the market confidence and expectations among domestic and international investors, on the one hand, and the economic and political regimes in the Asian region, on the other hand. However, there is almost universal consensus that the speed of the spread of the crisis from Korea to the entire South Asian region has put the importance of globalization to the forefront. For a good analysis of the crisis, *see* Paul Krugman, *What Happened to Asia?* (Conference paper, Jan. 1998), available at http://web.mit.edu/krugman/www/DISINTER.html, visited Aug. 1, 2005; Steven R. Pearlstein, *Background: Understanding the Asian Economic Crisis*, Washington Post, Jan 18, 1998, at A32.
51 *See supra* note 12.
52 *US – Subsidies on Upland Cotton*, WTO Doc. WT/DS267/AB/R, adopted Mar. 21, 2005. A similar case relating to the European Union's sugar subsidies is *EC – Export Subsidies for Sugar*, WTO Docs. WT/DS265/R & WT/DS265/AB/R (also DS266 and DS283, complainants are Australia, Brazil, and Thailand), adopted 19 May 2005. *See also EC – Export Subsidies on Sugar*, WTO Docs. WT/DS265/R, WT/DS266/R, WT/DS283/R, panel reports on complaints by Australia, Brazil, and Thailand, adopted 9 May 2005.
53 *US – Subsidies on Upland Cotton*, WT/DS267/AB/R.
54 *See* James R. Schlesinger, Final Report of the Independent Panel to Review DoD Detention Operations (William S. Hein, 2005); Anthony R. Jones, AR 15–6 Investigation of the Abu Ghraib Prison and 205th Military Intelligence Brigade (William S. Hein, 2005);

Karen J. Greenberg & Joshua L. Dratel, eds., The Torture Papers: The Road to Abu Ghraib (Cambridge University Press, 2005). More information on press coverage on the torture practices at the Abu Ghraib Prison is available at: www.washingtonpost.com/wp-dyn/world/mideast/gulf/iraq/ (includes references to a chronology of the prison events, pictures of the abuses, and testimonies of Abu Ghraib detainees, and the US Army Investigation Report), visited Jul. 20, 2005.

55 Thomas L. Friedman, The World Is Flat: A Brief History of the Twenty-First Century (Farrar, Straus & Giroux, 2005). For a somewhat contrary view, *see* Robert J. Samuelson, *The World Is Still Round*, Washington Post, Jul. 22, 2005, at A23; and Michael Lind, *Explode the Myths of Global Competition*, Financial Times (London), Jul. 28, 2005, at 13.

2.3 International law and its discontents

1 For an overview of the history of international law, *see* Nussbaum, section 2.1 *supra*, at note 2; David J. Bederman, International Law in Antiquity (Cambridge University Press, 2001).
2 *See* discussion and references to definitions in Chapter 1, *supra*.
3 *See* Hans Kelsen, General Theory of Law and State (Harvard University Press, 1945); Hans Kelsen, General Theory of Norms (Oxford University Press, 1990). Shaw criticizes Kelsen's concept of law, calling it "tautological" and incapable of justifying why customary international law is binding. Malcolm N. Shaw, International Law, 5th ed. (Cambridge University Press, 2003), at 49–50, 82–83.
4 *See, e.g.*, Jörg Kammerhofer, *Uncertainty in the Formal Sources of International Law: Customary International Law and Some of Its Problems*, European Journal of International Law 15 (2004): 523, 541: Kammerhofer argues that "to either assume a Grundnorm or to have a non-customary norm which would make customary law a formal source of law, then customary law could not itself create further 'steps' of the normative pyramid" and this "would exclude a hierarchy along the lines of jus cogens."
5 *Statute of the International Court of Justice*, June 26, 1945, 59 Stat. 1031, T.S. No. 993, Art. 38(1) (entered into effect Oct. 24, 1945) (ICJ Statute):

> "1. The Court, whose function is to decide in accordance with international law such disputes as are submitted to it, shall apply:
>   a. international conventions, whether general or particular, establishing rules expressly recognized by the contesting states;
>   b. international custom, as evidence of a general practice accepted as law;
>   c. the general principles of law recognized by civilized nations;
>   d. subject to the provisions of Article 59, judicial decisions and the teachings of the most highly qualified publicists of the various nations, as subsidiary means for the determination of rules of law."

Notes to pages 35–39

6 Kammerhofer, *Uncertainty, supra* note 4, at 536; A. D'AMATO, THE CONCEPT OF CUSTOM IN INTERNATIONAL LAW (Cornell University Press, 1971), at 91, stating that "there is no international 'constitution' specifying when acts become law."
7 JACK L. GOLDSMITH & ERIC A. POSNER, THE LIMITS OF INTERNATIONAL LAW (Oxford University Press, 2005). Another recent book by John F. Murphy is a careful and extensive analysis of the United States' views towards conforming to international law, with a series of modern case studies of US actions in that regard. *See* JOHN F. MURPHY, THE UNITED STATES AND THE RULE OF LAW IN INTERNATIONAL AFFAIRS (Cambridge University Press, 2004).
8 This classic doctrine of "consent" holds that "international legal rules emanate exclusively from the free will of states as expressed in conventions or by usages generally accepted as law." LORI F. DAMROSCH ET AL., INTERNATIONAL LAW – CASES AND MATERIALS, 4th ed. (West Group, 2001), at 58; OSCAR SCHACHTER, INTERNATIONAL LAW IN THEORY AND PRACTICE (Martinus Nijhoff, 1991), at 35–37; IAN BROWNLIE, PRINCIPLES OF PUBLIC INTERNATIONAL LAW, 6th ed. (Oxford University Press, 2003), at 3; ANTHONY C. AREND, LEGAL RULES AND INTERNATIONAL SOCIETY (Oxford University Press, 1999), at 87. Henkin writes that "the principle of consent is essentially intact but it has been softened." LOUIS HENKIN, INTERNATIONAL LAW: POLITICS AND VALUES (Kluwer Law International, 1995), at 26. *See also* PCIJ, *S.S. Lotus Case (France v. Turkey)*, 1927 PCIJ (Ser. A) No. 10 (Sept. 7).
9 Oscar Schachter, *Towards a Theory of International Obligation, in* THE EFFECTIVENESS OF INTERNATIONAL DECISIONS (Papers and Proceedings of a Conference of the American Society of International Law), Stephen M. Schwebel, ed. (Leyden: Oceana, 1971), at 9, 9–12, 30–31.
10 *Ibid.*
11 LOUIS HENKIN, HOW NATIONS BEHAVE, LAW AND FOREIGN POLICY, 2nd ed. (Columbia University Press, 1979), at 47.
12 The criticism and debate ranges from proposals for a reconceptualization to calls for a clear-cut elimination of customary international law. E.g., Simma and Alston suggest reframing current customary international law norms as general principles of international law under Art. 38(3) ICJ Statute. Bruno Simma and Philip Alston, *The Sources of Human Rights Law: Custom, Jus Cogens, and General Principles*, 12 AUSTRALIAN YEARBOOK OF INTERNATIONAL LAW (1992): 82. Kelly and D'Amato propose the elimination of customary international law. J. Patrick Kelly, *The Twilight of Customary International Law*, VIRGINIA JOURNAL OF INTERNATIONAL LAW 40 (2000): 449; A. D'Amato, *Customary International Law: A Reformulation*, INTERNATIONAL LEGAL THEORY 4 (1998):1.
13 International Law Association, Committee on Formation of Customary (General) International Law, *Final Report: Statement of Principles Applicable to the Formation of General Customary International Law*, available at http://www.ila-hq.org/pdf/CustomaryLaw.pdf, visited Aug. 1, 2005; The [US]

Restatement describes customary law as resulting "from a general and consistent practice of states followed by them from a sense of legal obligation" and adding in its commentary that "a practice that is generally followed but which states feel legally free to disregard does not contribute to customary international law." Rest. 3d FOREL Section 102, comm. c. BROWNLIE, PRINCIPLES OF PUBLIC INTERNATIONAL LAW, *supra* note 7, at 6–12.

14 Jack L. Goldsmith & Eric A. Posner, *A Theory of Customary International Law*, UNIVERSITY OF CHICAGO LAW REVIEW 66 (1999): 1113, 1115, write, using game theory and cases studies:

> States do not comply with norms of CIL because of a sense of moral or legal obligation; rather, CIL emerges from the states' pursuit of self-interested policies on the international stage.

See also Jack L. Goldsmith & Eric A. Posner, *Further Thoughts on Customary International Law*, MICHIGAN JOURNAL OF INTERNATIONAL LAW 23 (2001):191; Mark A. Chinen, *Game Theory and Customary International Law: A Response to Professors Goldsmith and Posner*, MICHIGAN JOURNAL OF INTERNATIONAL LAW 23 (2001):143; GOLDSMITH & POSNER, LIMITS OF INTERNATIONAL LAW, *supra* note 7.

15 ILA, *Final Report*, *supra* note 13. *See also* SHAW, INTERNATIONAL LAW, *supra* note 3, at 78–80; Michael Akehurst, *Custom as a Source of International Law*, British Yearbook of International Law 47(1977): 1, 40; M. Byers, *Custom, Power, and the Power of Rules: Customary International Law from an Interdisciplinary Perspective*, MICHIGAN JOURNAL OF INTERNATIONAL LAW 17 (1995): 109, 115 (1995).

16 However, Schachter notes the emerging tendency of states to consider law-declaring resolutions as evidence of a general *opinio iuris* that either reflects state practice or is expected to be followed in future practice. Oscar Schachter, *New Custom: Power, Opinio Juris and Contrary Practice*, in THEORY OF INTERNATIONAL LAW AT THE THRESHOLD OF THE 21ST CENTURY – ESSAYS IN HONOUR OF KRZYSZTOF SKUBISZEWESKI, J. Makarczyk, ed. (Kluwer Law International, 1996): 534. *See also* R. Kolb, *Selected Problems in the Theory of Customary International Law*, NETHERLANDS INTERNATIONAL LAW REVIEW L (2003):119, 125.

17 Kelly, *The Twilight of Customary International Law*, *supra* note 12.

18 *Ibid.*, at 457.

19 Curtis A. Bradley & Jack L. Goldsmith, *Customary International Law as Federal Common Law: A Critique of the Modern Position*, HARVARD LAW REVIEW 110 (1997): 815; Curtis A. Bradley & Jack L. Goldsmith, *Federal Courts and the Incorporation of International Law*, HARVARD LAW REVIEW 111 (1998): 2260; Phillip R. Trimble, *A Revisionist View of Customary International Law*, UC LOS ANGELES LAW REVIEW 33 (1986): 665. For opposing views, *see* Louis Henkin, *International Law as Law in the United States*, MICHIGAN LAW REVIEW 82 (1984): 1555; Harold Hongju Koh, *Is International Law Really State Law?*, HARVARD LAW REVIEW 111 (1998): 1824.

20 One of the most famous cases in which the US Supreme Court addressed customary international law is *The Paquete Habana* case. In his opinion, Justice Gray wrote "international law is part of our law" and "where there is no treaty, and no controlling executive or legislative act or judicial decision, resort must be had to the customs and usages of civilized nations; and, as evidence of these, to the works of jurists and commentators, who by years of labor, research and experience, have made themselves peculiarly well acquainted with the subjects of which they treat. Such works are resorted to by judicial tribunals, not for the speculations of their authors concerning what the law ought to be, but for trustworthy evidence of what the law really is." *The Paquete Habana*, 175 U.S. 677 (1900); *Filartiga v. Pena-Irala*, 630 F.2d. 876 (2d Circ. 1980). Interestingly, the Supreme Court relied on the *Charming Betsy* canon of interpretation as "plainest evidence that international law has an existence in the federal courts independent of acts of Congress." *Filartiga v. Pena-Irala*, 630 F.2d. 876, at 887 n. 20 (2d Circ. 1980). Koh referred to the *Filartiga* case as the "*Brown v. Board of Education*" of domestic human rights litigation. Harold Hongju Koh, *Transnational Public Law Litigation*, YALE LAW JOURNAL 100 (1991): 2347, 2366. Bradley argues that "Laws of the United States" was not intended to include the law of nations in Art. III or Art. VI of the US Constitution – neither of these articles mention customary international law. Curtis A. Bradley, *The Alien Tort Statute: Some Observations on Text and Context*, VIRGINIA JOURNAL OF INTERNATIONAL LAW 42 (2002): 587, 597. Cf. William S. Dodge, *The Constitutionality of the Alien Tort Statute: Some Observations on Text and Context*, VIRGINIA JOURNAL OF INTERNATIONAL LAW 42 (2002): 687.

21 *Banco Nacional de Cuba v. Sabbatino*, 376 U.S. 398, 84 S.Ct. 923, 11 L.Ed.2d 804 (1964).

22 *United States v. Alvarez-Machain*, 504 U.S. 655 (1992), holding that "the decision of whether respondent should be returned to Mexico, as a matter outside of the Treaty, is a matter for the Executive Branch."

23 *SOSA v. Alvarez-Machain*, No. 03-339 and 03-485, June 29, 2004, 124 S.Ct. 2739. See GARY C. HUFBAUER & NICHOLAS K. MITROKOSTAS, AWAKENING MONSTER: THE ALIEN TORT STATUTE OF 1789 (Institute for International Economics, 2003); Gary C. Hufbauer & Nicholas K. Mitrokostas, *International Implications of the Alien Tort Statute*, JIEL 7 (2004): 245; Harold Hongju Koh, *Separating Myth from Reality about Corporate Responsibility Litigation*, JIEL 7 (2004): 263.

24 *Alien Tort Claims Act*, 28 U.S.C. 1350 (2000); Act of 24 September 1789, ch. 20, 9(b), 1 Stat. 73, 77. The Alien Tort Claims Statute confers federal subject-matter jurisdiction when an alien sues for a tort committed in violation of the law of nations.

25 *See* JOHN H. JACKSON, WILLIAM J. DAVEY, & ALAN O. SYKES, LEGAL PROBLEMS OF INTERNATIONAL ECONOMIC RELATIONS: CASES, MATERIALS

AND TEXT ON THE NATIONAL AND INTERNATIONAL REGULATION OF TRANSNATIONAL ECONOMIC RELATIONS, 4th ed. (West Group, 2002), at 194.

26 *See* Stephen Zamora, *Is There Customary International Economic Law?* GERMAN YEARBOOK OF INTERNATIONAL LAW 22 (1989): 9; Georg Schwarzenberger, THE PRINCIPLES AND STANDARDS OF INTERNATIONAL ECONOMIC LAW, 117 RECUEIL DES COURS (1966-I): 1, 12, 14.

27 Reisman points out that *jus cogens* has come to be used in the human rights context in a different way than that intended by the drafters of the VCLT and that in this particular context, *jus cogens* is considered by some as "super-custom," based on trans-empirical sources. W. M. Reisman, *Unilateral Action and the Transformations of the World Constitutive Process: The Special Problem of Humanitarian Intervention*, EUROPEAN JOURNAL OF INTERNATIONAL LAW 11 (2000): 3, 15. For a discussion and critique of US courts' jurisprudence on *jus cogens*, see A. M. Weisburd, *American Judges and International Law*, VANDERBILT JOURNAL OF TRANSNATIONAL LAW 36 (Nov. 2003): 1474, 1494–1505.

28 *See* ANTHONY AUST, MODERN TREATY LAW AND PRACTICE (Cambridge University Press, 2000) at 257–258; G. E. do Nascimento e Silva, *The Widening Scope of International Law*, *in* THEORY OF INTERNATIONAL LAW, Makarczyck, ed., *supra* note 16, at 241. Kolb approaches *jus cogens* from a constitutional perspective and finds that the development of *jus cogens* norms is part of the emergence of a kind of constitutional international law, Kolb, *Selected Problems*, *supra* note 16, at 124.

29 Joost Pauwelyn, *A Typology of Multilateral Treaty Obligations: Are WTO Obligations Bilateral or Collective in Nature?* EUROPEAN JOURNAL OF INTERNATIONAL LAW 14 (2003): 907. *See also* JOOST PAUWELYN, CONFLICT OF NORMS IN PUBLIC INTERNATIONAL LAW (Cambridge University Press, 2003), at 101–106.

30 Data compiled as of Aug. 1, 2004. *See United Nations Treaty Collection Database*, at http://untreaty.un.org/, visited Aug. 1, 2005.

31 E.g., US Dept. of State, *Treaties in Force 2003: A List of Treaties and Other International Agreements of the United States in Force as of January 1, 2003* (US Dept. State, 2003), at www.state.gov/s/l/c8455.htm, visited Aug. 1, 2005. Regular updates are available at www.state.gov/s/l/c3428.htm, visited Aug. 1, 2005.

32 *VCLT*, *opened for signature* May 23, 1969, entered into force on Jan. 27, 1970, *reprinted in* 8 ILM 679 (1969). Art. 2.1(a) VCLT defines a treaty as "an international agreement concluded by States in written form and governed by international law, whether embodied in a single instrument or in two or more related instruments and whatever its particular designation." But gray areas exist between informal or personal agreements, and a true "treaty."

33 There are currently about 1,500 environmental treaties in force, of which 150 are multilateral and about 300 are regional, and there are approximately 1,000 bilateral treaties in force. *See* www.ecolex.org, visited Jul. 20, 2005. Section 7.3, *infra*, notes the number of "BITS" agreements as 2,200.

34 Often the definition from the VCLT is used, sometimes when that treaty is not strictly applicable (usually because of non-ratification), as an indication of the customary international law definition of "treaty." Other terms sometimes used include convention, agreement, protocol, covenant, charter, statute, act, declaration, concordat, exchange of notes, agreed minute, memorandum of agreement, memorandum of understanding, and *modus vivendi*. *See* the American Society of International Law Series, NATIONAL TREATY LAW AND PRACTICE, VOL. 1: FRANCE, GERMANY, INDIA, SWITZERLAND, THAILAND, UNITED KINGDOM (No. 27, 1995), Monroe Leigh & Merritt R. Blakeslee eds.; VOL. 2: AUSTRIA, CHILE, COLUMBIA, JAPAN, NETHERLANDS, UNITED STATES (No. 30, 1998) Monroe Leigh et al. eds.; VOL. 3: CANADA, EGYPT, ISRAEL, MEXICO, RUSSIA, SOUTH AFRICA (No. 33, 2003) Monroe Leigh et al. eds.

35 For example, the *Final Act of the Conference on Security and Cooperation in Europe*, signed at Helsinki on Aug. 1, 1975, the OECD Declaration on International Investment and Multinational Enterprises, the OECD Principles of Corporate Governance.

36 *See* section 4.5.b, *infra*.

37 Since 2000 the United States has been campaigning to convince ICC contracting parties and non-contracting parties to sign so-called "Article 98(2) Agreements" or "Bilateral Immunity Agreements" with the United States, which is making aid conditional upon signing such agreements. More than sixty states have signed such agreements, whereas more than thirty have publicly refused the invitation of the United States. It has been questioned whether these agreements are in fact consistent with Art. 98 ICC Statute.

38 *See The European Union constitution: Dead, But Not Yet Buried*, THE ECONOMIST (LONDON), Jun. 4, 2005; George Parker et. al., *After the Votes: Europe's Leaders Confront the Consequences of "the Wrong Answer"*, FINANCIAL TIMES (LONDON), 3 Jun. 2005, at 17.

39 *See* Chapter 5, especially section 5.12, *infra*.

40 *Uruguay Round Agreements Act*, s. 102, Pub. L. No. 103–182, 102, 107 Stat. 2057. *See* for discussion of the domestic effect of international treaties, FRANCIS G. JACOBS & SHELLEY ROBERTS EDS., THE EFFECT OF TREATIES IN DOMESTIC LAW: THE UNITED KINGDOM NATIONAL COMMITTEE OF COMPARATIVE LAW, Vol. 7 (Sweet & Maxwell, 1987), at XXIV; John H. Jackson, *Status of Treaties in Domestic Legal Systems: A Policy Analysis*, AJIL 86 (1992): 310. *See also* sections 4.6 and 5.9, *infra*.

Although the European Court of Justice and the Court of First Instance have continuously denied direct effect of the GATT and WTO Agreements, the European Courts have relied on the principle of consistent interpretation to these Agreements to argue that when more than one interpretation of the provisions of secondary Community legislation is available, preference should be given as much as possible to the interpretation which makes the provision consistent with the Treaty. For examples, see ECJ, *Interfood v.*

Hauptzollamt Hamburg, Case 92/71, 1972 E.C.R. 231, para. 6; E.C.J., *Commission v. Germany*, Case 61/94, 1996 E.C.R. I-3989, para 10; ECJ, *Hermès v. FHT*, Case C-53/96, 1998 E.C.R. I-3603. Eeckhout compares this approach by the European Courts with their case law on the legal impact of directives. Although the Courts have denied the horizontal direct effect of directives, Eeckhout writes that "the Court has undertaken some creative interpretation so as to give effect to directives, stretching the language and meaning of the interpreted provisions" and questions "whether the Court would be willing to do the same as regards international agreements which are not directly effective, in particular WTO agreements." PIET EECKHOUT, EXTERNAL RELATIONS OF THE EUROPEAN UNION: LEGAL AND CONSTITUTIONAL FOUNDATIONS (Oxford University Press, 2004), at 316.

41 *See* sections 4.4 and 4.5, *infra*.

2.4 International economic law

1 The Third (US) Restatement's comprehensive definition of international economic law reads, "The law of international economic relations in its broadest sense includes all the international law and international agreements governing economic transactions that cross state boundaries or that otherwise have implications for more than one state, such as those involving the movement of goods, funds, persons, intangibles, technology, vessels or aircraft." REST.3d Vol. 2 (1987), 261.
2 Donald M. McRae, *The Contribution of International Trade Law to the Development of International Law*, RECUEIL DES COURS 260 (1997): 103, at 122. McRae notes that an employee of the UK Ministry of Foreign Affairs estimated that between 50 and 70 percent of his time was spent on what were in fact economic matters.
3 There are over 300 tax treaties in force, predominantly bilateral treaties. Data available at Oceana Publications database, www.oceanalaw.com/, visited Jun. 30, 2005.
4 *See, e.g.*, LORI F. DAMROSCH ET AL., INTERNATIONAL LAW: CASES AND MATERIALS, 4th ed. (West Group, 2001).
5 *See, e.g.*, list generated at Amazon.com, section 1.1 *supra*, at note 11. Also note citations generally in Chapters 1–5 of this book.
6 *See, e.g.*, JOURNAL OF INTERNATIONAL ECONOMIC LAW (Oxford University Press); MANCHESTER JOURNAL OF INTERNATIONAL ECONOMIC LAW (Electronic Publications); WORLD TRADE REVIEW (Cambridge University Press).
7 A small sample of this literature can be browsed at the *International Law & Trade Abstracts*, Legal Scholarship Network, Social Science Research Network, Alan O. Sykes, ed., http://ssrn.com/lsn/index.html, visited Apr 26, 2005.
8 For recent discussion of this issue, *see* JAMES BACCHUS, TRADE AND FREEDOM (Cameron May, 2004); DEBRA STEGER, PEACE THROUGH TRADE: BUILDING THE WORLD TRADE ORGANIZATION (Cameron May, 2004).

9 Thomas Friedman, *"Golden Arches Theory of Conflict Prevention," Foreign Affairs Big Mac I*, NEW YORK TIMES, Dec. 8, 1996, at 15.
10 On the role of trade in the détente in US–Soviet relations, *see* HENRY KISSINGER, WHITE HOUSE YEARS (Little, Brown, 1979), at 153. For the more recent example of improved relations between India and Pakistan and the role of trade and the business community in the peace process, *see* Jo Johnson, *Relations with India: Peace Hopes Bring Trade Dividend*, FINANCIAL TIMES (London) 31 May 2005, at 24. *See also* THOMAS L. FRIEDMAN, THE WORLD IS FLAT: A BRIEF HISTORY OF THE TWENTY-FIRST CENTURY (Farrar, Straus & Giroux, 2005); section 1.2, *supra*, at note 7; and RAYMOND L. GARTHOFF, DÉTENTE AND CONFRONTATION: AMERICAN–SOVIET RELATIONS FROM NIXON TO REAGAN, rev. ed. (Brookings Institution Press, 1994).
11 *See* John Norton Moore, *Beyond the Democratic Peace: Solving the War Puzzle*, VIRGINIA JOURNAL OF INTERNATIONAL LAW 44 (2004): 341, 382; *Trade as an Agent of War*, presentation by Jan Kleinheisterkamp, Assistant Professor of Law, HEC School of Management, Paris, at *Trade as a Guarantor for Peace, Liberty and Security*, the Annual Conference of the International Economic Law Group of the American Society of International Law, Feb. 24–26, 2005, Washington, D.C., available at http://studies.hec.fr/object/SEC/file/A/FDDCNBTKGGYFVJSBPPKMARULLSPXZPMR/Trade%20&%20War%20speech.pdf, visited Jun. 30, 2005. *See also* Eric Allen Engle, *The Professionalization Thesis: The TBR, The WTO, and World Economic Integration*, INTERNATIONAL TRADE LAW JOURNAL 11 (2002): 16. For a recent example, *see Report of the Panel of Experts on the Illegal Exploitation of Natural Resources and Other Forms of Wealth of the Democratic Republic of the Congo* (2001), available at www.un.org/News/dh/latest/drcongo.htm, visited Jun. 30, 2005.
12 *See* John H. Jackson, *Global Economics and International Economic Law*, JIEL 1 (1998): 1.
13 *See* Chapters 4 and 5, *infra*.
14 Art. 31(1), VCLT. *See* Chapter 5, *infra*.
15 *Tunesia/Libya Continental Shelf Case*, 1982 ICJ Rep. 18, at 38; ICJ, *Nicaragua Case*, 1986 ICJ Rep. 3.
16 *Korea – Measures Affecting Government Procurement*, WTO Doc. WT/DS163/R, adopted 19 Jun. 2000, paras. 7.93-96, 7.100-101. JOOST PAUWELYN, CONFLICT OF NORMS IN PUBLIC INTERNATIONAL LAW: HOW WTO LAW RELATES TO OTHER RULES OF INTERNATIONAL LAW (Cambridge University Press, 2003), at 483–484.
17 McRae, *Contribution of International Trade Law*, *supra* note 2, at 109–111, & 121.

2.5 International institutional law

1 THOMAS M. FRANCK, RECOURSE TO FORCE: STATE ACTION AGAINST THREATS AND ARMED ATTACKS (Cambridge University Press, 2002), at 7–8. This practice has been endorsed by the ICJ *in Legal Consequences for States of the*

Continuing Presence of South Africa in Namibia (South West Africa) notwithstanding Security Council Resolution 276 (1970), Advisory Opinion 1971 ICJ Rep. 16, at 22, para. 22.
2 *See* Chapter 4, *infra*.
3 *Luxembourg Accords*, January 29, 1966, EEC Bulletin 8, No. 3 (1966).
4 Sutherland, *The Future of the WTO*, at para. 289, p. 64.
5 Art. 31(1) VCLT. The case law and literature on this issue is vast and too comprehensive to discuss and include for the purpose of the subject of this book. *See* IAN BROWNLIE, PRINCIPLES OF PUBLIC INTERNATIONAL LAW, 6th ed. (Oxford University Press, 2003), 602–607; ANTHONY AUST, MODERN TREATY LAW AND PRACTICE (Cambridge University Press, 2000), 184–206.
6 Chief Justice John Marshall, *McCulloch v. Maryland*, 4 Wheat. 316, 407 (1819).
7 ICJ, *Certain Expenses of the United Nations* (Art. 17, para. 2 of the Charter), *Advisory Opinion of 20 July 1962*, Statement of Mr. Chayes (USA), 1962 Vol. 21, 426. Judge Van Wyk also referred to Marshall in his separate opinion in ICJ, *South West Africa (Ethiopia v. South Africa/Liberia)*, 1966 ICJ Rep. 6, para. 2, n. 10.
8 *The Treaty Establishing a Constitution for Europe* 2004 O.J. (C 310), 1. *See also* Pavlos Eleftheriadis, *Constitution or Treaty?* THE FEDERAL TRUST ONLINE PAPER 12/04, Jul. 2004, at www.fedtrust.co.uk/default.asp?groupid=6, visited Aug. 31, 2004.
9 *See The Case of the S.S. Lotus (France v. Turkey)*, 1927 PCIJ (Ser. A) No. 10, and discussion *in* LORI F. DAMROSCH ET AL., INTERNATIONAL LAW: CASES AND MATERIALS, 4th ed. (West Group, 2001), at 68–76.
10 For example, the Appellate Body found in *Canada – Aircraft* that "although the word 'should' is often used colloquially to imply an exhortation, or to state a preference, it is not always used in those ways," and went on to find that "the word 'should' in the third sentence of Art. 13.1 is, in the context of the whole of Art. 13, used in a normative, rather than a merely exhortative, sense." Therefore the Appellate Body concluded that "members are, in other words, under a duty and an obligation to 'respond promptly and fully' to requests made by panels for information under Art. 13.1 of the DSU." *Canada – Measures Affecting the Export of Certain Aircraft*, WTO Doc. WT/DS70/AB/R, adopted Aug. 20, 1999, at para. 187; *see also* Rambod Behboodi, *"Should" Means "Shall": A Critical Analysis of the Obligation to Submit Information under Art. 13.1 of the DSU in the Canada – Aircraft Case*, JIEL 3 (2000): 563.
11 *See* section 5.6.c, *infra*.
12 *See* STEVEN GREER, THE MARGIN OF APPRECIATION: INTERPRETATION AND DISCRETION UNDER THE EUROPEAN CONVENTION ON HUMAN RIGHTS (Council of Europe, 2000); *cf.* Jeffrey A. Brauch, *The Margin of Appreciation and the Jurisprudence of the European Court of Human Rights: Threat to the Rule of Law*, COLUMBIA JOURNAL OF EUROPEAN LAW 11 (2004): 113.
13 For detailed statistics, *see* Union of International Associations, *Guide to Global*

Civil Society Networks: Statistics, Visualizations and Patters, YEARBOOK OF INTERNATIONAL ORGANIZATIONS 5 (2003–2004); Richard Blackhurst, *The Capacity of the WTO to Fulfill Its Mandate*, *in* THE WTO AS AN INTERNATIONAL ORGANIZATION, Anne Krueger ed., (Chicago University Press, 1998): 31; Richard Blackhurst & David Hartridge, *Improving the Capacity of WTO Institutions to Fulfill Their Mandate*, JIEL 7 (2004): 705; James Bacchus remarks that "the entire WTO annual budget of the WTO is less than the annual travel budgets of the International Monetary Fund." James Bacchus, *A Few Thoughts on Legitimacy, Democracy, and the WTO*, JIEL 7 (2004): 667.

14 A broad variety of aspects on good governance international institutions, focusing on the WTO, is addressed in ERNST-ULRICH PETERSMANN, ED., PREPARING THE DOHA DEVELOPMENT ROUND: CHALLENGES TO THE LEGITIMACY AND EFFICIENCY OF THE WORLD TRADING SYSTEM (Robert Schuman Centre for Advanced Studies, 2004); a selection of these papers is published in JOURNAL OF INTERNATIONAL ECONOMIC LAW 7 (2004): 585. *See also* generally, Sutherland, *The Future of the WTO*.

15 *See* Robert O. Keohane, *Governance in a Partially Globalized World* (Presidential Address, American Political Science Association, 2000), AMERICAN POLITICAL SCIENCE REVIEW 95 (2001):1; ROBERT O. KEOHANE, POWER AND GOVERNANCE IN A PARTIALLY GLOBALIZED WORLD (Routledge, 2002); ROBERT O. KEOHANE & JOSEPH S. NYE, JR., POWER AND INTERDEPENDENCE (Princeton University Press, 2001); LISA M. MARTIN, DEMOCRATIC COMMITMENTS: LEGISLATURES AND INTERNATIONAL COOPERATION (Princeton University Press, 2000); Robert A. Dahl, *Can International Organizations Be Democratic? in* DEMOCRACY'S EDGES, Ian Shapiro & Casiano Hacker-Cordon eds. (Cambridge University Press, 1999), at 19.

16 *See* section 6.5, *infra*. Alvarez describes the challenge of the Security Council as being "to secure the benefits of a diversity of insights and viewpoints, improve the quality of legislation, and avoid repeating mistakes," and recommends that "consultation and participation may require institutionalized mechanisms . . . as well as less formal approaches, such as greater attempts at transparency . . . Such mechanisms are also essential to securing continued multilateral cooperation in the future, whenever the hegemon and others require such cooperation." José E. Alvarez, *Hegemonic International Law Revisited*, AJIL 97 (2003): 873, 888. *See also* W. Michael Reisman, *The Constitutional Crisis in the United Nations*, AJIL 87 (1993): 83, 99; Paul C. Szasz, *The Security Council Starts Legislating*, AJIL 96 (2002): 901, 905.

2.6 Some conclusions: the international law system challenged

1 STEPHEN D. KRASNER, SOVEREIGNTY: ORGANIZED HYPOCRISY (Princeton University Press, 1999). *See* Chapter 3, *infra*.

2 *See* ANNE-MARIE SLAUGHTER, A NEW WORLD ORDER (Princeton University Press, 2004). *See also* section 2.2, *supra*.

Sovereignty-modern: a new approach to an outdated concept

1 INTERNATIONAL COMMISSION ON INTERVENTION AND STATE SOVEREIGNTY (ICISS), THE RESPONSIBILITY TO PROTECT (International Development Research Centre, Canada, 2001), at 7.

3.1 Sovereignty and the fundamental logic of international law

2 A preliminary version of parts of this chapter was first published in the American Journal of International Law. This chapter develops and extends that manuscript. See John H. Jackson, *Sovereignty-Modern: A New Approach to An Outdated Concept*, AJIL 97, (2003): 782. This author wishes to express his appreciation to AJIL for permission to use this text.

3 See *Arrest Warrant of 11 April 2000 (Dem. Rep. Congo v. Belg.)*, 41 ILM 536 (2002) (Int'l Ct. Justice, Feb. 14, 2002) (especially separate opinion of Judge ad hoc Bula-Bula, id. at 597 (in French)). See also IAN BROWNLIE, PRINCIPLES OF PUBLIC INTERNATIONAL LAW, 6th ed. (Oxford University Press, 2003), 319–322; HAZEL FOX, THE LAW OF STATE IMMUNITY (Oxford University Press, 2002).

4 One classic exception may be the end-of-a-war treaty, at least in some circumstances. In addition, there are sticky problems in connection with state succession, including whether the colonial imposition of obligations carries over to a newly independent state. See BROWNLIE, PRINCIPLES OF PUBLIC INTERNATIONAL LAW, *supra* note 3, at 622–623; MALCOLM N. SHAW, INTERNATIONAL LAW, 5th ed. (Cambridge University Press, 2003), 861–913; Oscar Schachter, *State Succession: The Once and Future Law, in* INTERNATIONAL LAW: CLASSIC AND CONTEMPORARY READINGS, 2d ed. Charlotte Ku & Paul F. Diehl eds. (L. Reiner Publishers, 2003), 127–134.

5 As discussed in Chapter 2, *supra*, an example of an "evolutionary approach" can be seen in some of Professor Thomas Franck's writings, particularly THOMAS M. FRANCK, RECOURSE TO FORCE: STATE ACTION AGAINST THREATS AND ARMED ATTACKS (Cambridge University Press, 2002) (noting the evolution of practice regarding the veto power under the UN Charter). See also *US – Import Prohibition of Certain Shrimp and Shrimp Products*, WTO Doc. WT/DS58/AB/R, adopted Nov. 6, 1998, at para. 130.

6 This article builds on several other published works by this author. See John H. Jackson, *The Great 1994 Sovereignty Debate: United States Acceptance and Implementation of the Uruguay Round Results, in* POLITICS, VALUES, AND FUNCTIONS: INTERNATIONAL LAW IN THE 21ST CENTURY – ESSAYS IN HONOR OF PROFESSOR LOUIS HENKIN, Jonathan I. Charney et al. eds. (Martinus Nijhoff, 1998): 149; John H. Jackson, *Sovereignty, Subsidiarity, and Separation of Powers: The High-Wire Balancing Act of Globalization, in* THE POLITICAL ECONOMY OF INTERNATIONAL TRADE LAW: ESSAYS IN HONOUR OF ROBERT E. HUDEC, Daniel L. M. Kennedy & James D. Southwick, eds. (Cambridge University Press, 2002): 13. See also John H.

Jackson, *Editorial Comment: International Law Status of WTO DS Reports: Obligation to Comply or Option to "Buy-Out"?* AJIL 98 (January 2004): 109; JOHN H. JACKSON, WILLIAM J. DAVEY, & ALAN O. SYKES, LEGAL PROBLEMS OF INTERNATIONAL ECONOMIC RELATIONS: CASES, MATERIALS AND TEXT ON THE NATIONAL AND INTERNATIONAL REGULATION OF TRANSNATIONAL ECONOMIC RELATIONS, 4th ed. (West Group, 2002).

7 John H. Jackson, *The WTO "Constitution" and Proposed Reforms: Seven "Mantras" Revisited*, JIEL 4 (2001): 67 (addressing "mantras" related to the WTO).

8 *See, e.g.*, MICHAEL ROSS FOWLER & JULIE MARIE BUNCK, LAW, POWER, AND THE SOVEREIGN STATE (Penn State University Press, 1995); THOMAS L. FRIEDMAN, THE LEXUS AND THE OLIVE TREE: UNDERSTANDING GLOBALIZATION (Farrar, Straus, Giroux, 1999); KAREN T. LIFTIN, ed., THE GREENING OF SOVEREIGNTY IN WORLD POLITICS (MIT Press, 1998); STEPHEN D. KRASNER, SOVEREIGNTY: ORGANIZED HYPOCRISY (Princeton University Press, 1999); GERALD KREIJEN et al. eds., STATE, SOVEREIGNTY, AND INTERNATIONAL GOVERNANCE (Oxford University Press, 2002); THOMAS J. BIERSTEKER & CYNTHIA WEBER, eds., STATE SOVEREIGNTY AS SOCIAL CONSTRUCT (Cambridge University Press, 1996); UTE COLLIER ET AL., eds., SUBSIDIARITY AND SHARED RESPONSIBILITY: NEW CHALLENGES FOR EU ENVIRONMENTAL POLICY 9 (European Center for Research on Federalism, Nomos, 1997); DAVID BEGG ET AL., MAKING SENSE OF SUBSIDIARITY: HOW MUCH CENTRALIZATION FOR EUROPE? Monitoring European Integration 4 (Centre for Economic Policy Research, 1993); ABRAM CHAYES & ANTONIA HANDLER CHAYES, THE NEW SOVEREIGNTY: COMPLIANCE WITH INTERNATIONAL REGULATORY AGREEMENTS (Harvard University Press, 1995); NEIL WALKER ed., SOVEREIGNTY IN TRANSITION (Hart, 2004); NEIL MACCORMICK, QUESTIONING SOVEREIGNTY: LAW, STATE, AND NATION IN THE EUROPEAN COMMONWEALTH (Oxford University Press, 1999); THOMAS L. FRIEDMAN, THE WORLD IS FLAT: A BRIEF HISTORY OF THE TWENTY-FIRST CENTURY (Farrar, Straus & Giroux, 2005).

9 *See, e.g.*, Sir Robert Jennings, *Sovereignty and International Law*, in STATE, SOVEREIGNTY, AND INTERNATIONAL GOVERNANCE, Gerald Kreijen et al. eds. (Oxford University Press, 2002), at.33; Marcel Brus, *The Authority of Law*, in Kreijen, at 19; INTERNATIONAL COMMISSION ON INTERVENTION AND STATE SOVEREIGNTY (ICISS), THE RESPONSIBILITY TO PROTECT (International Development Research Centre, Canada, 2001); LOUIS HENKIN, INTERNATIONAL LAW: POLITICS AND VALUES (Kluwer, 1995), discussed in Jackson, *Great 1994 Sovereignty Debate*, *supra* note 6; WOLFGANG FRIEDMAN, LAW IN A CHANGING SOCIETY, 2nd ed., at 465 (Columbia University Press, 1972); STÉPHANE BEAULAC, THE POWER OF LANGUAGE IN THE MAKING OF INTERNATIONAL LAW (Martinus Nijhoff, 2004).

10 *See* discussion in Chapters 1 and 2, *supra*.

11 *See* sections 1.2 (especially note 4) and 2.2, *supra*, which note the views that in

past periods, such as around 1900, the world was very integrated, perhaps more than at present. But, as noted in section 1.2, *supra*, circumstances are vastly different today, particularly in view of the factors mentioned in the text, which have an astonishingly different impact on globalization of world society than the factors involved one hundred years ago.

12 For example, the "just in time" inventory principles that have been introduced during the last few decades, calling for the smooth and efficient operation of communication transport, so that a factory can depend on the arrival of needed inputs just in time for production, without having to carry the interest impact of the purchase cost as well as the cost of storage. Clearly, recent events involving terrorism are changing that type of view of the globalized integration of production.

13 *See* works of this author, cited in Chapter 1, *supra*. *See also* Chapter 5, *infra*.

14 *See* section 5.5, *infra*.

15 Jennings, *Sovereignty and International Law*, supra note 9.

16 Brus, *The Authority of Law*, supra note 9.

17 ICISS, RESPONSIBILITY TO PROTECT, *supra* note 1, at 7.

18 National Intelligence Council, CIA, *Global Trends 2015: A Dialogue About the Future With Nongovernment Experts*, NIC 2000–02 (Dec. 2000), at 38. *See also Mapping the Global Future*, Report of the National Intelligence Council's 2020 Project, Dec. 2004 (avail. from the Government Printing Office, http://bookstore.gpo.gov); *The National Defense Strategy of the United States of America*, Department of Defense, March 2005, avail. at www.globalsecurity.org/military/library/policy/dod/nds-usa_mar 2005.htm, visited Jun. 28, 2005.

19 National Security Council, *National Security Strategy of the United States of America* (Sep 2002), at 1 and 3, avail. at www.whitehouse.gov/nsc/nss.html, visited Aug. 1, 2005.

20 Richard N. Haass, former ambassador and director of Policy Planning Staff, US Department of State, *Sovereignty: Existing Rights, Evolving Responsibilities*, remarks at the School of Foreign Service and the Mortara Center for International Studies, Georgetown University Jan. 14, 2003, transcript avail. at www.state.gov/s/p/rem/2003/16648.htm, visited Jul. 21, 2005. Ambassador Haass is currently president of the Council on Foreign Relations.

21 See Henkin in Jackson, *supra* note 9.

3.2 Traditional Westphalian sovereignty concepts: outmoded and discredited?

1 The "Treaty of Westphalia" is the *Peace Treaty Between the Holy Roman Emperor and the King of France and Their Respective Allies*, Oct. 24, 1648, *in* Clive Parry, Consolidated Treaty Series 1648–1919, Vol. 1 (Oceana Publications, 1969-81) at 319 (English trans.), also available at fletcher.tufts.edu/multi/texts/historical/westphalia.txt, last visited Mar. 18, 2005.

2 *See* STÉPHANE BEAULAC, THE POWER OF LANGUAGE IN THE MAKING OF INTERNATIONAL LAW (Martinus Nijhoff, 2004).

Notes to pages 63–68

3 Alfred van Staden & Hans Vollaard, *The Erosion of State Sovereignty: Towards a Post-Territorial World?* in STATE SOVEREIGNTY AND INTERNATIONAL GOVERNANCE, Gerald Kreijen et al. eds. (Oxford University Press, 2002).
4 Richard N. Haass, *Sovereignty: Existing Rights, Evolving Responsibilities*, Remarks at the School of Foreign Service and the Mortara Center for International Studies, Georgetown University (Jan. 14, 2003), at 2, avail. at www.georgetown.edu/sfs/documents/haass_sovereignty_20030114.pdf, visited Apr. 28, 2005.
5 STEPHEN D. KRASNER, SOVEREIGNTY: ORGANIZED HYPOCRISY (Princeton University Press, 1999).
6 *Id*, at 9.
7 MICHAEL ROSS FOWLER & JULIE MARIE BUNCK, LAW, POWER, AND THE SOVEREIGN STATE (Penn State University Press, 1995), at 21 (quoting QUINCY WRIGHT, MANDATES UNDER THE LEAGUE OF NATIONS (Greenwood Press, 1968), at 277–278).
8 Cynthia Weber & Thomas J. Biersteker, *Reconstructing the Analysis of Sovereignty: Concluding Reflections and Directions for Future Research*, in KREIJEN, STATE SOVEREIGNTY, *supra* note 3, at 278.
9 WOLFGANG FRIEDMAN, LAW IN A CHANGING SOCIETY (Columbia University Press, 1972), at 465.
10 THOMAS L. FRIEDMAN, THE LEXUS AND THE OLIVE TREE: UNDERSTANDING GLOBALIZATION (Farrar, Straus, Giroux, 1999), at 93.
11 *Id*. at 94.
12 *Id*. at 115.
13 KREIJEN, STATE SOVEREIGNTY, *supra* note 3.
14 Henry Schermers, *Different Aspects of Sovereignty*, in KREIJEN, STATE SOVEREIGNTY, *supra* note 3, at 185, 192.
15 NEIL WALKER, ed., SOVEREIGNTY IN TRANSITION (Hart Publishing, 2003).
16 An Agenda for Peace – Preventive Diplomacy, Peacemaking, and Peace-Keeping, Report of the Secretary-General, UN Doc. A/47/277-S/24111, para. 17 (1992), UN Sales No. E.95.1.15 (1995).
17 Kofi A. Annan, *Secretary-General's Speech to the 54th Session of the General Assembly*, UN Doc. SG/SM/7136 (1999).
18 *Ibid*.
19 *Doctrine of the International Community*, speech by the UK Prime Minister, Tony Blair, to the Economic Club, Chicago, Illinois, Apr. 24, 1999, avail. at www.number-10.gov.uk/output/Page1297.asp, visited Jul. 21, 2005.
20 MICHAEL J. GLENNON, LIMITS OF LAW, PREROGATIVES OF POWER: INTERVENTIONISM AFTER KOSOVO (Palgrave Macmillan 2001).
21 INTERNATIONAL COMMISSION ON INTERVENTION AND STATE SOVEREIGNTY, THE RESPONSIBILITY TO PROTECT 11 (International Development Research Centre, Canada, 2001).
22 *Id*. at Supplementary Volume, p. 8.

Notes to pages 68–70

23 Thomas M. Franck, *The Emerging Right to Democratic Governance*, AJIL 86 (1992): 46, 47, 49, 90. *See also* section 2.2.b, *supra*, at note 8.
24 *See* discussion at text in section 3.3.b.2, *infra*.
25 ROBERT H. JACKSON, QUASI-STATES: SOVEREIGNTY, INTERNATIONAL RELATIONS, AND THE THIRD WORLD (Cambridge University Press, 1990). Krasner elaborately describes many such anomalies, which led him to the title 'Sovereignty: Organized Hypocrisy'; *see supra* note 5.
26 One relatively recent example is the context of negotiations during the past few years, relating to the "Middle East settlement" and the role of Jerusalem. *See Wye River Memorandum*, Oct. 23, 1998, 1sr.-PLO, 37 ILM 1251(1998) (witnessed by President Bill Clinton); *see also* Michael Barnett, *Sovereignty, Nationalism, and Regional Order in the Arab State System, in* STATE SOVEREIGNTY AS SOCIAL CONSTRUCT, Thomas J. Biersteker & Cynthia Weber eds. (Cambridge University Press, 1996): 148 (containing a remarkable, brief account of the history of the "Arab state system" and its tensions with Westphalian notions of sovereignty). The history of Middle East negotiations, including the Wye Plantation discussions, is replete with references to the problem of Jerusalem, as well as other problems that challenge traditional notions of sovereignty with respect to territory, such as shared sovereignty for holy sites and allocation of governmental responsibilities, including control of security.
27 General Agreement on Tariffs and Trade, Oct. 30, 1947, Art. XXXIII, TIAS No. 1700, 55 UNTS 194; *UR Texts*.
28 Many examples of linkages exist, such as pressures by the European Union for human rights protection in the Cotonou Agreement, the Association Agreement with African, Caribbean, and Pacific States. *See* Elisabeth de Vos, *The Cotonou Agreement: A Case of Forced Regional Integration? in* KREIJEN, STATE SOVEREIGNTY, *supra* note 3, at 497; *see also* KRASNER, ORGANIZED HYPOCRISY, *supra* note 5, at 105 (for other human rights linkages); GARY CLYDE HUFBAUER, JEFFREY J. SCHOTT, & KIMBERLY ANN ELLIOTT, ECONOMIC SANCTIONS RECONSIDERED, 3rd ed. (Institute for International Economics, 2005) (for economic sanctions to promote human rights). On IMF conditionality, see, e.g., Deborah E. Siegel, *Legal Aspects of the IMF/WTO Relationship: The Fund's Articles of Agreement and the WTO Agreements*, AMERICAN JOURNAL OF INTERNATIONAL ECONOMIC LAW 96 (2002): 561, 572–75.
29 LOUIS HENKIN, INTERNATIONAL LAW: POLITICS AND VALUES (Kluwer, 1995), at 10, quoted in JOHN H. JACKSON, THE JURISPRUDENCE OF THE GATT AND THE WTO: INSIGHTS ON TREATY LAW AND ECONOMIC RELATIONS (Cambridge University Press, 2000), at 367.
30 *See* Louis Henkin, *That ASA Word: Sovereignty and Globalization, and Human Rights, et cetera*, FORDHAM LAW REVIEW 68 (1999):1.
31 Ernst A. Young, *The Rhenquist Court's Two Federalisms*, TEXAS LAW REVIEW 83 (2004):1.

32 As an exercise verifying this proposition, the author, with very able student research assistance, formulated a chart of the many news and other reports that touch on these allocation-of-power questions at various levels of government. This report involves too many instances to include in this article, but we could make it available to interested persons. *See, e.g.*, FINANCIAL TIMES (London), May 12, 2003, which, in this single issue, touches on seven or more topics of "allocating power or authority." These include the United Kingdom's consideration of joining the European single currency (*Sterling Falls From its Perch: Beginning of the Removal of the Main Obstacle to Euro Entry*, at 16); the role of international law in cases of unilateral use of armed force (Leon Fuerth, *America Need Not be a Law Unto Itself*, at 17); European Union measures relating to carbon emissions (Joanna Chung, *Action Urged to Limit Impact of Brussels Emissions Rules*, at 4); testing requirements for chemicals (Daniel Dombey, *US Concerned at EU Plan for Testing of Chemicals*, at 7); the control of Iraqi oil exports (Carola Hoyos, *Oil's New World Order Faces its First Test in Postwar Iraq*, at 12); WTO rulings on steel tariffs (Guy de Jonquieres, *Legal Moves Counter Steel Tariffs*, at 8); and ideas for a European common defense fund (*Britain's Views on a Common Defence Policy for Europe are as Central as Those of Paris*, at 16).

33 T. ALEXANDER ALEINIKOFF, SEMBLANCES OF SOVEREIGNTY: THE CONSTITUTION, THE STATE, AND AMERICAN CITIZENSHIP (Harvard University Press, 2002).

3.3 Potentially valid policy objectives of sovereignty concepts

1 *See* section 3.2, *supra*, and citations there.
2 This author also testified at this hearing. *See* John H. Jackson, *The Great 1994 Sovereignty Debate: United States Acceptance and Implementation of the Uruguay Round Results*, in POLITICS, VALUES, AND FUNCTIONS: INTERNATIONAL LAW IN THE 21ST CENTURY – ESSAYS IN HONOR OF PROFESSOR LOUIS HENKIN, Jonathan I. Charney et al. eds. (Martinus Nijhoff, 1998): 149, 174 n.31.
3 *The Uruguay Round of the General Agreement on Tariffs and Trade*, Hearing Before the Senate Comm. on Foreign Relations, 104th Cong. (Jun. 14, 1994), 1994 WL 266499.
4 *Id.* (prepared statement of Ralph Nader).
5 The author previously articulated these concepts in JOHN H. JACKSON, THE JURISPRUDENCE OF THE GATT AND THE WTO: INSIGHTS ON TREATY LAW AND ECONOMIC RELATIONS (Cambridge University Press, 2000), at 369. "Power" is used here similarly to the phrase "effective" or "legitimate authority," although these terms could be subject to considerable additional discussion.
6 *See* section 3.2, *supra*, and citations there.
7 As an exercise verifying this proposition, the author, with very able student research assistance, formulated a chart of the many news and other reports

Notes to pages 73–74

that touch on these allocation-of-power questions at various levels of government. This report involves too many instances to include in this article. Many current news articles can be added now. Section 3.2 *supra*, note 32, describes interesting examples.

8   *See* Cary Coglianese, *Globalization and the Design of International Institutions*, in GOVERNANCE IN A GLOBALIZING WORLD, Joseph S. Nye, Jr. & John D. Donahue eds. (Brookings Institution Press, 2000): 297, 299 (citing examples of differences in regulatory standards that tend to reduce competition and lead to inefficiencies).

9   Robert O. Keohane, *International Relations, Old and New*, in A NEW HANDBOOK OF POLITICAL SCIENCE, Robert E. Goodin and Hans-Dieter Klingemann, eds. (Oxford University Press, 1996): 462, 469.

10 John H. Jackson, *International Economic Law in Times That Are Interesting*, JIEL 3 (2000): 3. *See also* DANIEL C. ESTY & DAMIEN GERADIN, EDS., REGULATORY COMPETITION AND ECONOMIC INTEGRATION: COMPARATIVE PERSPECTIVES (Oxford University Press, 2001); and other articles in 3 JIEL (2000): 215–385.

11 RONALD W. JONES, GLOBALIZATION AND THE THEORY OF INPUT TRADE (MIT Press 2000), at 135.

12 *See* section 6.4, *infra*.

13 William C. Clark, *Environmental Globalization*, in NYE & DONAHUE, GOVERNANCE IN A GLOBALIZING WORLD, *supra* note 8, at 86. *See* section 7.4, *infra*.

14 *Making Sense of Subsidiarity: How Much Centralization for Europe*, ANNUAL REPORT: MONITORING EUROPEAN INTEGRATION 4 (Centre for Economic Policy Research, 1993); *see also* Paolo G. Carozza, *Subsidiarity as a Structural Principle of International Human Rights Law*, AJIL 97 (2003): 38 (a remarkably full account and history of the concept of subsidiarity, which elaborates an argument for its importance in the context of applying international human rights obligations, somewhat counter to the approach of many human rights advocates who argue that human rights norms are "universal").

15 For a succinct overview of the history of the concept of subsidiarity, with mention of sources that go back as far as Aristotle and a sixteenth-century book by the political philosopher Johannes Althusius, leading to nineteenth- and twentieth-century Catholic social thought, including the papal encyclical Quadragesimo Anno (fortieth year) in 1931, see Thomas Stauffer, *Subsidiarity as Legitimacy? in* Intergovernmental Fiscal Relations and Local Financial Management Program, topic 3, World Bank Institute (Jul. 26–Aug. 6, 1999), at www.worldbank.org/wbi/publicfinance/documents/stauffer.pdf.

16 *See, e.g.*, George W. Bush, *Campaign speech made to the Annual Convention of the National Conference of State Legislatures in Chicago* (July 18, 2000), quoted in Lisa B. Song, *Bush Pushes More State, Local Control of Schools*, CHICAGO TRIBUNE, July 18, 2000 (online ed.), transcript of speech was avail. at www.pbs.org/newshour/bb/politics/july-dec00/stump_7-20.html, visited Sept. 11, 2003.

17 Gerard Kreijen, *The Transformation of Sovereignty and African Independence: No Shortcuts to Statehood*, in STATE SOVEREIGNTY AND INTERNATIONAL GOVERNANCE, Gerald Kreijen et al. eds. (Oxford University Press, 2002): 45.
18 *See* THOMAS P. O'NEILL & GARY HYMEL, ALL POLITICS IS LOCAL (New York Times Books, 1994). For vivid descriptions of the colonial rule of the Belgian Congo in the late 1800s, *see* ADAM HOCHSCHILD, KING LEOPOLD'S GHOST (Mariner Books, 1999).
19 *See generally* Mark Tushnet, *Globalization and Federalism in a Post-Printz World*, TULSA LAW JOURNAL 36 (2000): 11 (and noted references).
20 Elaine Ciulla Kamarck, *Globalization and Public Administration Reform*, in Nye & Donahue, GOVERNANCE IN A GLOBALIZING WORLD, *supra* note 8, at 229, 250.
21 *See* Chapter 5, *infra*.

The WTO as international organization: institutional evolution, structure, and key problems

1 Senator Eugene Millikin on GATT, at the *Hearings on Reciprocal Trade Agreements Expansion Act of 1951*, before the Senate Committee on Finance, 82d Congress, 1st Sess., 92 (1951).
2 Winthrop Brown, Director, Office of Trade Policy, US Department of State, testifying at the 1951 Senate Hearings, *id.*, at 1061, 1076.

4.1 The WTO as international economic law and its relationship to general international law

3 For additional detail on the subject of this chapter, *see* works noted in section 1.1, *supra*.
4 *See* section 2.3, *supra*, and Donald M. McRae, *The Contribution of International Trade Law to the Development of International Law*, RECUEIL DES COURS 260 (1997): 103.
5 The WTO's first full-term Director-General, Renato Ruggiero, first described the WTO Dispute Settlement System in this way in 1997, but it has been repeated in many publications, and by many WTO officials. *See, e.g., Ten Years After Marrakech: The WTO and Developing Countries*, speech by WTO Director-General Supachai Panitchpakdi in Marrakech, Morocco, Jun. 9, 2004, available at www.wto.org/english/news_e/spsp_e/spsp29_e.htm; *The Post-Doha Multilateral Trading System*, remarks by WTO Director-General Mike Moore, at the Trilateral Commission Annual Meeting, 7 Apr. 2002, at www. Trilateral.org/AnnMtgs/trialog/trlgtxts/2002/pdf_folder/trade.pdf.
6 Jan. 1, 1948, to end of 1994: 1948–1957, 1958–1967, 1968–1977, 1978–1987, 1988–1994.
7 Examples include the US Constitution, the European Economic Community and evolving "constitution," the United Nations, the IMF and the World Bank. *See* section 2.5, *supra*, Chapter 6, *infra* (particularly section 6.5), and

Chapter 7, *supra* (particularly sections 7.7 and 7.8). *See also* JOSEPH E. STIGLITZ, GLOBALIZATION AND ITS DISCONTENTS (W.W. Norton & Company, 2002).
8 Sutherland, *The Future of the WTO*, 2005.

4.2 The policy objectives and preferences for a WTO

1 *See* JOHN H. JACKSON, THE WORLD TRADE ORGANIZATION: CONSTITUTION AND JURISPRUDENCE (Chatham House Papers, Royal Institute of International Affairs,1998).
2 "Charter" is an informal term, referring to the approximately fifteen pages of the Marrakesh Agreement Establishing the World Trade Organization which create the WTO.
3 *Havana Charter for an International Trade Organization*, 24 Mar. 1948 (never in force); *Final Act and Related Documents*, United Nations Conference on Trade and Employment, Havana Cuba, 21 Nov. 1947 to 24 Mar. 1948, UN Doc. ICITO/1/4 (1948).
4 *See* JACKSON, JOHN H. JACKSON, WORLD TRADE AND THE LAW OF GATT (The Bobbs-Merrill Company, Inc., 1969), at section 2.2, esp. at pp.38–39, for the general history of the ITO, GATT preparations.
5 Text based partly on this author's article: John H. Jackson, *Global Economics and International Economic Law*, JIEL 1 (1998): 1. *See also* RICHARD LIPSEY et al., MICROECONOMICS, 10th ed. (Harper Collins College Publishers, 1993); AVINASH K. DIXIT & BARRY J. NALEBUFF, THINKING STRATEGICALLY: THE COMPETITIVE EDGE IN BUSINESS, POLITICS, AND EVERYDAY LIFE (Norton Publishing Co., 1991); MAX CORDEN, TRADE POLICY AND ECONOMIC WELFARE (Clarendon Press, 1974); PETER B. KENEN, THE INTERNATIONAL ECONOMY (Cambridge University Press, 1994); PAUL KRUGMAN, INTERNATIONAL ECONOMICS: THEORY AND POLICY (Harper Collins College, 1994); JOSEPH E. STIGLITZ, GLOBALIZATION AND ITS DISCONTENTS (W.W. Norton & Company, 2002).
6 For an overview of the economic principles which support policies of liberal international trade rules, see Alan O. Sykes, *Comparative Advantage and the Normative Economics of International Trade Policy*, JIEL 1 (1998), 49–82.
7 *See, e.g.*, James Flanigan, *Turmoil is Free Market Watershed*, LOS ANGELES TIMES, 29 Oct. 1997, at 1.
8 RONALD H. COASE, THE FIRM, THE MARKET AND THE LAW (University of Chicago Press, 1988), at Ch. 5 (reprint of 1960 article).
9 DOUGLAS C. NORTH, INSTITUTIONS, INSTITUTIONAL CHANGE AND ECONOMIC PERFORMANCE (Cambridge University Press, 1990).
10 STIGLITZ, GLOBALIZATION AND ITS DISCONTENTS, *supra* note 5, at 219.
11 Sutherland, *The Future of the WTO*, at para. 3, p. .5.
12 JACKSON, WORLD TRADE AND THE LAW OF GATT, *supra* note 4. At least some credit for over fifty years of relative peace (avoiding a World War III)

can be attributed to reasonably successful activities of the International Monetary Fund and the World Bank.
13 *See* section 2.3, *supra*.
14 *See* the documentation of the 1999 *Symposium on Method in International Law* in Vol. 93 of the AJIL, and in particular, Steven R. Ratner & Anne-Marie Slaughter, *Appraising the Methods of International Law: A Prospectus for Readers*, at 291. *See* other works of Anne-Marie Slaughter, including, Slaughter et al., *International Law and International Relations Theory: A New Generation of Interdisciplinary Scholarship*, AJIL 92 (1998): 334; Slaughter, *Burley*, *International Law and International Relations Theory: A Dual Agenda*, AJIL 87 (1993): 205.
15 Louis Henkin's famous statement, quoted in section 2.3.a, *supra*.
16 *See* HENKIN, *id.*; ROGER FISHER, IMPROVING COMPLIANCE WITH INTERNATIONAL LAW (University Press of Virginia, 1981), at 12–16; ABRAM CHAYES & ANTONIA HANDLER CHAYES, THE NEW SOVEREIGNTY: COMPLIANCE WITH INTERNATIONAL REGULATORY AGREEMENTS (Harvard University Press, 1995).
17 *See, e.g.*, JACKSON, THE WORLD TRADING SYSTEM, 2nd ed. (MIT Press, 1997), at 109; JACKSON, THE WORLD TRADE ORGANIZATION, *supra* note 1, at Ch. 4.
18 *See, e.g.*, NORTH, INSTITUTIONS, *supra* note 9.
19 *See also* John H. Jackson, *Governmental Disputes in International Trade Relations: A Proposal in the Context of GATT*, JOURNAL OF WORLD TRADE LAW 13 (1979) 3–4, and Jackson, *The Crumbling Institutions of the Liberal Trade System*, JOURNAL OF WORLD TRADE LAW, 12 (1978) 98–101; JACKSON, THE WORLD TRADING SYSTEM, *supra* note 17.
20 Dr. Ernst-Ulrich Petersmann has written profoundly on this theme in some of his numerous writings; *see, e.g.*, CONSTITUTIONAL FUNCTIONS AND CONSTITUTIONAL PROBLEMS OF INTERNATIONAL ECONOMIC LAW (University Press, Fribourg, 1991); *Constitutionalism and WTO Law: From a State-Centered Approach Towards a Human Rights Approach in International Economic Law*, in THE POLITICAL ECONOMY OF INTERNATIONAL TRADE LAW: ESSAYS IN HONOR OF ROBERT E. HUDEC, Daniel Kennedy & James Southwick eds. (Cambridge University Press, 2002): 32; *The WTO Constitution and Human Rights*, JIEL 3 (2000): 19.
21 *See* sections 2.3 and 2.5, *supra*; section 6.5, *infra*.

4.3 Historical background: from Bretton Woods to Cancún and Hong Kong
1 *See* JOHN H. JACKSON, THE WORLD TRADING SYSTEM, 2nd ed. (MIT Press, 1997), at Ch. 1 (pp. 1–30). *See* section 2.5, *supra*, and section 6.5, *infra*.
2 *See* VCLT, Art. 31.
3 *See, e.g.*, JOHN H. JACKSON, WORLD TRADE AND THE LAW OF GATT (The Bobbs-Merrill Company, Inc., 1969); JOHN H. JACKSON, WILLIAM J. DAVEY,

AND ALAN O. SYKES, LEGAL PROBLEMS OF INTERNATIONAL ECONOMIC RELATIONS: CASES, MATERIALS AND TEXT ON THE NATIONAL AND INTERNATIONAL REGULATION OF TRANSNATIONAL ECONOMIC RELATIONS, 4th ed. (West Group, 2002)(hereinafter CASEBOOK); and JOHN H. JACKSON, JEAN-VICTOR LOUIS, AND MITSUO MATSUSHITA, IMPLEMENTING THE TOKYO ROUND (University of Michigan Press, 1984). *See also* ROBERT HUDEC, THE GATT LEGAL SYSTEM AND WORLD TRADE DIPLOMACY (Praeger, 1975). For an overview of GATT's troubled history, see WILLIAM DIEBOLD, THE END OF THE ITO (Princeton University Press, 1952); RICHARD N. GARDNER, STERLING–DOLLAR DIPLOMACY (Clarendon Press, 1969); WILLIAM A. BROWN, THE UNITED STATES AND THE RESTORATION OF WORLD TRADE (Brookings Institution, 1950); CLAIR WILCOX, A CHARTER FOR WORLD TRADE (Macmillan, 1949).
4 *See* JACKSON, WORLD TRADE, *supra* note 3; and JOHN H. JACKSON, THE WORLD TRADE ORGANIZATION: CONSTITUTION AND JURISPRUDENCE (Chatham House Papers, Royal Institute of International Affairs, 1998).
5 *See, e.g.*, JACKSON, WORLD TRADE, *supra* note 3.
6 The Bretton Woods Conference, officially called "The United Nations Monetary and Financial Conference," was held on July 1–22, 1944. Forty-four nations met to negotiate the establishment of the IMF and World Bank. *See* United Nations Monetary and Financial Conference (Bretton Woods, N.H., July 1–22, 1944), Proceedings and Documents 941 (US Dep't of State Pub. No. 2866, 1948).
7 *See* JACKSON, WORLD TRADE, *supra* note 3, at 37.
8 The documents are mostly part of the UN document series labeled EPCT, Preparatory Committee of the UN Conference on Trade and Employment. *See* JACKSON, WORLD TRADE, *supra* note 3, at Appendix E, pp. 901–912, for an explanation and list of the document series.
9 For an article by article presentation of relevant interpretative documents, *see* GATT ANALYTICAL INDEX.
10 *See, e.g.*, Richard N. Cooper, *Trade Policy as Foreign Policy*, in US TRADE POLICIES IN A CHANGING WORLD ECONOMY, Robert M. Stern ed. (MIT Press, 1987), at 291–336.
11 *See Act to Extend the Authority of the President under Section 350 of the 1930 US Tariff Act*, as amended, and for other purposes, 5 July 1945, Pub. L. 79–130, 59 Stat. 410.
12 *See* John H. Jackson, *Perspectives on the Jurisprudence of International Trade: Costs and Benefits of Legal Procedures in the United States*, MICHIGAN LAW REVIEW 82 (1984): 1570, 1573.
13 For example, if a tariff commitment for a maximum 10 percent tariff charge were made, a country might nevertheless decide to use a quantitative restriction to prevent imports and thus would evade the trade-liberalizing effect of the tariff commitment.

14 *See* Jackson, The World Trading System, *supra* note 1, at ch. 7 (pp.175–211). *See also* World Trade, *supra* note 3, at 20 et seq., 48–49.
15 A "binding" in a country's tariff schedule is an obligation under GATT Article II not to apply a tariff higher than the number stated in the binding, on imports of the product described in the binding. Large trading countries will have 10,000 or more bindings.
16 Susan A. Aaronson, Trade and the American Dream: A Social History of Postwar Trade Policy (University Press of Kentucky, 1996).
17 *See* World Trade, *supra* note 3, at 62; UN Doc. EPCT/TAC/7, 3 (1947).
18 *See Act to Extend the Authority*, *supra* note 11. The act expired on June 12, 1948. *See* World Trade, *supra* note 3, at 37.
19 *See* UN Doc. EPCT/TAC/4, 8 (1947).
20 55 UNTS 308 (1947).
21 *See* World Trade, *supra* note 3, at section 3.3.
22 *See* Edwin Vermulst and Marc Hansen, *The GATT Protocol of Provisional Application: A Dying Grandfather?* Columbia Journal of Transnational Law 27 (1987), 263–308.
23 *See* Jackson, The World Trading System, *supra* note 1, at Ch. 11 (pp. 279–303).
24 GATT, BISD 31 Supp. 74–94 (1985).
25 *See* World Trade, *supra* note 3, at 92, and Appendix D.
26 *See id.*, at 154.
27 *See id.*, at Ch. 6.
28 *See id.*, at 51.
29 *See* account of this development in *id.*, at 154.
30 The dates and locations are as follows: 1949 at Annecy, 1951 at Torquay, 1956 at Geneva, 1960–1961 at Geneva (Dillon Round), 1964–1967 at Geneva (Kennedy Round), 1973–1979 at Geneva (Tokyo Round), 1986–1994 at Geneva (Uruguay Round).
31 *See* Jackson, The World Trading System, *supra* note 1, at 154, for a list of over 800. Some governments have been compiling annual lists; *see* the extensive overviews of the trade barriers of the respective major trading partners by Japan (Industrial Structure Council METI, 2005 *Report on the WTO Inconsistency of Trade Policies by Major Trading Partners*, Tokyo 2005), the United States (United States Trade Representative, 2005 National Trade Estimate Report on Foreign Trade Barriers, available at www.ustr.gov/Document_Library/Reports_Publications/2005/2005_NTE_Report/section_Index.html) and the European Union (Market Access Database, available at http://mkaccdb.eu.int/mkaccdb2/indexPubli.htm).
32 *See* John H. Jackson, *The Great 1994 Sovereignty Debate: United States Acceptance and Implementation of the Uruguay Round Results*, Columbia Journal of Transnational Law 36 (1997): 157, 165–166.

Notes to pages 98–102

33 Protocol Amending the GATT to Introduce a Part IV on Trade and Development, GATT, BISD 13 Supp. 2 (1965).
34 *See* WORLD TRADE, *supra* note 3, at section 6.3.
35 *See Securing the Foothold*, TIME 91 (17 May 1968), 92; *The Kennedy Round: Sick, Sick, Six*, THE ECONOMIST 223 (1967); *The Politics of the Success*, THE ECONOMIST 223 (1967), 814. *See also* JOHN W. EVANS, THE KENNEDY ROUND IN AMERICAN TRADE POLICY: THE TWILIGHT OF GATT (Harvard University Press, 1971), at 235, 272.
36 *Marrakesh Agreement Establishing the World Trade Organization*, 15 Apr. 1994, WTO Doc. LT/UR/A/2. *in UR Texts*.
37 *See* JACKSON, WORLD TRADING SYSTEM, *supra* note 1, at 306.
38 But very much linked to the GATT, so not in practice very "stand alone."
39 *See* section 4.4, *infra*, discussing the structure of the WTO. *See also* CASEBOOK, *supra* note 3, at Ch. 6.
40 The PPA only required a sixty-day notice for withdrawal. It is not clear that all took the necessary action, but in effect all GATT contracting parties became WTO members.
41 For 1880 data, *see* DATAPEDIA OF THE UNITED STATES 1790–2005, 221–222, George Thomas Kurian ed. (Bernan, 2001). For 1995 data, *see* Linda Lobao & Katherine Meyer, *The Great Agricultural Transition: Crisis, Change, and Social Consequences of Twentieth Century US Farming*, ANN. REV. SOC. 27 (2001): 103, 108.
42 *See* ROBERT ACKRILL, THE COMMON AGRICULTURAL POLICY (Sheffield Academic Press, 2000): 25.
43 1951 Amendments to the Defense Production Act of 1950, 65 Stat. 131, 132 and to Sec. 22 (f) of the Agricultural Adjustment Act, 65 Stat. 75; *see* JACKSON, WORLD TRADE *supra* note 3, at 319.
44 GATT 1994, Art. XI.
45 *Treaty Establishing the European Economic Community*, Mar. 25, 1957 (Treaty of Rome). *See* ACKRILL, COMMON AGRICULTURAL POLICY, *supra* note 42, at 30–34; ROSEMARY FENNELL, THE COMMON AGRICULTURAL POLICY: CONTINUITY AND CHANGE (Oxford University Press, 1997), at 23–31.
46 *See* TIMOTHY E. JOSLING ET AL., AGRICULTURE IN THE GATT (St. Martin's Press, 1996): at 98–100.
47 *See* note 8, *supra*.
48 *See, e.g.*, TERENCE P. STEWART, ED., THE GATT URUGUAY ROUND: A NEGOTIATING HISTORY (1986–1992) (Kluwer Law and Taxation Publishers, 1993–1999), and list on www.WorldTradeLaw.Net.
49 *See, e.g.*, the *Derestriction of Uruguay Round Documents*, WTO Doc. MTN. TNC/47 of 6 Jan. 1997, as well as the *Decision of the General Council of 14 May 2002 Regarding Procedures for the Circulation and Derestriction of WTO Documents*, WTO Doc. WT/L/452, 16 May 2002.
50 *See* details and full list of Ministerial Conferences at www.wto.org, visited 29 Mar. 2005.

51 *See, e.g., Singapore Ministerial Declaration*, WTO Doc. WT/MIN(96)/DEC/, adopted 13 Dec. 1996.
52 The Fourth Ministerial Conference was held at Doha, Qatar, Nov. 9–14, 2001.
53 All Doha Ministerial Declarations and Decisions are available at www.wto.org/english/thewto_e/minist_e/min01_e/min01_e.htm, visited 29 Mar. 2005. *See also* CASEBOOK, *supra* note 3, at 1221.
54 The group included such countries as China, Brazil, and South Africa, and put pressure on the United States, Europe, and Japan to reduce or eliminate their agriculture subsidies. The size of the group seemed to vary.
55 *See, e.g., The EU, Cancún and the Future of the Doha Development Agenda*, Speech of EU Commissioner for External Trade, Pascal Lamy, Journal for Common Market Studies, London, Oct. 28, 2003; SUMMARY OF 14 SEPTEMBER 2003: *Day 5: Conference Ends Without Consensus Result*, available at www.wto.org/english/thewto_e/minist_e/min03_e/min03_14sept_e.htm, visited Mar. 29, 2005.
56 Comments of Pascal Lamy in Charlotte Denny, et al., *Brussels Urges Shakeup of "Medieval" WTO*, THE GUARDIAN (London), Sept. 16, 2003; *see also* Robert B. Zoellick, *America Will Not Wait for the Won't-do Countries*, FINANCIAL TIMES (London), Sept. 22, 2003.
57 The Trade Promotion Authority (TPA) contains a framework for close collaboration between Congress and the president. The TPA Act provides for Congress to vote without amendment and within a set period on trade-agreement-implementing legislation that the president submits. The TPA Act also calls for the president to notify, consult with, and report to the Congress on the negotiation of trade agreements that he seeks to implement through trade authorities procedures. The TPA Act also sets detailed objectives for trade negotiations on the multilateral, regional, and bilateral level.

Title XXI of the Trade Act of 2002 (Trade Act) contains the Bipartisan Trade Promotion Authority Act of 2002 which is valid until 1 Jul. 2005. The Act provides for extension of trade authorities procedures to include agreements concluded before1 Jul. 2007, if the president so requests in a report submitted to Congress by Apr. 1, 2005. The request was made on Mar. 30, 2005 (*see* the letter from the President to the Speaker of the House of Representatives and the President of the Senate at www.whitehouse.gov/news/releases/2005/03/20050330-5.html, visited Jul. 14, 2005). Congress extended the Trade Promotion Authority on 1 Jul. 2005, *see* www.ustr.gov/Document_Library/Press_Releases/2005/July/Statement_of_USTR_Rob_Portman_Regarding_Today's_Extension_of_Trade_Promotion_Authority_the_U.S._Trade_Agenda.html, visited Jul. 14, 2005.

In July 2004, the WTO General Council agreed on a framework for the future negotiations on agriculture in the Doha Round, *see Doha Work Programme – Decision Adopted by the General Council on 1 August 2004*, WTO Doc. WT/L/579, Aug. 2, 2004. The dynamics of a dispute settlement system can also extend very broadly beyond the particular disputants. Several recent cases regarding agricultural subsidies and trade restraints of the principal WTO membership (United States and European Union) resulted in findings in favor of the developing country complainants. *See US – Restrictions on Imports of Cotton and Man-Made Fibre Underwear*, WTO Doc. WT/DS24/AB/R, adopted Feb. 25, 1997; case brought by Brazil against the US: *US – Subsidies on Upland Cotton*, WTO Doc. WT/DS267/AB/R, adopted Mar. 21, 2005; and case brought by Thailand and Brazil (and Australia) against the EC: *EC – Export Subsidies on Sugar*, WTO Docs. WT/DS283/R and WT/DS/283/ AB/R, adopted May 19, 2005. *See* sections 5.5 and 6.6, *infra*.

On the role of agriculture in global trade, *see* MARTIN WOLF, WHY GLOBALIZATION WORKS (Yale University Press, 2004); JAGDISH BHAGWATI, IN DEFENSE OF GLOBALIZATION (Oxford University Press, 2004), at 215. *See also* DOUGLAS A. IRWIN, FREE TRADE UNDER FIRE (Princeton University Press, 2002); and various chapters in AGRICULTURAL TRADE POLICIES IN THE NEW MILLENNIUM, P. Lynn Kennedy & Won W. Koo eds. (Food Products Press, 2002). *See also* Kym Anderson, *The Future Agenda of the WTO*, *in* FROM GATT TO THE WTO: THE MULTILATERAL TRADING SYSTEM IN THE NEW MILLENNIUM, WTO Secretariat ed. (Kluwer Law International, 2000): 7, 12; WILL MARTIN & KYM ANDERSON EDS., AGRICULTURAL TRADE REFORM AND THE DOHA DEVELOPMENT AGENDA (World Bank Publications, forthcoming Oct. 2005). *See also* section 6.6, *infra*.

58 Sutherland, *The Future of the WTO, 2005*. *See also* section 4.1, *supra*, at note 8.

4.4 The World Trade Organization: structure of the treaty and the institution

1 *See* citations in section 1.1, *supra*, and in prior sections of this chapter.
2 *See UR Texts*.
3 *See* Appendix, *infra*.
4 *Trade Policy Review Mechanism: Programme of Reviews for 2005*, WTO Doc. WT/ TPR/157, Nov. 15, 2004, available at www.wto.org, visited Mar. 29, 2005.
5 Article X, para. 9, *WTO Charter*.
6 *See Accession of the People's Republic of China: Decision of 10 November 2001*, WTO Doc. WT/L/432, Nov. 23, 2001, available at www.wto.org, visited Mar. 29, 2005. *See also* NICHOLAS LARDY, INTEGRATING CHINA INTO THE GLOBAL ECONOMY (Brookings Institution Press, 2002), 101–102.
7 *See* the list of 148 members at www.wto.org/english/thewto_e/whatis_e/tif_e/org6_e.htm, visited Jun. 23, 2005.
8 Articles XI, XII, and XIII, *WTO Charter*.
9 Information on the status of individual accession processes is available on the official WTO website: http://www.wto.org/english/thewto_e/acc_e/status_e.htm, visited 1 Apr. 2005.
10 *See* GATT ANALYTICAL INDEX, at 1034.

11 Gabriel Marceau, Pratique et Pratiques dans le Droit de l'Organisation Mondiale du Commerce (Editions A. Pedone, 2004), at 197.
12 Lardy, Integrating China, *supra* note 6, at 163–164.
13 For a more complete overview of his views see Nicholas R. Lardy, Issues in China's WTO Accession, Congressional Testimony, U.S.–China Security Review Commission, May 9, 2001.

4.5 Institutional problems of the WTO

1 The following are particularly noted works evaluating the WTO and its world trading system (pro and con) (*see* notes in section 1.1 and Chapter 2, especially section 2.2, *supra*; Joseph E. Stiglitz, Globalization and its Discontents (W.W. Norton & Company, 2002); Gary Burtless et al., Globaphobia: Confronting Fears About Open Trade (Brookings Institution Press, 1998); Dani Rodrik, Has Globalization Gone Too Far? (IIE, 1997); Claude Barfield, Free Trade, Sovereignty, Democracy: The Future of the World Trade Organization (AEI Press, 2001); Douglas A. Irwin, Free Trade Under Fire (Princeton University Press, 2002); Steve Charnovitz, Trade Law and Global Governance (Cameron May, 2002).
2 Many of the problems discussed in this section have been addressed by the WTO Consultative Board Report – *see* section 4.1, *supra*, at note 8.
3 *See, e.g.,* Andrew T. Guzman, *Global Governance and the WTO*, Harvard International Law Journal 45 (Summer, 2004): 303–351; John O. McGinnis & Mark L. Movsesian, *Against Global Governance in the WTO*, Harvard International Law Journal 45 (2004): 353–365; Robert O. Keohane, Power and Governance in a Partially Globalized World (Routledge, 2002), at 271; Jürgen Habermas, Between Facts and Norms: Contributions to a Discourse Theory of Law and Democracy (MIT Press, 1996); Horst Siebert, ed., Global Governance: An Architecture for the World Economy (Springer, 2003); Joseph S. Nye & John D. Donahue, eds., Governance in a Globalizing World (Brookings Institution Press, 2000).
4 *See* other works by this author: John H. Jackson, *The WTO "Constitution" and Proposed Reforms: Seven "Mantras" Revisited,* JIEL 4 (March 2001): 67; John H. Jackson, The World Trade Organization: Constitution and Jurisprudence (Chatham House Papers, Royal Institute of International Affairs, 1998); and section 1.1, *supra*, at note 2.
5 The word "charter" is an informal term. *See* section 4.2 *supra*, at note 2.
6 In GATT, the EC was not formally recognized as a contracting party, but nevertheless by practice acted as one (representing and coordinating all EU member states that were GATT contracting parties). In the WTO, the EC is explicitly recognized as a member (Art. XI, *UR Texts*), but for voting purposes

the EC group shall have the number of votes equal to no more than the number of EC member states (Art. IX).
7 Art. IX, footnote 1, *WTO Charter*, which reads:
   The body concerned shall be deemed to have decided by consensus on a matter submitted for its consideration, if no Member, present at the meeting when the decision is taken, formally objects to the proposed decision.
8 DSU.
9 Art. IX(8), *WTO Charter*.
10 Jackson, *Mantras*, supra note 4; BARFIELD, FREE TRADE, supra note 1, at 141; Frieder Roessler, *The Institutional Balance Between the Judicial and the Political Organs of the WTO*, in NEW DIRECTIONS IN INTERNATIONAL ECONOMIC LAW: ESSAYS IN HONOR OF JOHN H. JACKSON, Marco Bronckers & Reinhard Quick eds. (Kluwer Law International, 2000): 325; Lorand Bartels, *The Separation of Powers in the WTO: How to Avoid Judicial Activism*, INTERNATIONAL AND COMPARATIVE LAW QUARTERLY 53 (2004): 861.
11 *See* the *Procedures for the Appointment of Directors-General*, adopted by the General Council on 10 Dec. 2002, WTO Doc. WT/L/509, Jan. 20, 2003; *WTO Members Choose Lamy as Organization's Fifth Director-General*, WTO Doc. Press/407, May 26, 2005.
12 Gregory C. Shaffer, *The World Trade Organization Under Challenge: Democracy and the Law and Politics of the WTO's Treatment of Trade and Environment Matters*, HARVARD ENVIRONMENTAL LAW REVIEW 25 (2001): 1.
13 *See* the *Chart of Acceptances of Tokyo Round Agreements*, in GATT ANALYTICAL INDEX, at 1056.
14 *See* Sutherland, *The Future of the WTO*, at para. 280.
15 *Annex on Financial Services* & *Annex on Negotiations on Basic Telecommunications*, General Agreement on Trade in Services, *in UR Texts*, at 310 and 319.
16 *Sixty Years On: The Bretton Woods Twins are Useful But Need Better Parents*, FINANCIAL TIMES (LONDON), Jul. 3, 2004, at 12. *See also* STIGLITZ, GLOBALIZATION AND ITS DISCONTENTS, supra note 1.
17 For more detail *see* chart of *Distribution of Staff Positions Within the WTO's Various Divisions* (2005), at www.wto.org/english/thewto_e/secre_e/div_e.htm, visited Jul. 7, 2005.
18 *See* 2005 budget details at www.wto.org/english/thewto_e/secre_e/budget05_e.htm, visited 7 Jul. 2005.
19 *See* Sutherland, *The Future of the WTO*, at para. 371.
20 Richard Blackhurst, *The Capacity of the WTO to Fulfill Its Mandate*, in THE WTO AS AN INTERNATIONAL ORGANIZATION, Anne Krueger ed. (Chicago University Press, 1998): 31; Richard Blackhurst & David Hartridge, *Improving the Capacity of WTO Institutions to Fulfill Their Mandate*, JIEL 7 (2004): 705.
21 *See* the internal assessment written by Mogens Peter Carl, Director-General for Trade, European Commission, Sept. 25, 2003, available at www.

insidetrade.com/secure/pdf4/wto2003_6250a.pdf, visited Jul. 7, 2005 (available to subscribers only). *See also Cancún Collapse: Where There's No Will, There's No Way*, BRIDGES DAILY UPDATES 6, Sept. 15, 2003, available at www.ictsd.org/ministerial/Cancún/wto_daily/ben030915.htm, visited 7 Jul. 2005; *Failure in Cancún Prompts Reflections, Interest in Possible Procedural Reform*, BNA WTO REPORTER, ISSN 1529–4153, Sept. 22, 2003.
22 *See* Sutherland, *The Future of the WTO*, at para 262.
23 *See* section 2.2, *supra*.
24 The Oxfam net income/expenditures for year 2003–2004 was approximately US$225 million, information available at www.oxfam.org.uk/about_us/downloads/moneytalk0304.pdf, visited Mar. 31, 2005. Compare with US$135 million 2004 budget of the WTO, information available at www.wto.org/english/thewto_e/secre_e/ budget04_e.htm, visited Mar. 31, 2005.
25 There are two main offices of the UN Secretariat dealing with NGO participation: the NGO Unit of the Department of Economic and Social Affairs (DESA) and the NGO section of the Department of Public Information. Formal interactions between NGOs and the United Nations are governed by the *UN Charter*, Ch. X, Art. 71, and related resolutions of ECOSOC, *e.g.*, *Consultative Relationship between the United Nations and Non-governmental Organizations*, UN Doc. E/1996/31 of July 25, 1996. In February 2003, the Secretary-General appointed a High Level Panel of Eminent Persons, who produced a report with a set of recommendations as to how the United Nations' work with civil society could be improved. The June 2004 report and Secretary-General's response are available at www.un.org/reform/panel.htm, visited Mar. 31, 2005. *See also "We, the Peoples: The Role of the United Nations in the Twenty-First Century"*, Report of the Secretary-General of March 27, 2000, UN Doc. A/54/2000 ("Millennium Report"), at paras. 312–361; *Reference Document on the Participation of Civil Society in United Nations Conferences and Special Sessions of the General Assembly During the 1990s* (Aug. 1, 2001) prepared by the Office of the President of the Millennium Assembly 55th session of the United Nations General Assembly, available at www.un.org/ga/president/55/speech/civilsociety1.htm, visited Mar. 31, 2005. The United Nations also has a Non-Governmental Liaison Service, established in 1975. See UN-NGLS website, at www.un-ngls.org/, visited Mar. 31, 2005. *Cf.* Jurij Daniel Aston, *The United Nations Committee on Non-Governmental Organisations: Guarding the Entrance to a Politically Divided House*, EUROPEAN JOURNAL OF INTERNATIONAL LAW 12 (Nov. 2001): 943.
26 *Arrangements and Practices for the Interaction of Non-Governmental Organisations in All Activities of the United Nations System*, Report of the Secretary-General of 10 July 1998, UN Doc. A/53/170, at para. 31. *See* WHO Principles Governing Relations with Nongovernmental Organizations, at www.who.int/civilsociety/relations/principles/en/index.html, visited Jul. 7, 2005. *See also Consultative*

Relationship Between the United Nations and Non-Governmental Organizations, ECOSOC Res. 1996/31, of Jul. 25, 1996.
27 Sutherland, *The Future of the WTO*, at para. 212.
28 The Sixth WTO Ministerial Conference was held in Hong Kong, China, on Dec. 13–18, 2005, *see Decision of the General Council of 21 October 2003*, Minutes of the Meeting, WTO Doc. WT/GC/M/83, at 4.
29 *See, e.g.*, the statement of the Hong Kong Legislative Council Panel on Commerce and Industry of Jul. 7, 2003, referring to "WTO Practice", www.legco.gov.hk/yr02–03/english/panels/ci/papers/ci0707cb1–2142–1e.pdf, visited Jul. 7, 2005.
30 *See* the recommendations of the Consultative Board, Sutherland, *The Future of the WTO*, at Chapter VII. *See also Commission Calls for WTO Reforms, Gets Cool Member State Response*, INSIDE U.S. TRADE, Nov. 7, 2003, available at www.insidetrade.com (by subscription).
31 Statistics compiled from United Nations, *2002 International Trade Statistics Yearbook, Volume II* (2004), at 467.
32 *See* list and each prospective member's status in accession process at www.wto.org/english/thewto_e/acc_e/status_e.htm, visited Apr. 1, 2005. If all applicants become WTO members, the WTO will cover about 98 percent of world trade. See World Development Indicators database, Sept. 2004, available at www.worldbank.org/data/databytopic/GDP.pdf, visited Apr. 11, 2005.
33 The Court of Justice of the European Communities was established in 1958, and sits in Luxembourg. It began as the joint court for the three treaty organizations that later became the European Communities in 1967. More information can be found at ww.curia.eu.int/, visited Apr. 1, 2005. In 1989, a Court of First Instance was created; in November 2004, the Council adopted a decision establishing the European Union Civil Service Tribunal, 2004 O.J. (L333) 7.
34 *See* section 2.5, *supra*.

4.6 WTO rules and members' domestic legal systems

1 *See* section 3.3, *supra*.
2 John H. Jackson, *Status of Treaties in Domestic Legal Systems: A Policy Analysis*, 86 AJIL 310 (1992); section 2.2.d, *supra*; John C. Yoo, *Globalism and the Constitution: Treaties, Non-Self-Execution, and the Original Understanding*, COLUMBIA LAW REVIEW 99 (1999): 1955; Martin S. Flaherty, *History Right? Historical Scholarship, Original Understanding, and Treaties as "Supreme Law of the Land," id.*, at 2095; Carlos Manuel Vázquez, *Laughing At Treaties, id.*, at 2154; John C. Yoo, *Treaties and Public Lawmaking: A Textual and Structural Defense of Non-Self-Execution, id.*, at 2218.
3 *See Bretton-Woods Agreements Act of 1945*, 22 U.S.C.A. sec. 286gg. *See also* JOHN H. JACKSON, WILLIAM J. DAVEY, AND ALAN O. SYKES, LEGAL PROBLEMS OF

INTERNATIONAL ECONOMIC RELATIONS: CASES, MATERIALS AND TEXT ON THE NATIONAL AND INTERNATIONAL REGULATION OF TRANSNATIONAL ECONOMIC RELATIONS, 4th ed. (West Group, 2002) (hereinafter CASEBOOK), at 200–203.

4 *US – sections 301–310 of the Trade Act of 1974*, WTO Doc. WT/DS152/R (Jan. 27, 2000) (not appealed).
5 *Murray v. The Schooner Charming Betsy*, 6 U.S. (2 Cranch) 64 (1804).
6 *United States v. Palestine Liberation Organization*, 695 F.Supp. 1456 (S.D.N.Y. 1988).
7 *See* CASEBOOK, *supra* note 3, at 102.
8 The United States, in 2000 under the Clinton administration, had signed the Rome Statute of the International Criminal Court, but shortly after the statute had acquired the number of ratifications needed to bring it into force, the Bush administration, in May 2002, notified the United Nations that it did not intend to become a party. This notification has been termed "unsigning" but rather expressed the intent not to ratify the treaty. *See* Diane F. Orentlicher, *Unilateral Multilateralism: United States Policy Toward the International Criminal Court*, CORNELL INTERNATIONAL LAW JOURNAL 36 (2004): 415, 421–422.
9 *See, e.g.*, Phillip R. Trimble, *The President's Foreign Affairs Power*, AJIL 83 (1989): 750; LOUIS HENKIN, FOREIGN AFFAIRS AND THE UNITED STATES CONSTITUTION, 2d ed. (Oxford University Press, 1996), at 31–62; CASEBOOK, at 90–95.
10 *See* John H. Jackson, *United States, in* THE EFFECT OF TREATIES IN DOMESTIC LAW – UNITED KINGDOM NATIONAL COMMITTEE OF COMPARATIVE LAW, Francis G. Jacobs & Shelley Roberts eds. (Sweet & Maxwell, 1987): 141, 144. For an up-to-date, extensive treatment of the politics of trade in the United States, *see* I. M. DESTLER, AMERICAN TRADE POLITICS, 4th ed. (Institute for International Economics, 2005).
11 *See* section 5.6, *infra*.
12 Jackson, *Status of Treaties*, *supra* note 2.
13 *Id.*, at 330–331.
14 *See* PIET EECKHOUT, EXTERNAL RELATIONS OF THE EUROPEAN UNION (Oxford University Press, 2004), at 170–175.
15 *See Treaty Establishing a Constitution for Europe*, signed in Rome on Oct. 29, 2004 and published in the OFFICIAL JOURNAL OF THE EUROPEAN UNION on Dec. 16, 2004 (C series, No 310). *See also* section 7.7 *infra*, and note 6 therein.
16 Commission of the European Communities, *Proposal for a Council Decision Concerning the Conclusion of the Uruguay Round of Multilateral Trade Negotiations* (1986–94) Com(94), 143 Final of Apr. 15, 1994, at Preface. For a recent, excellent overview and analysis of this extraordinarily complex subject, *see* Armin von Bogdandy, *Legal Effects of World Trade Organization Decisions within European Union Law*, JOURNAL OF WORLD TRADE 39 (2005): 45.

17 *See UR Texts*; Paolo Mengozzi, *The Marrakech DSU and its implications on the International and European Level*, in THE URUGUAY ROUND RESULTS: A EUROPEAN LAWYERS PERSPECTIVE, Jacques H. J. Bourgeois, Frédérique Berrod & Eric Gippini Fournier eds. (European Interuniversity Press, 1995): 115, 127–132. On the background of the Commission position, *see* Pieter J. Kuijper, *The Conclusion and Implementation of the Uruguay Round Results by the European Community*, EUROPEAN JOURNAL OF INTERNATIONAL LAW 6 (1995): 222.
18 *See Léon Van Parys NV v. Belgisch Interventie-en Restitutiebureau* (BIRB), Case C-377/02, Mar. 1, 2005 (not yet published); *Biret International SA v. Council*, Case C-93/02 P, 2003, ECR I-10497.
19 Yuji Iwasawa, *Constitutional Problems Involved in Implementing the Uruguay Round in Japan*, in IMPLEMENTING THE URUGUAY ROUND, John H. Jackson & Alan O. Sykes, Jr. eds. (Clarendon Press, 1997): 136; JOHN H. JACKSON, JEAN-VICTOR LOUIS, AND MITSUO MATSUSHITA, IMPLEMENTING THE TOKYO ROUND: NATIONAL CONSTITUTIONS AND INTERNATIONAL ECONOMIC RULES (University of Michigan Press, 1984).
20 *See* Donald C. Clarke, *China's Legal System and the WTO: Prospects for Compliance*, WASHINGTON UNIVERSITY GLOBAL STUDIES LAW REVIEW 2 (2003): 97; Jiangyu Wang, *The Application of WTO Law in China*, available at www.eastlaw.net/ research/wto/wto4.htm, visited 30 Jun. 2005.
21 *See, e.g., US – Measures Affecting Alcoholic and Malt Beverages*, GATT B.I.S.D. 39 (1992) 206; *Canada – Import, Distribution, and Sale of Alcoholic Drinks by Canadian Provincial Marketing Agencies*, GATT B.I.S.D. 37 (1989), Mar. 22, 1988, and GATT B.I.S.D. 27 (1993), Feb. 18, 1992.
22 Understanding on the Interpretation of Art. XXIV of the General Agreement on Tariffs and Trade 1994, *UR Texts*, para. 13:

> Each Member is fully responsible under GATT 1994 for the observance of all provisions of GATT 1994, and shall take such reasonable measures as may be available to it to ensure such observance by regional and local governments and authorities within its territory.

4.7 Scope of the subject matter agenda for the WTO: the question of competence

1 *Havana Charter for an International Trade Organization, 24 Mar. 1998*; Final Act and Related Documents, United Nations Conference on Trade and Employment, Havana, Cuba, Nov. 21, 1947, to Mar. 24, 1948, UN Doc. ICITO/1/4 (1948).
2 The Committee on Trade and Environment (CTE) was created following the adoption of the *1994 Ministerial Decision on Trade and Environment*, available at www.wto.org/english/docs_e/legal_e/56-dtenv_e.htm, visited Apr 5, 2005.
3 *Singapore Ministerial Declaration of 13 December 1996*, WTO Ministerial Conference, Singapore, Dec. 9–13, 1996, WTO Doc. WT/MIN(96)/DEC. See also the *Report of the Chairperson of the Governing Body of the ILO to the International*

Labour Conference for the year 1996–1997, at www.ilo.org/public/english/standards/relm/gb/refs/report97.htm, visited Jul. 5, 2005.
4 *See, e.g.*, Chakravarthi Raghavan, *WHO and WTO to Hold Expert Consultations on Cheap Drugs*, available at www.twnside.org.sg/title/expert.htm, visited Jul. 5, 2005.
5 *See* CLAUDE E. BARFIELD, FREE TRADE, SOVEREIGNTY, DEMOCRACY (AEI Press, 2001), at 37–69; Jeffrey L. Dunoff, *The Post-Doha Trade Agenda: Questions About Constituents, Competence and Coherence, in* THE WTO AND THE DOHA ROUND: THE CHANGING FACE OF WORLD TRADE, Ross P. Buckley ed. (Kluwer Law International, 2003): 59; Andrew T. Guzman, *Global Governance and the WTO*, HARVARD INTERNATIONAL LAW JOURNAL 45 (2004): 303.
6 The language is as follows:

Art. III
National Treatment on Internal Taxation and Regulation
. . .
4. The products of the territory of any contracting party imported into the territory of any other contracting party shall be accorded treatment no less favourable than that accorded to like products of national origin in respect of all laws, regulations and requirements affecting their internal sale, offering for sale, purchase, transportation, distribution or use.

7 *See Overview of Members' National Competition Legislation*, Note by the Secretariat, Revision, WTO Doc. WT/WGTCP/W/128/Rev.3, Nov. 27, 2003.
8 *See* section 6.4, *infra*.
9 *See* Danny Hakim, *G.M. Forecasts a Decline in its Earnings for 2005*, NEW YORK TIMES, Jan. 14, 2005, at 3 (noting the impact of medical costs on the earnings of General Motors).
10 *See US – Countervailing Measures Concerning Certain Products from the European Communities*, WTO Doc. WT/DS212/AB/R, adopted Jan. 8, 2003. *See also* Robert Lawrence, *Bush Had the Right To Impose Tariffs on Steel*, FINANCIAL TIMES (London), Jan. 29, 2003, at 17.
11 *General Agreement on Trade in Services, UR Texts*, at Annex 1B.
12 Regarding legal services, *see Annual Report of the Committee on Specific Commitments to the Council for Trade in Services (2004)*, WTO Doc. S/CSC/10, Nov. 25, 2004, at para. 4; the *Joint Statement on Legal Services*, Communication from Australia, Canada, et al., WTO Doc. TN/S/W/37, Feb. 24, 2005. On accounting services, *see, e.g., Communication from the United States: Accounting Services*, WTO Doc. S/CSS/W/20, Dec. 18, 2000 (including a negotiation proposal).
13 *Symposium: The Boundaries of the WTO*, AJIL 96 (2002) (contributions by Jose E. Alvarez; Kyle Bagwell, Petros C. Mavroidis, and Robert W. Staiger; Jagdish Bhagwati; Steve Charnovitz; Robert Howse; John H. Jackson; David W. Leebron; Debra P. Steger; and Joel P. Trachtman).

5 The WTO dispute settlement system

1 At the 1946 London meeting of the Preparatory Committee of the United Nations Conference on Trade and Employment, Harry Hawkins, representing the United States, speaking of the proposed ITO Charter. UN Doc. EPCT/C.II/PV.2, at 8 (1946). GATT, however, was probably not "self-executing" because it is applied through the Protocol of Provisional Application. *See* section 3.2, *supra*; *see also* John H. Jackson, *The General Agreement on Tariffs and Trade in United States Domestic Law*, MICHIGAN LAW REVIEW 66 (1967): 249, 285.
2 Chief Justice John Marshall, *McCulloch* v. *Maryland*, 4 Wheat. 316, 407 (1819).

5.1 The WTO dispute settlement system – unique, a great achievement, controversial

3 The US Department of State recognizes 192 independent countries in the world as of Jan. 28, 2005. *See* www.state.gov/s/inr/rls/4250.htm, visited Mar. 7, 2005.
4 Statistics of 93 percent and 87 percent, respectively, from: UNITED NATIONS, 2002 INTERNATIONAL TRADE STATISTICS YEARBOOK, Vol. II (UN, 2004): 467; World Bank, 2004 WORLD DEVELOPMENT INDICATORS 38 (2004).
5 *List of all WTO complaints brought pursuant to the Dispute Settlement Understanding (not including Article 21.5 disputes)*, at www.worldtradelaw.net, visited Jul. 20, 2005.
6 *See* www.worldtradelaw.net for statistics, visited Mar. 7, 2005; and *Update of WTO Dispute Settlement Cases*, WTO Doc. WT/DS/OV/24, 15 Jun. 2005, available at www.wto.org.
7 Author's calculations made as of Mar. 7, 2005.
8 John H. Jackson, *International Economic Law: Reflections on the 'Boiler Room' of International Relations*, AMERICAN JOURNAL OF INTERNATIONAL LAW AND POLICY 10 (1995):595.
9 *See generally* GIORGIO SACERDOTI ET AL. EDS., THE WTO AT TEN: THE ROLE OF THE DISPUTE SETTLEMENT SYSTEM (Cambridge University Press, 2006); RUFUS YERXA & BRUCE WILSON EDS., KEY ISSUES IN WTO DISPUTE SETTLEMENT: THE FIRST TEN YEARS (Cambridge University Press, 2005).

5.2 The bottom-up trial and error history of the GATT dispute settlement system and the Uruguay Round makeover

1 This section is derived from and builds upon the article by this author: *Dispute Settlement and the WTO: Emerging Problems*, JIEL 1 (1998): 329.
2 *Havana Charter for an International Trade Organization*, Arts. 92–97 in UN Conference on Trade and Employment – Final Act and Related Documents, UN Doc. E/Conf. 2/78 (1948). *See also* CLAIR WILCOX, A CHARTER FOR WORLD TRADE (Macmillan, 1949): 159, 305–308.
3 JACKSON, WTLG, at 167–71. Generally on the GATT dispute settlement procedure, *see also* William J. Davey, *Dispute-settlement in GATT*, FORDHAM INTERNATIONAL LAW JOURNAL 11 (1987): 51; Rosine Plank, *An Unofficial*

Notes to pages 138–140

Description of How a GATT Panel Works and Does Not, JOURNAL OF INTERNATIONAL ARBITRATION 4 (1987): 53.
4 *See, e.g.,* GATT ANALYTICAL INDEX, on Art. XXIII of GATT.
5 An action may also be brought under Art. XXIII when the attainment of any objective of the agreement is being impeded.
6 *See Australian Subsidy on Ammonium Sulphate,* Apr. 3, 1950, GATT B.I.S.D. (Vol. II) at 188 (1952). This case is sometimes called the *Marbury v. Madison* of GATT. See Robert E. Hudec, *Retaliation Against Unreasonable Foreign Trade Practices,* MINNESOTA LAW REVIEW 59 (1975): 461; ROBERT E. HUDEC, THE GATT LEGAL SYSTEM AND WORLD TRADE DIPLOMACY, 2d ed. (Butterworth, 1990), at 159–167; Robert E. Hudec, *GATT or GABB? The Future Design of the General Agreement on Tariffs and Trade,* YALE LAW JOURNAL 80 (1971): 1341.
7 *Australian Subsidy, id.,* and the *German Duty on Sardines case* (Oct. 31, 1952), GATT B.I.S.D. (1st Supp.) at 53 (1953), both endorse the view that GATT should be construed to protect "reasonable expectations" of the contracting parties. See HUDEC, THE GATT LEGAL SYSTEM, *supra* note 6, at 164, 167.
8 *See* HUDEC, THE GATT LEGAL SYSTEM, *supra* note 6.
9 Some of this information is developed from private conversations with senior GATT officials closely associated with the early development of GATT.
10 *Understanding Regarding Notification, Consultation, Dispute Settlement and Surveillance,* Nov. 28, 1979, GATT B.I.S.D. (26th Supp.) at 210 (1980), especially paragraphs 10–21.
11 *Netherlands Measures of Suspension of Obligations to the United States,* Nov. 8, 1952, GATT B.I.S.D. (1st Supp.) at 32 (1953). This was one fallout result of the US Congress's enactment of *1951 Amendments to Section 22 (f) of the Agricultural Adjustment Act,* 66 Stat. 75. *See* JACKSON, CASEBOOK, at 956.
12 The Netherlands never enforced the quota, arguably because of its ineffectiveness in removing the US quota on dairy products. *See* Hudec, *Retaliation, supra* note 6.
13 As a result of the panel decision in the so-called *Superfund (Oil Fee)* case, June 17, 1987, GATT B.I.S.D. (34th Supp.) at 136 (1988), the EC requested that the Contracting Parties authorize retaliation. *EC Superfund Tax Complaint,* INTERNATIONAL TRADE REPORTER (BNA) 5 (1988): 681; *EC Superfund Complaint,* INTERNATIONAL TRADE REPORTER (BNA) 5 (1988): 1303.
14 For example, in the *Citrus* case (*EEC – Tariff Treatment of Citrus Products from Certain Mediterranean Countries,* L/5776), as a result of the failure of the EC to accept the findings of a 1985 GATT panel. Proclamation 5354, 50 Fed. Reg. 26, 143 (1985). However, in the light of continuing discussion between the EC and the United States, the president issued Proclamation 5363 of Aug. 15, 1985, 50 Fed. Reg. 33, 711 (1985), suspending the application of the duty until Nov. 1, 1985. The duties became effective until Aug. 21, 1986, when the president revoked the increased rates of duty due to a settlement of the *Citrus* case. 51 Fed. Reg. 30, 146 (1986). However, it must be noted that

15 *Uruguayan Recourse to Article XXIII*, Nov. 16, 1962, GATT B.I.S.D. (11th Supp.) at 95 (1963).

The prima facie concept was also applied in situations involving quotas or domestic subsidies on products subject to agreed upon tariff limitations (i.e., tariffs bound under Art. II). *See generally* JACKSON, WTLG, at 182.

16 *See, e.g., French Assistance to Exports of Wheat and Wheat Flour*, Nov. 21, 1958, GATT B.I.S.D. (7th Supp.) at 46 (1959); *Spain – Measures Concerning Domestic Sale of Soybean Oil*, June 17, 1981, L/5142. *See also* GATT ANALYTICAL INDEX, at 171 (explaining several contracting parties' criticism of the Spanish Oil panel's conclusion that the term "like products" meant "more or less the same product").

17 *Understanding Regarding Notification, supra* note 10.
18 *See* section 4.3, *supra*.
19 GATT B.I.S.D. (29th Supp.) at 13 (1983).
20 See *Ministerial Declaration*, GATT B.I.S.D. (33rd Supp.) at 19, 25 (1987) and *Decision of 28 January 1987* GATT B.I.S.D. (33rd Supp.) at 31, 44–45 (1987). *See also, e.g.*, Clayton Yeutter, *The GATT Must Be Repaired – and Fast!*, THE INTERNATIONAL ECONOMY (Mar./Apr. 1988): 44, 47–48; *Address by Lamb*, US Department of State, CURRENT POLICY 585 (1984). Improvement of the dispute settlement procedures of GATT is also listed in the *Omnibus Trade and Competitiveness Act of 1988* (Pub. L. 100–418, Section 1101(b)(1), 102 Stat. 1121), as a US objective under the Uruguay Round.
21 JACKSON, CASEBOOK, at 287–288.
22 *EEC – Payments and Subsidies Paid to Processors and Producers of Oilseeds and Related Animal Feed Proteins*, Jan. 25, 1990, GATT B.I.S.D. (37th Supp.) at 37 (1990); JACKSON, ET AL, CASEBOOK, at 287–288.
23 *Agreement on Technical Barriers to Trade*, GATT B.I.S.D. (26th Supp.) at 8 (1980).
24 Art. 3(8), DSU, states:

> In cases where there is an infringement of the obligations assumed under a covered agreement, the action is considered prima facie to constitute a case of nullification or impairment. This means that there is normally a presumption that a breach of the rules has an adverse impact on other Members parties to that covered agreement, and in such cases, it shall be up to the Member against whom the complaint has been brought to rebut the charge.

25 DSU.
26 Reverse consensus means that the matter is adopted unless there is consensus against adoption. Since such consensus against adoption is defeatable by any member, the disputing member who "won" can prevent a blocking vote. *See* section 5.4, *infra*.

5.3 The multiple policy goals of international dispute settlement: dilemmas, balancing, and competing principles

1 This section is partially drawn from a presentation delivered at the conference in London, May 2003, on the WTO Dispute Settlement System, organized by the British Institute of International and Comparative Law (with participation of the *Journal of International Economic Law* (Oxford University Press) and the Institute of International Economic Law, of Georgetown University Law Center), May 2003. *See* John H. Jackson, *Policy Underpinnings of International Juridical Institutions, in* WTO LAW AND PROCESS, Mads Andenas & Federico Ortino eds. (BIICL, 2005).
2 DSU.
3 *US – Restrictions on Imports of Cotton and Man-made Fibre Underwear*, WTO Doc. WT/DS24/AB/R, adopted 25 Feb. 1997.
4 *See e.g.*, John H. Jackson, *Editorial Comment: International Law Status of WTO DS Reports: Obligation to Comply or Option to "Buy-Out"?* AJIL 98 (Jan. 2004): 109.
5 *See* section 5.7.a, *infra*.
6 *See* section 5.9, *infra*.

5.4 The current structure and operation of the WTO dispute settlement system

1 DSU. For more detail, *see generally* JACKSON, CASEBOOK, at Ch. 7. *See also* many articles of the JIEL.
2 Art. 5, DSU.
3 Art. 25, DSU.
4 Arts. 1 and 23, DSU.
5 *Rules of Conduct for the Understanding on Rules and Procedures Governing the Settlement of Disputes*, WTO Doc. WT/DSB/RC/1, 11 Dec.1996. *See generally* Gabrielle Marceau, *Rules on Ethics for the New World Trade Organization Dispute Settlement Mechanism*, JOURNAL OF WORLD TRADE 32 (June 1998): 57.
6 *See* William J. Davey, *WTO Dispute Settlement: Segregating the Useful Political Aspects and Avoiding Over-legalization, in* NEW DIRECTIONS IN INTERNATIONAL ECONOMIC LAW: ESSAYS IN HONOR OF PROFESSOR JOHN H. JACKSON, Marco Bronckers & Reinhard Quick eds. (Kluwer Law International, 2000): 291.
7 *EC – Measures Concerning Meat and Meat Products (Hormones)*, WTO Doc. WT/DS26 & 48/AB/R, adopted Feb. 13, 1998.
8 *Ibid.*, at para. 133.
9 *Ibid.*; *EC – Measures Affecting the Approval and Marketing of Biotech Products*, WTO Docs. WT/DS291/27, WT/DS292/21, WT/DS293/21 (The "GMO case" is an ongoing dispute. The panel, established on Aug. 19, 2003, estimates that it will issue its final report to the parties by the end of December 2005).
10 *U.S. Renews Call for More Transparency in WTO Disputes, Including Public Hearing*, INTERNATIONAL TRADE REPORTER 22, Jul. 21, 2005: 1196.
11 *US – Continued Suspension of Obligations in the EC – Hormones Dispute (WT/DS320)* and *Canada – Continued Suspension of Obligations in the EC – Hormones Dispute*

(WT/DS321), Communication from the Chairman of the Panels, WTO Docs. WT/DS320/8 & WT/DS321/8, of Aug. 2, 2005.

12 *EC – Regime for the Importation, Sale and Distribution of Bananas*, WTO Doc. WT/DS27/AB/R, adopted Sept. 25, 1997.

13 Often such counsel is based in Washington, DC; Brussels, Belgium; the United Kingdom; or increasingly in Geneva, Switzerland, itself.

14 Arts. 12, 15, 16, and Appendix 3 (which sets out an elaborate schedule of normal times), DSU.

15 Art. 16, DSU.

16 *Japan – Taxes on Alcoholic Beverages*, WTO Doc. WT/DS8, 10 & 11/AB/R, adopted 1 Nov. 1996

17 *See, e.g.*, Georg C. Umbricht, *An "Amicus Curiae Brief" on Amicus Curiae Briefs at the WTO*, JIEL 4 (Dec. 2001): 773; Petros C. Mavroidis, *Amicus Curiae Briefs Before the WTO: Much Ado About Nothing*, JEAN MONNET WORKING PAPER 2/01, available at: www.worldtradelaw.net/articles/mavroidisamicus.pdf; Geert Zonnekyn, *The Appellate Body's Communication on Amicus Curiae Briefs in the Asbestos Case – An Echternach Procession?* JOURNAL OF WORLD TRADE 35 (2001): 553. In the *Asbestos Case*, the Appellate Body developed a procedure for the submission of *amicus curiae* briefs, see *EC – Measures Affecting the Prohibition of Asbestos and Asbestos Products*, WTO Doc. WT/DS135/AB/R, adopted Apr. 5, 2001.

18 As an example of completing the analysis, see *US – Standards for Reformulated and Conventional Gasoline*, WTO Doc. WT/DS2/R, adopted Jan. 29, 1996. As an example of inability to take up an issue for lack of factual findings by the panel, see *Asbestos, id.*

19 See Claus-Dieter Ehlermann, *Reflections on the Appellate Body of the World Trade Organization*, AMERICAN SOCIETY OF INTERNATIONAL LAW PROCEEDINGS 97 (2003): 77. Note that the Vienna Convention on the Law of Treaties has not been ratified by some major WTO members, including the United States, France, and Brazil, but often VCLT language is said to represent customary international law regarding treaty interpretation. This issue is also discussed in section 5.8, *infra*.

20 Arts. 21, 22, and 26, DSU.

21 *See* Andrew T. Guzman, *The Design of International Agreements*, UC BERKELEY PUBLIC LAW RESEARCH PAPER No. 487662 (Nov. 2004), available at http://ssrn.com/abstract'487662, visited 8 Apr. 2005; John H. Knox, *Separated at Birth: The North American Agreements on Labor and the Environment*, LOYOLA OF LOS ANGELES INTERNATIONAL AND COMPARATIVE LAW REVIEW 26 (2004), available at http://ssrn.com/abstract'551602, visited Apr. 8, 2005; Daniel E. Ho, *Compliance and International Soft Law: Why Do Countries Implement the Basle Accord?*, JOURNAL OF INTERNATIONAL ECONOMIC LAW 5 (2002): 647; Naboth Van Den Broek, *Power Paradoxes in Enforcement and Implementation of World Trade Organization Dispute Settlement Reports*, JOURNAL OF WORLD TRADE 37

(Feb. 2003): 127; Harold Hongju Koh, *Review Essay: Why Do Nations Obey International Law?*, YALE LAW JOURNAL 106 (1997): 2599; Colter Paulson, *Compliance with Final Judgments of the International Court of Justice Since 1987*, AJIL 98 (Jul. 2004): 434.

22 *See* the developments after the first-level panel and Appellate Body rulings in *US – Tax Treatment for "Foreign Sales Corporations," (FSC)* WTO Docs. WT/DS108/R & WT/DS108/AB/R, adopted Mar. 20, 2000, and *FSC-Recourse to Article 21.5 of the DSU by the EC*, WTO Doc. WT/DS108/AB/RW, adopted Jan. 29, 2002, as well as *FSC – Recourse to Arbitration by the United States under Article 22.6 of the DSU and Article 4.11 of the SCM Agreement*, WTO Doc. WT/DS108/ARB, circulated Aug. 30, 2002 (awarding the EC the right to block $4 billion in exports from the United States). *See also* Robert Z. Lawrence, CRIME AND PUNISHMENTS? RETALIATION UNDER THE WTO (Institute of International Economics, 2003), 74–76; Sungjoon Cho, *The Nature of Remedies in International Trade Law*, UNIVERSITY OF PITTSBURGH LAW REVIEW 65 (2004): 763; Hale E. Sheppard, *Rethinking Tax-Based Export Incentives: Converting Repeated Defeats Before the WTO into Positive Tax Policy*, TEXAS INTERNATIONAL LAW JOURNAL 39 (2003): 111, 112–117.

5.5 A decade of WTO dispute settlement activity, 1995–2005

1 Often there are not present at WTO meetings sufficient numbers of country representatives to provide a two-thirds vote.
2 In private discussions, even private-sector persons (business people or lawyers) indicate that they or their clients follow the Appellate Body jurisprudence carefully because of the potential impact on investment and other decisions over the long term.
3 Statistics in this chapter were compiled as at October 2005.
4 *See* www.worldtradelaw.net, visited Oct. 3, 2005.
5 *See* www.worldtradelaw.net for statistics, visited Oct. 3, 2005; and *Update of WTO Dispute Settlement Cases*, WTO doc. WT/DS/OV/24, 15 Jun. 2005, available at www.wto.org.
6 *See* Kara Leitner & Simon Lester, *WTO Dispute Settlement 1995–2004: A Statistical Analysis*, JOURNAL OF INTERNATIONAL ECONOMIC LAW 8 (2005): 231.
7 The WTO recognizes as "least developed" those countries which have been designated as such by the United Nations. The UN definition includes three criteria: (i) an annual gross national income per capita under $750; (ii) a human resource weakness criterion (based on indicators of nutrition, health, education, and adult literacy); and (iii) an economic vulnerability criterion. *See* www.un.org/special-rep/ohrlls/ldc/ldcpercent20criteria.htm for the full definition, visited Jun. 15, 2005. Of the fifty countries on the UN list thirty-two have become WTO members.

8 *US – Standards for Reformulated and Conventional Gasoline*, WTO Doc. WT/DS2/AB/R, adopted Apr. 26, 1996.
9 *Japan – Taxes on Alcoholic Beverages*, WTO Docs. WT/DS8, 10 & 11/AB/R, adopted Nov. 1, 1996.
10 WON-MOG CHOI, "LIKE PRODUCTS" IN INTERNATIONAL TRADE LAW: TOWARDS A CONSISTENT GATT/WTO JURISPRUDENCE (Oxford University Press, 2003); Robert E. Hudec, *Like Product: The Differences in Meaning in GATT Articles I and III*, in REGULATORY BARRIERS AND THE PRINCIPLE OF NON-DISCRIMINATION IN WORLD TRADE LAW, Thomas Cottier & Petros Mavroidis eds. (University of Michigan Press, 2000): 101.
11 *EC – Measures Concerning Meat and Meat Products (Hormones)*, WTO Docs. WT/DS26/AB/R, WT/DS48/AB/R, adopted Feb. 13, 1998.
12 *Agreement on Sanitary and Phytosanitary Measures*, in *UR Texts*, at 59.
13 *US – Import Prohibition of Certain Shrimp and Shrimp Products*, WTO Doc. WT/DS58/AB/R, adopted Nov. 6, 1998.
14 *See, e.g.*, John H. Jackson, *Comments on Shrimp/Turtle and the Product/Process Distinction*, EUROPEAN JOURNAL OF INTERNATIONAL LAW 11 (2000): 303; Robert Howse, *The Appellate Body Rulings in the Shrimp/Turtle Case: A New Legal Baseline for the Trade and Environment Debate*, COLUMBIA JOURNAL OF ENVIRONMENTAL LAW 27 (2002): 49; Petros C. Mavroidis, *Trade and Environment After the Shrimp-Turtle Litigation*, JOURNAL OF WORLD TRADE 34 (2000): 73.
15 Statistics derived from www.worldtradelaw.net, visited Mar. 2005.
16 *See, e.g.*, the letter of Members of Congress Baucus, Rangel and Levin to the US Trade Representative Robert Zoellick of Nov. 19, 2003, protesting the renomination of three Appellate Body members, available on WORLD TRADE ONLINE, www.insidetrade.com (by subscription service only). *See also Opening Statement of The Honorable Sander M. Levin*, at the House Committee on Ways and Means, Feb. 26, 2003, at http://waysandmeans.house.gov/hearings. asp?formmode"printfriendly&id"122, visited Jun. 28, 2005.
17 *US – Measures Affecting the Cross-Border Supply of Gambling and Betting Services*, WTO Doc. WT/DS285/R, adopted Apr. 20, 2005 (subject to appellate changes).
18 *US – Measures Affecting the Cross-Border Supply of Gambling and Betting Services*, WTO Doc. WT/DS285/AB/R, adopted Apr. 20, 2005.
19 *US – Subsidies on Upland Cotton*, WTO Docs. WT/DS267/AB/R and WT/DS267/R, both adopted Mar. 21, 2005.
20 *EC– Export Subsidies on Sugar*, WTO Docs. WT/DS265, 266, 283/R and WT/DS265, 266, 283/AB/R, both adopted May 19, 2005.

5.6 Key jurisprudential questions I: the relation of WTO law to international law – sovereignty tensions

1 The most extensive current examination of this question of the relationship of general international law to the WTO is JOOST PAUWELYN, CONFLICT OF

NORMS IN PUBLIC INTERNATIONAL LAW: HOW WTO LAW RELATES TO OTHER RULES OF INTERNATIONAL LAW (Cambridge University Press, 2003). *See also* particularly the following WTO cases: *US – Restrictions on Imports of Tuna (Tuna II)*, GATT Doc. DS29/R, adopted Jun. 16, 1994, paras. 5.19–5.20. Fourteen other GATT panels also referred to the Vienna Convention on the Law of treaties. *See, e.g., US – Imposition of Countervailing Duties on Certain Hot-Rolled Lead and Bismuth Carbon Steel Products Originating in France, Germany and the United Kingdom,* WTO Doc. SCM/185, Nov. 15, 1994 (not adopted), at paras. 368 369; *EC – Imposition of Anti-Dumping Duties on Imports of Cotton Yarn from Brazil,* WTO Doc. ADP/137, adopted by the ADP Committee, Oct. 30, 1995, at para. 541.
2 *US – Standards for Reformulated and Conventional Gasoline,* WTO Doc. WT/DS2/AB/R, adopted May 20, 1996.
3 The only prior case was settled before coming to panel: *Malaysia – Prohibition of Imports of Polyethylene and Polypropylene,* WTO Doc. WT/DS1, requested Jan. 10, 1995, a complaint brought by Singapore against Malaysia.
4 US lawyers would probably use the rubric "legislative history" in this context.
5 *Japan – Taxes on Alcoholic Beverages,* WTO Docs. WT/DS8–DS11/AB/R, adopted Nov. 1, 1996. In this case, the Appellate Body considered whether Japan's taxation pattern on domestic and imported alcoholic beverages was discriminatory in violation of Art. III(2), GATT.
6 *Id.,* at footnotes 27 and 39.
7 GATT ANALYTICAL INDEX.
8 *See* Art. 26, VCLT ("Every treaty in force is binding upon the parties to it and must be performed by them in good faith"). *See* the *Annex of Important Panel and Appellate Body Decisions with References to Good Faith, in* Helge E. Zeitler, *"Good Faith" in the WTO Jurisprudence – Necessary Balancing or an Open Door to Judicial Activism?* JIEL 8 (2005): 721.
9 *See e.g.* the criticism expressed by the US representative in a Dispute Settlement Body Session on the Appellate Body Report on the Byrd Amendment and the panel report on Argentina – Poultry, WTO Doc. WT/DSB/M/150, 22 Jul. 2003, para. 44.
10 Draft articles on Responsibility of States for internationally wrongful acts adopted by the International Law Commission at its fifty-third session (2001), *Report of the International Law Commission on the work of its Fifty-third session,* OFFICIAL RECORDS OF THE GENERAL ASSEMBLY, FIFTY-SIXTH SESSION, SUPPLEMENT No. 10 (A/56/10).
11 *Japan – Alcoholic Beverages, supra* note 5.
12 Art. 31(3), VCLT:

> There shall be taken into account, together with the context: . . . (b) any subsequent practice in the application of the treaty which establishes the agreement of the parties regarding its interpretation.

13 For a detailed analysis of this problem, *see, e.g.,* John H. Jackson, *Editorial Comment: International Law Status of WTO DS Reports: Obligation to Comply or Option to "Buy-Out"?* AJIL 98 (2004):109. For further opinions on this subject, *see* notes in Jackson, article, *id.,* and more recently, Steve Charnovitz, *Recent Developments and Scholarship on WTO Enforcement Remedies, in* INTER-GOVERNMENTAL TRADE DISPUTE SETTLEMENT: MULTILATERAL AND REGIONAL APPROACHES, Julio Lacarte & Jaime Granados eds. (Cameron May, 2004): 151.

14 Art. 22(1), DSU.

15 Art. 22(2), DSU.

16 Arts. 21(6) and 21(1), DSU.

17 *Agreement on Implementation of Article VI of the General Agreement on Tariffs and Trade 1994, in UR Texts,* at 147.

18 *Id.,* at Art. 17(6):

> In examining the matter referred to in paragraph 5:
> in its assessment of the facts of the matter, the panel shall determine whether the authorities' establishment of the facts was proper and whether their evaluation of those facts was unbiased and objective. If the establishment of the facts was proper and the evaluation was unbiased and objective, even though the panel might have reached a different conclusion, the evaluation shall not be overturned;
>
> the panel shall interpret the relevant provisions of the Agreement in accordance with customary rules of interpretation of public international law. Where the panel finds that a relevant provision of the Agreement admits of more than one permissible interpretation, the panel shall find the authorities' measure to be in conformity with the Agreement if it rests upon one of those permissible interpretations.

19 *Id., Decision on Review of Article 17.6,* at 397:

> *Ministers decide as follows:*
> The standard of review in paragraph 6 of Article 17 of the Agreement on Implementation of Article VI of GATT 1994 shall be reviewed after a period of three years with a view to considering the question of whether it is capable of general application. With respect to dispute settlement pursuant to the Agreement on Implementation of Article VI of GATT 1994 or Part V of the Agreement on Subsidies.

20 *Id., Declaration on Dispute Settlement Pursuant to the Agreement on Implementation of Article VI,* at 397, footnote 17:

> Ministers recognize, with respect to dispute settlement pursuant to the Agreement on Implementation of Article VI of the General Agreement on Tariffs and Trades 1994 or Part V of the Agreement on Subsidies and Countervailing Measures, the need for the consistent resolution of disputes arising from antidumping and countervailing duty measures.

Notes to pages 169–174

21 *US – Imposition of Countervailing Duties on Certain Hot-Rolled Lead and Bismuth Carbon Steel Products Originating in the United Kingdom*, WTO Doc. WT/DS138/AB/R, adopted Jun. 7, 2000.
22 *Chevron U.S.A. Inc. v. Natural Resources Defense Council, Inc. et. al.*, 467 U.S. 837 (1984).
23 *See* Art. 17(6), *supra* note 18.
24 Many of the negotiators confirmed this intent.
25 *E.g.*, Art. 17(6), *supra* note 18, is *not* mentioned in *United States – Anti-Dumping Act of 1916*, WTO Docs. WT/DS136/AB/R & WT/DS162/AB/R, adopted Sept. 26, 2000.
26 *See e.g.*, the decisions of the Appellate Body in *EC – Measures Concerning Meat and Meat Products (Hormones)*, WTO Docs. WT/DS26/AB/R, WT/DS448/AB/R, adopted Feb. 25, 1997, at paras. 131–145; as well as the first-level panel reports in *United States – Restrictions on Imports of Cotton and Man-Made Fibre Underwear*, WTO Doc. WT/DS24/R, adopted Feb. 25, 1998, at paras. 7.10–7.13; and *US – Measures Affecting of Imports, Woven Wool Shirts and Blouses from India*, WTO Doc. WT/DS33/R, adopted 23 May 1997, at paras. 7.16–7.17.
27 *Hormones*, *id.*
28 MATTHIAS OESCH, STANDARDS OF REVIEW IN WTO DISPUTE RESOLUTION (Oxford University Press, 2003); Claus-Dieter Ehlermann & Nicolas Lockhart, *Standard of Review in WTO Law*, *in* A TRUE EUROPEAN: ESSAYS FOR JUDGE DAVID EDWARD, Mark Hoskins & William Robinson eds. (Hart Publishing, 2003): 267; Steven P. Croley & John H. Jackson, *WTO Dispute Procedures, Standard of Review and Deference to National Governments*, AJIL 90 (1996): 193.
29 William J. Davey, *Has the WTO Dispute Settlement System Exceeded Its Authority? A Consideration of Deference Shown by the System to Member Government Decisions and Its Use of Issue-Avoidance Techniques*, JIEL 4 (2001): 79.

5.7 Key jurisprudential questions II: structural doctrines channeling juridical techniques of decision

1 *See* Raj Bhala, *The Myth About Stare Decisis and International Trade Law (Part One of a Trilogy)*, AMERICAN UNIVERSITY INTERNATIONAL LAW REVIEW 14 (1999): 845; Raj Bhala, *The Precedent Setters: De Facto Stare Decisis in WTO Adjudication (Part Two of a Trilogy)*, FLORIDA STATE UNIVERSITY JOURNAL OF TRANSNATIONAL LAW & POLICY 9 (1999): 1; Raj Bhala, *The Power of the Past: Towards De Jure Stare Decisis in WTO Adjudication (Part Three of a Trilogy)*, GEORGE WASHINGTON INTERNATIONAL LAW REVIEW (2001): 873. *See also* Zhu Lanye, *The Effects of the WTO Dispute Settlement Panel and Appellate Body Reports: Is the Dispute Settlement Body Resolving Specific Disputes Only or Making Precedent at the Same Time?*, TEMPLE INTERNATIONAL AND COMPARATIVE LAW JOURNAL 17 (2003): 221.
2 This was based on the Montesquieu concept of a strict separation of powers, *see* Zenon Bankowski, et. al., *Rationales for Precedent*, *in* INTERPRETING

PRECEDENTS: A COMPARATIVE STUDY, D. Neil MacCormick & Robert S. Summers eds. (Ashgate/Dartmouth, 1997): 481, 482. For today's use of precedents in French law, *see* Art. 5 of the French Civil Code, which declares "it is prohibited for judges to decide by way of general provisions and rules on the cases that are brought before them." Art. 455 of the Code of Civil Procedure requires a judgment to be motivated; a decision making exclusive reference to a precedent has been considered a violation of the motivation requirement; *see* Michel Troper & Christophe Grzegorczyk, *Precedent in France*, in INTERPRETING PRECEDENTS, *id.* at 103, 115.

3 John Henry Merryman, THE LONELINESS OF THE COMPARATIVE LAWYER AND OTHER ESSAYS IN FOREIGN AND COMPARATIVE LAW (Kluwer Law International, 1999), at 17–52; Mathias Reimann, *The Progress and Failure of Comparative Law in the Second Half of the Twentieth Century*, AMERICAN JOURNAL OF COMPARATIVE LAW 50 (2002): 671.

4 *Planned Parenthood of Southeastern Pa. v. Casey*, 505 U.S. 833 (1992).

5 *Roe v. Wade*, 410 U.S. 113 (1973).

6 *SA CNL-SUCAL NV v. HAG GF AG*, Case C-10/89, 1990 E.C.R., *I-3711*, at para. 10. In this judgment, the court held: "the Court believes it necessary to reconsider the interpretation given in that judgment in the light of the case-law which has developed with regard to the relationship between industrial and commercial property and the general rules of the Treaty, particularly in the sphere of the free movement of goods." Opinion of the Advocate General, para. 67, p. 3749. Regarding the ECJ approach to precedent, *see* L. NEVILLE BROWN & TOM KENNEDY, THE COURT OF JUSTICE OF THE EUROPEAN COMMUNITIES, 5th ed. (Sweet & Maxwell, 2000), at 368; Alec Stone Sweet & Margaret McCown, *Discretion and Precedent in European Law*, in JUDICIAL DISCRETION IN EUROPEAN PERSPECTIVE, Ola Wiklund ed. (Kluwer Law International 2003): 84, 109.

7 *See* WALTER VAN GERVEN, THE EUROPEAN UNION: A POLITY OF STATES AND PEOPLES (Stanford University Press, 2005), at esp. Chs. 2 and 3. For the example of France, *see* Didier Maus, *The Birth of Judicial Review of Legislation in France*, in CONSTITUTIONAL JUSTICE UNDER OLD CONSTITUTIONS, Eivind Smith ed. (Kluwer Law International 1995): 113. For the example of the United Kingdom, *see* William Wade, *British Restriction of Judicial Review – Europe to the Rescue*, JUDICIAL REVIEW IN INTERNATIONAL PERSPECTIVE, Mads Andenas ed. (Kluwer Law International, 2000): 267. On the Dutch system of limited judicial review, *see* TIM KOOPMANS, COURTS AND POLITICAL INSTITUTIONS – A COMPARATIVE VIEW (Cambridge University Press, 2003), at 76.

8 *Statute of the International Court of Justice, June 26, 1945*, 59 Stat. 1031, T.S. No. 993, entered into effect Oct. 24, 1945.

9 *See* HENRY M. HART & ALBERT M. SACKS, THE LEGAL PROCESS: BASIC PROBLEMS IN THE MAKING AND APPLICATION OF LAW, tentative ed. (Harvard University, 1958), at 1348; H. L. A. HART, THE CONCEPT OF LAW

(Clarendon Press, 1961), at 131–132; INTERPRETING PRECEDENTS, *supra* note 2.
10 The word "charter" is an informal term. See section 4.2 *supra*, at note 2.
11 *Japan – Taxes on Alcoholic Beverages*, WTO Docs. WT/DS8, 10 & 11/AB/R, adopted Nov. 1, 1996, at 13–14.
12 *US – Definitive Safeguard Measures on Imports of Certain Steel Products*, WTO Docs. WT/DS248, 249, 251–254, 258, & 259/R, adopted Nov. 10, 2003.
13 JOHN H. JACKSON, THE JURISPRUDENCE OF GATT AND THE WTO: INSIGHTS ON TREATY LAW AND ECONOMIC RELATIONS (Cambridge University Press, 2000), at 118 – 132; John H. Jackson, *United States–EEC Trade Relations: Constitutional Problems of Economic Interdependence*, COMMON MARKET LAW REVIEW 16 (1979): 453.
14 *US – Import Prohibition of Certain Shrimp and Shrimp Products*, WTO Doc. WT/DS58/AB/R, adopted Nov. 6, 1998, at para. 119.
15 See *US – Sunset Reviews of Anti-Dumping Measures on Oil Country Tubular Goods from Argentina*, WTO Doc. WT/DS268/AB/R, adopted Dec. 17, 2004, at para. 188:

> Thus, it was appropriate for the panel, in determining whether the SPB is a measure, to rely on the Appellate Body's conclusion in that case. Indeed, following the Appellate Body's conclusions in earlier disputes is not only appropriate, but is what would be expected from panels, especially where the issues are the same.

16 *US – Taxes on Petroleum and Certain Imported Substances*, GATT B.I.S.D. (34th Supp.), adopted Jun. 17, 1987. This is sometimes referred to as the *Superfund Case*.
17 *Id. See also* section 5.2, *supra*.
18 *See* GATT ANALYTICAL INDEX, at 599–601.
19 *US – Sections 301–310 of the Trade Act of 1974*, WTO Doc. WT/DS152/R, adopted Jan. 27, 2000.
20 The author has heard this description during numerous private conversations.
21 *US – Sections 301, supra* note 19, at paras. 7.73, 7.75–7.77.
22 *US – Anti-Dumping Act of 1916*, WTO Docs. WT/DS136/R & WT/DS136/AB/R, adopted Sept. 26, 2000.
23 Arts. 22(4) and 22(6), DSU, which provides that the losing member can object to the level of suspension proposed.
24 *US – Continued Dumping and Subsidy Offset Act of 2000*, WTO Docs. WT/DS217 & 234/AB/R, adopted Jan. 16, 2003.
25 Art. 11, DSU.
26 Art. 17(6), DSU.
27 *EC – Measures Affecting Asbestos and Asbestos-Containing Products*, WTO Doc. WT/DS135/AB/R, adopted Apr. 5, 2001, at paras. 137–141.
28 *Japan – Measures Affecting Consumer Photographic Film and Paper*, WTO Doc. WT/DS44/R, adopted Apr. 22, 1998 (not appealed).

Notes to pages 181–183

29 Art. 17(6), DSU.
30 *Id.*, at 17(6)(i).
31 *EC – Measures Concerning Meat and Meat Products (Hormones)*, WTO Docs. WT/DS26/AB/R & WT/DS48/AB/R, adopted Feb. 13, 1998.
32 *EC – Measures Affecting the Approval and Marketing of Biotech Products*, WTO Docs. WT/DS291/27, WT/DS292/21, WT/DS293/21 (The "GMO case" is an ongoing dispute. The panel, established on Aug. 19, 2003, estimated that it would issue its final report to the parties by the end of June 2005, but by August it had not yet been issued.)
33 *Hormones, supra* note 31, at paras. 146–149.

5.8 Key jurisprudential questions III: treaty interpretation

1 *See* DAVID M. BEATTY, THE ULTIMATE RULE OF LAW (Oxford University Press, 2004); AHARON BARAK, PURPOSIVE INTERPRETATION IN LAW (Princeton University Press, 2005); and notes 6 and 20, *infra*.
2 The following are treaty interpretation concepts or approaches possibly relevant: priority to text and plain meaning; attention to the intent of the drafts persons; preparatory work (sometimes termed "legislative history"); the object and purpose of the agreement; a doctrine that no clause in a treaty should be without some impact, and therefore, the treaty should be interpreted to implement each treaty clause; questions of when there is conflict between different parts of a treaty, how to define "conflict," and whether the different treaty provisions can be "reconciled"; prior practice over time, or "practice under the agreement"; teleological interpretation; evolutionary interpretation; realist school of interpretation, focusing on the juridical preferences of the individuals who are the "judges"; a broader general policy motivation for interpreting the text (or interpreting the treaty relatively unconstrained by the text); standards of review (degree of deference to the nation state); situations where the text seems to imply further aspects of the treaty obligations not necessarily explicitly mentioned; general obligation of good faith in treaty implementation; reasonable expectations of the parties to the treaty; mandate to be "guided by" the decisions and dispute reports of other organizations or predecessor organizations (such as GATT); rules on burden of proof using presumptions and ideas about shifting burden of proof; notions of balancing some of the interpretation techniques by consideration of non-trade policies; ideas of interpreting a treaty in the direction of "multilateralism" rather than "unilateralism."
3 The WTO Member states who have *not* ratified the VCLT, are Angola, Antigua and Barbuda, Bahrain, Bangladesh, Belize, Benin, Bolivia, Botswana, Brazil, Brunei, Burkina Faso, Burundi, Cambodia, Chad, Côte d'Ivoire, Djibouti, Dominica, Dominican Republic, El Salvador, Fiji, France, Gambia, Ghana, Grenada, Guinea, Guinea Bissau, Guyana, Hong Kong, Iceland, India, Indonesia, Ireland, Israel, Jordan, Kenya, Macao, Madagascar, Maldives,

Malta, Mauritania, Namibia, Nepal, Nicaragua, Norway, Pakistan, Papua New Guinea, Qatar, Romania, Saint Kitts and Nevis, Saint Lucia, Sierra Leone, Singapore, South Africa, Sri Lanka, Swaziland, Taipei, Thailand, Trinidad and Tobago, Turkey, Uganda, United Arab Emirates, United States, Venezuela, Zambia, and Zimbabwe. *See* the current list of countries that have ratified the Vienna Convention, available at http://untreaty.un.org (by subscription), visited Jul. 18, 2005.

4 *See EC – Measures Concerning Meat and Meat Products (Hormones)*, WTO doc. WT/DS26/AB/R, adopted 13 February 1998, at footnote 154, page 67:

> [154]The interpretative principle of *in dubio mitius*, widely recognized in international law as a "supplementary means of interpretation," has been expressed in the following terms:
>
> The principle of *in dubio mitius* applies in interpreting treaties, in deference to the sovereignty of states. If the meaning of a term is ambiguous, that meaning is to be preferred which is less onerous to the party assuming an obligation, or which interferes less with the territorial and personal supremacy of a party, or involves less general restrictions upon the parties. [citations omitted]

As of July 2005, the phrase *in dubio mitius* has not appeared in the findings of any other WTO appellate report, but it has been argued in several disputant submittals, and has been mentioned in three panel reports, some citing the *Hormones* footnotes. Criticism of the *in dubio mitius* concept also parallels somewhat the criticisms of the famous *Lotus* case as representing "extreme positions"; *see* discussions in LORI F. DAMROSCH ET. AL., INTERNATIONAL LAW: CASES AND MATERIALS, 4th ed. (West Group, 2001), at 68–76.

5 The principle was not mentioned in the protocols of the UN Conference on the law of treaties during the discussion of Art. 31 of the VCLT. However, the rule of *in dubio mitius* was discussed during the drafting of the Resolution upon the Interpretation of Treaties, adopted by the Institute of International Law at Granada in 1956. During preparatory work of the respective committees, the members were unable to come to an agreement as to mention of this rule, with the result that it does not appear in the resolution. *See* LORD MCNAIR, THE LAW OF TREATIES (Clarendon, 1986), at 766. For relevant arguments related to the US Supreme Court "Chevron doctrine," *see* Steven P. Croley & John H. Jackson, *WTO Dispute Settlement Procedures, Standard of Review, and Deference to National Governments*, AJIL 90 (1996): 193.

6 *See* BARAK, PURPOSIVE INTERPRETATION, *supra* note 1, at Ch. 3. The word "proportionality" occurs over 100 times in WTO DS panel and Appellate Body reports (in approximately nineteen panel reports and three appellate reports).

7 *Japan – Taxes on Alcoholic Beverages*, WTO Docs. WT/DS8, 10 & 11/AB/R, adopted Nov. 1, 1996.

8 *See* GATT Art. III and interpretive note. The phrases "like product," "like or competitive product," and "competitive product," appear thirty times in the UR *Texts*.
9 *EC – Measures Affecting the Prohibition of Asbestos and Asbestos Products*, WTO Doc. WT/DS135/AB/R, adopted Apr. 5, 2001.
10 WON-MOG CHOI, "LIKE PRODUCTS" IN INTERNATIONAL TRADE LAW: TOWARDS A CONSISTENT GATT/WTO JURISPRUDENCE (Oxford University Press, 2003).
11 Claus-Dieter Ehlermann, *Reflections on the Appellate Body of the World Trade Organization*, AMERICAN SOCIETY OF INTERNATIONAL LAW PROCEEDINGS 97 (2003): 77.
12 *See* section 4.2, *supra*.
13 *US – Imports Prohibition of Certain Shrimp and Shrimp Products*, WTO Doc. WT/DS58/AB/R, adopted Nov. 6, 1998, at para. 130.
14 *See generally* Mark Tushnet, *Justification in Constitutional Adjudication: A Comment on Constitutional Interpretation*, TEXAS LAW REVIEW 72 (1994): 1707. For the "originalist" view, *see* Robert H. Bork, *Originalism, in* CONTEMPORARY PERSPECTIVES ON CONSTITUTIONAL INTERPRETATION, Susan J. Brison and Walter Sinnott-Armstrong eds. (Westview Press, 1993): 47. An example is Justice Antonin Scalia, *see* SCALIA, A MATTER OF INTERPRETATION (Princeton University Press, 1997), at 37–47 and 138–41; and the comment of Ronald Dworkin, *in id.*, at 119–127. The "evolutionary" approach is expressed by Justice Sandra Day O'Connor in O'CONNOR, THE MAJESTY OF THE LAW (Random House, 2003), at 58–64.
15 Hon. Justice Michael Kirby AC CMG, *7th Annual Grotius Lecture: International Law – The Impact on National Constitutions*, Delivered to the Annual Meeting of the American Society of International Law, Washington, DC, Mar. 29, 2005; Kirby, *Constitutional Interpretation and Original Intent – A Form of Ancestor Worship?* MELBOURNE UNIVERSITY LAW REVIEW 24 (2000): 2. The description derives from a comment of Justice William Ian Corneil Binnie, of the Supreme Court of Canada.
16 Teleology is, as defined by the OXFORD ENGLISH DICTIONARY, "The doctrine or study of ends or final causes, especially as related to the evidences of design or purpose in nature."
17 *US – Shrimp, supra* note 13.
18 Douglas A. Kysar, *Preferences for Processes: The Process/Product Distinction and the Regulation of Consumer Choice*, HARVARD LAW REVIEW 118 (2004): 525; OECD, *Processes and Production Methods (PPMs): Conceptual Framework and Considerations on Use of PPM-Based Trade Measures* 7, WORKING PAPER OCED/GD(97) 137 (Paris, 1997); Steve Charnovitz, *The Law of Environmental PPMs in the WTO: Debunking the Myth of Illegality*, YALE JOURNAL OF INTERNATIONAL LAW 27 (2002): 59; John H. Jackson, *The Limits of International Trade: Workers' Protection, the Environment and Other Human Rights*, AMERICAN SOCIETY OF INTERNATIONAL

LAW PROCEEDINGS 94 (2000): 222; Sanford E. Gaines, *Processes and Production Methods: How to Produce Sound Policy for Environmental PPM-Based Trade Measures*, COLUMBIA JOURNAL OF ENVIRONMENTAL LAW 27 (2002): 383.
19 *US – Import Prohibition of Certain Shrimp and Shrimp Products*, supra note 13, at para. 2.
20 *See* BEATTY, THE ULTIMATE RULE OF LAW, supra note 1, at 159. *See also* BARAK, PURPOSIVE INTERPRETATION, supra note 1, at 248, 432.
21 *US – Shrimp*, supra note 13, at para. 121.
22 *US – Prohibition of Imports of Tuna and Tuna Products from Canada*, GATT Docs. L/5198 – 29S/91, adopted Feb. 22, 1982; *US – Restrictions on Imports of Tuna*, GATT Docs. DS21/R – 39S/155, adopted Sept. 3, 1991); *US – Restrictions on Imports of Tuna (Tuna II)*, GATT Doc. DS29/R, adopted Jun. 16, 1994.

5.9 Key jurisprudential questions IV: dispute settlement reports and national law
1 For some detail, see section 4.6, *supra*.
2 *See, e.g., EC – Measures Affecting the Prohibition of Asbestos and Asbestos Products*, WTO Doc. WT/DS135/AB/R, adopted Apr. 5, 2001, at para. 374.
3 Art. 31(3)(b), *VCLT*.
4 *Murray v. The Schooner Charming Betsy*, 6 U.S. (2 Cranch) 64 (1804).
5 *See Japan – Taxes on Alcoholic Beverages*, WTO Docs. WT/DS8, 10 & 11/AB/R, adopted Nov. 1, 1996, at 12–14.
6 *Corus Staal BV v. Dept. of Commerce*, Fed. Cir. No. 04–1107, Jan. 21, 2005, 395 F.3d 1343; *The Timken Company v. United States*, Jan. 16, 2004, 354 F.3d 1334.

5.10 Key jurisprudential questions V: compliance and implementation
1 Edith Brown Weiss & Harold Jacobson, *Strengthening Compliance with International Environmental Accords*, in THE POLITICS OF GLOBAL GOVERNANCE: INTERNATIONAL ORGANIZATIONS IN AN INTERDEPENDENT WORLD, Paul F. Diehl ed. (Lynne Rienner Publishers, 1997): 305; ABRAM CHAYES & ANTONIA HANDLER CHAYES, THE NEW SOVEREIGNTY: COMPLIANCE WITH INTERNATIONAL REGULATORY AGREEMENTS (Harvard University Press, 1995); Robert O. Keohane et al., *Legalized Dispute Resolution: Interstate and Transnational*, INTERNATIONAL ORGANIZATION 54 (2000): 457. *See also* Anthony Clark Arend, *Do Legal Rules Matter? International Law and International Politics*, VIRGINIA JOURNAL OF INTERNATIONAL LAW 38 (1998): 107; William C. Bradford, *International Legal Compliance: An Annotated Bibliography*, NORTH CAROLINA JOURNAL OF INTERNATIONAL LAW AND COMMERCIAL REGULATION 30 (2004): 379.
2 *See* sections 1.3 and 2.3, *supra*. A few selected recent and useful works include PETROS C. MAVROIDIS & ALAN O. SYKES EDS., THE WTO AND INTERNATIONAL TRADE LAW (Edward Elgar, 2005); BUGGE THORBJØRN DANIEL, WTO ADJUDICATION (Forlaget Thomson, 2005); FEDERICO ORTINO & ERNST-ULRICH PETERSMANN EDS., THE WTO DISPUTE

SETTLEMENT SYSTEM 1995–2003 (Kluwer Law International, 2004); GIORGIO SACERDOTI, ET AL EDS., THE WTO AT TEN: THE ROLE OF THE DISPUTE SETTLEMENT SYSTEM (Cambridge University Press, 2006); RUFUS YERXA & BRUCE WILSON EDS., KEY ISSUES IN WTO DISPUTE SETTLEMENT: THE FIRST TEN YEARS (Cambridge University Press, 2005). Many articles on WTO DS can be found in the JOURNAL OF INTERNATIONAL ECONOMIC LAW.

3 An example is the standby arrangements of the IMF, by which a member is assured that it will be able to make purchases (drawings) up to a specified amount and during a specified period of time, usually one to two years, provided that the member observes the terms set out in the supporting arrangement. The periodic review reports show the extent to which the standby arrangements have influence on the fiscal, monetary and regulatory policy of the country concerned; *see e.g.* the *8th Review under the Standby Arrangement with Turkey*, IMF Country Report No. 05/163, May 2005, available at www.imf. org/external/pubs/ft/scr/2005/cr05163.pdf, visited Jul. 15, 2005. *See also* SUSAN SCHADLER ED., IMF CONDITIONALITY: EXPERIENCE UNDER STANDBY AND EXTENDED ARRANGEMENTS (International Monetary Fund, 1995).

4 *See, e.g.*, THE INTERNATIONAL LAW COMMISSION'S ARTICLES ON STATE RESPONSIBILITY: INTRODUCTION, TEXT, AND Commentaries, compiled by James Crawford (Cambridge University Press, 2002); *Agora: Future Implication of the Iraq Conflict*, AMERICAN JOURNAL OF INTERNATIONAL LAW 97 (Oct. 2003); *Agora: ICJ Advisory Opinion on Construction of a Wall in the Occupied Palestinian Territory*, AMERICAN JOURNAL OF INTERNATIONAL LAW 99 (Jan. 2005). Beth A. Simmons, *Compliance with International Agreements*, in INTERNATIONAL LAW: CLASSIC AND CONTEMPORARY READINGS, Charlotte Ku & Paul F. Diehl eds. (L. Rienner, 2003): 181.

5 Art. XVI(3), WTO Charter:

> In the event of a conflict between a provision of this Agreement and a provision of any of the Multilateral Trade Agreements, the provision of this Agreement shall prevail to the extent of the conflict.

6 *See* section 5.2, *supra*.
7 *See, e.g.*, Arts. 3(2), 19(2), DSU.
8 *See* discussion of non-violation cases in section 5.2, *supra*.
9 *See Netherlands Measures of Suspension of Obligations to the United States*, Nov. 8, 1952, GATT B.I.S.D. (1st Supp.) at 32 (1953) and subsequent authorizations to 1959. *See* GATT ANALYTICAL INDEX, at 645–649.
10 Art. 19(1), DSU.
11 Art. 3(8), DSU.
12 Art. 22, DSU.
13 Art. 22(6), DSU.
14 *Amendments to the Understanding on Rules and Procedures Governing the Settlement of Disputes*, Proposed Text by Mexico, WTO Doc. TN/DS/W/40, Jan. 27, 2003, at 4.

15 *See* the proposed retaliation list submitted by the European Communities to the WTO Council for Trade in Goods under Art. 12(5) of the Agreement on Safeguards, WTO Doc. G/C/10 G/SG/43, of May 15, 2002.
16 David E. Sanger, *A Blink From the Bush Administration*, THE NEW YORK TIMES, Dec. 5, 2003, at A28.
17 *See, e.g.*, ROBERT LAWRENCE, CRIMES AND PUNISHMENTS? RETALIATION UNDER THE WTO (Institute for International Economics, 2003). *See also* Sutherland, *Future of the WTO*, at para. 214, 221, etc. (expressing much satisfaction with the DS system, and warning against reforms that might "do harm," while nevertheless recommending some modest changes).
18 *See especially* William J. Davey, *The WTO Dispute Settlement System: The First Ten Years*, JIEL 8 (2005): 17. *See also* section 5.5, *supra*.
19 CHAYES, THE NEW SOVEREIGNTY, *supra* note 1. *See also* discussion in section 5.11, *infra*. *See also* section 4.2, *supra*, at note 14.

5.11 Dispute settlement structural problems and proposed reforms

1 *Decision on the Application and Review of The Understanding on Rules and Procedures Governing the Settlement of Disputes*, Uruguay Round ministerial decisions and declarations, available at: www.wto.org/english/docs_e/legal_e/legal_e.htm, visited Mar. 8, 2005.
2 *See* Report by the Chairman Ambassador Peter Balás to the Trade Negotiations Committee, WTO Doc. TN/DS/9, Jun. 6, 2003. *See also* the *Synopsis of Proposals for Reform of the DSU Made in the Course of the Doha Development Agenda, in* WTO LEGAL TEXTS, at 408, available at www.law.georgetown.edu/iiel/research/projects/dsureview/synopsis.html, visited Jul. 5, 2005; *Proposal to Amend Certain Provisions of the Understanding on Rules and Procedures Governing the Settlement of Disputes (DSU) Pursuant to Article X of the Marrakesh Agreement Establishing the World Trade Organization*, WTO Doc. WT/GC/W/410/Rev.1, Oct. 26, 2001 (and more Revs.), *VIII Summit Meeting of the Heads of State and Government of the Group of Fifteen*, WTO Doc. WT/MIN(98)/8, May 20, 1998; *World Trade Organization Issues in Dispute Settlement*, GAO Doc., GAO/NSIAD-00-210, Aug. 2000.
3 *See Doha Ministerial Declaration of 20 November 2001*, WTO Doc. WT/MIN(01)/DEC/1, at para. 47.
4 *See* Sutherland, *The Future of the WTO*. *See also* JIEL Vol. 8, Issues 2 and 3 (2005), each containing a *Mini-Symposium on the Consultative Board's Report on the Future of the WTO*, with introduction by William J. Davey, JIEL 8 (2005), at 287.
5 *See* discussions in sections 5.1 and 5.5, *supra*.
6 *See* the cost analysis of the European Commission, *Non-Paper: The Benefits of Moving from Ad Hoc to More Permanent Panellists*, Jul. 10, 2002, available at http://trade-info.cec.eu.int/doclib/docs/2003/october/tradoc_111221.pdf, visited Jul. 5, 2005.
7 *See Appellate Body Annual Report for 2004*, WTO Doc. WT/AB/3, 25 Jan. 2005.

8 *Negotiations on Improvements and Clarifications of the Dispute Settlement Understanding on Improving Flexibility and Member Control in WTO Dispute Settlement*, Textual Contribution by Chile and the United States, WTO Doc. TN/DS/W/52, Mar. 14, 2003, at 2.
9 *See* CLAUDE E. BARFIELD, FREE TRADE, SOVEREIGNTY, DEMOCRACY (AEI Press, 2001), at 127. *See also* Richard H. Steinberg, *Judicial Lawmaking at the WTO: Discursive, Constitutional and Political Restraints*, AJIL 98 (2004): 247, 273.
10 *See* section 4.5, *supra*.
11 *See* "consensus" discussion at section 4.5, *supra*.
12 Sutherland, *The Future of the WTO*, at para. 251:

> A more constructive approach might be to occasionally select particular findings for in-depth analysis by a reasonably impartial, special expert group of the DSB, so as to provide a measured report of constructive criticism for the information of the WTO system, including the Appellate Body and panels.

13 *See* section 5.7.a, *supra*.
14 *See, e.g.*, James McCall Smith, *Compliance Bargaining in the WTO: Ecuador and the Bananas Dispute*, prepared for a Conference on Developing Countries and the Trade Negotiation Process, UNCTAD, Geneva, Nov. 6–7, 2003, available at www.ruig-gian.org/conf/files/smith percent20paper.pdf, visited Jul. 5, 2005; *General Council – Minutes of Meeting – Held in the Centre William Rappard on 31 October and 1 November 2001*, WTO Doc. WT/GC/M/71, Dec. 13, 2001. Eliza Patterson, *The US-EU Bananas Dispute*, ASIL INSIGHTS (Feb. 2001), available at www.asil.org/insights/insigh63.htm, visited Jul. 5, 2005; Petros C. Mavroidis, *Proposals for Reform of Article 22 of the DSU: Reconsidering the Sequencing Issue and Suspension of Concessions*, in THE WTO DISPUTE SETTLEMENT SYSTEM, 1995–2003, Frederico Ortino & Ernst-Ulrich Petersmann eds. (Kluwer Law International, 2004): 61.

5.12 Perspectives and conclusions for Part II: the lessons of the GATT/WTO system
1 *See* section 5.2, *supra*.
2 *See* section 4.5, *supra*, and Sutherland, *The Future of the WTO*.
3 Georg C. Umbricht, *An "Amicus Curiae Brief" on Amicus Curiae Briefs at the WTO*, JIEL 4 (Dec 2001), 773–794. *See Minutes of the Special Session of the Dispute Settlement Body of 16–18 December 2002*, WTO Doc. TN/DS/M/7, Jun. 26, 2003; *also* section 5.4, *supra*.
4 *See* discussion at section 5.11, *supra*.

6 Policy analytical approaches and thought experiments

1 *US – Sections 301–310 of the Trade Act of 1974*, WTO Doc. WT/DS152/R, adopted 27 Jan. 2000, at paras. 7.71 & 7.73, at 320. *See* discussion in section 5.7, *supra*.

6.1 Introduction to Part III and Chapter 6

2 *See* discussion in section 2.3, *supra*.
3 *See* discussion in Chapter 3, *supra*.

6.2 The sovereignty conundrum: slicing the concept

1 *See* John Mikhail et al., *Toward a Universal Moral Grammar, in* PROCEEDINGS, TWENTIETH ANNUAL CONFERENCE OF THE COGNITIVE SCIENCE SOCIETY, Morton Ann Gernsbacher & Sharon J. Derry eds. (Lawrence Erlbaum, 1998): 1250; JOHN MIKHAIL, RAWLS' LINGUISTIC ANALOGY: UNIVERSAL MORAL GRAMMAR AND THE FOUNDATIONS OF HUMAN RIGHTS (forthcoming, Cambridge University Press); NOAM CHOMSKY, KNOWLEDGE OF LANGUAGE: ITS NATURE, ORIGIN AND USE (Praeger, 1986).
2 *See* Schachter list in section 2.3, *supra*.
3 *See* IAN BROWNLIE, PRINCIPLES OF PUBLIC INTERNATIONAL LAW, 6th ed. (Oxford University Press, 2003), at 553–555; *see generally*, as a general reference on the history of the right to self-determination: MICHELINE ISHAY, THE HISTORY OF HUMAN RIGHTS: FROM ANCIENT TIMES TO THE GLOBALIZATION ERA (University of California Press, 2004), at 173–244.
4 *See* sections 3.1 and 3.2, *supra*.
5 The ASIL president, Anne-Marie Slaughter, is one of the few to recognize the importance of this question and to offer preliminary thoughts on an answer. She suggests that the United Nations must face up to this question, particularly in the context of human rights, and she enumerates three conditions that should be present as prerequisites to UN action, namely "1) possession of weapons of mass destruction or clear and convincing evidence of attempts to gain such weapons; 2) grave and systematic human rights abuses sufficient to demonstrate the absence of any internal constraints on government behavior; and 3) evidence of aggressive intent with regard to other nations." Anne-Marie Slaughter, *Opinion, A Chance to Reshape the U.N.*, WASHINGTON POST, Apr. 13, 2003, at B7. *See also* section 7.8, *infra*.
6 *Doctrine of the International Community*, speech by British Prime Minister Tony Blair to the Economic Club, Chicago, Illinois, Apr. 24, 1999, available at www.number-10.gov.uk/output/Page1297.asp, visited Jul. 21, 2005, quoted in section 3.2, *supra*.

6.3 Towards a policy analysis matrix: a three-dimensional puzzle (at least)

1 *See* sections 2.5 and 3.3, *supra*.
2 *See* discussion of power allocation in section 3.3, *supra*.
3 *See* section 3.3, *supra*.
4 *See, e.g., The Emergence of Collective Preferences in International Trade: Implications for Regulating Globalisation*, speech by Pascal Lamy, EU Trade Commissioner, at the *Conference on Collective preferences and global governance: what future for the multilateral trading system?*, Brussels, Sept. 15, 2004, available at http://tradeinfo.cec.eu.int/doclib/docs/2004/september/tradoc_118929.pdf;

Steve Charnovitz, *An Analysis of Pascal Lamy's Proposal on Collective Preferences*, GWU LAW SCHOOL PUBLIC LAW RESEARCH PAPER, No. 122 (Dec. 2004), available at http://ssrn.com/abstract'639322, visited Apr. 12, 2005; Letter from Jurgen Strube, of UNICE, to Commissioner Lamy, of Apr. 26, 2004, available at http://wto.unice.org/Content/Default.asp?PageID'12, visited Jun. 28, 2005. *See also* Reinhard Quick & Andreas Blüthner, *Has the Appellate Body Erred? An Appraisal and Criticism of the Ruling in the WTO Hormones Case*, JIEL 2 (1999): 603.

5 *See* discussions of balancing in sections 5.3 and 5.12, *supra*. Often the term "proportionality" is used in ways similar to "balancing." There is substantial literature on these concepts, particularly in national supreme court contexts. *See, e.g.*, Vicki C. Jackson, *Ambivalent Resistance and Comparative Constitutionalism: Opening up the Conversation on Proportionality, Rights and Federalism*, UNIVERSITY OF PENNSYLVANIA JOURNAL OF CONSTITUTIONAL LAW 10 (1999): 583; EVELYN ELLIS (ED.), THE PRINCIPLE OF PROPORTIONALITY IN THE LAWS OF EUROPE (Hart Publishing, 1999); DAVID M. BEATTY, THE ULTIMATE RULE OF LAW (Oxford University Press, 2004). The word "proportionality" has been used in the WTO jurisprudence frequently (in at least nineteen first-level panel reports and three Appellate Body reports), *Results of word match search of all WTO Jurisprudence*, undertaken by the author, July 2005.

6.4 Economics and markets: a thought experiment about market failure in the era of globalization

1 For a previous article on the economic analysis of power allocation, see John H. Jackson, *Global Economics and International Economic Law*, JIEL 1 (1998): 1.
2 See, e.g., RICHARD LIPSEY, PAUL COURANT, DOUGLAS PURVIS, & PETER STEINER, MICROECONOMICS, 12th ed. (Addison Wesley, 1998), at 207. *See also* JOSEPH E. STIGLITZ, GLOBALIZATION AND ITS DISCONTENTS (W.W. Norton, 2002).
3 International Competition Policy Advisory Committee, *Final Report to the Attorney General and Assistant Attorney General for Antitrust* (US Department of Justice, 2000), available at www.usdoj.gov/atr/icpac/finalreport.htm, visited Apr. 12, 2005.
4 Eleanor M. Fox, *International Anti-Trust and the Doha Dome*, VIRGINIA JOURNAL OF INTERNATIONAL LAW 43 (2003): 911.
5 Based on word match searches for occurrences of *monopoly, competition*, and *competitive*, undertaken by the author, July 2005.
6 Art. 13, *WTO Agreement on Agriculture, in UR Texts*. *See also* Richard H. Steinberg & Timothy E. Josling, *When Peace Ends: the Vulnerability of EC and US Agricultural Subsidies to WTO Legal Challenge*, JIEL 6 (2003): 369. On the scope of the Peace Clause, *see also US – Subsidies on Upland Cotton*, WTO Doc. WT/DS267/AB/R, adopted Mar. 21, 2005, at 318–394.

Notes to pages 222–224

6.5 Thinking constitutional

1 The term "acquis" is most frequently used in the context of the European Union, where it refers to the entire body of European law that needs to be respected by every member state. During the process of enlargement, the *acquis* was divided into thirty-one chapters for the purpose of negotiation between the European Union and the candidate member states. *See* http://news.bbc.co.uk/1/hi/in_depth/europe/euro-glossary/1216329.stm, visited Jul. 7, 2005. The term has also been used e.g. to describe the achievements of the Council of Europe (*Section 12, Parliamentary Assembly of the Council of Europe Resolution 1290*).

2 For example, the term is often used for structural documents of business entities, non-governmental organizations, sub-federal or regional government levels, super-national regions (e.g., the European Union), and relatively informal societies such as gardening clubs or stamp collectors' associations. A considerable literature regarding "constitutionalism" is developing. A small selection of recent interesting works relevant to "international" subjects includes: Thomas Cottier & Maya Hertig, *The Prospects of 21st Century Constitutionalism, in* MAX PLANCK YEARBOOK OF UNITED NATIONS LAW 7, Armin von Bogdandy & Rüdiger Wolfrum eds. (Brill, 2004); CHISTIAN JOERGES ET AL. EDS., TRANSNATIONAL GOVERNANCE AND CONSTITUTIONALISM (Hart, 2004); DAN SAROOSHI, INTERNATIONAL ORGANIZATIONS AND THEIR EXERCISE OF SOVEREIGN POWERS (Oxford University Press, 2005); DEBORAH Z. CASS, THE CONSTITUTIONALIZATION OF THE WORLD TRADE ORGANIZATION (Oxford University Press, 2005).

3 *Treaty Establishing a Constitution for Europe*, 2004 O.J. (C 310), 1. On the treaty process, *see, e.g.*, Manuel Medina-Ortega, *A Constitution for an Enlarged Europe*, GEORGIA JOURNAL OF INTERNATIONAL AND COMPARATIVE LAW 32 (2004): 393; *The European Union's Constitutional Treaty: The Voters' Charter*, THE ECONOMIST (LONDON), 24 Apr. 2004; *One Summit Conquered but it is Still a Hard Climb to the Peak of Ratification*, FINANCIAL TIMES (LONDON), 21 Jun. 2004; *The European Union Constitution: Dead, But Not Yet Buried*, THE ECONOMIST (LONDON), 4 Jun. 2005; George Parker, et al., *After the Votes: Europe's Leaders Confront the Consequences of "the Wrong Answer"*, FINANCIAL TIMES (LONDON), 3 Jun. 2005, at 17.

4 *See* section 5.12, *supra*.

5 *See* section 2.3, *supra*.

6 *See* Jörg Kammerhofer, *Uncertainty in the Formal Sources of International Law: Customary International Law and Some of Its Problems*, EUROPEAN JOURNAL OF INTERNATIONAL LAW 15 (2004): 523; Hugh Thirlway, *The Sources of International Law, in* INTERNATIONAL LAW, Malcolm D. Evans (Oxford University Press, 2003): 117; various articles in MARTTI KOSKENNIEMI ED., SOURCES OF INTERNATIONAL LAW (Ashgate, 2000); OSCAR SCHACHTER,

337

INTERNATIONAL LAW IN THEORY AND PRACTICE (M. Nijhoff Publishers, 1982), at 58.
7 VICKI C. JACKSON & MARK TUSHNET, COMPARATIVE CONSTITUTIONAL LAW (Foundation Press, 1999), at 709–987; LAURENCE H. TRIBE, AMERICAN CONSTITUTIONAL LAW, 3rd ed. (Foundation Press, 2000).
8 T. ALEXANDER ALEINIKOFF, SEMBLANCES OF SOVEREIGNTY: THE CONSTITUTION, THE STATE, AND AMERICAN CITIZENSHIP (Harvard University Press, 2002).
9 KAREN J. ALTER, ESTABLISHING THE SUPREMACY OF EUROPEAN LAW: THE MAKING OF AN INTERNATIONAL RULE OF LAW IN EUROPE (Oxford University Press, 2001). *See also* WALTER VAN GERVEN, THE EUROPEAN UNION: A POLITY OF STATES AND PEOPLES (Stanford University Press, 2005).
10 *See also* discussion in section 5.8, *supra*.
11 *See Articles of Agreement of the International Monetary Fund*, Jul. 22, 1944, 60 Stat. 1301; 2 U.N.T.S. 39; *Articles of Agreement of the International Bank for Reconstruction and Development*, Jul. 22, 1944, 60 Stat. 1440, 2. U.N.T.S. 134, amended Dec. 16, 1965, 16 U.S.T. 1942, 606 U.N.T.S. 294. *See also* section 4.3, *supra*.
12 THOMAS M. FRANCK, RECOURSE TO FORCE: STATE ACTION AGAINST THREATS AND ARMED ATTACKS, Hersch Lauterpacht Memorial Lectures Series (Cambridge University Press, 2002).
13 *See* sections 4.2, 5.8, and 5.12, *supra*. *See also* JOHN H. JACKSON, THE WORLD TRADE ORGANIZATION: CONSTITUTION AND JURISPRUDENCE (Chatham House Papers, 1998).
14 *See, e.g.*, Robert O. Keohane, *Governance in a Partially Globalized World*, in GOVERNING GLOBALIZATION: POWER, AUTHORITY, AND GLOBAL GOVERNANCE, David Held & Anthony McGrew, eds. (Polity, 2002): 325; and Robert O. Keohane, *Governance in a Partially Globalized World: Presidential Address, American Political Science Association, 2000*, AMERICAN POLITICAL SCIENCE REVIEW 95 (2001): 1.
15 CLARE OVEY & ROBIN WHITE, JACOBS & WHITE, the EUROPEAN CONVENTION ON HUMAN RIGHTS, 3d ed. (Oxford University Press, 2002), at 210–215; STEVEN GREER, THE MARGIN OF APPRECIATION: INTERPRETATION AND DISCRETION UNDER THE EUROPEAN CONVENTION ON HUMAN RIGHTS (Council of Europe, 2000). For a critical perspective, *see* Jeffrey A. Brauch, *The Margin of Appreciation and the Jurisprudence of the European Court of Human Rights: Threat to the Rule of Law*, COLUMBIA JOURNAL OF EUROPEAN LAW 11 (2004): 113.
16 *See, e.g.*, the *Second Interim Report of the Independent Inquiry Committee into the United Nations Oil-For-Food Programme*, Mar. 29, 2005, available at www.iic-offp.org/documents/InterimReportMar2005.pdf, visited Jul. 7, 2005, or the Second Report by the Committee of Independent Experts, *Reform of the*

Commission – *Analysis of current practice and proposals for tackling mismanagement, irregularities and fraud*, 10 Sept. 1999, available at www.europarl.eu.int/experts/pdf/rep 2–1en.pdf, visited Jul. 7, 2005.

17 *See* Chapters 2 and 3 and section 5.12, *supra*. *See also* PAUL HIRST & GRAHAME THOMPSON, GLOBALIZATION IN QUESTION: THE INTERNATIONAL ECONOMY AND THE POSSIBILITY OF GOVERNANCE (Polity Press, 1996), at 170–194; James Bacchus, *A Few Thoughts on Legitimacy, Democracy, and the WTO*, JIEL 7 (2004): 667.

18 *See* section 7.6, *infra*, and section 5.6, *supra*. *See also* John H. Jackson, *Status of Treaties in Domestic Legal Systems: A Policy Analysis*, AJIL 86 (1992): 310.

6.6 The growing importance of juridical institutions

1 Motivations for including new subject matters under GATT (and now the WTO) often include the desire for better treaty implementation. This was manifested in the 1980s activity to include services and intellectual property in the Uruguay Round negotiations. On this topic, *see* JOHN CROOME, RESHAPING THE WORLD TRADE SYSTEM – A HISTORY OF THE URUGUAY ROUND, 2d ed. (Kluwer Law International, 1999), at 99–116; Lynne Saylor & John Beton, *Why the TRIPS Agreement?*, *in* INTELLECTUAL PROPERTY & INTERNATIONAL TRADE, International Chamber of Commerce ed. (International Chamber of Commerce, 1996): 12.

2 *See* Chapter 5, *supra*.

3 In 1967, the three European Communities (European Coal and Steel Community (established in 1951), and the 1957 European Atomic Energy Community and European Economic Community) were merged into the European Community. There was established a single Commission and a single Council of Ministers as well as the European Parliament. In 1992, the Treaty of Maastricht created the European Union by adding intergovernmental co-operation to the existing Community system. *See* WALTER VAN GERVEN, THE EUROPEAN UNION: A POLITY OF STATES AND PEOPLES (Stanford University Press, 2005); MICHAEL BURGESS, FEDERALISM AND EUROPEAN UNION: THE BUILDING OF EUROPE, 1950–2000 (Routledge, 2000); WIM F.V. VANTHOOR, A CHRONOLOGICAL HISTORY OF THE EUROPEAN UNION 1946–1998 (Edward Elgar, 1999).

4 One might argue, however, that the European Union has developed into an organization closer to a federalist state than an "international" organization in the traditional sense. *See* SIONAIDH DOUGLAS-SCOTT, CONSTITUTIONAL LAW OF THE EUROPEAN UNION (Longman, 2002), at 155–198; Gretchen M. MacMillan, *The European Union: Is It a Supranational State in the Making? in* FEDERALISM DOOMED?: EUROPEAN FEDERALISM BETWEEN INTEGRATION AND SEPARATION, Andreas Heinemann-Grüder ed. (Berghahn, 2002): 63.

5 The International Tribunal for the Law of the Sea has so far decided thirteen cases. More information is available at www.itlos.org, visited Jul. 11, 2005.

6 The rules for arbitration and mediation of intellectual property disputes between private parties at the WIPO Arbitration and Mediation Center are available at www.wipo.int/freepublications/en/arbitration/446/ wipo_pub_446.pdf, visited Jul. 11, 2005. So far, the Center has received thirty-five requests for mediation and twenty-six requests for arbitration (http://arbiter.wipo.int/center/caseload.html, visited Jul. 11, 2005). *See also* Frederick M. Abbott, *Distributed Governance at the WTO – WIPO: An Evolving Model for Open-Architecture Integrated Governance, in* NEW DIRECTIONS IN INTERNATIONAL ECONOMIC LAW – ESSAYS IN HONOUR OF JOHN H. JACKSON, Marco Bronckers & Reinhard Quick, eds. (Kluwer Law International, 2000): 291.

7 *North American Free Trade Agreement*, Dec. 17, 1992. Can.-Mex.-U.S., 32 ILM 289 & 605 (1993) (entered into force Jan. 1, 1994), at Chapters 19 & 20. Chapter 11 allows a NAFTA investor who alleges that a host government has breached its investment obligations under this chapter to have recourse to the World Bank's International Centre for the Settlement of Investment Disputes (ICSID); ICSID's Additional Facility Rules; the rules of the United Nations Commission for International Trade Law (UNCITRAL); or to choose the remedies available in the host country's domestic courts. Chapter 19 contains notably a mechanism to provide an alternative to judicial review by domestic courts of final determinations in antidumping and countervailing duty cases, with review by independent binational panels whose decisions may be reviewed by independent binational panels. Chapter 20 contains government-to-government dispute settlement provisions that are applicable to all disputes regarding the interpretation or application of NAFTA. In consultation with the parties, the panels may be assisted by scientific review boards which can provide a written report on any factual issue concerning environmental, health, safety, or other scientific matters.

8 *See* Chapter 22, *US – Chile Free Trade Agreement* (Final Text) (Jun. 6, 2003), entered into force Jan. 1, 2004, available at www.ustr.gov/assets/Trade_ Agreements/Bilateral/Chile_FTA/Final_Texts/asset_upload_file683_4016. pdf, visited Jul. 11, 2005; Chapter 15, *US – Singapore Free Trade Agreement* (Final Text) (6 May 2003), entered into force Jan. 1, 2004, available at www.ustr.gov/assets/Trade_Agreements/Bilateral/Singapore_FTA/Final_T exts/asset_upload_file708_4036.pdf, visited Jul. 11, 2005; Chapter 21, *US – Australia Free Trade Agreement* (Final Text) (May 18, 2004), entered into force Jan. 1, 2005, available at www.ustr.gov/assets/Trade_Agreements/Bilateral/ Australia_FTA/Final_Text/asset_upload_file959_5166.pdf, visited 11 Jul. 2005; Chapter 20, *Central America-Dominican Republic-United States Free Trade Agreement* (Final Text) (28 May 2004), available at www.ustr.gov/ assets/ Trade_Agreements/Bilateral/CAFTA/CAFTA-DR_Final_Texts/asset_ upload_file85_3940.pdf,visited Jul. 11, 2005

9 *Treaty Establishing a Common Market between the Argentine Republic, the Federal Republic of Brazil, the Republic of Paraguay and the Republic of Uruguay*,

Mar. 26, 1991, 30 I.L.M. 1041 (establishing Mercosur – Mercado Comun del Sur).

10 *Mercosur Protocol of Brasilia for the Solution of Controversies*, Decision 1/91, Art. 23 (Dec. 17, 1991) 36 I.L.M. 691 (1997) (English Translation); the Protocol provides for an arbitral procedure (Chapter IV) and a procedure for private party complaints (Chapter V).

11 Based on private conversations with the author.

12 *See, e.g.*, Art. 56 on the Settlement of Disputes, in the revised International Health Regulations of 2005, WHO Doc. A58/55 of May 23, 2005.

13 Jonathan I. Charney, Is International Law Threatened by Multiple International Tribunals, Hague Academy of International Law 271 (Martinus Nijhoff, 1999). *See also Symposium: Diversity or Cacophony?: New Sources of Norms in International Law,* Michigan Journal of International Law 25 (Summer 2004): 845, including John H. Jackson, *Varied Policies of International Juridical Bodies – Reflections on Theory and Practice*, at 869. Further, the International Law Commission has established the *Study Group on Fragmentation of International Law: Difficulties arising from the Diversification and Expansion of International Law. See* its current work, e.g., the *Report on the Work of the International Law Commission*, 55th Session 2003, General Assembly Official Records Fifty-eighth Session, Supplement No. 10 (A/58/10), Chapter X.

14 Claude E. Barfield, Free Trade, Sovereignty, Democracy: The Future of the World Trade Organization (AEI Press, 2001), at 112–114; William A. Davey, *WTO Dispute Settlement: Segregating the Useful Political Aspects and Avoiding Over-Legalization, in* New Directions in International Economic Law, *supra* note 6, at 291. *See also* (especially with regard to the TRIPS agreement) Kal Raustiala, *Compliance and Effectiveness in International Regulatory Cooperation,* Case Western Reserve Journal of International Law 32 (2000): 387.

15 *See, e.g., US – Subsidies on Upland Cotton*, WTO Doc. WT/DS267/R, adopted Mar. 25, 2005, which first-level panel report, with addenda, amounts to 2,051 pages and *US – Definitive Safeguard Measures on Imports of Certain Steel Products*, WTO Docs. WT/DS248, 249, 251, 252, 253, 254, 258, 259/R, which first-level panel report amounts to 970 pages including addenda.

16 *See, e.g.*, case brought by Costa Rica against the United States: *US – Restrictions on Imports of Cotton and Man-Made Fibre Underwear*, WTO Doc. WT/DS24/AB/R, adopted Feb. 25, 1997; case brought by Brazil against the United States: *US – Subsidies on Upland Cotton*, WTO Doc. WT/DS267/AB/R, adopted Mar. 21, 2005; and case brought by Thailand and Brazil (and Australia) against the EC: *EC – Export Subsidies on Sugar*, WTO Docs. WT/DS283/R and WT/DS/283/AB/R, adopted May 19, 2005. *See* sections 4.3 & 5.5, *supra*.

17 *See* section 5.11, *supra*.

Notes to pages 229–234

18 *See* WTO *Cotton* & *Sugar* cases, *supra* note 16.
19 *See* developments in current Doha Round, sections 4.3 and 5.5, *supra*.
20 *See* section 4.3, *supra*, at note 57.
21 *US – Tax Treatment for "Foreign Sales Corporations,"* WTO Doc. WT/DS108/AB/R, adopted 20 Mar. 2000. Canada was a Third Party in this case.
22 *See* section 5.4, *supra*, at note 20.
23 *See* discussion of rule orientation in section 4.2, *supra*.
24 *See* section 5.3, *supra*.
25 This can be contrasted on the one hand to the very significant, yet more specialized jurisprudence of the European and the Inter-American Courts of Human Rights and the International Criminal Tribunals for Rwanda and the former Yugoslavia or, on the other hand, the more technical International Claims Tribunals and the International Tribunal for the Law of the Sea. On the various international courts, *see* MARK W. JANIS ED., INTERNATIONAL COURTS FOR THE TWENTY-FIRST CENTURY (Martinus Nijhoff, 1992); JEAN ALLAIN, A CENTURY OF INTERNATIONAL ADJUDICATION: THE RULE OF LAW AND ITS LIMITS (T.M.C. Asser Press, 2000).
26 *See* section 5.5, *supra*.
27 *See* sections 5.6–5.10, *supra*.

6.7 Interface theory: managing globalization in a world of wide variation

1 *See* section 3.2, *supra*.
2 In his book THE LEXUS AND THE OLIVE TREE (Anchor Books, 2000), Thomas Friedman describes the "electronic herd" (a combination of institutions and millions of individuals), whose investment decisions, carried out by the click of a mouse, affect the fortunes of nations, having impacts as significant as triggering the downfall of governments. *See, e.g., Co-existence Between Public Policy and Free Trade: Can We Achieve Good Protectionism?*, speech of Pascal Lamy, at Conference of the Greens/European Free Alliance at the European Parliament, Brussels, Mar. 5, 2004, available at http://europa.eu.int/comm/archives/commission_1999_2004/lamy/speeches_articles/spla21_en.htm, visited Apr. 12, 2005. Many examples exist. See DALE D. MURPHY, THE STRUCTURE OF REGULATORY COMPETITION: CORPORATIONS AND PUBLIC POLICIES IN A GLOBAL ECONOMY (Oxford University Press, 2004).
3 JACKSON ET AL., CASEBOOK, at 679, 678–680. *See also* John H. Jackson, *Perspectives on the Jurisprudence of International Trade: Costs and Benefits of Legal Procedures in the United States*, MICHIGAN LAW REVIEW 82 (1984): 1570.
4 *See* Sutherland, *The Future of the WTO*, at Chapter VII.

7 Illustrative applications

1 Sutherland, *The Future of the WTO*, at 29, para. 112.

7.1 Illustrative applications – grappling with detail and diversity

7.2 The WTO and its "constitution": institutional detail and dynamic evolution

1. Art. IX.2, WTO Charter.
2. Art. X, WTO Charter.
3. John H. Jackson, *Dispute Settlement and the WTO: Emerging Problems*, JIEL 1 (1998): 329. *See also* various articles by this author collected in JOHN H. JACKSON, THE JURISPRUDENCE OF THE GATT AND THE WTO: INSIGHTS ON TREATY LAW AND ECONOMIC RELATIONS (Cambridge University Press, 2000). *See* sections 2.3 and 5.8, *supra*.
4. John H. Jackson, *The WTO "Constitution" and Proposed Reforms: Seven "Mantras" Revisited*, JIEL 4 (2001): 67.
5. *See* section 5.10, *supra*.
6. *See* section 5.7, *supra*. *See also* Claus-Dieter Ehlermann, *Some Personal Experiences as Member of the Appellate Body of the WTO*, POLICY PAPER 2002/9 (European University Institute, Robert Schuman Centre, 2002).

7.3 Investments and international rules

1. For an overview of the rule governing foreign investment and expropriation of foreign property under international law, *see* IAN BROWNLIE, PRINCIPLES OF PUBLIC INTERNATIONAL LAW, 6th ed. (Oxford University Press, 2003), at 497–527; LORI F. DAMROSCH, ET AL, INTERNATIONAL LAW: CASES & MATERIALS, 4th ed. (West Group 2001), at 775–787; Gerhard Loibl, *International Economic Law*, in INTERNATIONAL LAW, Malcolm D. Evans ed. (Oxford University Press, 2003): 689.
2. AMERICAN LAW INSTITUTE, RESTATEMENT OF THE LAW (Third), Foreign Relations Law of the United States (1987), § 712.
3. *See* Oscar Schachter, *Compensation for Expropriation*, AMERICAN JOURNAL OF INTERNATIONAL LAW 78 (1984): 121; Andrew T. Guzman, *Why LDCs sign treaties that hurt them: Explaining the Popularity of Bilateral Investment Treaties*, VIRGINIA JOURNAL OF INTERNATIONAL LAW 38 (1999): 639, 644–651; A. F. M. Maniruzzaman, *Expropriation of Alien Property and the Principle of Non-Discrimination in International Law on Foreign Investment: An Overview*, JOURNAL OF TRANSNATIONAL LAW & POLICY 8 (1998): 57.
4. *See* David Kinley & Junko Tadaki, *From Talk to Walk: The Emergence of Human Rights Responsibilities for Corporations at International Law*, VIRGINIA JOURNAL OF INTERNATIONAL LAW 44 (2004): 931; Elisa Westfield, *Globalization, Governance, and Multinational Enterprise Responsibility: Corporate Codes of Conduct in the 21st Century*, VIRGINIA JOURNAL OF INTERNATIONAL LAW 42 (2002): 1075, 1082; PETER MUCHLINSKI, MULTINATIONAL ENTERPRISES AND THE LAW (Blackwell, 1995): 3; Steven R. Ratner, *Corporations and Human Rights: A Theory of Legal Responsibility*, YALE LAW JOURNAL 111 (2001): 443, 460.
5. *See, e.g.*, MARTIN WOLF, WHY GLOBALIZATION WORKS (Yale University Press, 2004): 221–248; JAGDISH BHAGWATI, IN DEFENSE OF GLOBALIZATION (Oxford University Press, 2004): 51–195.

6 The first bilateral investment treaty was signed by Germany and Pakistan in 1959. *See* for the history of BITs RUDOLF DOLZER & MARGRETE STEVENS, BILATERAL INVESTMENT TREATIES (M. Nijhoff, 1995), at 1–19. For an overview of existing BITs *see* the database maintained by the UN Conference on Trade and Development (UNCTAD) at www.unctadxi.org/templates/DocSearch____779.aspx, visited Oct. 6, 2004.

7 There are currently over 2,200 bilateral investment treaties in force, data available at www.unctad.org/Templates/WebFlyer.asp?intItemID'3150&lang'1, visited Aug. 1, 2004. *See also* UNCTAD, World Investment Report 2004: The Shift Towards Services, avail at www.unctad.org/Templates/webflyer.asp?docid'5209&intItemID'3235&lang'1&mode'highlights, visited Sep. 2, 2004.

8 On the history of FCNs, *see* Kenneth J. Vandevelde, The Bilateral Investment Treaty Program of the United States, CORNELL INTERNATIONAL LAW JOURNAL 21 (1988): 201, 203–208; for the FCN treaties still in force, *see* www.tcc.mac.doc.gov/cgi-bin/doit.cgi?207:64:104662438, visited Oct. 14, 2004.

9 Founded in 1960 through the Convention on the Organisation for Economic Cooperation and Development. *See* www.oecd.org, visited Oct. 13, 2004.

10 The draft Multilateral Investment Agreement can be found at www.oecd.org/dataoecd/46/40/1895712.pdf, visited Oct. 6, 2004.

11 The OECD currently has thirty member states, nineteen of which are EU member states. Mexico and Turkey are the only members that qualify as developing countries, *see* www.oecd.org/about/, visited Jun. 22, 2005. South Korea has been a member of the OECD since 12 Dec. 1996; as a "more advanced developing country in transition," it is still recognized by the OECD on the list of country recipients of aid.

12 *See, e.g.*, The Contribution of Japan: Consideration Of The Necessity Of Multilateral Investment Rules From Diversified Viewpoints, WTO Doc. WT/WGTI/W/158, Apr. 7, 2003; Submission by the European Community and its Member States of May 30, 1997, WTO Doc. WT/WGTI/W/1; and The Position Laid Out Regarding a Future MIA in the WTO Framework at http://europa.eu.int/comm/trade/miti/invest/ecprop_mai.htm, visited Oct. 14, 2004.

13 The third WTO Ministerial Conference was held in Seattle, United States, on Nov. 30–Dec. 3, 1999. Further documents regarding this Ministerial Conference can be found at www.wto.org/english/thewto_e/minist_e/min99_e/min99_e.htm, visited Oct. 13, 2004. *See also* section 4.3, *supra*.

14 The fourth WTO Ministerial Conference was held in Doha, Qatar, on Nov. 9–14, 2001. *See* Concluding Ministerial Statement WTO Doc. WT/MIN(01)/DEC/1, 20 Nov. 2001. For the terms of the declaration regarding trade and investment *See* www.wto.org/english/thewto_e/minist_e/min01_e/mindecl_e.htm#tradeinvestment, visited 6 Oct. 2004. *See also* section 4.3, *supra*.

Notes to pages 242–245

15 JACKSON, ET AL, CASEBOOK, at 1223. *See also* Doha Ministerial Declaration, *id.*
16 The Fifth WTO Ministerial Conference was held in Cancun, Mexico, from Sept. 10 to 14, 2003. *See* Concluding Ministerial Statement, WTO Doc. WT/MIN(03)/20, 23 Sept. 2003. *See also* section 4.3, *supra*.
17 The so called "Singapore Issues" comprise investment, competition policy, transparency in government procurement, and facilitated market access. Their denomination stems partly from their mention in the Ministerial Declaration of the First WTO Ministerial Conference in Singapore in 1996; *see* www.wto.org/english/thewto_e/minist_e/min96_e/wtodec_e.htm, visited Oct. 14, 2004). The issues were mandated to working groups for further examination.
18 Decision Adopted by the General Council on August 1, 2004, WTO Doc. WT/L/579, Aug. 2, 2004.
19 Thomas Wälde, *Treaties and Regulatory Risk in Infrastructure Investment*, JOURNAL OF WORLD TRADE 32 (2000): 1,12. Daniel Schwanen, Chilling Out: The MAI is on Ice but Global Investment Remains Hot at www.cdhowe.org/pdf/Sch-03.pdf, visited Oct. 14, 2004.
20 *See* section 4.7, *supra*.
21 *See Developing Countries Cool to All Singapore Issues but Trade Facilitation*, INSIDE U.S. TRADE, Dec. 19, 2003, and *Developing Countries Maintain Rigid Opposition to Singapore Issues* (Sept.12, 2003), at www.insidetrade.com, visited Oct. 13, 2004.

7.4 Environmental policies

1 DOUGLAS IRWIN, FREE TRADE UNDER FIRE (Princeton University Press, 2002), at 53, also quoting Gene M. Grossman and Alan B. Krueger, *Economic Growth and the Environment*, QUARTERLY JOURNAL OF ECONOMICS 110 (1995): 353.
2 *See* the overview at http://untreaty.un.org/English/bible/titles/english.pdf, visited Jun. 27, 2005. The IEA Database of the University of Oregon lists over 700 multilateral environmental agreements (405 Agreements, 152 Protocols, and 236 Amendments), *see* http://darkwing.uoregon.edu/~iea/, visited Jun. 27, 2005.
3 *See* United Nations, Report of the World Summit on Sustainable Development, Johannesburg, South Africa, 2002. UN Doc. A/CONF.199/20, available at: www.johannesburgsummit.org/html/documents/documents.html, visited 9 Apr. 2003. Readers will note that no organization was established. *See also* Steve Charnovitz, *A World Environment Organization*, COLUMBIA JOURNAL OF ENVIRONMENTAL LAW 27 (2002): 323.

7.5 Health, globalization, and international institutions

1 *See Preamble of the World Health Organization Constitution*, repr. in WORLD HEALTH ORGANIZATION, Gian Luca Burci & Claude-Henri Vignes (Kluwer Law

International, 2004) (hereinafter BURCI, WHO), at Annex 1, p. 225. *See also* Jeremy Shiffman, *Orchestrating Collaboration Among Contending States: The World Health Organization and Infectious Disease Control in Southeast Asia*, in SOVEREIGNTY UNDER CHALLENGE, John D. Montgomery & Nathan Glazer eds. (Transaction Publishers, 2002): 143, 157–160; David P. Fidler, *Constitutional Outlines of Public Health's "New World Order,"* TEMPLE LAW REVIEW 77 (2004): 247.

2 Several international sanitary conferences were held in the mid-1800s, *see* BURCI, WHO, *id.*, at 16. *See, e.g.*, David Brown. *World Not Set to Deal With Flu*, WASHINGTON POST, 31 Jul. 2005, at 1.

3 In 1920, the Health Organization of the League of Nations was founded, BURCI, WHO, *supra* note 1, at 16.

4 WILLIAM NAPHY & ANDREW SPICER, THE BLACK DEATH: A HISTORY OF PLAGUES 1345–1730 (Tempus, 2000); BURCI, WHO, *supra* note 1, at 16.

5 *See, e.g., How Big a Dent in economy?*, THE ECONOMIST (London), 17 May 2003; *For Better, for Worse*, THE ECONOMIST (London), 10 May 2003.

6 *See Preamble of the Revision of International Health Regulations*, WHO Doc. WHA58.3 of 23 May 2005. *See also* Lawrence O. Gostin, *International Infectious Disease Law – Revision of the World Health Organization's International Health Regulations*, JOURNAL OF THE AMERICAN MEDICAL ASSOCIATION 291 (2004): 2623.

7 *See Preamble of the WHO Constitution*, repr. in BURCI, WHO, *supra* note 1, at 225; and YVES BEIGBEDER, THE WORLD HEALTH ORGANIZATION (M. Nijhoff, 1998), at 45.

8 *Resolution of the Economic and Social Council of the United Nations of 15 February 1946*, United Nations Doc. E/9, *see* Official Records of the World Health Organization 1, p. 40.

9 Official Records of the World Health Organization 2, p. 100.

10 *See* BEIGBEDER, WHO *supra* note 7, at 2.

11 *See* sections 2.5 and 7.2, *supra*.

12 WHO Constitution, Art. 19, reprinted in BURCI, WHO, *supra* note 1, at 230.

13 *Chair's Text of a Framework Convention on Tobacco Control*, WHO Doc. A/FCTC/INB2/2, 9 Jan. 2001.

14 Rules 71 and 73 of the *Rules of Procedure of the World Health Assembly*.

15 Art. 22 of the WHO Constitution, reprinted in BURCI, WHO, *supra* note 1, at 230.

16 *See* in particular BURCI, WHO, *supra* note 1, at 72 for the agreements with States and p. 92 for the relation to non-governmental organizations; *See also* BEIGBEDER, WHO, *supra* note 7, at 190.

17 BEIGBEDER, WHO, *supra* note 7, at 35.

18 *See* BURCI, WHO, *supra* note 1, at 55; BEIGBEDER, WHO, *supra* note 7, at 57 – 59.

19 BURCI, WHO, *supra* note 1, at 107.

20 Private interview at the World Health Organization, June 2004.

21 *See* WHO Constitution, Art. 75, reprinted in Burci, WHO, *supra* note 1, at 239.
22 *See Settlement of Disputes, in Revision of International Health Regulations*, WHO Doc. A58/55, 23 May 2005, at Art. 56, available at www.who.int/ gb/ebwha/ pdf_files/WHA58/A58_55_en.pdf, visited Jul. 6, 2005.
23 The current *Complete List of Standards Adopted by the Codex Alimentarius Commission Up to 2001* is available at www.codexalimentarius.net/web/standard_l ist.do?lang'en, visited Jul. 6, 2005.
24 *See* for the cooperation of the WHO with other relevant international organizations in the field of health Burci, WHO, *supra* note 1, at 73–88, and Beigbeder, WHO, *supra* note 7, at 171–184. The WHO has observer status in the WTO Committee on Technical Barriers to Trade and the Committee on Sanitary and Phytosanitary Measures, as well as ad hoc observer status in the Council for Trade-related Aspects of Intellectual Property Rights, and the Council for Trade in Services, *see* lists of observer status at www.wto.org/ english/thewto_e/igo_obs_e.htm, visited Jul. 6, 2005.
25 *See* on the link in general, *WTO Agreements and Public Health: A Joint Study by the WHO and the WTO Secretariat* (World Health Organization and World Trade Organization, 2002), available at http://www.who.int/media/homepage/ en/who_wto_e.pdf, visited 6 Jul. 2005.
26 *Agreement on Sanitary and Phytosanitary Measures*, in UR Texts, at 59.
27 *Agreement on Technical Barriers to Trade*, in *id.*, at 121.
28 *EC – Measures concerning Meat and Meat Products*, WTO Doc. WT/DS26, 48/AB/R, adopted Feb. 13, 1998, at para. 124; *Australia – Measures affecting Importation of Salmon*, WTO Doc. WT/DS18/AB/R, adopted Nov. 6, 1998, at para. 125.
29 *Agreement on Trade-Related Aspects of Intellectual Property Rights*, in UR Texts, at 321.
30 *See WTO Agreements and Public Health*, *supra* note 25, at 87–111; and articles in Volume 7, Issue 2 (2004) of the Journal of International Economic Law related to the symposium held on 24–26 April 2003 at Duke University School of Law "Conference on International Public Goods and Transfer of Technology under a Globalized Intellectual Property Regime". E.g. Gregory Schaffer, *Recognizing Public Goods in WTO Dispute Settlement: Who Participates? Who Decides?*, JIEL 7 (2004): 459. *See also* Carmen Otero Garcia-Castrillon, *An Approach to the WTO Ministerial Declaration on the TRIPS Agreement and Public Health*, JIEL 5 (2002): 212; Duncan Matthews, *WTO Decision on Implementation of Paragraph 6 of the Doha Declaration on the Trips Agreement and Public Health: A Solution to the Access to Essential Medicines Problem?*, JIEL 7 (2004): 73; Frederick M. Abbott, *The Doha Declaration on the TRIPS Agreement and Public Health: Lighting a Dark Corner at the WTO*, JIEL 5 (2002): 469; Frederick M. Abbott, *The WTO Medicines Decision: World Pharmaceutical Trade and the Protection of Public Health*, AJIL 99 (2005): 317.

31 *See* Lawrence O. Gostin & Center for Law and the Public's Health, *A Conflict Analysis of the Draft Revised Health Regulations and Existing International Law: A Report to the World Health Organization* (Center for Law and the Public's Health, 2004). *See also* Lawrence O. Gostin, *World Health Law: Toward a New Conception of Global Health Governance for the 21st Century*, YALE JOURNAL OF HEALTH POLICY, LAW, AND ETHICS 5 (2005): 413. *See also* CATHERINE BUTTON, THE POWER TO PROTECT: TRADE, HEALTH and UNCERTAINTY IN THE WTO (Hart, 2004).

7.6 Human rights and nation-state sovereignty

1 *See* on the discussion e.g. COUNCIL OF EUROPE, UNIVERSALITY OF HUMAN RIGHTS IN A PLURALISTIC WORLD (Kehl, 1990); Thomas M. Franck, *Is Personal Freedom a Western Value?*, AJIL 91 (1997): 593; EVA BREMS, HUMAN RIGHTS: UNIVERSALITY AND DIVERSITY (Kluwer Law International, 2001); *See also* for a confirmation of the universal character the Vienna Declaration and Programme of Action of the World Conference on Human Rights, Vienna, 14–25 June 1993, UN Doc. A/CONF. 157/23.
2 *See* Gerda Kleijkamp, *Comparing the Application and Interpretation of the United States Constitution and the European Convention on Human Rights*, TRANSNATIONAL LAW AND CONTEMPORARY PROBLEMS 12 (2002): 307.
3 *See Convention for the Protection of Human Rights and Fundamental Freedoms*, signed in Rome on November 4, 1950; Council of Europe, CETS No. 005, reprinted in JACOBS & WHITE, THE EUROPEAN CONVENTION ON HUMAN RIGHTS, 3d ed., Clare Ovey and Robin White eds. (Oxford University Press, 2002): 455. See also A.W. BRIAN SIMPSON, HUMAN RIGHTS and the END OF EMPIRE: BRITAIN AND THE GENESIS OF THE EUROPEAN CONVENTION (Oxford University Press, 2001); THOMAS COTTIER, JOOST PAUWELYN & ELISABETH BÜRGI, EDS., HUMAN RIGHTS AND INTERNATIONAL TRADE (Oxford University Press, 2005).
4 *See* statistics available at www.echr.coe.int/Eng/InfoNotesAndSurveys.htm, visited Jul. 6, 2005.
5 *See, e.g.*, HOWARD CHARLES YOUROW, THE MARGIN OF APPRECIATION DOCTRINE IN THE DYNAMICS OF THE EUROPEAN HUMAN RIGHTS JURISPRUDENCE (Kluwer Law International, 1996); MIREILLE DELMAS-MARTY, ED., THE EUROPEAN CONVENTION FOR THE PROTECTION OF HUMAN RIGHTS (Kluwer Academic Publishers 1992) at 8–14 and 305–309; for a critical perspective *see* Eyal Benvenisti, *Margin of Appreciation, Consensus, and Universal Standards*, NEW YORK UNIVERSITY JOURNAL OF INTERNATIONAL LAW & POLITICS (Summer 1999): 843.
6 So far, the Charter of Fundamental Rights is only politically and not legally binding on Member States. However, the European Court of Justice and in particular the Court of First Instance has begun referring to it in their decisions, to support their findings. *See* e.g., *Regione autonoma Friuli-Venezia Giulia and Agenzia regionale per lo sviluppo rurale (ERSA) v. Ministero delle Politiche Agricole e Forestali*, Case C-437/03, Judgment of May 12, 2005 (not yet published)

(regarding the right to property) and *Jégo-Quéré et Cie SA v. Commission of the European Communities*, Case T-177/01, E.C.R. 2002, p.II-2365 (regarding the right to be heard and the right to an effective remedy).

7 *Draft Treaty Establishing a Constitution for Europe*, OFFICIAL JOURNAL OF THE EUROPEAN UNION, 2004 O.J. (C 310). After negative referenda in France and the Netherlands, the ratification process might not continue as previously planned, *see Declaration by the Heads of State or Government of the Member States of the European Union on the Ratification of the Treaty Establishing a Constitution for Europe, at the European Council in Brussels, 16 & 17 Jun. 2005*, available at http://ue.eu.int/ueDocs/cms_Data/docs/pressData/en/ec/85325.pdf, visited 7 Jul. 2005 (calling for a "period of reflection").

8 *See* briefings by the Federal Trust on www.fedtrust.co.uk/policybriefs, visited 26 Jul. 2005.

9 Bill of Rights passed by Congress September 25, 1789, ratified December 15, 1791.

10 Described by Louis Henkin, *U.S. Ratification of Human Rights Conventions: The Ghost of Senator Bricker*, AJIL 89 (1995): 341; and LOUIS HENKIN, THE AGE OF RIGHTS (Columbia University Press, 1990): 65–80.

11 At least, this is what is argued. *See, e.g.*, Mark Tushnet, *Marbury v. Madison Around the World*, TENNESSEE LAW REVIEW 71 (2004): 251; TIM KOOPMANS, COURTS AND POLITICAL INSTITUTIONS – A COMPARATIVE VIEW (Cambridge University Press, 2003), at 51, 271.

12 *See* for a critical view J. Patrick Kelly, *The Twilights of Customary International Law*, VIRGINIA JOURNAL OF INTERNATIONAL LAW 40 (2000): 449; T. Alexander Aleinikoff, *International Law, Sovereignty, and American Constitutionalism: Reflections on the Customary International Law Debate*, AJIL 98 (2004): 91; Curtis A. Bradley, *The Costs of International Human Rights Litigation*, CHICAGO JOURNAL OF INTERNATIONAL LAW 2 (2001): 457. For an arguably too broad approach to formation of customary international law, *see, e.g.*, KAROL WOLFKE, CUSTOM IN PRESENT INTERNATIONAL LAW, 2d ed. (Martinus Nyhoff Publishers, 1993) at 116–160.

13 Michael J. Dennis, David P. Stewart, *Justiciability of Economic, Social and Cultural Rights: Should there be an international complaints mechanism to adjudicate the rights to food, water, housing, and health?*, AJIL 98 (2004): 462; *Righting Wrongs*, THE ECONOMIST (London), Aug. 16, 2001; *The Politics of Human Rights: Does It Help To Think of Poverty or Inadequate Health Care as Violations of Basic Rights?*, THE ECONOMIST (London), Aug. 16, 2001.

14 *See, e.g.*, COTTIER, ET AL, HUMAN RIGHTS AND INTERNATIONAL TRADE, *supra* note 3; Ernst-Ulrich Petersmann, *How to Reform the UN System? Constitutionalism, International Law, and International Organizations*, LEIDEN JOURNAL OF INTERNATIONAL LAW 10 (1997): 427; FRANZ CEDE AND LILY SUCHARIPA-BEHRMANN, EDS., THE UNITED NATIONS: LAW AND PRACTICE (Kluwer Law International, 2001); JEAN E. KRASNO, ED., THE UNITED NATIONS:

CONFRONTING THE CHALLENGES OF A GLOBAL SOCIETY (Lynne Rienner Publishers, 2004); JAMES P. MULDOON, JR. ET AL. EDS., MULTILATERAL DIPLOMACY AND THE UNITED NATIONS TODAY (Westview Press, 1999).
15 COTTIER ET AL., HUMAN RIGHTS, *supra* note 3.
16 GARY CLYDE HUFBAUER ET AL, ECONOMIC SANCTIONS RECONSIDERED: HISTORY AND CURRENT POLICY, 2d ed. (Institute for International Economics, 1990); HOSSEIN ASKARI, ET AL, ECONOMIC SANCTIONS (Praeger, 2003); ERNEST H. PREEG, FEELING GOOD OR DOING GOOD WITH SANCTIONS (Center for Strategic and International Studies, 1999).
17 *See, e.g.*, Michael P. Malloy, *Reconciling Political Sanctions with Globalization and Free Trade*, CHICAGO JOURNAL OF INTERNATIONAL LAW 4 (2003): 371. For an overview over the general international legal framework for economic sanctions, *see* HAGUE ACADEMY OF INTERNATIONAL LAW, ECONOMIC SANCTIONS IN INTERNATIONAL LAW (M. Nijhoff, 2000); and VERA GOWLLAND-DEBBAS, UNITED NATIONS SANCTIONS AND INTERNATIONAL LAW (Kluwer Law International, 2001).
18 *See, e.g.*, Steve Charnovitz, *The Globalization of Economic Human Rights*, BROOKLYN JOURNAL OF INTERNATIONAL LAW 25 (1999): 113; and *WTO Cosmopolitics*, NEW YORK UNIVERSITY JOURNAL OF INTERNATIONAL LAW & POLICY 34 (2002): 299; Ernst-Ulrich Petersmann, *Theories of Justice, Human Rights, and the Constitution of international markets*, LOYOLA OF LOS ANGELES LAW REVIEW 37 (Fall 2003): 407.

7.7 Federalism examples: US and EU struggles with the allocation of power
1 *See Bush v. Gore*, 531 U.S. 98, 111–12, 141–42 (2000).
2 *Id.* at 111.
3 *Id.* (Rehnquist, C.J., concurring, at 112).
4 *Id.* (Ginsburg, J., dissenting, at 141).
5 *Id.* (Ginsburg, J., dissenting, at 142).
6 *See, e.g.*, Pascal Lamy, *Europe's Policymakers Live in the Real World*, FINANCIAL TIMES (London), 28 Oct. 2002, at 5 (editorial); Daniel Dombey & George Parker, *Plan for a New Europe "Will Last 50 Years,"* FINANCIAL TIMES (London), Oct. 7, 2002, at 4; *The Future of the European Union: Can These Bones Live?* ECONOMIST (London), Nov. 2, 2002, at 51; British Prime Minister Tony Blair, A Clear Course for Europe, Keynote Speech, Cardiff, Wales, 28 Nov. 2002, transcript available at www.number10.gov.uk/output/Page1739.asp, visited Apr. 13, 2005. The *Treaty Establishing a Constitution for Europe 2004* O.J. (C 310), 1, also discussed in sections 2.5 and 6.5 (at footnote 3), *supra*. *See also* WALTER VAN GERVEN, THE EUROPEAN UNION: A POLITY OF STATES AND PEOPLES (Stanford University Press, 2005).
7 *See Treaty Establishing a Constitution for Europe*, *Id.*
8 *See, e.g.*, NEIL WALKER, ED., SOVEREIGNTY IN TRANSITION (Hart Publishing, 2004). Many of the essays within this book struggle with some of these issues.

7.8 The United Nations and the use of force: constitutionalism evolving
1. This chapter has been partially adapted from John H. Jackson, *Sovereignty Modern: A New Approach to an Outdated Concept*, AJIL 97 (2003): 782.
2. Major works include MICHAEL J. GLENNON, LIMITS OF LAW, PREROGATIVES OF POWER: INTERVENTIONISM AFTER KOSOVO (Palgrave Macmillan, 2001); Legal Opinion for the Government of the United Kingdom, Letter of the British Foreign Minister, Jack Straw, containing a statement of the Attorney General Lord Goldsmith, on the legal basis for the use of force against Iraq, Mar. 17, 2003, available at: www.fco.gov.uk/Files/kfile/Iraq%20-%20use%20of%20force.pdf, visited Jun. 23, 2005, and a document leaked by Lord Goldsmith of 7 Mar. 2003, excerpts of which can be found at: http://news.bbc.co.uk/1/hi/uk_politics/vote_2005/frontpage/4491801.stm, visited 23 Jun. 2005; *Agora: Future Implications of the Iraq Conflict*, AMERICAN JOURNAL OF INTERNATIONAL LAW 97 (July 2003): 553; Sean D. Murphy, *Taking Multinational Corporate Codes of Conduct to the Next Level*, COLUMBIA JOURNAL OF TRANSNATIONAL LAW 43 (2005): 389.
3. See Chapter 6.2, notes 5 and 6, *supra*.
4. INTERNATIONAL COMMISSION ON INTERVENTION AND STATE SOVEREIGNTY [ICISS], THE RESPONSIBILITY TO PROTECT 11 (International Development Research Centre, 2001).
5. *See* Henry Schermers, *Different Aspects of Sovereignty*, in STATE SOVEREIGNTY AND INTERNATIONAL GOVERNANCE, Gerald Kreijen et al. eds. (Oxford University Press, 2002): 185.

8 Perspectives and implications: some conclusions

1. JOSEPH E. STIGLITZ, GLOBALIZATION AND ITS DISCONTENTS (W.W. Norton & Company, 2002), at 224.
2. *See* section 1.1, *supra*.
3. *See* section 5.8, *supra*, at note 4 and discussion in the text.
4. *See* Don Greig, "*International Community,*" "*Interdependence*" *and All That . . . Rhetorical Correctness?*, in STATE, SOVEREIGNTY AND INTERNATIONAL GOVERNANCE, Gerard Kreijen ed. (Oxford University Press, 2002): 521.
5. THOMAS M. FRANCK, FAIRNESS IN INTERNATIONAL LAW AND INSTITUTIONS (Oxford University Press, 1995), at 41.
6. THOMAS HOBBES, LEVIATHAN (orig. 1651) (Viking Press, 1982) ("[In a state of nature] No arts; no letters; no society; and which is worst of all, continual fear and danger of violent death; and the life of man, solitary, poor, nasty, brutish, and short").
7. Robert O. Keohane, *Governance in a Partially Globalized World*, Presidential address, American Political Science Association, 2000, THE AMERICAN POLITICAL SCIENCE REVIEW (Menasha, Mar. 2001).

8 Paul Kennedy, *The Eagle Has Landed*, FINANCIAL TIMES (London), Feb. 2, 2002, at 1.
9 *See* STIGLITZ, GLOBALIZATION AND ITS DISCONTENTS, *supra* note 1.
10 *See* section 6.5, *supra*.
11 *See* sections 2.3 and 5.12, *supra*.
12 The Chicago Council on Foreign Relations, *Global Views 2004: American Public Opinion and Foreign Policy (2004)*, available at www.ccfr.org/globalviews 2004/index.htm, visited Apr. 13, 2005.
13 THOMAS P. O'NEILL AND GARY HYMEL, ALL POLITICS IS LOCAL (New York Times Books, 1994), and Peter F. Drucker, *Trade Lessons from the World Economy*, FOREIGN AFFAIRS, 73 (Jan./Feb. 1994): 99.

Appendix: Outline of the Uruguay Round treaty agreement establishing the World Trade Organization

1 *Marrakesh Agreement Establishing the World Trade Organization, UR Texts. See also* JOHN H. JACKSON, WILLIAM J. DAVEY, & ALAN O. SYKES, 2002 SUPPLEMENT TO LEGAL PROBLEMS OF INTERNATIONAL ECONOMIC RELATIONS: CASES, MATERIALS AND TEXT ON THE NATIONAL AND INTERNATIONAL REGULATION OF TRANSNATIONAL ECONOMIC RELATIONS, 4th ed. (West Group, 2002).

Index

Note: Page references in *italics* indicate tabulated materials

acquis communautaire, 263
aggregation of nation-states, 20–21
agricultural goods
  at Doha Round, 31, 163, 229
  EU CAP (Common Agricultural Policy), 101
  EU import restrictions, 163, 229
  FAO (UN Food and Agriculture Organization), 247
  as global issue, 30–31, 163
  GMOs (genetically modified foodstuffs), 182, 218, 319n9, 328n32
  Japanese import restrictions, 163
  Tokyo Round's failure to establish discipline for, 101
  at UR, 100–101
  US import restrictions, 30–31, 100, 101, 139–40, 164, 229
AIDS/HIV, 245, 247
Aleinikoff, Alex, 70
allocation of power. *See* power allocation analysis
American Indian tribes, sovereignty of, 70, 224
amicus curiae briefs and dispute settlement at WTO, 155, 181, 207
Annan, Kofi, 18, 60, 65–66, 67
antidumping
  domestic and international law, interaction of, 194
  "effect" or "measure," actual occurrence of, 179
  as exceptional WTO measure answering specific nation-state needs, 237
  fact-finding issues and, 181–182
  interface theory (variable geometry) and, 231, 233

policy goals and, 147
standard of review and, 169, 171
WTO dispute settlement activity involving, 95, 162
Antigua and Barbuda, 163
appellate process and Appellate Body, WTO dispute settlement, 156–58, 159, 200–202
Asian financial crisis (1997–98), 6
ASIL (American Society of International Law), 4
Austin, John, 18, 32
authority to make decisions, allocation of. *See* power allocation analysis

balance of power theories, 13, 266
bankruptcy laws, WTO subject matter competence regarding, 133
Belgium, fragmentation and aggregation of government in, 21
Berlin Wall, fall of (1989), 5, 6, 12
bilateral investment treaties (BITs), 241
bilateral treaties, 44
Blackhurst, Richard, 116
Blair, Tony, 66
Bosnia, 65
Boutros-Ghali, Boutros, 65
Brazil, 30–31, 161, 163, 165–66
Bretton Woods Conference (1944), 6, 92, 147, 274n9
Bretton Woods institutions. *See* General Agreement on Tariffs and Trade; International Monetary Fund; World Bank
Breyer, Stephen G., 253
Britain. *See* United Kingdom
Brown, Winthrop, 81

Index

Canada, 117, 142–43, 163
Cancún Ministerial Conference (2003), 12, 27, 103, 118, 121, 130
CAP (Common Agricultural Policy), EU, 101
"Charming Betsy" principle, 124–25, 193
Charney, Jonathan, 228
Chevron doctrine, 170
Chile, 201, 340n8
China, 109, 110, 127, 231
Chomsky, Noam, 216
Coase, Ronald, 86
Codex Alimentarius Commission, 247
Common Agricultural Policy (CAP), EU, 101
communications, effects of developments in, 10–11, 31–32
competition policy, disputes as to internationalization of, 221–22
compliance and implementation requirements, WTO dispute settlement, 158–59, 195–99
consensus approach
  dispute settlement at WTO, 113
  in international governmental organizations, 24, 43, 50
  sovereignty and, 58, 216
  at WTO, 43, 50, 112–16, 206, 237–38, 262
consent theory for international law norms, 36, 58, 206, 215
consequential immunity, 58
constitutional issues
  international law, "constitutional" approach to, 224–27, 268
  power allocation analysis and constitutionalism, 222–27
  treaties with constitutional functions, 44, 51–52
  "treaty rigidity" as "constitutional" question, 45, 50
constitutions. *See also* Table of Statutes and Regulations
  EU draft constitution, 44, 51, 223, 249, 254 (*see also* Table of Statutes and Regulations)
  Netherlands, 23
  UK, unwritten constitution of, 222
  UN Charter, constitutional character of, 223, 225
  WHO, 246
  WTO, 236–40
consultations as part of dispute settlement at WTO, 152–53
contractual treaties, 44
Costa Rica, 148–149
customary international law, 35, 39–42, 58–59, 212

decision-making authority, allocation of. *See* power allocation analysis
deference, degree of (standard of review)
  dispute settlement at WTO, 169–72, 239–40
  "margin of appreciation" concept, 52, 226, 240, 249, 254–55
"democratic entitlement," 21
democratic legitimacy of international system, 216, 226
developing countries' involvement in WTO dispute settlement activity, 160–61, 229
Dewey, John, 264
disease, rapid transmittal of, 31
dispute settlement at WTO, 134–37, 204–08
  amicus curiae briefs, 155, 181, 207
  appellate process and Appellate Body, 156–58, 159, 200–202
  consensus approach, 113
  consultations, 152–53
  domestic and international law, relationship between, 192–95
  domestic law affected by, 124
  DSB (Dispute Settlement Body), 107
  DSU (Dispute Settlement Understanding) (*see* Table of Statutes and Regulations)
  "effect" or "measure," actual occurrence of, 177–180
  fact-finding issues, 180–82, 240
  general international law and, 164–68
  growing importance of, 227–29
  historical background under GATT and UR, 137–45
  implementation and compliance requirements, 158–59, 195–99
  issue avoidance, 172–73
  obligation to perform, 168
  panel process, 153–56, 202–03
  policy goals, 145–51
  power allocation analysis and, 238–40
  precedent, 173–77, 195, 239
  reform proposals, 199–204
  remedies and relief, 203–204
  review of activity (1995–2005), 159–63
  review of process, 199–200
  rule-oriented *vs.* power-oriented systems, 146–47
  sovereignty issues, 163–73
  standard of review or degree of deference, 169–72, 239–40
  stare decisis, 173–77, 193, 239
  structural doctrines, 173–82
  structural problems faced by, 199–204
  structure and operation of system, 152–59
  treaty interpretation and, 182–92
Doha Ministerial Conference (2001)
  "Consultants to the Chair" at, 118
  declarations, 103

354

Index

relative success of, 102–03, 121
two-track approach used at, 130
World Trade Organization (WTO), 242
Doha Round
  agricultural subsidies as issue for, 31, 163, 229
  designation as development round, 103
domestic and international law, relationship between. *See also* sovereignty
  dispute settlement at WTO and, 192–95
  human rights protections and sovereignty principle, 217, 248–52
  "margin of appreciation" given to federal states, 254–55
  monist *vs.* dualist view of, 23, 123
  "self-executing" effect of international norms in domestic context, 123, 126, 134, 151, 192
  sovereignty, 60, 69
  sub-federal units, applicability of international law to, 127–28
  treaties, 21–23, 45
  WTO rules, 122–28
Drucker, Peter, 268
DS. *See* dispute settlement at WTO
dualist view of relationship between international and national law, 23, 123
dumping. *See* antidumping

EC/EEC (European Community/European Economic Community). *See* European Union
ECJ. *See* European Court of Justice
economic law, international. *See* international economic law
ECOSOC (UN Economic and Social Committee), 245
Ehlermann, Claus-Dieter, 187
enforcement requirements, WTO dispute settlement, 158–59, 195–99
England. *See* United Kingdom
environmental policies, international, 243–44
"equality of nations" doctrine, 24, 50, 112, 216, 262
erga omnes treaties, 44
European Court of Justice (ECJ)
  establishment and purpose of, 227, 312n33
  on relationship between international and domestic law, 23, 127
  stare decisis vs. precedent, 174–76
European Union (EU)
  agricultural import restrictions, 163, 229
  CAP (Common Agricultural Policy), 101
  competition policy, disputes as to internationalization of, 221
  dispute settlement activity at WTO (*see also* specific cases involving EC/EEC, in Table of Cases)

dispute settlement activity at WTO, involvement in, 160, 163, 170–71, 198, 229
domestic application of international norms in, 127, 255
draft constitution, 44, 51, 223, 249, 254 (*see also* Table of Statutes and Regulations)
federalism in, 253–54
greater unity as response to world circumstances, 5
human rights tradition of, 249
legal application of international norms in, 123
MIAs (multilateral investment agreements), development of, 242
organizational evolution of, 122, 205
power allocation as major issue in, 224
sovereignty, sub-national use of term in, 70
US petroleum product import tax, GATT dispute settlement regarding, 142–43
voting and majority requirements, 25, 51
voting block powers in international organizations, 24, 115
WTO Ministerial Conference reforms called for by, 121
as WTO Quad Group member, 117
extraterritorial effects of domestic government regulation, 22

fact-finding issues in WTO dispute settlement mechanism, 180–82, 240
failed states, 21–22, 257
FCN (friendship, commerce, and navigation) agreements, 241
federalism issues, 69–70, 252–55
Food and Agriculture Organization (FAO), 247
fragmentation of governments, 20–21
France's referendum on EU constitution, 44, 349n7
Franck, Thomas, 21, 40, 51, 68, 72, 225, 264
free trade agreements as types of governmental aggregation, 21
Friedman, Thomas L., 3, 13, 64
Friedman, Wolfgang, 64
friendship, commerce, and navigation (FCN) agreements, 241

gambling on Internet, WTO dispute settlement regarding US restrictions on, 163
General Agreement on Tariffs and Trade (GATT). *See also* Table of Statutes and Regulations, for specific sections of treaty
  dispute settlement under, 137–45
  grandfather rights under, 96
  "green room" meetings, 103, 116, 117
  institutional evolution of, 82, 96–98, 205

355

Index

General Agreement on Tariffs and Trade
  (GATT). (*cont.*)
  interface theory (variable geometry), 230–31
  ITO draft charter and, 92–94
  provisional application of, 94–96
  Rounds of, 305n30 (*see also* specific
    negotiating rounds, e.g. Uruguay
    Round)
  significance of, 91
  sovereignty and membership criteria, 69
  WTO and, 91, 105
General Agreement on Trade in Services
  (GATS). *See* Table of Statutes and
  Regulations
genetically modified foodstuffs (GMOs), 182,
  218, 319n9, 328n32
Geneva Ministerial Conference (1998), 102,
  121
Ginsburg, Ruth, 253
globalization
  criticism of and challenges to, 6, 13
  defined and described, 8–10
  exogenous and endogenous, 9
  of health issues, 245–248
  interface theory (variable geometry) and, 25,
    226, 230–33, *232*, 254
  international law and, 54–56
  international legal principles challenged by,
    3, 5
  market economy and, 30–31, 220–22
  sovereignty affected by, 60, 61, 69
  "transmittals," increasing effects of rapidity
    of, 31–32
  WTO subject matter competence and, 133
GMOs (genetically modified foodstuffs), 182,
  218, 319n9, 328n32
Goldsmith, Jack L., 35–36
good governance
  as basis for legitimation of international law
    norms, 216
  in international organizations, 25, 53–54,
    263, 267–68
  WTO ideals, 118–21, 203
governments. *See* nation-states
grandfather rights under GATT, 95, 96
Great Britain. *See* United Kingdom
"green room" meetings, 103, 116, 117
Grotius, Hugo, 18
Gulf War (1991), 5

Haass, Richard N., 63
Havana Charter of ITO, 84, 92–93, 129. *See
  also* Table of Statutes and Regulations
Hawkins, Harry, 134, 138
health issues, international aspects of, 245–48
Henkin, Louis, 38, 61, 69, 265
HIV/AIDS, 245, 247

Hobbes, Thomas, 264
"holdout" states, 59
Hong Kong Ministerial Conference (2005),
  103, 121
Hong Kong's membership in WTO, 109
human rights
  international protections and sovereignty
    issues, 217
  "margin of appreciation" concept, 226
  nation-state sovereignty and, 248–52
  policy analysis matrix and, 218

ICITO (Interim Commission for the
  International Trade Organization), 97
ICJ or International Court of Justice (World
  Court), 135, 246. *See also* Table of Cases
  and Table of Statutes and Regulations
IMF. *See* International Monetary Fund
immunity, 58, 205
implementation and compliance requirements,
  WTO dispute settlement, 158–59,
  195–99
in dubio mitius, 184–85, 262
India, 109
Indian tribes in America, sovereignty of, 70,
  224
information technology, effects of
  developments in, 10–11, 31–32
institutional international law, 49–54. *See also*
  international governmental
  organizations
institutional structures' importance to market,
  214
intellectual property rights
  subject matter competence of WTO
    regarding, 130
  TRIPS (WTO Agreement on Trade-Related
    Aspects of Intellectual Property Rights),
    105, 227, 247, 347n29
  UR introducing WTO involvement in, 99,
    144
  WIPO, 227
interdependence, concept of, 8–13, 264. *See also*
  globalization
interface theory (variable geometry), 25, 226,
  230–33, *232*, 254
Interim Commission for the International
  Trade Organization (ICITO), 97
internal governance, international involvement
  in. *See* domestic and international law,
  relationship between
International Commission on Intervention and
  State Sovereignty (2001), 57, 67
International Court of Justice or ICJ (World
  Court), 135, 246. *See also* Table of Cases
  and Table of Statutes and Regulations
international economic law, 46–49

356

Index

general international law concepts and, 4, 13, 46–49, 81–82, 234
  implications of current situation, 13–15
  investment flows, 240–43
  transactional and regulatory aspects of, 47
international governmental organizations. *See also* specific institutions, e.g. World Trade Organization
  consensus approach, 24, 43, 50
  constitutional treaties of, 51–52
  diplomatic and governance activities of, 24–26
  "equality of nations" doctrine, 24, 50
  good governance ideals, 25, 53–54, 263, 267–68
  international institutional law, 49–54
  public support for, 268
  "treaty rigidity," 45, 50
  voting systems, 24, 43, 50–51
international investment flows, 240–43
international law, 32–35
  basis for legitimation of, 215–17, 263–68
  changing circumstances and challenges, 3–7
  conclusions regarding, 260–268
  "constitutional" approach to, 224–27, 268
  criticisms of, 18–19, 34–35
  current landscape of, 6–13, 20
  customary international law, 35, 39–42, 58–59, 212
  dispute settlement at WTO and, 164–68
  domestic law, relationship to (*see* domestic and international law, relationship between)
  economic (*see* international economic law)
  environmental policies, 243–44
  foundations of, 35–39
  future challenges, possible responses to, 211–14
  globalization, challenges posed by, 54–56
  health issues, 245–48
  implications of current situation, 13–15
  of institutions, 49–54 (*see also* international governmental organizations)
  interface theory (variable geometry), 25, 226, 230–33, *232*, 254
  juridical institutions, growing importance of, 227–30
  sovereignty's relationship to, 57–62 (*see also* sovereignty)
  "state consent" theory and, 36, 58, 206, 215
  treaty law (*see* treaties)
  unified theory, impossibility of constructing, 258
international law associations, 4, 273n3
International Monetary Fund (IMF)
  Asian financial crisis testing capacity of, 6
  "conditionality," 69

inception of, 274n9
  "treaty rigidity" in, 45
  weighted voting system, 24, 115–16
  WTO resources compared, 116, *117*
International Trade Organization (ITO)
  dispute settlement mechanism intended for, 138
  failure of, 94, 107, 205
  GATT Secretariat evolving from staff of, 97
  Havana Charter, 84, 92–93, 129, 138 (*see also* Table of Statutes and Regulations)
  historical background, 82, 92–94
  subject matter agenda, 129
Internet gambling restrictions, WTO dispute settlement regarding, 163
investment flows, international, 240–243
Iraq
  current war in (2003–), 31, 256–57
  Gulf War (1991), 5
issue avoidance and dispute settlement at WTO, 172–173
ITO. *See* International Trade Organization

James, William, 264
Japan
  agricultural import restrictions, 163
  domestic application of international norms in, 127
  membership in WTO, 109
  MIAs (multilateral investment agreements), development of, 242
  as WTO Quad Group member, 117
juridical institutions
  constitutionalism and, 225
  ECJ (*See* European Court of Justice)
  growing importance of international systems, 227–230
  ICJ (International Court of Justice or World Court), 135, 246
  Law of the Sea Tribunal, 227, 280n28
  standard of review or degree of deference dispute settlement at WTO, 169–172, 239–240
  "margin of appreciation" concept, 52, 226, 240, 249, 254–255
  WHO system, 246
  WTO system (*See* dispute settlement at WTO)
jus cogens, 42, 48, 250, 287n27–28

Kant, Immanuel, 32
Kelly, J. Patrick, 40
Kelsen, Hans, 32, 35, 264
Kennedy Round, 98
Keohane, Robert, 265
Kosovo crisis, 6, 65, 263
Krasner, Stephen, 63

357

Index

Lamy, Pascal, 114
Law of the Sea Tribunal, 227, 280n28
lex specialis, 167

"margin of appreciation" concept, 52, 226, 240, 249, 254–55
market economy
    failure of markets, power allocation in cases of, 220–22
    globalization of, 30–31, 220–22
    institutional structures, importance of, 214
    socialist collapse and upsurge in market economic thinking, 12
Marshall, John, 51, 134
McRae, Donald, 49
Mercosur, 21, 227–228
Mexico, 142–143
MFN (Most Favored Nation) obligations, 95, 96, 115
MIAs (multilateral investment agreements), 242–43
Millikin, Eugene, 81
Ministerial Conferences of WTO, 102–04, 106, 121–122. *See also* individual conferences, e.g. Singapore
MNCs (multinational corporations), 29–30, 241. *See also* nongovernment actors and organizations
monist view of relationship between international and national law, 23, 123
Monterrey Conference 2002 (International Conference on Financing for Development), 27
Most Favored Nation (MFN) obligations, 95, 96, 115
multilateral investment agreements (MIAs), 242–43
multilateral treaties, 44
multinational corporations (MNCs), 29–30, 241. *See also* nongovernment actors and organizations

Nader, Ralph, 70
nation-states. *See also* domestic and international law, relationship between; sovereignty
    democratic protections afforded by, 226
    extraterritorial effects of domestic actions of, 22
    fragmentation or aggregation of, 20–21
Native American tribes, sovereignty of, 70, 224
natural law or natural reason, 216
Netherlands
    EU constitution, referendum on, 44, 349n7
    monist legal system of, 23, 123
    US dairy import restrictions, 139–140

NGOs. *See* nongovernmental actors and organizations
non-contractual treaties, 44
non-interference/non-intervention principle, 217, 263
non liquet, 172–173
non-tariff barriers (NTBs), 96, 98, 131
nongovernmental actors and organizations, 26–29
    environmental policies, international, 244
    illicit operators, 29
    increase in number and participation, implications of, 11–12, 14–15, 24, 26–28, 120
    non-profits, 26–28
    profit organizations and businesses, 28–29
North American Free Trade Agreement (NAFTA), 126, 227
NTBs (non-tariff barriers), 96, 98, 131

obligation to perform as feature of WTO dispute settlement, 168
OECD. *See* Organisation for Economic Co-operation and Development
O'Neill, Tip, 268
opinio juris, 39, 59, 263, 265
opt-out clause in WTO charter, 109
Organisation for Economic Co-operation and Development (OECD)
    member states, 344n11
    MIAs (multilateral investment agreements) development of, 242
    WTO resources compared, 116, *117*
Organization for Trade Cooperation (OTC), 97, 107
OXFAM, 27, 311n24

panel process, WTO dispute settlement, 153–56, 202–03
Panitchpakdi, Supachai, 83, 114
participation as good governance ideal, 25, 120–21
Peirce, Charles Sanders, 264
plurilateral agreements, 106, 115
policy objectives
    of dispute settlement at WTO, 145–51
    of international law, 37–39
    matrix for analysis of, 217–20
    power allocation analysis and, 70–76, 217–20
    of sovereignty concept, 70–76
    of WTO, 84–91
Posner, Eric A., 35–36
power allocation analysis
    constitutionalism and, 222–27
    federalism issues (sub-national sovereignty), 69–70, 252–55

Index

future challenges involving, 211–14
illustrative examples invoking, 235
interface theory (variable geometry), 25, 226, 230–33, *232*, 254
juridical institutions, growing importance of, 227–30
market failure in global economy, response to, 220–22
policy objectives and, 70–76, 217–20
sovereignty concepts and, 70–77, 212–13, 214–17, 252 (*see also* sovereignty)
UN, use of force by, 256–57
WTO and, 238–40
pragmatism, 264
precedent, 173–77, 195, 239
public support for international institutions, 268
Punta del Este Conference (1986), 5, 99, 141

Quad Group, 117–18

reciprocity, concept of
  in international law, 30, 51
  in WTO, 88, 131, 148, 149, 196, 199, 237
Rehnquist, William, 253
remedies and relief, WTO dispute settlement, 203–04
rights. *See* human rights
"risk premium," rule-oriented approach lowering, 15, 38–38, 88, 187, 205, 262
rogue states, 21–22, 217, 226–27
Roosevelt, Franklin Delano, 251
Ruggiero, Renato, 114
rule-oriented approach
  of dispute settlement of WTO, 146–47, 206
  of GATT and ITO charter, 138, 205, 206
  importance of juridical institutions and, 229
  importance of structures based on, 214
  of international law, 37–39
  "risk premium," lowering, 15, 38–38, 88, 187, 205, 262
  of WTO, 88–90, 205, 206
Rwanda, 6, 65

SARS, 245
Scalia, Antonin, 253
Schachter, Oscar, 36–37, 216
Schermers, Henry, 64, 257
Seattle Ministerial Conference (1999), 6, 102–03, 118, 121, 130
"self-executing" effect of international norms in domestic context, 123, 126, 134, 151, 192
September 11, 2001 attacks, impact of, xi, 4, 6
services, trade in
  GATS (General Agreement on Trade in Services) (*see* Table of Statutes and Regulations)
  subject matter competence of WTO regarding, 133
  UR introducing WTO involvement in, 99, 144
"Singapore issues," 103, 131, 242, 345n17
Singapore Ministerial Conference (1996), 102, 121
single undertaking arrangement at UR, 100
Slaughter, Anne-Marie, 335n5, 351n3
socialist structures, decline and fall of, 12
Somalia, 6, 65
Souter, David, 253
South Africa, 109
sovereign immunity, 58, 205
sovereignty
  "anomaly examples" of, 68–69, 214
  challenges to entire concept of, 13–14, 214
  changing fundamentals of international law and, 76–78
  conclusions regarding, 260–68
  and constitutionalism, 222–27
  continuing usefulness of concept, 69–70, 214–15, 217
  disaggregation or "slicing" of concept, 215
  dispute settlement at WTO and, 163–73
  domestic and international law, tension between, 60, 69
  future challenges regarding, 214–17
  globalization affecting, 60, 61, 69
  human rights and, 217, 248–52
  of Native American tribes, 70, 224
  policy objectives and, 70–76
  power allocation analysis and, 70–77, 212–13, 214–17, 252
  relationship to international law, 57–62
  "state consent," concept of, 36, 58, 206, 215
  sub-national (federalism issues), 69–70, 252–55
  UN, use of force by, 256–57
  Westphalian concept, criticism of, 14, 57, 62–70, 260–61
  WTO and, 69, 237, 261–62
standard of review
  dispute settlement at WTO, 169–72, 239–40
  "margin of appreciation" concept, 52, 226, 240, 249, 254–55
stare decisis, 173–77, 193, 239
"state consent," concept of, 36, 58, 206, 215
states. *See* nation-states
Stephens, John Paul, 253
Stiglitz, Joseph E., 258
Stone, Christopher D., 32
structural doctrines and dispute settlement at WTO, 173–82

Index

sub-national units
　applicability of international law to, 127–28
　sovereignty or federalism issues, 69–70, 252–55
subsidiarity, concept of, 25, 68, 226, 230
subsidies, agricultural. *See* agricultural goods

Taiwan, 109
Thirty Years War, 62
Thomas, Clarence, 253
Tokyo Round
　agricultural discipline, failure to establish, 101
　consensus approach, problems created by, 114
　dispute settlement at, 140, 142, 143–44
　grandfather rights and US position during, 96
　NTBs, focus on, 98, 131
　single-sector agreements *vs.* single undertaking of UR, 100
　Trade Policy Review Mechanism (TRPM), 105, 107
　trade remedy cases, 162
"transmittals," increasing effects of rapidity of, 31–32
transparency as good governance ideal, 25, 53, 118–21, 203
transportation, effects of developments in, 10, 31–32
treaties, 35, 42–45. *See also* Table of Statutes and Regulations, for specific treaties
　bilateral, 44, 241
　challenges to continued viability of, 14–15
　with constitutional functions, 44, 51–52
　customary international law and, 41–42
　differential treatment of, 44, 51
　dispute settlement at WTO involving interpretation of, 182–92
　domestic law impacts of, 21–23, 45
　FCN (friendship, commerce, and navigation) agreements, 241
　foundations of law regarding, 35
　MIAs (multilateral investment agreements), 242–43
　multilateral, 44, 242–43
　opt-out clause in WTO charter, 109
　sovereignty and, 58
"treaty rigidity," 45, 50, 206, 262
TRPM (Trade Policy Review Mechanism), 105, 107

underwear imports, Costa Rican protest of US restrictions on, 148–149
United Kingdom (UK)
　dualist legal system of, 123
　GATT, initiatives leading to establishment of, 92

　unwritten constitution of, 222
United Nations (UN)
　constitutional character of Charter, 223, 225 (*see also* UN Charter, in Table of Statutes and Regulations)
　ECOSOC (Economic and Social Committee), 245
　FAO (Food and Agriculture Organization), 247
　force, use of, 256–57
　Gulf War (1991), prosecution of, 5
　human rights protection, role in, 251
　international law challenges currently faced by, 4
　number of treaties registered with, 42
　organizational evolution of, 122
　veto powers in, 24, 51
United States (US)
　agricultural import restrictions, 30–31, 100, 101, 139–40, 164, 229
　Appellate Body reform proposal, 201
　Chevron doctrine and standard of review, 170–171
　competition policy, disputes as to internationalization of, 221
　constitutionalism in, 223–24
　customary international law arguments in US Supreme Court, 40–41
　dispute settlement activity at WTO, involvement in, 160, 162, 163, 170–71, 184–95, 198, 229 (*see also* specific cases involving US, in Table of Cases)
　distinctions between treaties made by, 43
　domestic application of international norms in, 45, 123–27, 255
　federalism in, 252–53
　GATT, initiatives leading to establishment of, 92–93
　human rights tradition of, 249–51
　mixed monist/dualist legal system of, 23, 123
　public support for international institutions in, 268
　as sole superpower, 5, 12–13
　sovereignty, sub-national use of term in, 69–70
　stare decisis vs. precedent, 173–75
　WTO, domestic law impact of, 45
　as WTO Quad Group member, 117
universal jurisdiction, treaties calling for, 44
Uruguay, GATT violations of industrial countries alleged by, 140
Uruguay Round (UR)
　dispute settlement and, 137–45
　historical outline of, 99–102
　impact of, 5–6
　subject matter competence of WTO expanded at, 99, 131, 133, 144

360

Index

treaty agreements at, 269–70
treaty structure for WTO, 104–06
WTO established at, 99, 269–70

variable geometry (interface theory), 25, 226, 230–33, *232*, 254
Venezuela, 161, 165–66
voting systems in international organizations, 24, 43, 50–51, 112–16, 237

"Washington Consensus," 267
weapons, effects of developments in, 11
weighted voting systems, 24, 115–16
Westphalian sovereignty, criticism of, 14, 57, 62–70, 260–61
WHO (World Health Organization), 29, 245–248
Wilcox, Clair, 138
WIPO (World Intellectual Property Organization), 227
World Bank
  Asian financial crisis testing capacity of, 6
  inception of, 99, 274n9
  "treaty rigidity" in, 45
  weighted voting system, 24, 115–16
  WTO resources compared, 116, *117*
World Court (International Court of Justice or ICJ), 135, 246. *See also* Table of Cases and Table of Statutes and Regulations
World Health Organization (WHO), 29, 245–48
World Intellectual Property Organization (WIPO), 227
World Summit on Sustainable Development (2002), 11, 26
World Trade Organization (WTO)
  agricultural subsidies as major issue in, 30–31
  Charter, 104–106, 269–70, 306n36 (*see also* Table of Statutes and Regulations, for specific sections)
  competition policy, disputes as to internationalization of, 221–22
  consensus approach at, 43, 50, 112–16, 206, 237–38, 262
  "constitution" of, 236–40
  criticism of and challenges to, 6
  decision-making processes, 107–108
  dispute settlement mechanism (*see* dispute settlement at WTO)
  GATT and, 91, 105
  good governance ideals of, 118–21, 203
  health issues, involvement with, 247
  inception of, 5–6
  interface theory (variable geometry), 230–31
  internal domestic legal systems and rules of, 122–28
  link to general international law, 3–4, 13, 81–84
  membership and membership accession, 107, 108–10
  MIAs (multilateral investment agreements) development of, 242–43
  Ministerial Conferences, 102–04, 106, 121–22 (*see also* individual conferences, e.g. Singapore)
  nongovernmental actors' participation in, 12, 15, 27–28
  policy objectives of, 84–91
  power allocation analysis and, 238–40
  problems and criticisms, 110–12, 262
  reasons for use as case study, 16–17, 261–62
  resources of, 116, *117*
  sovereignty and, 69, 237, 261–62
  steering group issues, 116–18
  structure and organization of institution, 106–07, 122
  subject matter competence of, 128–33, 236–40
  super-majority requirements at, 237
  UR agreements establishing, 99, 269–70
Wyndham-White, Eric, 98, 139